Starting Lines in Scottish, Irish, and English Poetry

Starting Lines
in Scottish, Irish, and
English Poetry

From Burns to Heaney

FIONA STAFFORD

OXFORD
UNIVERSITY PRESS

OXFORD
UNIVERSITY PRESS

Great Clarendon Street, Oxford, OX2 6DP
Oxford University Press is a department of the University of Oxford.
It furthers the University's objective of excellence in research, scholarship,
and education by publishing worldwide in

Oxford New York

Athens Auckland Bangkok Bogotá Buenos Aires Calcutta
Cape Town Chennai Dar es Salaam Delhi Florence Hong Kong Istanbul
Karachi Kuala Lumpur Madrid Melbourne Mexico City Mumbai
Nairobi Paris São Paulo Shanghai Singapore Taipei Tokyo Toronto Warsaw

and associated companies in Berlin Ibadan

Oxford is a registered trade mark of Oxford University Press
in the UK and certain other countries

Published in the United States
by Oxford University Press Inc., New York

© Fiona Stafford 2000

The moral rights of the author have been asserted

Database right Oxford University Press (maker)

First published 2000

British Library Cataloguing in Publication Data

Data available

Library of Congress Cataloging in Publication Data

Data available

ISBN 0-19-818637-1

1 3 5 7 9 10 8 6 4 2

Typeset by Regent Typesetting, London
Printed in Great Britain
on acid-free paper by
Biddles Ltd
Guildford and King's Lynn

For
DOMINIC *and* RACHAEL

Acknowledgements

For permission to reproduce the texts included in the chapters below, I am grateful to: Ciaran Carson, The Gallery Press and Wake Forest University Press for 'The Irish for No' from *The Irish for No* (1987); to Seamus Heaney, Faber and Faber Ltd. and Farrar Straus Giroux, LLC. for 'xliv' from 'Crossings' from *Seeing Things*, Copyright © 1991 by Seamus Heaney; to Methuen for Noel Coward's 'The Stately Homes of England' from *Operette* (1938); to John Murray (Publishers) Ltd. and the Estate of George Mackay Brown for 'All Souls' from *Northern Lights: a Poet's Sources* (1999). An earlier version of chapter seven originally appeared in *Bullán* 1 (Spring 1994), 63–74; I am grateful to the editor, Ray Ryan, for allowing me to include the extended discussion that now forms the final chapter of this study.

I would also like to record my thanks to the staff of the Bodleian Library, Somerville College Library, and the English Faculty Library in Oxford; the British Library; the Royal Irish Academy; and the National Library of Ireland.

For encouragement in the early stages of the project, I would like to thank Jason Freeman, and for continuing interest and support, Sophie Goldsworthy. Frances Whistler has offered extremely helpful editorial advice in the later stages, while for judicious and tactful copyediting, I am indebted to Dorothy McCarthy.

Many of the critical and scholarly works that have informed this study are acknowledged in the footnotes and references below. However, my thinking has also been greatly enriched by conversations over a number of years with friends in Scotland, England, and Ireland, which have revealed to me how differently things appear, when viewed from different directions. I am also particularly indebted to the following for drawing my attention to, or supplying copies of, books, articles and other invaluable resources: David Bradshaw, Kelvin Everest, Roy Foster, Luke Gibbons, Andrew Noble, Matthew Scott, Gill

Stafford, Neil Vickers, Tim Webb. For perceptive and constructive comments on individual chapters, I am very grateful indeed to Stephen Gill, Lucy Newlyn, Bernard O'Donoghue and Tim Webb.

My greatest debts, as always, are to Malcolm, Dominic, and Rachael, whose contributions at every stage have been too many and various to quantify.

Contents

'What's Past is Prologue'

'Begin at the beginning, and go on till you come to the end: then stop.'[1] It wouldn't really matter what the task in hand might be—as an instruction on how to proceed, this could hardly be clearer. The words are simple, the sequence straightforward, and the action, complete. And yet, as every reader of *Alice's Adventures in Wonderland* knows, this advice is given in the face of misunderstanding and general mayhem. Words which, when taken out of context, seem entirely lucid, become charged with vexation and difficulty when restored to their original setting in the surreal courtroom drama where the search for any truth, let alone the whole, seems forlorn and faintly absurd. To ask another witness to 'begin' risks reopening the kind of confusion that had beset the Mad Hatter, as his attempt to recount an adventure that 'began with tea' turned instantly into an exchange about words beginning with 'T'. The question of what things begin with (other than 'T') is far from simple, and so the King of Hearts' request that the White Rabbit should 'begin at the beginning' is not easily obeyed.

Even behind the King's own apparently straightforward words lies a history of literary associations long enough to unsettle his effort to bring direction through directness. For when Byron launched his ironic epic, *Don Juan*, on unsuspecting readers of 1819, he made his narrator inform them that his way was 'to begin with the beginning'.[2] Again, if the line is heard outside the context of the poem, it seems to be articulating something too obvious to need putting into words. Readers of Byron's opening canto, however, know that the remark is made in explicit contrast to the 'usual methods' of

[1] Lewis Carroll (Charles Lutwidge Dodgson), *Alice's Adventures in Wonderland* (1865), *The Annotated Alice*, ed. Martin Gardner, rev. edn. (Harmondsworth, 1970), 158.
[2] *Don Juan*, I. 7, *The Complete Works of Lord Byron*, ed. Jerome J. McGann, 7 vols. (Oxford, 1980–93).

poets, who generally prefer to plunge '*in medias res*' (into the middle of things). The apparently obvious, casual decision to begin with the beginning is thus a comic refusal to comply with advice offered more than eighteen centuries earlier by the Latin poet, Horace, who was himself basing his observations on a reading of the much older Greek poet, Homer. Whether Byron's emphasis on the 'beginning' rather than the 'middle' also carries resonances of the ultimate 'beginning' in the Book of Genesis is open to debate, but to evoke such a narrative model for the story of Don Juan would certainly accord with the irreverent tone of the new epic as well as effectively overturning the authority that had come to be invested in classical literary criticism.[3] The narrator's statement of intent is nevertheless undermined as he speaks, through his own inveterate tendency to digression and also because he is embarking on a story with which all his readers would already have been familiar. By choosing Don Juan, whose legendary character was so well known, Byron is himself plunging into the middle, because the beginning is not really the beginning if the whole has been told many times before.[4]

What should be emerging from this rather bewildering train of associations is that the King's command is far less simple than it might initially appear, not least because of the perennial problem of establishing 'the beginning'. For if the beginning is not easily identified, how can anyone confidently begin there? Even without exploring the more abstract dimensions of the problem of beginning, a task already undertaken ably and memorably by Edward Said, the question of where writers begin and how they proceed from their chosen beginning is a complicated one.[5] Many poets, and especially those belonging to the generation or two before Lewis Carroll, would probably have gone along with the King of Hearts' advice as an ideal for composition, if not for narrative strategy. To begin at the beginning

[3] For a perceptive and learned discussion of Horace's advice in *Ars poetica*, 146–9, and the complexities attendant on even the 'natural beginning' of Genesis, see A. D. Nuttall, *Openings: Narrative Beginnings from the Epic to the Novel* (Oxford, 1992), to which my own opening is indebted.

[4] On the popularity of the Don Juan legend in early nineteenth-century Britain, see Moyra Haslett, *Byron's* Don Juan *and the Don Juan Legend* (Oxford, 1997).

[5] Edward W. Said, *Beginnings: Intention and Method* (1975), The Morningside Edition (New York, 1985).

and go on until you come to the end smacks of the simplicity and spontaneity that has traditionally been associated with Romantic aesthetics. It implies an unproblematic re-creation of experience by someone who has the capacity to relate his material clearly, concisely, directly. John Keats's description of poetry coming as naturally as the Leaves to a Tree (or 'it had better not come at all') implies a similar ideal of creativity: one which does not involve stumbling about to find a suitable starting point or wasting time deciding on which idea, moment or fine phrase should come first.[6] If poetic composition is, as Coleridge once described it, a 'hot fit', then careful structuring or the incorporation of rhetorical devices seems inappropriately calculated or unattractively plodding.[7] Shelley's image of the poet's mind as 'a fading coal which some invisible influence, like an inconstant wind, awakens to transitory brightness' suggests a process beyond the conscious control of the individual writer who apparently cannot say 'I will compose poetry.'[8] His own legacy of numerous unfinished fragments seems to testify to his view of the poet seized by inspiration and compelled to write furiously, lest the moment pass.

It is not surprising that readers have been happy to surrender to these high Romantic images of the poet. The figure of the youthful visionary, compulsively creative and frequently wrecked by the intensity of his special experience, is in itself compelling. Poets seem, when viewed in such an imaginative way, to acquire the haloes of semi-divine beings, mediating between the mysterious sources of creation and the more mundane world of the reading public. The desire to revere poets and to set them slightly apart from the community is by no means exclusively Romantic, even if the poets we now group

[6] Keats to John Taylor, 27 Feb. 1818, *The Letters of John Keats 1814–1821*, ed. Hyder E. Rollins, 2 vols. (Cambridge, Mass., 1958), i, 238–9.

[7] Coleridge to John Rickman, 28 Feb. 1804, *The Collected Letters of Samuel Taylor Coleridge*, ed. E. L. Griggs, 6 vols. (Oxford, 1956–71), ii, 1075. For the significance of this remark, and an illuminating discussion of Coleridge's (and Keats's) methods of composition see Jack Stillinger, *Coleridge and Textual Instability: The Multiple Versions of the Major Poems* (New York and Oxford, 1994), 100–17. See also Zachary Leader, *Revision and Romantic Authorship* (Oxford, 1996).

[8] P. B. Shelley, 'A Defence of Poetry' (composed 1821), *Shelley's Poetry and Prose*, ed. Donald H. Reiman and Sharon B. Powers (New York and London, 1977), 503–4.

under this term were more inclined to draw attention to their special status than others have been. When Thomas Carlyle announced to an early Victorian audience that poets and prophets were originally the same, he drew on the Latin 'vates' to support his claim that the task of the great poet had always been to reveal 'that sacred mystery which he more than others lives ever present with'.[9] For the young Carlyle, emerging from the era of Coleridge and Shelley, it seemed that poets had traditionally fulfilled a quasi-religious role in society, and with this prophetic status came the visionary ideal of unpremeditated expression.

Academic readers are now more sceptical of Romantic claims about the nature of poetry, but perhaps because of the recent onslaught on 'Romanticism', it is still rather reassuring to find that, in the case of Keats at least, actual practice seems to have come close to the optimistic ideal of natural composition.[10] His 'Ode to a Nightingale', a quintessentially 'Romantic' poem, was apparently written in the garden at Hampstead in the space of two or three hours; and the biographical account of his friend Brown is corroborated by the surviving manuscript, which shows every sign of haste and rapid composition.[11] Apart from a couple of revisions to isolated words, Keats does indeed appear to have begun at the beginning, gone on until he reached the end, and stopped. It was probably this rare facility to compose remarkable poetry at remarkable speed which made him willing to engage in sonnet-writing competitions with his rather less

[9] Thomas Carlyle, 'Lecture III: The Hero as Poet', 12 May 1840, On Heroes, Hero-Worship and the Heroic in History (London, 1841), 130.

[10] Important challenges to traditional ideas about Romanticism appeared in the 1980s, in Jerome J. McGann's The Romantic Ideology: A Critical Investigation (Chicago, 1983) and Marilyn Butler's Romantics, Rebels, and Reactionaries: English Literature and its Background 1760–1830 (Oxford, 1981). Further contributions include Stephen Copley and John Whale's Beyond Romanticism: New Approaches to Texts and Contexts 1780–1832 (London, 1992) and Mary Favret and Nicola Watson's At the Limits of Romanticism: Essays in Cultural, Feminist and Materialist Criticism (Bloomington, Ind., 1994). For a useful survey, see Michael O'Neill, 'General Studies of the Romantic Period', Literature of the Romantic Period: A Bibliographical Guide (Oxford, 1998), 1–26.

[11] The Keats Circle: Letters and Papers, 1816–1878, ed. Hyder E. Rollins, 2 vols. (Cambridge, Mass., 1948), ii, 65. For discussion of the manuscripts, see The Poems of John Keats, ed. Jack Stillinger (London, 1978), 651–3. See also Stillinger, Coleridge and Textual Instability, 102–3; id., 'Keats's Extempore Effusions and the Question of Intentionality' in Robert Brinkley and Keith Hanley (eds.), Romantic Revisions (Cambridge, 1992), 307–20.

gifted friend, Leigh Hunt, who was apt to take a little longer than the fifteen minutes allotted for the game.[12]

Not all poets have been so fortunate. Leigh Hunt's experience of toiling on into the early hours on a sonnet which his friends Keats and Shelley had dashed off in a matter of minutes is perhaps the more common. For it is clear from both manuscripts and memoirs that many of the most talented writers have laboured long and hard before their embryonic first draft could finally be delivered to an editor or publisher. There is nothing particularly leaf-like about Dylan Thomas's method of composition, for example: 'I write a poem on innumerable sheets of scrap paper, write it on both sides of the paper, often upside down and criss cross ways unpunctuated, surrounded by drawings of lamp posts and boiled eggs, in a very dirty mess; bit by bit I copy out the slowly developing poem into an exercise book; and, when it is completed, I type it out.'[13] Neither have those who most admired spontaneity necessarily refrained from repeated revisions of their own work, as is apparent from a glance into *The Notebook of William Blake* or any of the volumes of *The Cornell Wordsworth* (as Stephen Gill has commented, revision was for Wordsworth 'compulsive and continuous'[14]). Nor has the act of putting 'the poem to bed' always proved as final as it might have seemed at the time, for many poets have revised the published texts of their poems for later editions. Dante Gabriel Rossetti's 'Blessed Damozel', for example, underwent a series of facelifts between her début in *The Germ* in 1850 and her final appearance in *Poems* in 1870. Such revisions have sometimes been made in response to adverse criticism, as in Tennyson's reworkings of the poems he had published and seen savaged in 1833. Often they reflect the maturing taste or technique of the poet, however, as is evident from W. H. Auden's description of his work on a new *Collected Poems*: 'I have been going through everything, revising and gnashing my teeth at my clumsiness in the old days.'[15]

[12] Stillinger, 'Keats's Extempore Effusions', 309–10; id., *Coleridge and Textual Instability*, 101–2.

[13] *Poet in the Making: The Notebooks of Dylan Thomas*, ed. Ralph Maud (London, 1965), 9.

[14] Stephen Gill, 'Wordsworth's Poems: The Question of Text', in Brinkley and Hanley (eds.), *Romantic Revisions*, 43–63, 46.

[15] Quoted in Humphrey Carpenter, *W. H. Auden: A Biography*, rev. edn. (London, 1983), 415.

Few poets can have invested quite as much energy in revising their published work as Coleridge, however. Whatever the impression given by 'Kubla Khan' and its prefatory account of the poet waking from his reverie and eagerly writing down the lines, the meticulous work of Jack Stillinger has established that Coleridge revised his texts 'not just once or twice, but again and again (seemingly obsessively) over a long lifetime'.[16] Despite his admiration for literature that embodied natural unpremeditated growth, Coleridge subjected his own compositions to revision, expansion and incessant tinkering. While this may be quite consistent with a view of art as organic, in that it suggests a deep unwillingness to regard the poem as fixed, inert, or resistant to future growth, it is nevertheless hard to reconcile with the notion of the 'hot fit'—the spontaneous inspired creation that begins without reflection, plan, or an eye to its rhetorical effect.

It is particularly interesting that Coleridge should have expended so much care on the beginnings of his poems, not necessarily altering the first lines, but frequently modifying his titles, adding or removing prefatory details or inserting lines from other writers at the head of his own verses. In such instances, he often appears to be revealing or concealing something about the poem's origins, and, in the process, emphasizing that the memorable opening line is not, after all, the true beginning. 'This Lime Tree Bower my Prison' begins with the offhand, colloquial 'Well, they are gone, and here must I remain', which seems to place the reader directly in the presence of the speaker. The subsequent inclusion of detail about the poet's accident, which disabled him from walking with 'long-expected Friends', may help to explain both the situation and mood, but it also imposes retrospect, pushing the present-tense monologue into the completeness of the past.[17] The poem is evidently not beginning at the beginning, but plunging readers into the middle of something that has already happened.

When the additional material takes the form of a Latin epigraph, as in the later versions of 'The Rime of the Ancient Mariner', the distancing effect is more pronounced. For while a note on the composition of 'This Lime Tree Bower' has obvious connection with the poem it prefaces, Coleridge's decision to

[16] *Coleridge and Textual Instability*, 107.
[17] For the headnote, and details of textual variants, see ibid. 148.

begin his most famous poem with a quotation from one of the lesser-known works of a seventeenth-century prose writer is less easy to comprehend. Although readers of 1817 who first encountered the transformed 'Mariner' would have been more accustomed than later audiences to the use of classical mottoes, the incongruity of juxtaposing Thomas Burnet's philosophical ruminations with the arresting 'It is an ancient Mariner | And he stoppeth one of three' must still have been striking. Burnet's speculation on the visible and the invisible, the certain and uncertain, is an appropriate enough caution to readers embarking on Coleridge's dazzling narration, but its appearance imposes a sudden distance, exploding the illusion of orality that seemed conjured up by the poem in its original position at the beginning of an anonymous collection of *Lyrical Ballads*.[18] The Latin epigraph underlines the condition of the poem as a written text, something created for readers who will implicitly be well enough versed in classical languages and capable of engaging in metaphysical speculation.

The addition of the Latin passage under the title of 'The Rime of the Ancient Mariner' probably says as much about Coleridge's preoccupations in 1816–17 as it does about the poem itself. It is a good example, nevertheless, of the way in which poems can change radically over time, not merely because new readers bring fresh understanding to the text, but also because writers who remain alert and alive have the capacity and often the inclination to alter their early work. (We do not know what Keats might have done to his poems had he lived to become the great poet of the Victorian era, but the existence of 'The Fall of Hyperion', with its careful reworking of passages from the published 'Hyperion', suggests that his early thoughts on spontaneous composition might themselves have undergone some revision in time.) The question of how poems begin is thus complicated not only by the essential difficulty of defining the

---

[18] 'The Rime of the Ancyent Marinere' was first published in Wordsworth and Coleridge's joint collection *Lyrical Ballads* (Bristol, 1798). It was republished in the expanded versions of the collection, but not in its original position as the opening poem. Coleridge also reprinted it many times, with significant revisions; for these, and the text of the epigraph from Thomas Burnet's *Archaeologiae Philosophicae* (1692), see Stillinger, *Coleridge and Textual Instability*, 158–84. Michael Mason includes a translation of the quotation in his invaluable edition of *Lyrical Ballads* (London, 1992), 363–4.

beginning, but also by the knowledge that many poems origin-
ally begin in one way but, within days, months, or years, turn
out to begin with something quite different.

This book is not an attempt to determine the 'real' beginnings
of poems, nor is it a study of the process of composition. Instead
I am concerned with the published texts of poems and the
ways in which they appear to begin (and may have appeared
to readers of the early printed editions). In particular, I am
interested in those poems which appear to begin with other
poems. Although it could be argued that every poem starts with
an earlier poem simply by adopting an established literary form,
this discussion focuses on those poems which make the presence
of predecessors obvious from the first. Again, numerous poems
begin with an obvious reference to an earlier work or tradition,
a technique adopted perhaps most famously by Milton for
Paradise Lost, and subsequently played upon by Pope in his
mock epic, *The Rape of the Lock*. In other works the allusion is
less formulaic, as for example in Wordsworth's evocation of
Milton's elegiac sonnet for his own 'Methought I saw the foot-
steps of a throne', or in Paul Muldoon's rather more surreal
recollection of Yeats in the opening line of his poem, 'Louis':
'Both beautiful, one a gazebo'.[19] Numerous examples could be
added and analysed; my concern in this study is, however, with
poems that begin not with a conventional device or submerged
allusion, but with direct quotation.

Some of these quotations take the form of epigraphs, but in
most of the poems under discussion, the quotation is embedded
in the first line of the new poem. Ciaran Carson's 'The Irish for
No', for example, takes its opening line from Keats's 'Ode to a
Nightingale': 'Was it a vision or a waking dream?' This is not an
adaptation, but a clear signal that the new poem is beginning
with a line from an extremely well-known canonical text that
many readers will instantly identify as the source. The line is

---

[19] William Wordsworth, *Poems, in Two Volumes, and Other Poems, 1800–
1807*, ed. Jared Curtis, *The Cornell Wordsworth* (Ithaca, 1983), 148–9; Milton,
'Sonnet xix', *The Complete Shorter Poems*, ed. John Carey (London, 1968), 413–
14. Paul Muldoon, 'Louis', *Meeting the British* (London, 1987), 55, which evokes
'In Memory of Eva Gore-Booth and Con Markiewicz', 'both | Beautiful, one a
gazelle' (lines 3–4, 19–20) and 'We the great gazebo built' (line 30), *W. B. Yeats:
The Poems*, ed. Daniel Albright (London, 1990), 283–4.

Keats's, but it is also an intrinsic part of the new poem, which could not continue (or begin) without it, any more than Muldoon's sequence '7, Middagh Street' could begin without its borrowed first line 'Quinquereme of Nineveh from distant Ophir'.[20] Such practice is very different from the revised 'Ancient Mariner', where the additional lines from Burnet have often been excised again by later editors, who presumably regard them as extraneous material and not an essential part of the poem.

Late twentieth-century poets, and especially those from Ireland, who choose to weave quotations into the texture of their own work are influenced by different literary models and political developments from those affecting writers two centuries ago. Among T. S. Eliot's contributions to literary tradition was the foregrounding of direct quotation in his poetry, a technique which ironically seemed to mark his work out as different from the heavily allusive texts he inherited. Although those who have followed (or resisted) Eliot and his contemporaries may have adopted different ways of incorporating existing lines into their poetry, the basic practice of employing quotation rather than a more ingested form of allusion or echo has become commonplace in the twentieth century. Contemporary poems which open with other poems thus seem quite different from the eighteenth-century texts that were published with accompanying epigraphs. And yet, there are often surprising parallels between the practices of those earlier poets who adorned their work with epigraphs and the late twentieth-century writers whose use of quotation may initially seem more ironic and unreverential. For although some epigraphs initially seem rather detached from the poem below, further investigation often reveals the important and pervasive contribution that they are making to the new text. To ignore them is to close off whole avenues of possibility. The typographical completeness of an epigraph may set it apart like the label beside a painting in an art gallery, but if the lines are affecting the entire poem, working through the new composition and into the reader's experience, the epigraph may be just as much a part of the poem as the quotation embedded in a

[20] *Meeting the British*, 36. The line is the opening of John Masefield's well-known 'Cargoes', *Poems* (London and Toronto, 1946), 906.

twentieth-century text. Indeed, when this is the case (as will be clear in subsequent chapters) the technique is all the more subtle and exciting, since both the motto and the poem appear closed and independent but then surprise the reader by turning out to be open and dynamically engaged.

This is not a comprehensive survey of the transformation of formal epigraph to postmodern quotation in poetry, but rather an exploration of a small selection of texts that initially seem quite different, but on reflection reveal surprising similarities. In the discussions of the individual poems which follow, this emerges through the consideration of the various ways in which the poem in question is engaging with a predecessor whose presence is signalled by an excerpt at the beginning. In the book as a whole, similarities emerge through the juxtaposition of diverse writers who have adopted the same strategy of presenting a poem to readers which appears to begin with another poem. In order to examine both the parallels and distinctions, I have attempted to bring together periods that are usually treated independently by critics working in different fields. For although contemporary poetry is in many ways far removed from that usually considered 'Romantic', many of the concerns explored by poets working in Ireland in the twentieth century can be fruitfully compared with those that fascinated British writers in the late eighteenth and early nineteenth, as they came to terms with their experience of the newly United Kingdom. In both periods, poetry was engaging with turbulent political change, and driven by a sense of the importance of nationhood, and of the responsibilities of literature to a new national consciousness. Although the establishment of the modern Irish nation has compelled writers to free themselves from English forms and literary traditions, many of the attendant concerns— with poetic inheritance, identity, and independence—produce ironic echoes of late eighteenth-century English and Scottish poetry when similar issues were so much to the fore. What may appear in a late twentieth-century poem as a sardonic allusion can thus possess the further irony of revealing preoccupations similar to those of the apparently rejected tradition. Conversely, awareness of the integration of poetry and politics in modern Ireland can help to illuminate the poetic encounters which were taking place within these islands two centuries before.

My own starting point for this investigation was the poem by Seamus Heaney which forms the focus of Chapter 7: the ending, as is often the case, being in one sense the beginning (and vice versa). As I went beyond the immediate fascination of Heaney's poem, I found myself moving back through the centuries—not only to Henry Vaughan's beautiful elegy, which also opens with the image of going 'into the world of light', but also to a host of other texts beginning with other poems. These poems were not of the same kind, but ranged from nonsense ('Twinkle, twinkle, little bat') and parody ('Two voices are there') to profound self searchings ('Thou art indeed just, Lord').[21] Some were darkly ironic, like 'Verses on the Death of Dr Swift', others more play-ful, though similarly witty, such as Donne's 'The Bait', in which the seductive power of Marlowe's passionate shepherd is so cleverly inverted.[22] Especially noticeable in this enjoyable, if slightly desultory, pursuit was the discovery of poems in the Romantic period which began with lines from other poems. For such practice not only seemed at odds with the late eighteenth-century emphasis on spontaneity and unmediated recreation of experience, but also with the related aesthetic preoccupation with originality.

Since the need to be original or, as Heaney has James Joyce say in *Station Island*, 'to swim | out on your own', is as urgent in

[21] 'Twinkle, twinkle, little bat!' in *Alice's Adventures in Wonderland*, *The Anno-tated Alice*, 98–9, parodies Jane Taylor's 'The Star', from *Rhymes for the Nursery* (1806), which has been described as the most 'memorized' poem in English by Anne K. Mellor, *Romanticism and Gender* (New York and London, 1993), 10–11. Wordsworth's 'Thought of a Briton on the subjugation of Switzerland' (1807) begins 'Two Voices are there; one is of the Sea, | One of the Mountains'; J. K. Stephen starts his own Wordsworthian parody 'A Sonnet' with the same words, though the voices turn out to be those of 'the deep' and of 'an old half-witted sheep'. For these and other parodies, see *Parodies: An Anthology from Chaucer to Beerbohm and After*, ed. Dwight Macdonald (London, 1961); Graeme Stones and John Strachan (eds.) *Parodies of the Romantic Age*, 5 vols. (London, 1998). Hopkins's sonnet begins with a translation of Jeremiah 12: 1, 'justus quidem tu es, Domine, si disputem tecum', *The Poetical Works of Gerard Manley Hopkins*, ed. Norman H. Mackenzie (Oxford, 1990), 201.

[22] 'Verses on the Death of Dr Swift D.S.P.D., Occasioned by reading a Maxim in Rochefoulcault' (written in 1731), *The Poems of Jonathan Swift*, ed. Harold Williams, 3 vols. (Oxford, 1937), ii, 551–72. 'The Bait' begins with 'Come Live with me and be my Love', the opening line of Christopher Marlowe's 'The Passionate Shepherd to his Love' (1599), which had already provoked Walter Raleigh's 'The Nymph's Reply' (1600), John Donne, *The Complete English Poems*, ed. A. J. Smith, corrected edn. (Harmondsworth, 1973), 43–4, 357.

twentieth-century Irish writing as in British Romantic literature, it is worth pausing to examine this question in a little more detail.[23] For it is not immediately obvious why a poet who wishes to be seen as, or indeed to *be* an 'original genius' should continue to quote from other writers, or revise his own composition to make it appear to begin with a line from someone else. Why did Coleridge, for example, want readers to encounter 'The Ancient Mariner' in the company of Thomas Burnet? Since the very notion of originality is now commonplace, a brief investigation of the period when it was a relatively new concept may be helpful. For 'Originality' is often singled out as a defining characteristic of the late eighteenth-century shift in cultural values. Where writers had traditionally sought perfection irrespective of the novelty of their subject ('What oft was *Thought*, but ne'er so well *Exprest*'), from the 1750s and 1760s onwards they were more inclined to aim for difference: for new styles, new themes, and new ways of representing the world.[24] The reasons for this are complicated and different scholars have laid emphasis on various philosophical, social, economic, and political changes, with explanations ranging from a fundamental revolution in the way the world is perceived by the artist to more material developments such as the expansion of the book trade and a number of milestone cases affecting the law of copyright.[25] Whatever the causes, the effects of these multiple changes included a widespread reaction against the forms inherited from the classical past, a new interest in the mind of the writer and the imaginative experience of the reader, and an association between literary texts and personal property. At the confluence of all these important, if now unexceptional developments, was the idea of originality.

That the new cultural values were perceptible not merely

---

[23] *Station Island*, XII (London, 1984), 93–4.

[24] Alexander Pope, *An Essay on Criticism*, 298; *The Twickenham Edition of the Works of Alexander Pope*, ed. John Butt, 11 vols. (London, 1938–68), Vol. I: *Pastoral Poetry and An Essay on Criticism*, ed. E. Audra and Aubrey Williams (London and New Haven, 1961), 273.

[25] Among the classic accounts of the aesthetic revolution in the eighteenth century are W. J. Bate, *From Classic to Romantic* (Cambridge, Mass., 1946) and M. H. Abrams, *The Mirror and the Lamp* (London, 1953). On the book trade, copyright laws, and changing reading practices, see Mark Rose, *Authors and Owners: The Invention of Copyright* (Cambridge, Mass., 1993), Jon Klancher, The *Making of English Reading Audiences, 1790–1832* (Madison, Wisc., 1987).

with hindsight but also at the time is obvious from the explosion of influential mid-century essays on aesthetic subjects. The notion of 'originality' was expressed most succinctly by the poet Edward Young, whose *Conjectures on Original Composition* also articulate the burgeoning emphasis on spontaneous growth. His short essay makes the memorable comparison between 'the mind of a man of genius' and a fertile meadow enjoying a 'perpetual spring', in which '*Originals* are the fairest flowers'. The metaphor then develops in language that anticipates Keats's poetic 'Leaves' and Coleridge's later thoughts on organic form: 'An *Original* may be said to be of a *vegetable* nature; it rises spontaneously from the vital root of genius; it *grows*, it is not *made*: *Imitations* are often a sort of *manufacture* wrought up by those *mechanics*, *art*, and *labour*, out of pre-existent materials not their own.'[26] Young's essay is a virtual manifesto for the Romantic poet, stressing the importance of natural growth over careful toil, of individual, innate genius over trained craftsmanship. Above all, the poet must produce works of originality, to 'extend the republic of letters, and add a new province of its dominion'.[27] The genius not only had the power to create spontaneously, but also to open up new territories for others, and to venture alone into uncharted waters— ideas that seem to link the new aesthetic to contemporary exploration and the expansion of British interests abroad.

The association between the new idea of originality and the equally new idea of the nation was also developing from other directions. In France, for example, Voltaire's *Lettres philosophiques* had done much to establish England as the home of liberty and originality, ideas reinforced by the popularity of Sterne's highly innovative texts. Since the sense of being different from the French appears also to have been a major factor in the internal development of a distinctly British consciousness, it is not surprising to find the new defining characteristics of liberty and originality beginning to pervade discussions of the national language.[28] Perhaps the most famous

---

[26] Edward Young, *Conjectures on Original Composition* (1759), ed. Edith Morley (Manchester, 1918), 7. Lucy Newlyn has discussed Young's influence in the period in *Paradise Lost and the Romantic Reader* (Oxford, 1993), 46–9.

[27] Young, *Conjectures*, 6–7.

[28] Linda Colley has emphasized the importance of the series of wars with France

publication of the 1750s was Johnson's *Dictionary*, which reveals the growing association between ideas of the 'original' and the 'native' in its Preface:

Our language, for almost a century has, by the concurrence of many causes, been gradually departing from its original Teutonic character, and deviating towards a Gallic structure and phraseology, from which it ought to be our endeavour to recall it, by making our ancient volumes the ground-work of style, admitting among the additions of later times only such as may supply real deficiencies, such as are readily adopted by the genius of our tongue, and incorporate easily with our native idioms.[29]

For Johnson, 'originality' is connected with the roots of the English language, its recovery part of a vital defensive strategy against the threat posed by French to 'the spirit of English liberty'.[30] Although his own method of defining meaning through the use of carefully chosen quotation may suggest an approach to the truth that differs widely from Young's rousing call to the individual artist, the implications of their observations had similar tendencies. The very celebration of national character in the *Dictionary*, which was founded upon reference to the finest writers in the English language, inevitably encouraged the contemporary reaction against classical models, which were closely associated with French neoclassicism. Though apparently conservative in his return to the '*wells of English undefiled*' and himself a master of Latin composition, then, Johnson was also indirectly adding his not inconsiderable weight to Young's advice to young authors, to shake off the burden of 'illustrious examples' and be 'original'.[31]

With such inspiring ideals to fire the imagination, it is not surprising to find English writers of the late eighteenth and early nineteenth centuries turning to areas that had not been visited by their immediate predecessors, and developing forms that were consciously different from those fashionable in the earlier part of the century. Stuart Curran has analysed the Romantic

in the development of Britishness in her influential *Britons: Forging the Nation, 1707–1837* (London and New Haven, 1992).

[29] 'Preface to the Dictionary of the English Language' (1755), *The Oxford Authors: Samuel Johnson*, ed. Donald Greene (Oxford, 1984), 319.

[30] Ibid. 326.

[31] Ibid. 319 (Johnson is quoting Edmund Spenser's tribute to 'Dan *Chaucer*, well of English undefyled', *The Faerie Queene*, IV. ii. 32); Young, *Conjectures*, 9.

revival of poetic genres, seeing the late eighteenth-century movement as possessing 'much of the fervor, the aggressive creation and dismantling of conventions . . . that accompanied its predecessor in the sixteenth century'.[32] Just as Renaissance poets had wrested distinctively English forms from Italian, French, and Latin models, so Romantic poets attempted to recover the energy of the Elizabethans in their own reaction against the neoclassical values imported after the Restoration. Wordsworth's preface to *Lyrical Ballads* probably contains the best-known statements about the deliberate rejection of 'poetic diction', while Shelley explicitly emphasized the political dimension of the new aesthetic, seeing the great writers of his own age as 'the companions and forerunners of some unimagined change in our social condition'.[33] By 1819, when Shelley composed *Prometheus Unbound*, the confluence of aesthetic and political events seemed all too plain, as the late eighteenth-century revolution in taste could now be seen as the herald of cataclysmic changes in the constitution and society of America and France. Although contemporary writers responded to political events and to each other in very different ways, the association between original genius and independence was firmly established. It is not surprising, then, that when Irish writers a century later were attempting to free themselves from the Union with England, Scotland, and Wales and to develop a distinct national literature, the idea of originality should have been so important. As will become clear a little later on, however, the modern aesthetic ideal has proved deeply problematic for writers whose own situation renders the eighteenth-century equation between England and liberty decidedly unconvincing.

To return, however, to the apparent contradiction of the survival of epigraphs and quotations in periods when originality and independence were especially prized. Why, at such moments, should any poet striving to be original still choose to place someone else's words at the head of a new poem? One fairly obvious explanation is the phenomenon that has

---

[32] Stuart Curran, *Poetic Form and British Romanticism* (Oxford, 1986), 31.
[33] Preface to *Lyrical Ballads*, 68; Preface to *Prometheus Unbound* (1820), *Shelley: Poetical Works*, ed. Thomas Hutchinson, rev. edn. G. M. Matthews (Oxford, 1970), 206.

variously been analysed as 'the anxiety of influence' or 'the burden of the past'. In the early 1970s, when notions of revolution and originality were once again much in the air, two influential critical accounts appeared, highlighting the problems bequeathed to poets in the shape of their great predecessors' works. Harold Bloom's *The Anxiety of Influence* drew a striking picture of 'strong writers' locked in an Oedipal struggle with their literary forefathers, and wrestling to liberate their own independent voices through a variety of complicated strategies.[34] Taking a less overtly psychoanalytical approach, Walter Jackson Bate addressed the related difficulty which he identified as being of central importance to those unlucky enough to be writing in the wake of Shakespeare and Milton— 'What is there left to say?'[35] Bate's account is not that of the spectator at a wrestling match, or, indeed, a Greek tragedy, but rather the voice of the modern intellectual, sympathetic to the plight of talented writers who saw the scope for their genius narrowing, receding, or simply being exhausted. In both accounts, however, past writers pose a serious problem—representing figures to be wrestled into submission or acknowledged as debilitatingly superior.

In such views of the past, the use of an epigraph makes perfect sense. A line or two from a great master can act as the gauntlet spurring the newcomer to excellence, and making him (or, less appropriately, her) assert his own powers in contest with the illustrious dead. The 'potentially strong poet', according to Bloom, must somehow capture his precursor in order to avoid being overwhelmed by the past, and so the epigraph functions as a reminder of the heroic struggle. Equally plausible, however, would be the reading that views quotations as signs of vanished magnificence, fragments of an earlier age under which the literary latecomer must forever lie prostrate, rather like Fuseli's memorable image of 'The Artist Moved by the Magnitude of Antique Fragments'. For if the past is a 'burden', quotation from a literary elder may effectively crush the life from the younger poem beneath. With this attitude dominant,

[34] Harold Bloom, *The Anxiety of Influence: A Theory of Poetry* (New York, 1973). See also his later *A Map of Misreading* (Oxford and New York, 1975), and the useful collection of essays, *Poetics of Influence*, ed. J. Hollander (New Haven, 1988).

[35] W. J. Bate, *The Burden of the Past and the English Poet* (London, 1971).

the epigraph serves as a reminder that despite the struggles of the new poet, any quest for originality is futile because everything has been said before: discovery is merely the re-articulation of an old truth.

Such critical approaches shed helpful light on the strange survival of the epigraph and the use of quotation in Romantic poetry and have helped to illuminate some of the discussion of individual poems below. For the work of both Bloom and Bate, and that of the critics on whom they have themselves exerted a powerful influence, is more complicated than my brief paraphrase might suggest, the critical analyses being much richer and subtler when read in conjunction with the poems on the couch. Bate's book opens, for example, with Dryden's verse epistle 'To My Dear Friend Mr Congreve, on his Comedy called The Double Dealer', whose title signals at once that the self-deprecations of the modern poem are not entirely straightforward. The past may be rather burdensome ('Strong were our sires, and as they fought they writ . . . what we gained in skill we lost in strength'), but it is also a source of inspiration, not least because the very articulation of the sense of belatedness is not a topic that has been exhausted by the strong sires. The modern writer's predicament of being without a subject turns out to be a subject in itself, and one that demands all the wit and ingenuity of the extraordinary poem on 'Nothing' by Dryden's contemporary, Rochester.[36] Despite the personal tone of the letter form, the attempt to write about the difficulty of writing is characteristic of the paradoxical and intelligent age that Dryden appears to berate, and so to read his poem as emotionally self-revelatory is fraught with problems. Like the modern author of *The Battle of the Books*, Dryden's own words counter what he appears to be arguing, thus complicating the sense of the age's supposed inferiority to the past.[37]

That earlier writers were treated by Dryden and his con-

---

[36] John Wilmot, Earl of Rochester, *The Complete Works*, ed. Frank H. Ellis (Harmondsworth, 1994), 201–4; 'To My Dear Friend Mr Congreve', *The Oxford Authors: John Dryden*, ed. Keith Walker (Oxford and New York, 1987), 455–7.

[37] Jonathan Swift's *The Battle of the Books* (1704) satirized contemporary debate about the relative value of Ancient and Modern Learning. For useful discussions of the controversy, see J. Levine, *The Battle of the Books: History and Literature in the Augustan Age* (London, 1991); R. F. Jones, *Ancients and Moderns: A Study of the Rise of the Scientific Movement in Seventeenth Century England* (St Louis, 1936).

temporaries not only with reverence or antagonism but also wit is equally clear from the explosion of parody and mock forms in the early eighteenth century. It could be argued, of course, that mockery is essentially defensive, and that poems whose jokes rely on the evocation of great predecessors are just as anxiety-driven as those by Romantic writers who attempted the higher literary kinds with the highest seriousness. The resulting poetry is very different, however, and so are its effects on the reader. *The Rape of the Lock*, for example, does not immediately strike as a poem about Milton's influence, any more than *Tom Jones* seems to be Fielding's way of dealing with the 'problem' of Homer. Evocation of earlier texts in the eighteenth century can often be a fairly relaxed business because the poems were so well known that writers could assume their readers' familiarity with the original. The games are then played on the assumption that everyone knows the rules. With direct quotation, too, the canonical text frequently provides a familiar base against which the new piece can bounce incongruous ideas, as when Robert Burns adapts a line from *Paradise Lost* to introduce his poem on the Scotch Distillery Act of 1786, 'Dearest of distillation! Last and best'.[38]

To assume that quotation from a literary classic in the eighteenth century was always reverential or anxious would be a mistake; but so would the related notion that quotation always had the power to impress an audience. Although Addison began each of his famous *Spectator* essays with a line from Horace or Virgil, Ovid or Cicero, he was well aware of the potential absurdities, and sent himself up in No. 221, by recounting the tale of two country clergymen whose competition for the larger congregation was settled by their use of Latin. At first the more learned preacher attracted greater numbers by filling his sermons with passages from the early Church Fathers. Once his rival discovered a Latin grammar, however, he was able to quote from it just as profusely and thus 'filled his Church, and routed his Antagonist'.[39] The anecdote may appear

---

[38] 'The Author's Earnest Cry and Prayer, to the Scotch Representatives in the House of Commons', *The Poems and Songs of Robert Burns*, ed. James Kinsley, 3 vols. (Oxford, 1968), i. 185. Burns adapts Adam's address to the fallen Eve, 'O fairest of creation, last and best', *Paradise Lost*, IX. 896.

[39] Joseph Addison, *Spectator* 221 (13 Nov. 1711), *The Spectator*, ed. Donald F. Bond, 5 vols. (Oxford, 1965), ii. 360. Cf. Mr Dilly's anecdote about the

to reveal the power of quotation, but is in fact a gently self-deprecating comment on Addison's own practice and the misplaced vanity of his readers: 'The natural Love to *Latin* which is so very prevalent in our common People, makes me think that my Speculations fare never the worse among them for that little Scrap which appears at the Head of them; and what the more encourages me in the use of Quotations in an unknown Tongue is, that I hear the Ladies, whose Approbation I value more than that of the whole Learned World, declare themselves in a more particular manner pleas'd with my *Greek* Motto's.' Jane Austen presumably had this in mind when she wrote to her sister Cassandra of a new acquaintance, 'She has an idea of your being remarkably lively; therefore get ready the proper selection of adverbs, & due scraps of Italian and French', or when she made the socially aspiring Mrs Elton try to impress Emma with Italian phrases.[40] James Macaulay's praise of Burns's first volume of poems is similarly tongue-in-cheek: 'For by the scraps o' French an' Latin, | That's flung athort your buik fu' thick in, | It's easy seen you've aft been flitting | Frae school to school'.[41] Detached quotation, especially from other languages, was a perennial source of humour, even though in a different context the very same lines might be employed to embody a profound truth. Often the underlying purpose is to expose ostentation and false appearances—Mrs Elton's 'parade', Addison's 'Ladies' who pretend to more knowledge than they possess.

The tradition reaches its apogee in Byron's audacious mock epic, where the English school diet of rote learning and copious translation is mercilessly attacked by a narrator whose own diction reveals the enduring after-effects of such an education. Classical quotations are embedded in *Don Juan* with an apparent casualness that makes them all the more startling:

'presbyterian parson, who for eighteen-pence would furnish any pamphleteer with as many scraps of Greek and Latin, as would pass him off for an accomplished classic', as reported by Richard Cumberland, *Memoirs* (London, 1806), 475.

[40] Jane Austen to Cassandra Austen, 26 May 1801, *Jane Austen's Letters*, 3rd edn., ed. Deirdre Le Faye (Oxford, 1995), 90.

[41] 'Rhyming Epistle to Mr. R—— B——, Ayrshire', *Edinburgh Evening Courant*, 23 June 1787; see also Carol McGuirk, *Robert Burns and the Sentimental Era* (Athens, Ga., 1985), 37.

> But Virgil's songs are pure, except that horrid one
> Beginning with *Formosum pastor Corydon*.[42]

Although such moments are part of the larger attempt to
ironize the continuing adherence to classical precedent, for the
poet who rhymed 'Plato' with 'potato', and 'Odysseys' with
'goddesses' and 'bodices', quotation from classical authors was
obviously a rich source of merriment. Much of the humour
nevertheless relies on the continuing attitude of reverence
towards classical authors, for the narrator's capacity to shock
would be much diminished if his readers were equally dismissive
of the great Latin poets. Resounding in the background of
Byron's irreverent usage is the still more prevalent view
epitomized by Dr Johnson's opinion that 'classical quotation is
the *parole* of literary men all over the world'.[43] It is clear, never-
theless, from the numerous references to 'scraps' and 'mottoes'
that although quotations were part of the normal currency,
their purpose was almost as varied as those who enjoyed
them. In familiar conversation they seem to have floated freely,
unanchored by sources or mental footnotes, and ready for any
occasion that should arise.

The offhand manner in which Byron's narrator quotes
Horace or Virgil may seem very different from the detached
epigraph which stood above so many contemporary poems,
apparently looking down on the performance below. However,
it is clear from eighteenth-century accounts of rhetorical
techniques that the use of quotation to introduce more formal
discourse could seem equally spontaneous. Hugh Blair's best-
selling *Lectures on Rhetoric and Belles Lettres*, for example,
had much advice to offer on appropriate introductions, which
should ideally seem 'natural and easy', avoiding any kind of
ostentation. Taking his own cue from Cicero and Quintilian,
who had neatly summed up the aims of an exordium—'Reddere
auditores benevolos, attentos, dociles' ('to make the audience
kind, attentive, and open to persuasion'), Blair advocates
devotion of the greatest care to opening passages, in order
for them to seem natural, spontaneous, and integral to the

---

[42] *Don Juan*, I. 42. The reference is to the first line of Virgil's 'Eclogue II', which
describes the love of Corydon for the young Alexis.

[43] As quoted by Boswell on 8 May 1781, in his *Life of Samuel Johnson* (1791),
ed. G. B. Hill, rev. L. F. Powell, 6 vols. (Oxford, 1934–50), iv. 102.

rest.[44] He also recommends the use of someone else's words as an effective starting point, observing that 'Quinctilian makes an observation which is very worthy of notice: that Introductions, drawn from something that has been said in the course of the Debate, have always a peculiar grace'. Although this relates specifically to public speaking, Blair's approval of quotation as a starting point for the new speech sheds more light on the apparently contradictory discovery of a predilection for epigraphs and quotations in an age obsessed with originality. For he goes on to quote Quintilian at some length, explaining that when a speech is introduced by a reference to the other speaker's discourse, 'it appears not to have been meditated at home, but to have taken rise from the business, and to have been composed on the spot'. Such spontaneity at the outset then makes the whole speech seem 'artless and unlaboured', however many hours had gone into its preparation: 'though all the rest of his Oration should be studied and written, yet the whole Discourse has the appearance of being extemporary, as it is evident that the Introduction to it was unpremeditated'.[45] In order to appear simple and unplanned, then, great attention must be paid to the words of others; and the ironies of Blair's advice to authors are matched by his own adherence to classical texts in the promotion of a supposedly new aesthetic of spontaneity and naturalness.

It may seem inappropriate to relate Blair's analysis of effective oratory to the presentation of published poetry. But there is an interesting parallel between the speech whose seeming spontaneity depends on reference to an earlier speaker and that of the poem which begins with an existing poem, especially at a time when many poems seemed to yearn for the conditions of oral discourse. It could be argued, for example, that Coleridge's 'Dejection: An Ode' has the 'appearance of being extemporary' because it opens with a reference to the lines that form its epigraph:

> Well, if the Bard were weather-wise
> That made the grand old ballad of Sir Patrick Spence.

---

[44] Hugh Blair, 'Lecture 31', *Lectures on Rhetoric and Belles Lettres*, 2 vols. (London and Edinburgh, 1783), ii. 158–69.

[45] Ibid. 168.

The ode (whose form was itself traditionally associated with public orations) appears to respond directly to thoughts triggered by the old ballad, and thus to follow Romantic ideals of spontaneous composition based on individual experience, even though it begins with an earlier poem. Here the introductory quotation is indeed essential to the whole, whose aspiration towards orality is signalled loudly by the colloquial 'Well'. For the expression suggests that the ballad has come to mind not from the speaker's reading, but from the sight of the sky, which has jogged the memory of long familiar words. The apparently simple process demonstrates that even immediate perception of the external world is often complicated and that the re-creation of such first-hand experience in poetry will not necessarily involve a straightforward record of physical objects and details. Spontaneous composition is not therefore at odds with quotation, if perception is partially conditioned by earlier experience, and if experience includes memories of poetry.

One of the main reasons behind the recommendation by Blair (or rather Quintilian) to start with the words of another, however, is to win the audience away from the opponent who is being quoted. By using part of the argument against its author, the subsequent speaker not only appears quick-witted and open to new ideas, but also cleverer. It is a technique that continues to be popular with politicians, barristers, and students whose essays open with a comment from an uncongenial critic. Other people's words can provide a useful Aunt Sally, erected in order to prove the skill and strength of the person bent on demolition. While few of the poetic encounters below are as aggressive as this rhetorical strategy might suggest, it is occasionally possible to see the opening quotation serving as a point against which the responding writer develops an alternative perspective, as when Robert Burns offers a rather different view from *King Lear*, or James Clarence Mangan appears to take issue with Shelley's eloquent statement on life and death. In neither case does the response work to diminish the power of the quoted words, but nor is it in any way submissive in attitude.

Hugh Blair, though obviously indebted to the classical rhetoricians, was also a minister in the Church of Scotland and an effective preacher. But although some of the same principles might apply as readily to the pulpit as the Bar, the differences were also important. Immediately after recommending Quintilian's advice on beginning with the words of an adversary, for example, Blair states emphatically that 'in Sermons, such a practice as this cannot take place'. Sermons also begin routinely with quotation, but the text is biblical and therefore not a line to be taken out of context and turned against its source. The quotation is of course the starting point for the new discourse, but here the response assumes a position of reverence and humility. Blair published the most popular sermons of the late eighteenth century and many of his addresses begin with a direct reference to the day's text. On Good Friday, for example, he takes John 17: 1, 'Jesus lifted up his eyes to heaven, and said, Father! The hour is come', and then proceeds, 'These were the words of our blessed Lord on a memorable occasion.'[46] The Bible is the starting point for a stirring oration on the crucifixion, throughout which Christ's words are cited again and again, forming a linguistic counterpart to the event that provided the 'centre' of human history. There can be no question here about the relative powers of the originating text and the response—the Bible is eternally primary, the sermon, however accomplished, secondary. This unchanging order leads not to antagonism or to the intimidation of the secondary author, however. The model is the source of inspiration, its words an inexhaustible resource on which to draw and be refreshed.

The differences between the attitude of the classical rhetorician and the Christian minister, which merge so interestingly in the work of Hugh Blair, offer helpful ways into the often confusing practices of poetic citation. For while the classical orator had his eye fixed firmly on the audience, the minister is concerned, first and foremost, with obedience to God. If the orator quotes from an opponent to display his own superior knowledge and ingenuity, the preacher, ideally, invokes the Bible for personal guidance and help for his congregation. Both speakers might also resort to quotation to find authority for their own views, but again the orator is largely attempting to persuade and impress, while the minister is seeking to demonstrate the universality of the truths he is attempting to convey. However indebted to classical principles the sermon might be, and

[46] Hugh Blair, 'Sermon V', *Sermons*, 5 vols. (Edinburgh and London, 1777–1801), i, 114.

however frequently clergymen (like those in Addison's account) failed to measure up to the high ideals of humility and obedience, the fundamental differences between the two kinds of discourse remain, and can also be discerned in poetic practice.

While some poems use quotation to convey a sense of the author's wit or erudition, others adopt a more humble stance and seem content that the opening passage should embody some profound truth that the ensuing poem develops. Indeed, it is possible to see both classical and Christian attitudes in the work of T. S. Eliot, as Christopher Ricks has pointed out. In the earlier works, and most obviously *The Waste Land*, Eliot's allusions are, according to Ricks, 'an act of hostility, demanding surrender from the enemy', while after his conversion to Christianity the references to earlier writers become 'an act of self-surrender'.[47] 'Journey of the Magi' thus begins with an extended quotation from Lancelot Andrewes, but there is no sense of rebellion towards the source or the desire to impress or alienate readers. It is a kind of meditation on a biblical source, different in character from Hopkins's dark musing on Jeremiah, 'Thou art indeed just, Lord', but similarly bent on the inner truth and not on displaying the personal achievement of the poet.

If the Christian ideal of humility is not easily reconciled with the aims of classical rhetoric, neither is it entirely compatible with the aesthetic creed of originality. For although originality was often celebrated in quasi-religious language by Romantic poets who presented themselves as prophetic figures, revealing divine truths to the less gifted, it was also associated with pride and self-aggrandisement. The admiration for Milton's Satan that emerges in the work of late eighteenth-century radical writers reveals a new enthusiasm for the revolutionary figure who overturns convention and opens the way to a new society. Satan is, in a sense, an original genius, with the capacity to rebel against authority and change the world for ever. Interestingly, he is also, in Milton's representation, a gifted speaker who employs classical rhetoric with consummate skill. For all his persuasiveness and self-confidence, however, Satan is also the

---

[47] Christopher Ricks, *T. S. Eliot and Prejudice* (London, 1988), 258.

embodiment of pride. In the eyes of Christian readers, Satan's motives have always seemed primarily selfish and vindictive, thus making his seductive activities extremely dangerous. By analogy, the actions of the political or poetic revolutionary, though seemingly noble and generous, could in fact reflect personal ambition and a lust for power. Milton's own some-what uneasy parallels between the course of the narrator of *Paradise Lost* and that of Satan indicate an awareness of the potential hubris of the aspiring poet in the very text that seemed to equate the roles of prophecy and poetry most eloquently. For the Romantic poet, the compelling ideal of originality was thus attended by nagging doubts about the underlying motives, and whether the real attraction might lie in personal glory rather than in the revelation of truth. Was the genius who had the capacity to 'extend the republic of letters, and add a new province of its dominion' working for the good of all mankind, or merely for himself? Hence perhaps the frequent emphasis on the role of the poet in society, and the justification of the most ambitious poems in terms of their benefits to others, serving like Wordsworth's proposed epic 'to chear | Mankind in times to come!'[48]

If the aesthetic demand for originality brought the additional hazard of pride, an epigraph could provide a degree of protec-tion. For the Christian ideal of self-sacrifice could be symbolized by the adoption of an earlier text, even if this were added later as with 'The Rime of the Ancient Mariner'. In its later versions, Coleridge's strange poem ceases to seem the work of a radical poet attempting to chart unmapped waters, and is transformed into a meditation on questions which had occupied the finest minds of the past. The revised 'Ancient Mariner' thus embodies not just the late eighteenth-century ideal of originality, but also the more devotional attitude displayed in Coleridge's 'To William Wordsworth', in which the experience of hearing *The Prelude* leads to prayer. A passage from an earlier author which is somehow connected with the new poem emphasizes a collect-ive quest for truth, whereas the poem alone might be more likely to direct the attention of readers towards the author. For

---

[48] William Wordsworth, *Home at Grasmere: Part First, Book First of The Recluse*, ed. Beth Darlington, *The Cornell Wordsworth* (Ithaca, 1977), 106–7; 'Prospectus to the Recluse', MS 2, 267.

although self-promotion was attractive to some, there were others for whom traditional teachings about pride and ostentation went very deep. If a poem expressing a private emotion were presented with an introductory quotation from elsewhere, it would seem less narrow and self-indulgent, and thus to take on an air of universality, even as it retained the intensity of the personal feeling.

Originality carried the further risk of being self-authenticating: if no one had perceived things in this way before, how could the poet or his readers be confident that the new view was a true one? This is part of the difficulty that Peacock is exposing in *The Four Ages of Poetry*, when he ridicules the Lake Poets by pointing out that their 'new principle' is but another name for falseness and fantasy: 'They wrote verses on a new principle; saw rocks and rivers in a new light . . . and contrived, though they had retreated from the world for the express purpose of seeing nature as she was, to see her only as she was not.'[49] Traditional associations between poetry and madness had also been strengthened in the eighteenth century by Locke's influential diagnosis of the 'mad Men' whose violent Imaginations led them to mistake 'Fancies for Realities'; and although his ideas had been challenged, the disturbing image of the eccentric who saw things differently from the saner members of society still lingered.[50] In the face of such concerns, the poet who strove for originality might well decide to frame his work with reference to more recognizable sources: quotation from an earlier writer could have the effect of validating a new creation, of reassuring a sceptical audience that it was convincing, and worthy of their attention. It is another sign of anxiety, but not one that derives from the fear of powerful predecessors—instead, the predecessors themselves can be exploited to prove that the original poem is all right after all.

Gradually the co-presence of quotation and an aesthetic of originality begins to seem less odd. It is not just that old habits of wit and recourse to classical authority died hard, but that the new ideals of spontaneity and naturalness actually encouraged

[49] *The Four Ages of Poetry* (1820), *The Halliford Edition of the Works of Thomas Love Peacock*, ed. H. F. Brett-Smith and C. E. Jones, 10 vols. (London and New York, 1924–34), viii. 18.

[50] John Locke, *An Essay Concerning Human Understanding* (1690), ed. P. H. Nidditch (Oxford, 1975), 161.

opening reference to earlier observations, in imitation of the immediacy of oral debate or conversation. Attempts at novelty also required external validation, and so a quotation had the additional benefit of pre-empting hostile criticism by demonstrating that the new poem was still articulating something of value to others. Above all, the hubristic tendencies of the revolutionary imagination could be tempered and kept on altruistic tracks if the originality of the poem was shown to reveal the truth, rather than just the brilliance of the poet. In addition to these defensive activities, the epigraph or quotation could also provide a creative catalyst through underlining the continuing power of older texts—the 'strong sires', the 'wells of English undefiled'. As a symbol of an earlier poem, a quotation provided a specific touchstone on which to test the newcomer and stimulate his energies in the wrestle for an independent identity. At the same time, the epigraph served as a clear reminder to poet and readers alike of the great achievements and wisdom of the past. While this might inspire reverence and thus lead to further meditation upon the profoundest questions, it could also prove intimidating enough to discourage the fledgling poet. In the case of published poems, however, any sense of such overpowering greatness is partially checked by the very decision to appear in print, thus introducing an ironic element into the engagement. And it is only a short step from ironic engagement with a past master to parody, where the new poem's entire *raison d'être* is the response to a well-known text.

In the discussion of individual poems which follows, the relationship between the texts and their starting lines are inevitably mixed. Past masters, as is already apparent, can inspire a host of different feelings, ranging from admiration to envy, amusement to anxiety, depending on the mood, the moment, and identity of the reader. When the response to an earlier work takes the form of a poem, all of these reactions might come into play, but the analysis of the resulting text is further complicated by its own readers' perceptions of the new poem's relationship with the past and with the contemporary moment. The poems chosen for detailed discussion below exhibit a great variety of tendencies in their engagements with earlier poems, some reflecting the complicated workings of literary influence, others rather more idiosyncratic factors. In each case, though, the relationship with the opening quotation is complicated, and often seems to change on further investigation. While none take an unequivocally hostile approach to the earlier text, few are content to follow meekly; even when an epigraph appears to have been chosen as a way of highlighting an important thought, the ensuing poem invariably offers an alternative perspective, not necessarily attacking the quotation, but rather responding to changed circumstances and different contemporary demands. Mangan's encounter with Shelley's *Adonais*, for example, is complicated by his position as a Catholic in early nineteenth-century Dublin, while Burns's engagement with Shakespeare is deeply affected by the conflicting contexts in which he was working: his native Ayrshire and post-Enlightenment Edinburgh. In a slightly different way, a text that strikes initially as parodic, such as Noel Coward's 'The Stately Homes of England', rapidly begins to demonstrate a much more subtle and ambivalent relationship to its ancestral poem, influenced by the very different social structures of twentieth-century Britain.

The variety of literary encounters below has meant that the poems as a group seem resistant to any single theory of influence or intertextuality. Since the selection is small and the writers diverse, I have not attempted to establish any helpful, all-purpose model for understanding these poems. Instead, each engagement is explored independently, with detailed attention being given to the new poem and its context. Through close reading of the language and a recognition of the importance of its historical moment, I have attempted to uncover some of the ways in which the chosen poem responds to, grows from, or coexists with the earlier text. To overplay the similarities between the various encounters would be to detract from the interest of the particular engagement under discussion, and to diminish the individuality of the two texts. Nevertheless, the issues which emerge in the series of analyses have a cumulative interest, demonstrating aspects of the development of poetry in response to cultural and political influences, as well as the changing relationships between the literary traditions of these islands.

One of the key questions implicit in this study is whether the quotation that introduces the poem is in itself a mini-text, or whether it is always to some degree allusive? At times the quoted lines seem to have acquired a life of their own, irrespective of their earlier (and continuing) position in a larger text, but often the quotation is a kind of shorthand for the rest of the work from which it was plucked. This means that the older text is constantly there if only in the background, rather like a close friend or famous person at a party: we may not spend the whole evening engaged in conversation, but we are always conscious of the powerful presence. When viewed in this way, the quotation may cease to represent the great tradition or intimidating predecessor, and adopt a more subsidiary role akin to that played by Horatio, Marcellus, and Bernardo in Coleridge's reading of *Hamlet*: 'The knowledge,—the *unthought-of* consciousness,—the *Sensation*, of human Auditors,—of Flesh and Blood Sympathists—acts as a support, a stimulation *a tergo*, while the *front* of the mind, the whole Consciousness of the Speaker, is filled by the solemn Apparition.'[51] Rather than fulfilling the role of the ghost, spurring the speaker into action or agonized introspection, the opening quotation may thus become a kind of background 'support and stimulation', making the dynamics of poetic influence rather more complicated than a linear genealogy might suggest. For since poems often engage with more than one predecessor, different metaphors are needed to describe the various encounters. The epigraph or opening line may be only one quotation among many, and if this is so its pre-eminent position is challenged by subsequent competing influences. The Oedipal model becomes rather more difficult to apply when a poet has several 'fathers', taking the form of poetic predecessors, important role models, *and* the 'real' man known since infancy.

This complication informs the poem by Seamus Heaney discussed in Chapter 7, which was published in *Seeing Things*, a volume haunted by Dante, Virgil, Larkin, Joyce, and, perhaps most powerfully, by the poet's own father. The preoccupation with fathers and sons can also be discerned in another poem written in 1991, the year that *Seeing Things* was published: George Mackay Brown's 'All Souls':

---

[51] Coleridge, Lecture 3, Lectures on Shakespeare, 1818–19, *Lectures 1808–1819 On Literature*, ed. R. A. Foakes, Vol. V of *The Collected Works of Samuel Taylor Coleridge*, 2 vols. (Princeton, 1987), ii. 299.

> 'There are more Hamnavoe
> Folk in the kirkyard
> Than there are walking the
> Hamnavoe street'—
> My father used to say that,
> And I a child.[52]

The opening lines quote the words of Mackay Brown's father, turned into poetry by the son; but the poem goes on to meditate upon a 'throng of good ghosts' that visit the living. Although the poet Edwin Muir appears, he is only one among a 'host so numerous I | can't name them all': for Mackay Brown, influence is not an exclusively literary matter.

Mackay Brown's relationship with the past grows from his special experience in Orkney, whose history sets it apart from the rest of the country. The metaphors of poetic inheritance in such a community seem quite different from those that inform academic analyses of the English literary tradition. Although Brown's work also demonstrates the influence of his wide reading and familiarity with twentieth-century poetics, the importance of his own island's story is paramount, as he explains in the opening passage of his own autobiography: 'These historical events form the backdrop to much of the narrative and verse that I have written. Without the violent beauty of those happenings eight and a half centuries ago, my writing would have been quite different.'[53] The ancient battle of King Hakon and Earl Magnus stands as a kind of epigraph to Mackay Brown's own story, not because it provides a parable for the individual or a typological analogue, but because it has been foundational to the entire community of the island for centuries. Just as the kirkyard of Hamnavoe throngs with good ghosts, so the island community progresses collectively, Mackay Brown's writings being part of the larger cultural tradition. When he composed his most famous book, he adopted a metaphor of craftsmanship, of creating something from existing materials, as is obvious from the title: *An Orkney Tapestry*. Years later he was to describe his task as a poet and storyteller as being 'to rescue the centuries'

---

[52] 'All Souls', 2 Nov. 1991, *Northern Lights: A Poet's Sources* (London, 1999), 67. The poem is reprinted in the Epilogue below.

[53] George Mackay Brown, *For the Islands I Sing: An Autobiography* (London, 1997), 9.

treasure before it is too late'.[54] For such a writer, growing up in a close-knit community where the local legends and happenings continued to live on for hundreds of years, the ideas of influence that illuminate published works by named authors are often unsuitable. The awareness of the past as a living present makes the linearity implicit in so many discussions of poetic tradition inappropriate. The old men of Orkney, who say 'the name Robbie Burns | As if he'd farmed | Very recently, in Cairston or Stenness or Hoy', would find the idea of Burns fulfilling the role of a dominant father figure decidedly odd, for 'Robbie was a poor man | Like themselves'.[55]

Although Mackay Brown's situation as an Orcadian may set him apart from the mainstream of twentieth-century poetry, his approach to poetry and narrative has something in common with the work of a younger, Irish contemporary. For when Ciaran Carson was interviewed about his poetry in 1995 he also stressed the connection between writing verse and storytelling, suggesting that the impulse to write comes not from 'needing to release your psyche', but from 'the urge to invent a story'.[56] He then went on to describe the structure of his own poems:

I would describe them as being based on the structure of a reel, for instance the line is based on the length of four bars of a reel, or it's the long line of the Irish song, or it's the long line when somebody embarks on a story when you're at the bar—'well, there was this man now I'll tell ye and there was this man now . . .'

Although this may seem far removed from the mythic roots of Mackay Brown's work, the parallels with local music and personal conversation reveal a similar integration with a distinctive community, which is providing the larger texture for the poet's work. Carson's deep and practical knowledge of Irish music has helped him to develop a distinctive attitude to the creation of poetry, and the adaptation of sources. In a passage in his prose collection, *Last Night's Fun*, he argues that song-writing is a 'highly artificial construct', but one 'underwritten by the assumptions of the authenticity of universal feelings, as embodied in the speech of common beings', and invokes

[54] *Northern Lights*, 4.
[55] 'January the Twenty-fifth', *Northern Lights*, 11–13.
[56] 'Ciaron Carson: Interview with Niall McGrath', *Edinburgh Review*, 93 (Spring 1995), 61–6, 61.

Wordsworth's Preface to *Lyrical Ballads* in support.[57] However, other aspects of Romantic theory—ideas of organic growth and spontaneity—are dismissed with the observation that 'writing simply is not easy'. The organic metaphors so pervasive in the late eighteenth century are wittily employed in a defence of 'cliché' and 'stock phrases'—the very kinds of imitative language rejected by Wordsworth and his contemporaries: 'If "stock" at one point in its history meant a tree-trunk, it is augmented by a family tree of branching limbs and leafy ornament; and if "cliché" was a stereotype plate or bank of type, then an impression taken from it can come out freshly minted as an original print.' This is a deliberate rejection of Romantic ideas of originality, and one which celebrates the kind of creative achievement that acknowledges, and indeed draws strength from, earlier song-writing:

The words must emerge from a deep awareness of all the floating lines and verses that inhabit songs like these, flitting through the centuries and reverberating in the mouths of generations; and the maker must surrender herself to that authority. She must walk the thin line stretched above the chasm of the past.

As a metaphor for the poet's relationship with her predecessors, the tightrope walk is certainly not free from anxiety, but it is perhaps the absence of distinctive figures that makes it seem so different from the images informing critical works in the tradition of Bloom or Bate. Here it is the songs that survive, rather than the idea of their composer, while the task of the maker seems as much performative as creative. Each new song is constituted by and contributes to the lyrics that have been reverberating for centuries, and yet the limelight is now on the piece that is emerging from the shadows.

The ways in which traditional stories develop nevertheless depend on a sense of the singer, the present audience, and the earlier performers. Just as Carson's father is described in *The Star Factory*, remembering his narrative through 'rhythmic clusters and motifs', which contain 'implications of its past and future' and serve as '*aides-mémoires* for both audience and teller', so his own writing seems to unfold before an imagined

---

[57] Ciaran Carson, *Last Night's Fun: A Book About Irish Traditional Music* (London, 1996), 158.

audience.[58] Like Mackay Brown, with his 'store of symbols', Carson has a rich supply of 'constellations' to light his tale on its way. His work is studded with significant images and recurrent words, which readers can gradually begin to recognize and interpret through the deepening associations gathered through the text. The organization is not a linear, logical progression, but conveys a sense of the existence of many stories, which the individual teller picks up and weaves into a new pattern—'the hook-and-eye principle' of writing, as Carson describes it.[59] Oral tradition renders the idea of beginning with the beginning redundant, for all tales must start at the point chosen by the teller. The story has already been told many times before, and so it is the craft of the latest narrator that makes the tale worth hearing. The whole story is an extended quotation, and often the skill lies in the choice of which lines to retain, and which passages to import from other existing tales. In Carson's prose texts, several pages are often devoted to a series of passages from different sources, all knitted into a startling new pattern.

Metaphors of knitting and weaving evoke craftsmanship, and are thus in accord with the deep sense of community that emerges from the writings of both Mackay Brown and Ciaran Carson. For despite the important differences between the poet who lived on the remote island off the north-east coast of Scotland and his younger contemporary who grew up in the broken industrial city of Belfast, both are strongly influenced by oral poetry and its methods. But each inhabits other worlds as well, which means his distinctive compositions incorporate not only local symbols and stories, but also cultural traditions that seem quite alien. The 'floating lines and verses' that make their way into Carson's work are often drawn from his wide reading, and thus the traditions of storytelling and song-writing collide with published texts, resulting in a dynamic, and often ironic mixture, that is quite distinct from any individual source.

Although the collision of the oral and the literary is often very fruitful and exciting, it can also be painful, complicated as it is by the internal history of these islands. For twentieth-century

[58] Ciaran Carson, *The Star Factory* (London, 1997), 66.
[59] Ibid. 226.

Irish writers, the great poems of the English tradition represent a colonial as well as a literary burden. When Yeats used the memorable phrase later adopted by Bate in *The Burden of the Past*, it was in a context in which literature was inseparable from history:

You ask what I have found, and far and wide I go:
Nothing but Cromwell's house and Cromwell's murderous crew,
The lovers and the dancers are beaten into clay,
And the tall men, and the swordsmen and the horsemen, where are
    they?
And there is an old beggar wandering in his pride,
His fathers served their fathers before Christ was crucified.
    O what of that, O what of that,
    What is there left to say?[60]

And yet, as Edward Callan has shown, Yeats singled out this stanza in the draft of his 'General Introduction for my Work' as representative of the kind of hatred that sometimes possesses those, like himself, in whom 'the past is always alive'.[61] He then went on to confess that he owed his soul 'to Shakespeare, to Spenser and to Blake, perhaps to William Morris, and to the English language in which I think, speak, and write'. As a Protestant property-owner and a founder member of the Irish Free State, Yeats's political position was deeply ambiguous, but his literary dilemma is one that has been shared by many Irish writers, caught between a desire to resist English culture as both symbol and instrument of an oppressive colonial power, and an often deep attachment to the familiar literature and language. In a stirring essay of the late 1970s, Sean Golden observed that 'the colonized native *cannot* have the same relationship with the English tradition that the native Englishman has', and as a result, the Irish writer 'casts a cold eye on all the monuments of the English tradition'.[62] But despite Golden's understandable

---

[60] 'The Curse of Cromwell', *W. B. Yeats: The Poems*, 351.

[61] W. B. Yeats, 'A General Introduction for my Work', *Yeats on Yeats: The Last Introductions and the 'Dublin' Edition*, ed. Edward Callan (Mountrath, 1981), 62–3. On the significance of this passage, see W. J. McCormack, *Ascendancy and Tradition in Irish Literary History from 1789 to 1939* (Oxford, 1985); George J. B. Watson, *Irish Identity and the Literary Revival: Synge, Yeats, Joyce and O'Casey*, 2nd edn. (Washington, DC, 1994), 31.

[62] Sean Golden, 'Post-Traditional English Literature: A Polemic', *The Crane Bag*, 3/2 (1979), 7–18, 13–14. I am indebted to Luke Gibbons for drawing my attention to this article.

wish to consign the English tradition to the grave, it is clear
that generations of Irish writers have displayed more ambiva-
lent responses to English texts, often drawing on them with
admiration and affection, even in the process of creating some-
thing quite distinct. The preoccupation with political questions
in twentieth-century Ireland has meant that no poet has been
able to allude to an English writer unselfconsciously, however,
and so references are often ironic or deeply uncomfortable, like
Yeats's 'my hatred tortures me with love, my love with hate'.[63]

For a modern Irish writer to begin a poem with a line from an
English writer is thus overtly political. The colonial burden
means that such quotation is not merely threatening to lingering
Romantic ideals of originality, but also to the painfully won
independence of the free writer. If in the aesthetic climate of the
late eighteenth century imitation had become undesirable, how
much more problematic has it been in the postcolonial culture
of the late twentieth century, in its newly designated form of
'mimicry'. For if, as Frantz Fanon argued, the imitation of
established authority is a sign of the deeply colonized subject,
the idea of an Irish poet being guided by English models is
inevitably fraught with internal resistance.[64] Seamus Deane has
accordingly pointed to the significance of Joyce's Stephen
Dedalus, who refuses those forces 'that threaten to make him
nothing more than an inheritor, with a language or discourse
that is theirs, not his'.[65] Dedalus has, therefore, to 'create him-
self'.

At the same time, the very ideal of originality, with its roots
in a Protestant culture of economic individualism, is somewhat
alien to Ireland. Even if Stephen Dedalus is refusing 'Mother
Ireland' and 'Mother Church' along with 'Mother England', the
oral traditions of Ireland (and indeed Catholic ideals of 'self-
surrender') make submission to earlier narrative and song a
natural way to proceed for much of the population.[66] Questions
of influence and inheritance are therefore deeply contradictory.
The difficulties are further increased by the linguistic and
historic complexity of the modern Irish nation. For although

---

[63] Yeats, 'A General Introduction for my Work', *Yeats on Yeats*, 63.
[64] Frantz Fanon, *Black Skin, White Masks* (London, 1991), 103.
[65] Seamus Deane, *Strange Country: Modernity and Nationhood in Irish Writing since 1790* (Oxford, 1997), 96–7.
[66] Ibid.

many twentieth-century writers have been, and continue to be, uneasy with the English language and its forms, the 'native' Irish tradition can sometimes seem equally foreign. Since many Irish writers have grown up in English-speaking households, English is the natural language for composition, and yet its use has to be negotiated and considered, never taken for granted.

The contemporary Irish poems chosen here for detailed discussion reveal the complexity of their encounter with the English tradition individually and through the implicit comparison between the two. Both Seamus Heaney and Ciaran Carson come from Catholic families in the North, both know Irish as well as English, and both have written poems which begin with a line from a poem in English. The results are, however, very different in form, tone, and resolution. Despite the poets' shared cultural experience, their creations are still distinctive, reflecting their own individuality and that of the particular poem which has triggered a response. If reference to English literature is inherently political in a modern Irish context, the range and kind of comment is wide and varied. In some cases, awareness of the colonial aspects of imitation can lead to dark irony, but at times the irony is intensified by the more complicated effects of 'mimicry', which Homi Bhabha has revealed as being profoundly disturbing to the colonial power.[67] In other cases, a lingering Yeatsian 'love' for English literature emerges in ways that are not negatively fraught, but can rather be punning and playful, acknowledging history, recognizing difference, but still looking forward as well as back.

Although I have been discussing Irish experience in the twentieth century, this should not be taken to imply that the use of English quotation by Irish writers has only recently become a political matter. The editors of a radical Dublin newspaper, *The Comet*, launched in the early 1830s during the anti-tithe campaign, were certainly aware of the political potential when they urged their readers to send in examples of those 'apt quotations' which seemed particularly ironic in the contemporary Irish context.[68] Although they were especially interested in the inappropriate application of biblical texts, they also ran a

---

[67] Homi Bhabha, 'Of Mimicry and Men', *The Location of Culture* (London, 1994), 85–92.
[68] 'Apt Quotations', *The Comet* (29 May 1831), 38.

series of Byronic parodies, the 'Ecclesiastical Melodies', which routinely used the *Hebrew Melodies* to provide the form for a satirical lyric on the Established Church. Here the target was not the late Lord Byron, who was well known for his radical sympathies and support for Catholic Emancipation; his extremely popular poetry could nevertheless provide a vehicle for attack through parody. There is thus nothing new about the use of English poetry by Irish writers for explicitly political purposes, but this does not mean that such use necessarily implies hostility towards the English poet. Indeed, the 'Ecclesiastical Melodies' demonstrate the ways in which an established voice can be mimicked ironically, his own affinities with the colonized being exposed as part of the imitative process.

The political charge of an encounter with English poetry is not of course peculiar to the Irish experience. Although the problems confronting a nation struggling to develop an independent culture in the wake of colonial experience may be rather different from those facing other kinds of political change, interesting comparisons can be made between Ireland in the twentieth century and Scotland in the eighteenth. For both in a sense have had to grapple with 'post-Union' experience, even though for twentieth-century Ireland this meant independence, and for eighteenth-century Scotland, union with England. Despite this obvious and massive difference, the respective preoccupations with language and national identity have much in common, and it is quite instructive to contrast the efforts of Scots to master the new 'state language' with the modern Irish desire to break free from the authority of the old colonial power. In both instances, English provides a powerful challenge to which different writers have responded in a variety of ways. In both situations, too, the existence of a completely separate Celtic language has served as a problematic opposite, leaving many poets caught between their awareness of the English tradition and their unfamiliarity with the older, indigenous Gaelic forms. Since my concern here is with the use of quotation in English, I have focused on poems written in English, or, in the case of Burns's 'A Winter Night', in a rich linguistic hybrid. Nevertheless, the use of English by several of the poets

represented below is conditioned by their awareness of alterna-
tives, and often by backgrounds that have contributed to a
fluctuating unease about the dominant language.

It might be assumed that when writers from beyond the
borders of England have chosen to introduce their own words
with those from a canonical English author, they have done
so with a degree of irony, hostility, anxiety, or admiration.
This would, however, indicate a sense of the unquestionable
superiority of English writings. It should already be clear from
the general discussion of the relationship between poems and
epigraphs that, in fact, the power dynamics are rarely pre-
dictable or stable. Once further complicated by linguistic dis-
junctions, the balance becomes even more uncertain and, again,
resistant to any clear pattern of influence. When Burns adopts a
passage from Shakespeare in a volume of poems 'chiefly in the
Scottish Dialect', for example, the difference between the
epigraph and the poem is especially marked, and thus draws
attention to the language of both. Burns's vocabulary signals at
once that his composition belongs to a tradition quite distinct
from that of Shakespeare, and much of his poem repeats this
through the deft shifts between Scots and English. Far from see-
ing this as an expression of the inferiority of his own culture,
however, it is more fruitful to see Burns engaging in a process
of exploration, of weighing different poetic techniques and
cultural values, and finding poetry emerging from the heart of
the encounter.

It would also be mistaken to assume that when Coleridge
quotes from a Scottish source, he is necessarily asserting the
superiority of English poetry. For, as will become clear in the
opening chapters, the very attitudes that led to the promotion
and inhibition of Burns also seem to have obstructed Coleridge,
even as they served as a creative stimulus. Although Coleridge's
employment of an epigraph from a 'grand old ballad' may seem
to contrast strongly with Burns's quotation from Shakespeare,
both 'Dejection' and 'A Winter Night' are grappling with
the contradictory implications of the aesthetic attitudes that
demanded originality and natural growth. Since the Romantic
discourse of originality employed organic metaphors and
emphasized the 'native', it also prized those who seemed rooted
in congenial soil. Consequently, those who, like Coleridge, were

acutely conscious of being restless travellers, untied by childhood or by family tradition to a particular place, were apt to feel disadvantaged when it came to creativity. This sense of deficiency, which made old country ballads seem so attractive, inevitably complicates the question of poetic quotation and the use of epigraphs. According to Edward Said, 'although quotation can take many forms, in every one the quoted passage symbolizes other writing as encroachment, as a disturbing force moving potentially to take over what is presently being written'.[69] The idea is similar in some ways to Bloom's 'anxiety' or Bate's 'burden', but the language used by Said suggests a force more spatial than temporal in its progress. For he continues by observing that even a passing allusion is 'a reminder that other writing serves to displace present writing, to a greater or lesser extent, from its absolute, central, proper place'. This is the language of conquest rather than inheritance, and thus serves as an important corrective to ideas of literary encounter that focus exclusively on linear traditions and poetic genealogies. For Said in *Beginnings*, quotation assumes the role of the colonizing power, alarming the poet who adopts this particular device by its power to 'displace' and 'encroach'. In the light of this, Coleridge's choice of a verse from 'Sir Patrick Spens' should be seen as a sign of deep anxiety about the superior power of the ballad over a poem which deals explicitly with the difficulties of writing.

At the same time, however, it is equally possible to interpret the encounter rather differently, especially given the tendency of so many eighteenth-century English gentlemen to collect miscellaneous treasures from abroad and arrange them in their own houses. If Coleridge is cast as an eclectic collector and member of an expanding world power, his chosen quotations might be seen as the riches of empire—exotic exhibits on display in an English context. His own source, Thomas Percy, seems to have seen himself very much in this light when he described his search for ancient poetry in terms of 'ransacking the whole British Empire'.[70] The subsequent success of 'Dejection', too,

---

[69] *Beginnings*, 22.
[70] Percy to Shenstone, 19 July 1761, *The Percy Letters: The Correspondence of Thomas Percy and William Shenstone*, ed. Cleanth Brooks (New Haven and London, 1977), 109.

has tended to marginalize the lines from the ballad, which now hang above the ode while critical interest continues to be warmed by the poem beneath.

Of course the relationship between 'Dejection' and 'Sir Patrick Spens' does not fit neatly into either perspective, though both have some bearing on the interpretation. As with all the poems under discussion, here, the two texts engage in fine balancing acts, whose tensions contribute greatly to the excitement of the reader. For the ambiguities are not peculiar to the English poets who quote from Scottish or Irish sources—in the texts by Burns, Mangan, Carson, and Heaney, the encounters with English lines are equally complicated. The English quotations often seem to provoke a certain anxiety which might fruitfully be seen as the effects of an encroaching, colonial literature, but, in every case, the responding poem replies triumphantly. The poems below, whether by English, Scottish, or Irish writers, all demonstrate the capacity of their creators to ransack other literature and find whatever is necessary for their own purposes. Epigraphs or quotations placed in prime positions may appear to dominate the poems beneath them, but since the poems are invariably larger and more substantial, the balance keeps shifting, especially in those poems whose structure does not conform to notions of linear, hierarchical, or chronological progression.

Metaphors of colonial encounter indicate an uneasy and even violent relationship, which may be appropriate in some cases. However, it is also clear from many of the discussions below that the disputes with earlier poems are as often affectionate as acrimonious. Despite a difficult political history, many writers still have the capacity to respond positively to other literatures and points of view. Quotation may be a warning sign of encroachment, but very often it offers the possibility of amusement, secret communication, and even deep consolation. Keats, who according to Bate was one of the most 'burdened poets' ever, could still 'look upon fine Phrases like a Lover',[71] and many share his sense of admiration and delight. For Burns, quotations were an essential part of the mental equipment, as he explained to his friend Mrs Dunlop: 'I pick up favorite quotations, & store them in my mind as ready armour, offen-

[71] Keats to Bailey, 14 Aug. 1819, *Letters*, i. 277.

sive, or defensive, amid the struggle of this turbulent exist-
ence.'[72] A similar belief in the power of words is still shared by
Seamus Heaney, who has commented on the way in which one
of Ford Madox Ford's characters manages to deal with his
experience in the trenches by recollecting George Herbert: 'his
sense of value in the face of danger is both clarified and verified
by the fleeting recollection of a couple of his favourite lines'.[73]
And it is this profound sense of the personal importance of
particular lines and phrases that perhaps emerges from this
study as the real common ground, irrespective of other
differences.

When Bernard Darwin introduced *The Oxford Dictionary of
Quotations* to its first readers in 1941, he began with the
startling assertion that 'Quotation brings to many people one of
the intensest joys of living'. Although this may seem somewhat
exaggerated, it is immediately substantiated through reference
to the recent deployment of quotation by the wartime leaders
and especially Winston Churchill, who had stirred a vast
audience with the words of Arthur Hugh Clough. But it was not
apparently Clough's poetry that helped Darwin through the
dark hours, as much as the fact of recognizing Churchill's
quotation—'he had chosen what we knew and what, if we had
thought of it, we could have quoted ourselves'.[74] Quotation in
this instance, it seems, was acting as a kind of code or common
understanding, binding together the English-speaking people
against the advancing menace.

Darwin's little essay is a masterpiece of whimsy, but it never-
theless demonstrates that even in times of intense conflict the
uses of quotation are many and various, including defence just
as readily as attack. In a similar context, it is perhaps also worth
pausing to consider the reaction of Picasso to the news of the
eventual victory of the Allies. Throughout most of the war, he
had been confined to his apartment in Paris, painting still lifes
and portraits of his companion. As the Nazis retreated, how-
ever, Picasso turned to the great masters of the past and began a

---

[72] Burns to Mrs Dunlop, 6 Dec. 1792, *The Letters of Robert Burns*, ed. J. De
Lancey Ferguson, rev. 2nd edn., ed. G. Ross Roy, 2 vols. (Oxford, 1985), ii. 165.
[73] Foreword to *Lifelines: An Anthology of Poems Chosen by Famous People*, ed.
Niall Macmonagle (Harmondsworth, 1993), p. xiii.
[74] Bernard Darwin, Introduction, *The Oxford Dictionary of Quotations*
(Oxford, 1941), p. iii.

series of exuberant adaptations from Poussin and Manet.[75] It is an extraordinary form of quotation, but clearly not one that perceived earlier art forms as threatening or displacing. Just as Van Gogh confessed to drawing deep personal pleasure and 'consolation' from the imitation of great paintings, so Picasso seems to have celebrated the moment of liberty by beginning a highly individual dialogue with the past.[76] With this in mind, it is interesting to speculate on whether the use of quotation by the most able poets is not also, first and foremost, an expression of delight and liberation.

[75] Hans L. C. Jaffé, *Picasso* (New York, n.d. [1973?]), 40–1.
[76] *The Complete Letters of Vincent Van Gogh*, 3 vols. (Greenwich, Conn., 1958), iii. 216, cited by Jaffé, *Picasso*, 148.

2

Scottish Bards and English Epigraphs: Robert Burns's 'A Winter Night'

A Winter Night

Poor naked wretches, wheresoe'er you are,
That bide the pelting of this pityless storm!
How shall your houseless heads, and unfed sides,
Your loop'd and window'd raggedness, defend you
From seasons such as these—

SHAKESPEARE

When biting *Boreas*, fell and doure,
Sharp shivers thro' the leafless bow'r;
When *Phoebus* gies a short-liv'd glow'r,
⟶ Far south the lift,
Dim-dark'ning thro' the flaky show'r,
⟶ Or whirling drift.

Ae night the Storm the steeples rocked,
Poor Labour sweet in sleep was locked,
While burns, wi' snawy wreeths up-choked,
⟶ Wild-eddying swirl,
Or thro' the mining outlet bocked,
⟶ Down headlong hurl.

List'ning, the doors an' winnocks rattle,
I thought me on the ourie cattle,
Or silly sheep, wha bide this brattle
⟶ O' winter war,
And thro' the drift, deep-lairing, sprattle,
⟶ Beneath a scar.

Ilk happing bird, wee, helpless thing!
That, in the merry months o' spring,

Delighted me to hear thee sing,
　　　　What comes o' thee?
Whare wilt thou cow'r thy chittering wing,
　　　　An' close thy e'e?

Ev'n you on murd'ring errands toil'd,
Lone from your savage homes exil'd,
The blood-stain'd roost, and sheep-cote spoil'd,
　　　　My heart forgets,
While pityless the tempest wild
　　　　Sore on you beats.

Now *Phoebe*, in her midnight reign,
Dark-muffl'd, view'd the dreary plain;
Still crouding thoughts, a pensive train,
　　　　Rose in my soul,
When on my ear this plaintive strain,
　　　　Slow-solemn, stole—

　'Blow, blow, ye Winds, with heavier gust!
　'And freeze, thou bitter-biting Frost!
　'Descend, ye chilly, smothering Snows!
　'Not all your rage, as now, united shows
　　'More hard unkindness, unrelenting,
　　'Vengeful malice, unrepenting,
'Than heaven-illumin'd Man on brother Man bestows!

　'See stern Oppression's iron grip,
　　'Or mad Ambition's gory hand,
　'Sending, like blood-hounds from the slip,
　　'Woe, Want, and Murder o'er a land!
　'Ev'n in the peaceful rural vale,
　'Truth, weeping, tells the mournful tale,
'How pamper'd Luxury, Flatt'ry by her side,
　'The parasite empoisoning her ear,
　'With all the servile wretches in the rear,
'Looks o'er proud Property, extended wide;
　'And eyes the simple, rustic Hind,
　　'Whose toil upholds the glitt'ring show,
　'A creature of another kind,
　'Some coarser substance, unrefin'd,
'Plac'd for her lordly use thus far, thus vile, below!

　'Where, where is Love's fond, tender throe,
　'With lordly Honor's lofty brow,
　　'The pow'rs you proudly own?

'Is there, beneath Love's noble name,
'Can harbour, dark, the selfish aim,
  'To bless himself alone!
'Mark Maiden-innocence a prey
  'To love-pretending snares,
'This boasted Honor turns away,
  'Shunning soft Pity's rising sway,
'Regardless of the tears, and unavailing pray'rs!
'Perhaps, this hour, in Mis'ry's squalid nest,
'She strains your infant to her joyless breast,
'And with a Mother's fears shrinks at the rocking blast!

  'Oh ye! who, sunk in beds of down,
'Feel not a want but what yourselves create,
'Think, for a moment, on his wretched fate,
  'Whom friends and fortune quite disown!
'Ill-satisfy'd, keen Nature's clam'rous call,
  'Stretch'd on his straw he lays himself to sleep,
'While thro' the ragged roof and chinky wall,
  'Chill, o'er his slumbers, piles the drifty heap!
'Think on the dungeon's grim confine,
'Where Guilt and poor Misfortune pine!
'Guilt, erring Man, relenting view!
'But shall thy legal rage pursue
'The Wretch, already crushed low
'By cruel Fortune's undeserved blow?
'Affliction's sons are brothers in distress;
'A Brother to relieve, how exquisite the bliss!'

    I heard nae mair, for *Chanticleer*
      Shook off the pouthery snaw,
    And hail'd the morning with a cheer,
      A cottage-rousing craw.

    But deep this truth impress'd my mind—
      Thro' all his works abroad,
    The heart benevolent and kind
      The most resembles GOD.[1]

Few volumes of poetry can have had as decisive an impact on their first readers or, indeed, on the lives of their authors as Robert Burns's *Poems, Chiefly in the Scottish Dialect*. The little

---

[1] 'A Winter Night' was first published in the enlarged edition of Robert Burns's *Poems Chiefly in the Scottish Dialect* (Edinburgh, 1787), 199–204. The text included here and all further references to Burns's poetry are taken from *The Poems and Songs of Robert Burns*, ed. James Kinsley, 3 vols. (Oxford, 1968).

collection was published in Kilmarnock, a small town in Ayrshire, in July 1786, but news of its extraordinary quality spread rapidly. Within weeks, the first edition had more or less sold out and plans for a second were under way. Instead of Jamaica, which had been the destination of a rather desperately planned escape from financial ruin and very messy emotional entanglements, Burns found himself heading for Edinburgh to dazzle, and be fêted by, literary high society. It was a remarkable turn of fortune, but one so swift that its effect seems to have been as much unsettling as uplifting. In the capital city, Burns may not have been faced with a failing farm or lovers carrying his children, but there were new, and unexpected pressures. A second edition of the poems would require more material, but for the first time in his life Burns was writing at the demand of others. The original pieces that had attracted so much favourable attention were composed for his own satisfaction or for friends, but anything written in the wake of the Kilmarnock edition bore the full weight of public expectation. If Burns had been saved from emigration in August, December found him writing to William Greenfield, the Professor of Rhetoric and Belles Lettres at the University of Edinburgh, to acknowledge grave misgivings about the future:

Never did Saul's armour sit so heavy on David when going to encounter Goliah, as does the encumbering robe of public notice with which the friendship and patronage of some 'names dear to fame' have invested me.—I do not say this in the ridiculous idea of seeming self-abasement, and affected modesty.—I have long studied myself, and I think I know pretty exactly what ground I occupy, both as a Man, & a Poet; and however the world, or a friend, may sometimes differ from me in that particular, I stand for it, in silent resolve, with all the tenaciousness of Property.—I am willing to believe that my abilities deserved a better fate than the veriest shades of life; but to be dragged forth, with all my imperfections on my head, to the full glare of learned and polite observation, is what, I am afraid, I shall have bitter reason to repent.—

I mention this to you, once for all, merely, in the Confessor style, to disburthen my conscience, and that—'When proud Fortune's ebbing tide recedes'—you may bear me witness, when my buble of fame was at the highest, I stood, unintoxicated, with the inebriating cup in my hand, looking forward, with rueful resolve, to the hastening time when the stroke of envious Calumny, with all the eagerness of vengeful triumph, should dash it to the ground.[2]

This remarkable letter is peculiarly characteristic of Burns, because while it apparently looks forward with humility to less auspicious days, the tone is elevated and extravagantly literary. The echoes of Shakespeare and Shenstone reveal a self-dramatizing persona whose awareness of his audience adds a certain irony to the supposed fear of 'the full glare of learned and polite observation'. The highly rhetorical parallel with David, too, is unlikely to make his correspondent conclude that Burns is doomed to failure. The identification with the shepherd boy who triumphed on his own terms is nevertheless telling, especially in the winter of 1786–7 when Burns was wrestling to produce more poems for an increasingly unfamiliar audience. For although it conveys a sense of inner strength and ingenuity sufficient to conquer the most unfavourable odds, it also reveals an acute awareness of the potentially obstructive effects of fame and patronage. In an ironic reversal, typical of Burns, the 'confessor' figure stands accused.

Burns's anxieties about his future as a poet were partly a natural response to sudden, overnight success. But they were also aggravated by the immediate reception of his work, which was unusually complicated and contradictory. Readers of his first collection of poetry seem to have been variously overwhelmed with pleasure, astonishment, or exhaustion, depending on where they happened to live. Perhaps not surprisingly, the acclaim in Ayrshire was universal, as Robert Heron, who lived in neighbouring Galloway at the time, recalled some years later: 'Old and young, high and low, grave and gay, learned or ignorant, all were alike delighted, agitated, transported.'[3] Further afield in rural Northamptonshire, however, the volume

---

[2] Burns to Greenfield, Dec. 1786, *Letters*, i. 73–4. In the event, Greenfield had more to fear with regard to sudden loss of reputation than did Burns, as Martin Moonie has discovered, 'William Greenfield: Gender and the Transmission of Literary Culture', in Robert Crawford (ed.), *The Scottish Invention of English Literature* (Cambridge, 1998), 103–15.

[3] Robert Heron, 'Memoirs of the Life of the Late Robert Burns', *Monthly Magazine*, 3 (1797), 213–16, 552–62, 215. Extracts from Heron's 'Memoir', and many other responses to Burns have been helpfully assembled by Donald A. Low in *Robert Burns: The Critical Heritage* (London and Boston, 1974).

did not go down so well: William Cowper had the greatest difficulty in finding a friend to share his enthusiasm for Burns ('I lent him to a very sensible neighbour of mine, but his uncouth dialect spoiled all and before he had half read him through, he was quite *ramfeezled*'[4]). But it was in Edinburgh that the poems seemed to pose particular problems, leaving readers torn between their excitement over a newly discovered Scottish genius and a rather paradoxical regret that he should have chosen to write in his local dialect. As Henry Mackenzie observed in his influential periodical, the *Lounger*, 'Even in Scotland, the provincial dialect which Ramsay and he have used is now read with a difficulty which greatly damps the pleasure of the reader: in England it cannot be read at all, without such a constant reference to a glossary, as nearly to destroy that pleasure.'[5] Mackenzie articulated the dilemma of many when he praised the natural genius of Burns, and yet acknowledged the linguistic 'bar' to the reader's enjoyment, helpfully pointing out as he did so those pieces that were 'almost English'.

In the *Monthly Review*, James Anderson combined high praise of the poetry with serious doubts about its general intelligibility. 'The Cotter's Saturday Night' is singled out as a 'beautiful picture of that simplicity of manners, which still, we are assured, on the best authority, prevails in those parts of the country where the Author dwells', and yet the selected passages of the poem are introduced with the following comment: 'We have used the freedom to modernise the orthography a little, wherever the measure would permit, to render it less disgusting to our Readers south of the Tweed.'[6] In the same review, the comic pieces are praised, while the 'Odes, Dirges, &c' are dismissed as 'very poor', which leaves a somewhat confusing impression of the volume as a whole. For the comic pieces, in Scots, though supposedly superior, are yet deemed unintelligible and even 'disgusting'. The English odes and dirges, on the other hand, may be universally accessible, but are nevertheless of a most inferior quality. It is perhaps not surprising in the face of

---

[4] Cowper to Samuel Rose, 27 Aug. 1787, *The Letters and Prose Writings of William Cowper*, ed. J. King and C. Ryskamp, 5 vols. (Oxford, 1979–86), iii. 18.
[5] *Lounger*, 97 (9 Dec. 1786), 386.
[6] 'Poems Chiefly in the Scottish Dialect. By Robert Burns', *Monthly Review*, 75 (1786), 442.

such responses that when Burns began to consider his new material in the winter of 1786, he felt somewhat uncertain about his future. To write in Scots, it seems, was to limit the audience and attract further comment about his lack of education and general ignorance, but to write in English was to risk accusations of downright failure.

The very aspects of his life that most excited readers were threatening to stunt his development as a poet because of the curious logic that influenced the reception of his work: as a 'simple Bard' he must be unfamiliar with the language and culture of the wider world, and consequently any attempts at 'higher' kinds of literature struck educated readers as inappropriate or derivative. These are the kinds of difficulty being confronted in a poem such as 'A Winter Night', which Burns wrote in Edinburgh in November 1786, as he grappled with the conflicting influences on his poetry and agonized about his future.

To what extent the critical response to Burns was determined solely by the Kilmarnock edition is difficult to assess because of the complicated position of the Scots language at the time of its composition. The Edinburgh men of letters who enthused over Burns's genius clearly found their desire to praise compromised by a tradition of awkwardness surrounding the Scottish tongue. The problem was expressed most memorably by James Beattie, in a letter whose very eloquence contradicts the feelings to which it confesses:

We who live in Scotland are obliged to study English from books, like a dead language. Accordingly, when we write, we write it like a dead language, which we understand but cannot speak; avoiding, perhaps, all ungrammatical expressions, and even the barbarisms of our country, but at the same time without communicating that neatness, ease, and softness of phrase, which appears so conspicuously in Addison, Lord Lyttleton, and other elegant English authors. Our style is stately and unwieldy, and clogs the tongue in pronunciation, and smells of the lamp. We are slaves to the language we write, and are continually afraid of committing *gross* blunders; and, when an easy, familiar, idiomatical phrase occurs, dare not adopt it, if we recollect no authority, for fear of Scotticisms. In a word, *we* handle English, as a person who cannot fence handles a sword; continually afraid of hurting ourselves with it, or letting it fall, or making some awkward motion that shall betray our ignorance. An English author of learning is the master, not the slave, of his language, and wields it gracefully, because he wields it with ease, and with full assurance that he has the command of it.[7]

Although the very problem appears to have stimulated Beattie to vivid metaphors of slavery and swordsmanship, his deep anxiety about the spoken word, and the related difficulty of giving a 'vernacular cast' to his written English, is only too apparent.

As many twentieth-century scholars have pointed out, eighteenth-century Scotland was caught in a paradoxical situation wherein its intellectuals were leading the world in philosophical and scientific advances, and yet suffering from an acute embarrassment about the way in which they spoke.[8] David Hume, for example, possessed not only the most brilliant brain of the period, but also a distinct lack of confidence about his prose style, and still sent work to friends to have it purged of 'Scoticisms'.[9] The difficulty appears to have had its origins in 1603 when the court of James VI moved south; even more significant, though, was the 1707 Act of Union which completed the shift of political power from Edinburgh to London. As affairs of state came to be conducted entirely in England, so the language of Scotland began to seem provincial and subordinate. The growth of literacy, the vast expansion of the publishing trade, and the enormous improvement in transport and communications, all combined to assist the spread of English as the standard language of the United Kingdom, thus accentuating perceptions in North Britain of a great gulf between Scottish speech and the acceptable written word.[10] The

[7] Beattie in response to a proposed essay on 'Scottish barbarisms' by Sylvester Douglas, Lord Glenbervie, 5 Jan. 1778, William Forbes, *An Account of the Life and Writings of James Beattie*, 2 vols. (Edinburgh, 1806), ii. 17.

[8] See especially David Daiches, *The Paradox of Scottish Culture* (London, 1964); David Craig, *Scottish Literature and the Scottish People 1630–1830* (London, 1961); Tony Crowley, *Language in History* (London, 1996); Robert Crawford, *Devolving English Literature* (Oxford, 1992); James Basker, 'Scotticisms and the Problem of Cultural Identity in Eighteenth-Century Britain', in John Dwyer and Richard B. Sher (eds.), *Sociability and Society in Eighteenth-Century Scotland* (Edinburgh, 1993), 82–95.

[9] Hume to David Mallet (Anglicized form of 'Malloch'), 8 Nov. 1762, *The Letters of David Hume*, ed. J. Y. T. Greig, 2 vols. (Oxford, 1932), i. 370; cited in Basker, 'Scotticisms', 85.

[10] For a variety of approaches to the issue of the Union and its implications for Scottish writers, see Kenneth Simpson, *The Protean Scot: The Crisis of Identity in Eighteenth-Century Scottish Literature* (Aberdeen, 1988); Colin Kidd, *Subverting*

benefits of the Union were celebrated in the first *Edinburgh Review*; but the very recognition of the rapid 'progress of knowledge' also brought an increased awareness of what seemed a major obstacle to further improvement—'the difficulty of a proper expression in a country where there is either no standard of language, or at least one very remote'.[11] It was in this climate of cultural embarrassment that the Irish elocutionist, Thomas Sheridan, was invited to Edinburgh to lecture to packed houses on the 'Reading and Speaking of the English Language'.[12]

The sense of difference highlighted by the Union also encouraged linguistic activity of another kind, however, by stimulating interest in the native languages of Scotland. The removal of Parliament from Edinburgh prompted a new awareness of what was essentially *Scottish* rather than British, thus alerting people to the riches of the home-grown tradition.[13] Although the Jacobite Risings led to concerted efforts to eradicate Gaelic, the popularity of poetry collections in Scots was growing from 1707 onwards.[14] At the same time, however, the powerful vernacular revival was somewhat circumscribed by the steady diminishment of the literary standing of the Scots language, a decline which even those most energetically involved in its preservation seem to have accelerated. As Harriet

Scotland's Past: Scottish Whig Historians and the Creation of an Anglo-British Identity, 1689–c.1830 (Cambridge, 1993); Leith Davis, *Acts of Union: Scotland and the Literary Negotiation of the British Nation 1707–1830* (Stanford, 1999).

[11] *Edinburgh Review*, I (1755), Preface, pp. ii–iii. Despite distinguished contributors such as Adam Smith and Hugh Blair, the journal was short-lived and is much less well known than its namesake, founded by Francis Jeffrey in 1802.

[12] Sheridan published his lectures the year after their oral delivery as *A Course of Lectures on Elocution* (London, 1762).

[13] On the crucial role of Allan Ramsay in this period, see *Poems by Allan Ramsay and Robert Fergusson*, ed. A. M. Kinghorn and A. Law (Edinburgh and London, 1974). See also John Butt, 'The Revival of Scottish Vernacular Poetry in the Eighteenth Century', in F. W. Hilles and Harold Bloom (eds.), *From Sensibility to Romanticism: Essays Presented to Frederick A. Pottle* (New York, 1965), 219–37; Douglas Dunn, ' "A Very Scottish Kind of Dash": Burns's Native Metric', in Robert Crawford (ed.), *Robert Burns and Cultural Authority* (Edinburgh, 1997), 58–85.

[14] Charles Withers has examined the retreat of Gaelic in *Gaelic in Scotland, 1698–1981* (Edinburgh, 1984). Interestingly, the decades of suppression also saw a flowering of Gaelic poetry, in the work of Alasdair Mac Mhaighstir Alasdair, Donnchadh Ban Mac t-Saoir, Rob Donn, and Iain MacCodrum. For useful discussion, see Derick S. Thomson, *An Introduction to Gaelic Poetry* (London, 1977), 156–217; William J. Watson (ed.) *Bardachd Ghaidhlig: Gaelic Poetry 1550–1900*, 3rd edn. (repr. Inverness, 1976).

Harvey Wood has observed in her edition of James Watson's important *Choice Collection of Comic and Serious Scots Poems*,

It is the ultimate irony that Watson, whose avowed intention it was to preserve Scots poetry and make it more widely known, should have contributed unwittingly to the provincialization of the language. For the message transmitted by the *Collection*, taken as a whole, to later poets is clear: Scots for *Christ's Kirk*, for *The Mare of Collingtoun*, for the homely proverbs of *The Cherry and the Slae* and for the vigorous bawdy and invective of *The Flyting of Polwart and Montgomerie*; English for the poems of gentility.[15]

As the century progressed, Scots was increasingly associated with low life, rusticity, and humour, suitable for certain purposes and readers, but heavily restricted in its scope. The vogue for sentimental literature in the latter half of the century may have helped to encourage the market for poetry in 'Scottish dialect' but, as Carol McGuirk has shown, with the middle-class cult of sensibility came an attitude of pity towards dialect poets and their subject matter.[16] By the time Burns published his first volume of poetry, the division between the language used by the Anglo-aspiring critics in the literary periodicals and that of the untutored bards whom they patronized was wide indeed. When Burns was hailed as a 'Heaven-taught ploughman' by Edinburgh's leading literary light, the praise of his passion, genius, and fire thus came packaged with assumptions about rusticity, ignorance, and low birth.[17]

Characteristically, however, the ploughman poet achieved with his first collection not only instant fame, but also a curious inversion of the assumptions of many of his readers. Even as his collection fulfilled certain expectations about the subject and style of a rural bard, it also seems to have wrong-footed many readers by surreptitiously challenging their positions of assumed authority. For while the literati marvelled at the outpourings of the labouring poet, their own reading experience was far from easy, natural, and spontaneous. Though hardened by 'toil and fatigues', Burns still emerges in the reviews and letters of the period as a poet whose 'simple strains, artless and unadorned,

---

[15] Harriet Harvey Wood (ed.), *James Watson's Choice Collection of Comic and Serious Scots Poems*, 2 vols. (Edinburgh and Aberdeen, 1977, 1991), ii, p. xxvii.

[16] McGuirk, *Robert Burns and the Sentimental Era*, 59–83.

[17] Mackenzie's famous remark appeared in the *Lounger*, 97 (9 Dec. 1786), 388.

seem to flow without effort from the native feelings of the heart'.[18] His more comfortable readers, on the other hand, were faced with the hard task of working out exactly what these simple strains might mean. And the further from Ayrshire, the harder the labour of reading.

In the short preface to the Kilmarnock edition, Burns drew attention to his lack of a classical education, but it is done in such a way that the superiority of his own knowledge seems indisputable. Unlike the poet who 'amid the elegancies and idlenesses of upper life, looks down for a rural theme, with an eye to Theocritus or Virgil', Burns presents himself as singing 'the sentiments and manners, he felt and saw in himself and his rustic compeers around him'.[19] What appears to be a confession of ignorance is in fact a statement of authority, as he makes clear that in contrast to those bookish writers who search for inspiration among dead languages, his own knowledge of rural life is authentic, first-hand, and continuing. The acknowledgement that he has not been taught to compose poetry 'by rule' is equally double-edged, since his desire to 'transcribe the various feelings, the loves, the griefs, the hopes, the fears, in his own breast' not only seems a rather more interesting motivation, but also emphasizes an innate capacity for deep feeling. As Burns admits certain limitations to his audience, he indirectly asserts his possession of strong passions and associated powers of creativity—qualities that were increasingly being seen as essential to great poetry.

The decades immediately preceding the publication of Burns's work had seen a steady shift in taste from the neoclassical ideals of harmony, order, and rational control to a new aesthetic that placed a higher value on wildness, originality, creative energy, and feeling. Burns's poetry was released into a culture increasingly conditioned to admire poets such as Homer and Shakespeare for their innate 'fire' and brilliant capacity to draw intuitively on 'nature'.[20] His preface is thus both soaked in and

---

[18] *Monthly Review*, 75 (1786), 440.

[19] Burns, Preface to the Kilmarnock edition, *Poems and Songs*, iii. 971.

[20] On the changing attitudes to Homer and Shakespeare in this period, see D. M. Foerster, *Homer in English Criticism: The Historical Approach in the Eighteenth Century* (New Haven, 1947); K. Simonsuuri, *Homer's Original Genius: Eighteenth-Century Notions of the Early Greek Epic 1688–1798* (Cambridge, 1979); Michael Dobson, *The Making of the National Poet: Shakespeare,*

appealing to readers similarly immersed in the aesthetic ideals of the mid-eighteenth century, even though some of these were ultimately problematic. For the use of Scots, which created such difficulties for Burns's urban readers, is part of the same aesthetic trend to celebrate spontaneity and naturalness. In the preface, the issue is treated casually, in the explanation for the choice of subject: Burns responds to his local community and therefore 'sings . . . in his and their native language'. His practice is entirely consistent with prevailing aesthetic theory; but the corollary seems to have been that those less close to his sources had more difficulty in understanding his art. In another odd inversion of normal assumptions, Burns seems to demonstrate that the further from 'nature', the more strenuous the effort of reading and the slower the enjoyment of the spontaneous effusions. The 'simple Bard' emerges from the volume not only as an intuitive genius, but also as a teacher ready to assist more remote readers with a glossary and occasional explanatory notes. Since the emotional centre of his work was firmly located in south-west Scotland, it followed that those long-distance readers who were prepared to battle with unfamiliar vocabulary found themselves placed in a peripheral position. 'David' was thus demonstrating his ability to conquer those who might think themselves in a position to look down on his efforts.

The same surface humility and underlying assertion of superiority can be read into the very title of Burns's volume. For while the description of his poems as being 'in the Scottish dialect' suggests the use of provincial, non-standard language, the qualifying 'chiefly' provides a possible counterbalance. Its obvious meaning is to indicate that most of the poems in the collection will be in Scots—that they are *largely* in dialect. But the choice of 'chiefly' carries the additional associations of leadership and, in the Scottish context, of intimacy. While some readers might see the extensive presence of dialect as a sign of uncouthness and lack of sophistication, then, there were others who would respond more sympathetically, understanding that by being in Scots these poems are 'chiefly'. And it would be

Adaptation and Authority, 1660–1769 (Oxford, 1992); S. Schoenbaum, *Shakespeare's Lives* (Oxford, 1970).

those closest to Burns in terms of language and experience—his 'chief' friends—who would be most able to appreciate the poems. Even in the title, Burns can exploit his familiarity with alternative cultural traditions, playing to an audience who regard English as the gold standard for writing, and also to other readers who would warm to the secret celebration of the native, oral tongue.[21]

At the same time, the very qualification that the poems are 'chiefly' in dialect gives out a strong signal that other elements are there to be found. This is consistent with the preface, which, despite its emphasis on immediate, local inspiration, also reveals the author's familiarity with English literature by quoting 'that celebrated Poet', William Shenstone. The short essay is in itself testimony to Burns's own facility in the standard written language, being, as Alexander Kinghorn pointed out long ago, 'couched in elegant English which ought to have given a lie to any pretence on his part to a lack of formal education'.[22] As the volume unfolds it also becomes clear that Burns's poetry is by no means exclusively Scottish, for in addition to the songs, the poems in 'Standard Habbie' or those in the tradition of 'Christ's Kirk on the Green' or 'Bonnie Heck', the collection also contains prayers, odes, and dirges in the language of eighteenth-century English poetry.[23] Even the poems employing Scottish metre and matter are frequently, as Thomas Crawford has

[21] Cf. Tom Paulin on the local words of Northern Ireland which act 'as a secret sign and serve to exclude outsiders', *A New Look at the Language Question*, in *Ireland's Field Day* (London, 1985), 3–22, 16. For further discussion see Ch. 6, below.

[22] A. M. Kinghorn, 'The Literary and Historical Origins of the Burns Myth', *Dalhousie Review*, xxxix (1959), 76–85. Though see also Kinsley's refutation in his 'Textual Introduction', *Poems and Songs*, iii. 972–3.

[23] 'Standard Habbie', so called from Robert Sempill's use of the form for 'The Life and Death of the Piper of Kilbarchan, or the Epitaph of Habbie Simson', is often referred to as the 'Burns stanza'. It consists of four four-beat lines (iambic tetrameters) interspersed with two two-beat lines (dimeters) and rhymes accordingly—aaabab. For useful discussion see Dunn, ' "A Very Scottish Kind of Dash": Burns's Native Metric', and Derek Attridge, *The Rhythms of English Poetry* (London, 1982), 84–8. 'Christ's Kirk on the Green' is a well-known comic poem, often ascribed to James V; for text and details see Wood (ed.), *Watson's Choice Collection*, i. 1–7, ii. 1–15; see also Allan H. MacLaine, 'The Christ's Kirk Tradition: Its Evolution in Scots Poetry to Burns', *Studies in Scottish Literature*, II (1964–5), i. 3–18. William Hamilton of Gilbertfield's 'The Last Dying Words of Bonny Heck, a Famous Grey-Hound in the Shire of Fife', a model for Burns's 'Death and Dying Words of Poor Mailie', also appears in *Watson's Choice Collection*, i. 68–70, ii. 63–4.

shown, 'shot through with English, a favourite pattern being the movement from a vernacular or "particular" beginning to an English or generalised conclusion'.[24] The sporadic presence of English epigraphs also means that this 'movement' can be seen less in terms of linear development and more as a complicated dynamic through which alternative traditions play off each other. At times, Burns seems to be engaged almost in a linguistic game, except that the ground rules were constantly shifting and being reinvented as the traditions of North Britain readjusted themselves to neighbouring influences.

Poems, Chiefly in the Scottish Dialect contains not only the original poetry of Robert Burns, but also a series of dislocated lines from earlier writers, generally sandwiched between the title and first line of the poem. The quotations, drawn from well-known English poets such as Pope, Gray, and Milton, take the form of epigraphs, standing above the poem and introducing a central theme. At first glance, they are merely part of the normal presentation of poetry in the period: quotations had served as fashionable headpieces for various kinds of literature throughout the century, from the satires and pastorals of the opening decades to the chapter headings of Gothic novels in the last. But while it was commonplace for a young poet to evoke more established authorities on his first venture into print, the linguistic jump in some of the poems between the epigraphs and the verse that follows is so startling that it accentuates both the presence of the quotation and the very different style of the verse:

Address to the Deil

> *O Prince, O chief of many throned pow'rs,*
> *That led th'embattl'd Seraphim to war—*
>   MILTON

> O THOU, whatever title suit thee!
> Auld Hornie, Satan, Nick, or Clootie,
> Wha in yon cavern grim an' sooty
>   Clos'd under hatches,

---

[24] Thomas Crawford, *Burns: A Study of the Poems and Songs* (Edinburgh and London, 1960), 193.

> Spairges about the brunstane cootie,
> To scaud poor wretches![25]

The contrast is almost as extreme as that between the classical mottoes in the *Spectator* and the English essays they adorned. For some readers, Burns might thus seem to be using great English writers in the same way that others had turned to classical texts—to evoke authority and confer respectability on his own compositions. The English epigraphs might be serving as mediators between the raw Scottish dialect and the sensibility of the reader, even performing the role of interpreter by offering clues as to what was to follow. 'The Cotter's Saturday Night', for example, begins with a stanza from Gray's 'Elegy written in a Country Churchyard', which prepares the ground for the ensuing celebration of rural life and places the new poem in a recognizable tradition despite the unfamiliar language.

In many cases, however, the movement from epigraph to poem is a little more complicated. 'Address to the Deil', for example, sets up the high, heroic tone of *Paradise Lost* only to puncture it immediately with the vigorous colloquialism of a Scottish speaker, apparently quite unawed by his well-known interlocutor. This is hardly an apologetic concession to English readers, but seems closer to the attitude of the writer who compared himself with David going out to meet Goliath. Although the incongruity between the epigraph and the verses may seem very different from the use of Gray for 'The Cotter's Saturday Night', the juxtaposition is nevertheless an appropriate prelude to the rest. For if the poem itself startles readers by the speaker's irreverent self-possession in the face of the Prince of Darkness, the encounter has already been played out by the implicit mockery of Milton by Burns.

More interesting perhaps than the juxtaposition of Milton's Satan with 'Auld Hornie', however, is the much less obvious debt to Pope which stands as bridge between the two. For beneath the acknowledged citation from *Paradise Lost* is a more subtle allusion to *The Dunciad*:

> O thou! Whatever title please thine ear,
> Dean, Drapier, Bickerstaff, or Gulliver![26]

---

[25] 'Address to the Deil', *Poems and Songs*, i. 168.
[26] *The Dunciad*, I. 19–20, *The Twickenham Edition of the Works of Alexander Pope*, Vol. V, ed. James Sutherland (London, 1943), 62.

If Scottish readers see in 'Address to the Deil' a straightforward challenge to Milton's authoritative creation, it is also worth bearing in mind that the first words of the Scottish speaker indicate a less openly articulated allegiance to the satirical, but also mutually sustaining, writings of Pope and Swift. Burns was more than capable of conveying coded references to his Scottish-speaking circle, but he was equally adept at evoking literary friendships from other parts of the islands. The recollection of Pope's mock-heroic masterpiece and its address to the mercurial, multi-voiced Swift not only introduces an interesting literary dimension to Burns's poem, hinting humorously perhaps at links between satire and Satan, but also accentuates the tone of comic insult between close companions. Burns's poem undoubtedly draws on the folklore and flyting traditions of Scotland but, at the same time, it represents a response to Milton as mediated through the comic writings of Pope.

One of the poems that Burns, perhaps wisely, decided to omit from the Kilmarnock edition is 'Holy Willie's Prayer', which combines a similar sense of being written for a private circle with a curious debt to Pope. This time the debt is more pronounced, taking the form of an epigraph from *The Rape of the Lock*: 'And send the godly in a pet to pray'.[27] Again the English quotation is being used for comic purposes, and again there is a striking contrast between the Ayrshire village where Burns's speaker is at prayer and the glittering aristocratic world of Pope's poem. Rather than challenge Pope's well-known masterpiece in the way that 'Address to the Deil' seems to defy Milton, however, Burns allows *The Rape of the Lock* to play quietly in the background of his poem, surprising through analogy rather than incongruity. For while Holy Willie could hardly seem more different from Pope's Belinda in terms of gender, character, and circumstances, both are figures whose sense of power has grown to vast proportions in the confined society in which it operates. Both, too, are protagonists whose pride, sexual secrets, and splenetic dispositions are mercilessly exposed by an invisible poet with an 'eavesdropping Muse'.[28] Though Holy Willie's

---

[27] 'Holy Willie's Prayer', *Poems and Songs*, i. 74. The poem was written in early 1785, after Burns's friend Gavin Hamilton had been called before the Kirk session by the Reverend William Auld, the model for Holy Willie.

[28] Susan Manning notes that the 'idiom of the eavesdropping Muse is Popean' in

rhetorical energy derives from the Kirk rather than the classics, Burns's attack on hypocrisy and inflated language gives his poem a mock-heroic quality that might well have been inspired by the Muse of *The Rape of the Lock*. An epigraph that initially seems to provide comedy through contrast thus turns out to be much closer in spirit to the poem it adorns, while also revealing aspects of the new poem that might not immediately be obvious. This is not a question of a Scottish poem either rebuffing or seeking authority from an established English master, but represents a far more animated and equal exchange. Though polarized in terms of place, language, religion, and gender, 'Holy Willie's Prayer' nevertheless speaks to *The Rape of the Lock* and finds common ground.

Although epigraphs and allusions were commonplace in the literature of the period, there can have been nothing accidental or merely decorative about Burns's usage. His fascination with particular lines of poetry emerges clearly in his correspondence, as has already been seen in the strange letter to Professor Greenfield. His fondness for quotation was not merely on display in correspondence with the learned and the literary, however, nor was it confined to ironic contexts. Even when addressing those who were less well known for their knowledge of *belles-lettres* and for whom satire was not likely to prove the most successful mode of approach, Burns frequently chose to adapt the words of others. When he met Agnes M'Lehose in Edinburgh, for example, he may have felt it sensible to agree with her that 'a friendly correspondence goes for nothing, except one write their undisguised sentiments', but the very next day he was penning a letter that moved from Genesis to Thomson's *Alfred* to *Paradise Lost* in a matter of sentences.[29] Incapable, it seems, of addressing his new-found 'Clarinda' in simple terms, Burns had to frame even the occasional moments of direct intent with poetry:

---

her essay on 'Burns and God', in Crawford (ed.), *Robert Burns and Cultural Authority*, 120. For interesting comment on the importance of Pope to Burns, see R. D. S. Jack, 'Burns as Sassenach Poet', in Kenneth Simpson (ed.), *Burns Now* (Edinburgh, 1994), 150–66.

[29] Burns to Agnes M'Lehose, 4 and 5 Jan. 1788, *Letters*, i. 195, 198.

I am determined to see you, if at all possible, on Saturday evening.
Next week I must sing—

> The night is my departing night,
>   The morn's the day I maun awa';
> There's neither friend nor foe o' mine
>   But wishes that I were awa'!
>
> What I hae done for lack o' wit,
>   I never, never can reca';
> I hope ye're a' my friends as yet—
>   Gude night, and joy be wi' you a'![30]

The same letter contains two stanzas from another anonymous
eighteenth-century song beginning 'What art thou love!', and
manages to fit in a couplet from *The Deserted Village* before
concluding with a brief progress report on the leg he had injured
by falling from a coach.

Ian McIntyre has voiced a common sense of irritation when
he describes the letters to Clarinda as 'Burns at his most
tedious—quotations from Thomson and Young, and a great
deal of nonsense about his life reminding him of a ruined
temple'.[31] The extravagant language strikes many as insincere,
while the repeated literary reference seems tiresome, and osten-
tatious. That the practice was deliberate is clear, however, from
Burns's accompanying comments: 'I like to have quotations
ready for every occasion.—They give one's ideas so pat, and
save one the trouble of finding expression adequate to one's
feelings.'[32] He then goes on to align himself with those who have
enriched the world with reusable turns of phrase: 'I think it is
one of the greatest pleasures attending a Poetic genius, that we
can give our woes, cares, joys, loves, &c, an embodied form in
verse, which, to me, is ever immediate ease.' Good lines were for
Burns 'embodied' feelings, and once incarnate they could be
recalled whenever occasion demanded. Their ability to fascinate
and flatter was also part of his rhetorical strategy, whose success
is obvious not only from the warmth of his relationship with
Clarinda, but also by the sorry image of her showing off his love
letters to friends, years after the poet's death.[33]

[30] Burns to Agnes M'Lehose, 14 Jan. 1788, ibid. 206. The lyric is a traditional
Scottish song of parting.
[31] Ian McIntyre, *Dirt and Deity: A Life of Robert Burns* (London, 1995), 189.
[32] Burns to Agnes M'Lehose, 14 Jan. 1788, *Letters*, i. 207.
[33] McIntyre, *Dirt and Deity*, 417.

Burns was a compulsive and self-conscious quoter of others' words. Throughout his correspondence, constant reference is made to earlier writings, while his own prose is repeatedly interrupted by inverted commas and indented passages. Some of the passages seem to be particular favourites, occurring in more than one letter. The Popean description of his father, William Burnes, for example, which was sent to Dr John Moore in a long autobiographical letter of August 1787, 'I have met with few who understood "Men, their manners and their ways" equal to him', echoes an earlier representation to John Murdoch of the poet himself: 'In short, the joy of my heart is to "Study men, their manners, and their ways".'[34] The phrase appears again in a later letter to Captain Richard Brown: 'I have much to tell you, of "Men, their manners & their ways", perhaps a little of t'other Sex.'[35] In each case, Burns is reflecting on his own life and special development into 'the character of a Poet',[36] but the recurring line from Pope suggests not so much conscious allusion as the kind of mental shorthand described to Clarinda ('quotations . . . give one's ideas so pat, and save the trouble of finding expression adequate to one's feelings').

Burns's memory was well stocked with lines of poetry, ready to be added to his own compositions whenever occasion demanded. Whether the lines carried their context with them or not, is difficult to assess. If Burns had his reading of Pope in mind when writing to Murdoch, the evocation of Placebo's voice from 'January and May' is playful and ironic:

> Sir, I have liv'd a Courtier all my Days,
> And study'd Men, their Manners, and their Ways;
> And have observ'd this useful Maxim still,
> To let my Betters always have their Will.[37]

While keen to please his former teacher, Burns hardly saw himself as a courtier ('as a man of the world, I am most miserably

---

[34] Burns to Moore, 2 Aug. 1787, Burns to Murdoch, 15 Jan. 1783, *Letters*, i. 134, 17. His fondness for the line may have increased after Mackenzie's comments on the 'uncommon penetration and sagacity' with which Burns had 'looked upon men and manners', *Lounger*, 97 (1786), 388.

[35] Burns to Brown, 30 Dec. 1787, *Letters*, i. 192.

[36] Ibid.

[37] 'January to May; or The Merchant's Tale from Chaucer', 156–9, *The Twickenham Edition of the Works of Alexander Pope*, Vol. II, *The Rape of the Lock and Other Poems*, ed. G. Tillotson (London and New Haven, 1940), 22.

deficient').[38] Even less like Pope's Placebo was Burns's father, whose study of 'men, their manners and their ways' was apparently accompanied not by 'mild . . . looks' and a 'pleasing . . . tone', but by 'stubborn, ungainly Integrity, and headlong, ungovernable Irrascibillity'.[39] It is in the letter to Brown that an allusion to 'January and May' would be least appropriate, however, since the Captain had recently married and so to recall Pope's version of 'The Merchant's Tale', with its humorous account of an elderly husband cuckolded by his lovely young wife, would be risky even by Burns's standards of irreverence. The much-quoted phrase, then, appears to have developed a special personal meaning over years of familiarity and could be applied independently or ironically, according to whether Burns's correspondent would be expected to recognize its original source.

Certain lines and passages of poetry had an inherent quality that seemed to render them independent of their origins and, once lodged in Burns's extraordinarily retentive memory, they lived on quietly, ready to be called upon from time to time. Far from indicating a lack of originality or inability to transform unruly thoughts into neat turns of phrase (his own capacity in this area being abundantly evident from any dictionary of quotations), these peculiar lines of poetry were deeply embedded in his psyche and apt to resurface in particular circumstances. It was not in moments of creative exhaustion that he fell back on familiar words, but at times when deep feelings seemed to prompt recollection rather than invention, as he explained to Mrs Dunlop, after citing some favourite lines from Thomson: 'Probably I have quoted some of these to you formerly, as indeed when I write from the heart, I am apt to be guilty of these repetitions.'[40] Just as the simple lyrics of the traditional songs collected by Burns had deepened through generations of singing, so the power of those scattered lines he had been absorbing throughout his life seemed to increase with repetition.[41] It was as if there were some ideal correspondence

---

[38] Burns to Murdoch, 15 Jan. 1783, *Letters*, i. 16–17.

[39] Burns to Moore, 2 Aug. 1787, ibid. 134–5.

[40] Burns to Mrs Dunlop, 6 Dec. 1792, ibid. ii. 165. He had quoted the same lines in a letter to her of 9 July 1790, ibid. 33.

[41] For a useful discussion of Burns's debts to the oral tradition, see Mary Ellen Brown, *Burns and Tradition* (London, 1984).

between certain emotional states and particular passages of verse, so that at any moving moment, the poetry was there to celebrate or make it bearable. Quotations provided a psychological shield, protecting the protagonist from life's unanticipated developments, and offering not only the comfort of familiarity and experience, but also a sense of being in control. The most difficult circumstance could be combated or at least endured, if only the right words were on hand.

Burns's habit of quotation is not a passive mode, but rather an active means of fending off the unknown or unsettling. It is 'ready armour, offensive, or defensive', or, in other words, a kind of intellectual weaponry poised to safeguard the bearer.[42] The strategic deployment of his reading was part of Burns's defiant attitude to existence, and even when dealing with less sombre subjects than those discussed in the letter cited above, select lines of verse are carefully marshalled. In August 1786, when still planning to sail for Jamaica, he wrote vigorously to his drinking friend, James Smith:

Where I shall shelter, I know not, but I hope to weather the storm.— Perish the drop of blood of mine that fears them! I know the worst, and am prepared to meet it—

> 'I'll laugh, an' sing, an' shake my leg,
> As lang's I dow.'[43]

He is quoting one of his own poems on this occasion, but it is a good illustration of his psychological tactics. The quotation is serving as armour, protecting a speaker who is well aware of the tragicomic figure he is cutting.

Very different in tone, but equally careful and self-dramatizing in its use of remembered verses, is the letter he was to send a few months later to James Sibbald, whose *Edinburgh Magazine* had carried extensive reviews of the Kilmarnock edition:

so little am I acquainted with the Modes & Manners of the more publick and polished walks of life, that I often feel myself much embarrassed how to express the feelings of my heart, particularly Gratitude.—

---

[42] Burns to Mrs Dunlop, 6 Dec. 1792, *Letters*, ii. 165.
[43] Burns to James Smith, 14 Aug. 1787, ibid. i. 47. The lines are from the 'Second Epistle to John Lapraik', stanza 9, *Poems and Songs*, i. 91.

'   —Rude am I in speech,
'And little blest with the set, polish'd phrase,
'For since these arms of mine had seven's year's pith, [*sic*]
'Till now, some nine moons wasted, they have us'd
'Their dearest effort in the rural field;
'And therefore, little can I grace my cause
'In speaking for myself—'[44]

Here, Shakespeare is available to rescue Burns from the embarrassment of saying 'Thank you' to a stranger, providing famous lines to convey him over awkward terrain. Othello's speech, its military 'tented field' beaten into an image of ploughing, enables Burns to project a complicated, paradoxical image of himself as a rude, rural bard, who nevertheless possesses something of the heroic. Like the speaker in 'Address to the Deil', Burns presents himself here as being so unawed by mighty power that he feels able to adapt Shakespeare's words to fit himself—a form of armour that he was to wear increasingly, as the object of wonder and patronage in Edinburgh literary circles.

When confronted with a poem by Burns that begins with an epigraph, then, there are a number of different things to take into account. As we have seen already, the role of the epigraph in the eighteenth century was surprisingly varied, ranging from the anxiety-producing fragment of past majesty to the authoritative quasi-biblical source of inspiration, and even to the comic stooge set up by a younger poet keen to play off new, ironic ideas. When it came to introductory devices, Burns, like every other well-read poet of his day, inherited a rich tradition of allusiveness and rhetorical play. At the same time, his knowledge of local songs and ballad-making gave him an additional wealth of materials and methods, quite different from the printed, literary culture of the eighteenth century. Some of his finest work consists of adaptation rather than creation *ex nihilo*—a song such as 'John Anderson, my Jo', for example, existed in several versions before Burns took hold of it and made it his own.[45] With regard to quotation, then, it is worth bearing in mind that

[44] Burns to Sibbald, Jan. 1787, *Letters*, i. 77–8. Cf. his adaptation of the same speech from *Othello*, I. iii. 81–9, with a rather different tone, in a letter to Mrs Dunlop, 15 Apr. 1787, *Letters*, i. 104–5.

[45] See Brown, *Burns and Tradition*; Donald A. Low, *The Songs of Robert Burns* (London, 1993); Kirsteen McCue, 'Burns, Women, and Song', in Crawford (ed.), *Robert Burns and Cultural Authority*, 40–57.

in addition to late eighteenth-century aesthetic attitudes, Burns was influenced by song-writing techniques not unlike those described more recently by Ciaran Carson, who remains so deeply aware of the 'floating lines and verses . . . reverberating in the mouths of generations'.[46] Although the collision of the oral and literary tradition might prove problematic, it appears that the song-writer's capacity to absorb 'floating lines and verses' also affected the ways in which Burns responded to published poems. As is obvious from his surviving correspondence, his mind was chock full of stray verses, many of which seemed to embody particular feelings and thus provide a mental currency for sharing the riches of his own mind with others. Since quotations could represent the embodiment of a feeling, rather than merely being reminders of an earlier narrative, they were well suited to alerting readers to the emotional significance of a new poem. Again, apparently distinct traditions fused in Burns's work, as the late eighteenth-century discourse of sympathy and sensibility combined with the traditional assumptions of popular song.

The success of the Kilmarnock edition demonstrates that Burns's situation at the confluence of alternative traditions seems to have been entirely positive. His knowledge of local forms and culture mixes with his reading of literary works to produce a highly volatile and exciting collection. As he moved to Edinburgh, however, the creative tensions seem to have turned to obstructive contradictions. Critical praise of naturalness, spontaneity, and feeling could translate quickly into contempt for ignorance, Scotticisms, and lack of intellect; and it is clear from the poem composed in November 1786 that these distinctly double-edged tributes were registering on Burns's new work. This does not mean that the poet in Burns was snuffed out by critical articles, but 'A Winter Night' nevertheless reflects a new awareness of the complexity of poetic allegiances, identity, and linguistic choices. The move from Ayrshire and exposure to Edinburgh's literary circles seems to have accentuated Burns's sense of the peculiarities of his own verse and personal experience, introducing a self-consciousness into his poetry similar to that evident in the letters of the period. Burns

[46] See Ch. 1, above.

was on show in the capital; and the attention seems to have increased both his self-dramatizing and secretive tendencies. At the same time, the variety of poetic forms, traditions, and vocabulary that had simply been there for the taking now presented difficult artistic choices, fraught with the new awareness of the relative associations of Scots and English, songs and odes.

In 'A Winter Night', Burns's sense of poetry as performance emerges in the complicated presentation of the persona, whose words are introduced by part of a highly dramatic speech from *King Lear*. The consciousness that composition, far from being artless and spontaneous, involves careful selection from competing traditions is also apparent in the poem's strange structure and linguistic variation. Much of the energy is generated by the curious internal shifts between Scots and English, which affect not only the language, but also the form, tone, voice, and meaning. Although it appears to follow the pattern described by Thomas Crawford of the vernacular beginning which leads into more generalized thoughts expressed in English, the presence of the epigraph and brief conclusion means that instead of a simple movement from Scots to English, 'A Winter Night' alternates between the two poetic languages and demonstrates the complexity of both. The poem may begin with a cold Scottish night described in Standard Habbie, but it is prefaced by a passage from Shakespeare. It is the voice of Lear on the heath, experiencing the shock of physical suffering and thus reflecting on those 'Poor naked wretches' who are without food or shelter. Though the words are those of a thoroughly English author, however, they express just the kind of sentiment that would appeal to readers nursed on novels such as Henry Mackenzie's *The Man of Feeling*, a book prized by Burns 'next to the Bible'.[47]

The lines chosen by Burns stop just short of Lear's self-punishing admonishment to 'take physic' and 'expose thyself to feel what wretches feel', leaving the reader with the direct address to those suffering poverty and starvation:

> Poor naked wretches, wheresoe'er you are,
> That bide the pelting of this pityless storm!

[47] Burns to Murdoch, 15 Jan. 1783, *Letters*, i. 17.

> How shall your houseless heads and unfed sides,
> Your loop'd and window'd raggedness, defend you
> From seasons such as these?[48]

Shakespeare's image of the 'poor naked wretches' is thus extracted from the compelling scene on the heath to emphasize the universal significance of the lines, and their powerful emotional charge. Burns seems to be directing the sympathy of his readers towards the homeless and the hungry, whose unenviable situation is not confined to Shakespeare's imaginary depiction of a pre-Christian world, but is just as common in modern Britain. In doing so, he anticipates the interpretations of *King Lear* that have been popular in the late twentieth century, which have given 'special weight' to this very speech and, as R. A. Foakes has commented, represent a 'radical critique of political power and social injustice'.[49] As such, it is a peculiarly powerful choice of epigraph, and one that seems to dare the new poem to compete in seriousness.

The opening stanzas are thus something of a surprise. For although the temperature remains sub-zero, there is no arresting image of human beings caught without shelter in the storm. Instead, the chilling north wind of the first line seems to have little effect on those whose occupations render them completely oblivious to the nocturnal weather:

> Ae night the Storm the steeples rocked,
> Poor Labour sweet in sleep was locked . . .

While Lear's storm 'drenched . . . steeples' and 'drowned the cocks' in its apocalyptic fury, the effects of biting Boreas seem far less destructive: 'rocked' suggesting not only gale force winds, but also the far more gentle, domestic idea of being rocked off to sleep. The image of 'Poor Labour' could hardly be further from that of the 'Poor naked wretches' envisaged by the King, and suggests a rather more down-to-earth and resilient attitude towards the storm. The refusal to be overwhelmed by uncontrollable forces recalls the speaker in 'Address to the Deil', where a similar contrast is set up between the elevated language of the epigraph and the defiant colloquialism of the poem. Here,

---

[48] *King Lear*, III, iv. 28–32.
[49] William Shakespeare, *King Lear*, ed. R. A. Foakes, *The Arden Shakespeare* (London, 1997), 28.

Burns is also taking up the challenge of a great text, but rather than strive to outdo Shakespeare he seems bent instead on revealing that the truth of the epigraph is not the whole truth, that it is only one aspect of man's relationship with the natural world, or, indeed, one view of the condition of the poor.

Although the epigraph commands the reader's sympathy from the outset, the image of the sleeping farm workers simply offers an alternative view of the situation and, in doing so, seems to suggest a certain narrowness attendant upon judgements made from a position too distant from the people under discussion. However benevolent the sentiments expressed in the epigraph, the pitying tone indicates an assumption of superiority to the 'wretches', who are not only 'houseless' but also nameless and voiceless. As Burns relocates Lear's words into the more general eighteenth-century discourse of feeling, the gulf between the well-meaning voice of the epigraph and those who are the objects of pity seems uncomfortably wide. By adopting Scots for the opening of his own verses, Burns is thus able to capitalize on the contemporary association between the Scottish language and low or rustic life in order to indicate that his speaker has a much better understanding of the poor in winter than the English voice of the epigraph, and can thus describe their experience with far greater authority. The use of the present tense in the first stanza suggests habitual experience rather than the unique and shocking encounter implied by the epigraph's 'this pitiless storm':

> When biting *Boreas*, fell and doure,
> Sharp shivers thro' the leafless bow'r;
> When *Phoebus* gies a short-liv'd glow'r,
>   Far south the lift,
> Dim-dark'ning thro' the flaky show'r
>   Or whirling drift.

Neither the snowstorm, nor the biting north wind, nor the short-lived glimpse of winter sunlight, cause this speaker much surprise, seeming rather the normal features of a Scottish winter. It is not '*The* Winter Night', but '*A* Winter Night'.

The opposition between the voice of the epigraph and that of the main poem is, however, less absolute than it might initially appear; for although the speaker demonstrates his knowledge of rural Scotland in the winter, he nevertheless sets himself apart from 'Poor Labour'. It is obvious from the third stanza, in which he is 'List'ning, the doors an' winnocks rattle', that the speaker is neither 'houseless' like those envisaged in the epigraph, nor 'in sleep . . . locked' like those in the second stanza. Indeed, his own reaction to the storm is to contemplate the plight of the creatures for whom such a night could prove fatal: the sheep and cattle who might be caught in drifts, the wild birds probably freezing to death, and even the foxes whose nocturnal habits will have sent them out on a futile search for food. Though accustomed to stormy nights, the speaker is, after all, no more able to sleep than King Lear. His reflections on the sufferings of lower beings caught in the storm even give him a curious affinity with the fallen monarch whose description of the 'pitiless storm' is echoed in the fifth stanza:

> Ev'n you on murd'ring errands toil'd,
> Lone from your savage homes exil'd,
> The blood-stain'd roost, and sheep-cote spoil'd,
>   My heart forgets,
> While pityless the tempest wild
>   Sore on you beats.

As the poem unfolds, it becomes clear that the epigraph is not as detached from its source as it might have seemed. Just as Holy Willie possesses curious parallels with Pope's Belinda, so the speaker of 'A Winter Night', though a native Scots speaker, shares certain characteristics with Shakespeare's tragic monarch.

The sympathy for suffering creatures continues in stanza four with 'Ilk happing bird, wee, helpless thing!' This image is strongly reminiscent of 'To a Mouse', the poem placed immediately before 'A Winter Night' in the new edition, which also explores the prospect of being left without shelter in freezing conditions.[50] Interestingly, Seamus Heaney has also perceived in Burns's address to the mouse a startling parallel with *King Lear*. In Heaney's reading, the interruption to winter ploughing caused by the discovery of the smashed nest provokes

---

[50] 'To a Mouse' begins 'Wee sleekit, cowran, tim'rous beastie'. Thomas Carlyle quoted from 'A Winter Night' to demonstrate Burns's capacity for 'sympathy' in his review of '*The Life of Burns. By J. G. Lockhart*', *Edinburgh Review*, 48 (1828), 267–312, 283.

an 'involuntary outrush of fellow feeling' and leads to an intense identification with the evicted mouse:

What has happened here is truly, almost literally, a discovery. From a hiding place in the foggage of the poet's own consciousness, his wee, cowran, tim'rous soul has been panicked out into a bleak recognition of its destiny. The sturdy, caring figure who overshadowed and over-saw the panic of the mouse at the beginning has been revealed to him-self as someone less perfectly firm, less strong and robust than he or the reader would have ever suspected. In other words, Burns's mouse gradually becomes a sibylline rather than a sentimental element in the poem—so much so that, by the end, the reader feels that the bleakness of Lear's heath must have overtaken the field at Mossgiel on that wintry November day in 1785 when 'crash! The cruel coulter passed | Out thro' thy cell'.[51]

Burns's imaginative sympathy with the suffering creature is so strong that he seems to experience fears as overwhelming as those he has induced in the mouse. As Heaney points out, this is not a self-soothing sentimentality, but a moment of bleak insight into the human condition and, as such, akin to Lear's experience on the heath. And it is this that makes Burns's mouse 'sibylline'—or, in other words, prophetic of man's unhappy destiny.

In Heaney's essay, the 'outrush of fellow feeling' derives as much from the language as the situation, however, as he describes his own discovery of the poem many years ago and the liberating effect of encountering dialect in a school anthology: 'The word 'wee' put its stressed foot down and in one pre-emptive vocative strike took over the emotional and cultural ground, dispossessing the rights of written standard English and offering asylum to all vernacular comers.'[52] Burns's poem is levelling, therefore, not merely because it reveals the fate common to all living things, be they kings, ploughmen, or mice, but also because it authorizes speech that does not conform to eighteenth-century notions of standard English. The truth of the

[51] Seamus Heaney, 'Burns's Art Speech', in Crawford (ed.), *Robert Burns and Cultural Authority*, 216–33, 220.

[52] Ibid. 218. Although Heaney mentions the poem in connection with *The Ambleside Book of Verse*, he may be remembering another collection, as E. W. Parker's anthology contains 'To a Daisy', which begins 'Wee, modest, crimson-tipped flower', but not 'To A Mouse'. For further discussion of Heaney's reading and attitudes to language, see Chs. 6 and 7, below.

poem is both emotional and moral, but the true language, here, is Scots. The prevailing association of dialect with naturalness and spontaneity works to authenticate the speaker's response to the suffering mouse, revealing strengths even as the poem appears to expose human weakness. Like Lear's experience on the heath, the racking moment of surprised humility is also a moment of bleak hope, as the capacity for fellow-feeling and self-knowledge is simultaneously discovered. Ironically, the language of Burns's ploughman brings him close to Shakespeare's king, as it challenges attitudes towards traditional social divisions while upholding the power of universal human emotions.

Although in 'A Winter Night' the speaker's situation indoors may seem to work against any possible identification with Lear on the heath, his capacity for sympathy with lesser beings is plain. The first-person pronoun appears for the first time in stanza three, along with the shivering cattle and sheep. Like the bird in the following stanza, the stormy night seems to prevent the speaker from closing his eyes, even if the cause of his restlessness is not the mere physical fact of the weather. Indeed, the strange parallel between the experience of the bird and the situation of the speaker invites further reflection, especially since birds are traditionally images of the poet. As the speaker reflects on the contrasting fortunes of songbirds through the year:

> Ilk happing bird, wee, helpless thing!
> That in the merry months o' spring,
> Delighted me to hear thee sing,
>   What comes o' thee?
> Whare wilt thou cow'r thy chittering wing,
>   An' close thy e'e?

it is easy to be reminded of Burns's anxieties about his own success. As is apparent from the letter written soon afterwards to Professor Greenfield, Burns was suffering from profound misgivings about his future as a poet. Within weeks of composing 'A Winter Night', he expressed his feelings even more directly in a letter to his friend, Robert Aiken: 'Various concurring circumstances have raised my fame as a Poet to a height which I am absolutely certain I have not merits to support; and I

look down on the future as I would into the bottomless pit.'[53]
With such anxieties in mind, it is perhaps not surprising that
Burns should have been particularly affected by the plight of the
bird in winter, whose songs now seem redundant in the face of a
hostile environment.

Burns's strong sense of the precariousness of his current good
fortune suggests a further disturbing parallel with Shakespeare's
tragic ruler and his sudden fall from power. Indeed, the thought
of Lear in the fourth Act, adorned with a crown of flowers, has
a peculiar resonance in the new edition of Burns's poems, where
'A Winter Night' seems to revisit not only 'To a Mouse', but
also one of the other more celebrated pieces in the original
volume, 'The Vision'. Like 'A Winter Night', 'The Vision'
describes the solitary poet on a cold night, but on this occasion
he is visited by the Scottish Muse, Coila, who addresses him as
her '*own* inspired Bard' and concludes by bestowing a crown:

> '*And wear thou this*'—She solemn said,
> And bound the *Holly* round my head:
> The polish'd leaves, and berries red,
>   Did rustling play;
> And, like a passing thought, she fled,
>   In light away.[54]

In the Kilmarnock edition, the final crowning with holly berries
suggests a witty appropriation of the classical laurels for a
Northern bard. When 'The Vision' is read in the enlarged
edition, alongside 'A Winter Night', however, the image begins
to acquire darker overtones, deepened by the thought of Lear's
weedy crown.

With this irony in mind, it is then possible to read a covert
reference to the poet in the second stanza of 'A Winter Night'.
For although on first reading, the 'burns, wi' snawy wreeths up-
choked' may seem merely part of the winter landscape-painting,
the line might also suggest (for readers already familiar with
'The Vision') a disturbing echo of the concluding image of
Burns the poet, crowned with the holly wreath. Burns's skilful
use of two literary languages means that apparently simple
words can be loaded with extra possibilities, and so 'wreeths',

---

[53] Burns to Aiken, 16 Dec. 1786, *Letters*, i. 73.
[54] 'The Vision', 271–6, *Poems and Songs*, i, 113.

which seems in the Scottish context to refer to drifts of snow, can also carry the entirely different meaning that is more common in English. With the epigraph from *King Lear* and the similarity between the situation in 'A Winter Night' and that of 'The Vision', the notion of the wreath referring not merely to snow but also to the poetic circlet of woven leaves seems only too persuasive. And once the possibility of wordplay is recognized, the pun on Burns is also hard to ignore: this is not merely an image of a stream in winter, but a coded reference to the poet.

The self-naming in the second stanza suggests that the question of human suffering underlined in the epigraph may have a more personal dimension than might be obvious at first. For while 'The Vision' concluded with an optimistic image of the 'Rustic Bard' crowned by Coila and tasked with the creation of a particular kind of Scottish poetry, the revised version of the image in 'A Winter Night' seems much less clear and assured. Now the wreath is 'snawy' or, in other words, cold, ephemeral, and unlikely, perhaps, to survive the return of the sun the following morning. Though ultimately transient, it is nevertheless capable of causing a serious blockage: the 'burns' are choked, and forced into wild eddies or unnatural courses. As a sequel image to that in 'The Vision', this might suggest that the pressures on the emerging poet lead not to further creative outpourings, but rather to frustration, confusion, and even diversion through artificial and unsuitable outlets. Given the contradictory signals emitted by the contemporary reviews, it is not surprising to find this kind of uncertainty, though it is characteristic of Burns to confront it through metaphor and, indeed, to turn it into a subject for poetry. 'The Vision' had already explored the value of poetry as an occupation, so 'A Winter Night' could turn to the difficulties facing a poet who has achieved some success but remains extremely doubtful about the future. The linguistic swings that mark the poem seem to embody the very uncertainties, representing the competing literary traditions and critical readings that combine to drive the poet hither and thither.

Although the personal difficulties facing the poet are articulated rather covertly in the opening stanzas through imagery and double meanings, the juxtaposition of alternative traditions becomes extremely apparent in the sixth stanza where the 'plaintive strain' suddenly seems to sweep away the Scottish voice with Englishness:

> 'Blow, blow, ye Winds, with heavier gust!
> 'And freeze, thou bitter-biting Frost!
> 'Descend, ye chilly, smothering Snows!
> 'Not all your rage, as now, united shows
>   'More hard unkindness, unrelenting,
>   'Vengeful malice, unrepenting,
> 'Than heaven-illumin'd Man on brother Man bestows!'

Whereas 'The Vision' depicted the solitary poet being visited by a Scottish muse whose physicality is sufficiently convincing to allow for admiration of her leg ('Sae straught, sae taper, tight and clean'), the words that steal on the speaker's ear in the later poem seem bodiless and almost ghostly. They contrast strongly with the Scottish cadences of the opening, with the obvious shift to English vowel sounds 'Blow', 'snows', 'shows', 'bestows'. Even if, as Thomas Crawford has suggested, the central passages are meant to be read aloud in a Scottish accent, the signals given off by Burns's spelling suggest a marked shift from the 'snawy' diction of the earlier stanzas.[55]

It is not merely the language, however, that indicates a significant shift in the poem, but also the reintroduction of Shakespeare. The 'plaintive strain' takes the reader back to *King Lear* and the opening lines of the scene on the heath from which Burns's epigraph is taken ('Blow winds and crack your cheeks'). It is almost as if the unsleeping speaker of 'A Winter Night' is catching the voice of Lear out in the storm, railing against the cruelty and ingratitude of man. And yet the strain is 'plaintive' and 'slow-solemn', suggesting the melancholic voice of Macpherson's *Ossian* more readily than that of Shakespeare's raging king. Nor does the echo of *King Lear* extend beyond the first words of the stanza, which rapidly begins to recall instead Amiens's song in *As You Like It*:

---

[55] Thomas Crawford, *Burns*, 194. On the relationship between English and Scots in Burns's poetry, see David Murison, 'The Language of Burns', in Donald A. Low (ed.), *Critical Essays on Robert Burns* (London, 1975), 54–69.

Blow, blow, thou winter wind,
Thou art not so unkind
    As man's ingratitude.
Thy tooth is not so keen,
Because thou art not seen,
    Although thy breath be rude.
Heigh-ho' sing heigh-ho, unto the green holly
Most friendship is feigning, most loving mere folly.
Then heigh-ho, the holly,
    This life is most jolly.

Freeze, freeze, thou bitter sky,
That does not bite so nigh
    As benefits forgot.
Though thou the waters warp,
Thy sting is not so sharp,
    As friend remember'd not.[56]

The same creative memory that enabled Burns to quote from *Othello* in his letters or adapt traditional Scottish songs seems to be at work here, as familiar lines from both *King Lear* and *As You Like It* are refashioned into something entirely new. Indeed, the double allusion unsettles the recollection of both plays, by revealing similarities in speeches that seem quite unalike when seen in their original contexts. For although the plight of Orlando and Adam, or of the exiled Duke Senior, may have something in common with Lear and the 'homeless wretches' he evokes, the contrast between the two plays is such that the response of the audience to Lear on the heath is inevitably very different from that inspired by Amiens's song. This mixing of tragedy and comedy is nevertheless highly appropriate for Burns's poem, with its exploration of competing cultural traditions, of contrasting voices and perceptions. Just as his image of 'Poor Labour sweet in sleep' seems to challenge the apocalyptic despair of the epigraph, so too the recollection of *As You Like It* seems to balance the attitude of the tragic hero towards the storm. Amiens does not deny the magnitude of man's ingratitude, but rather than take this as a cue to call for the destruction of the entire human race, he concludes with cheerful irony:

[56] *As You Like It*, II, vii. 174–89.

Then heigh-ho the holly,
This life is most jolly.

The jingling rhyme of 'holly' and 'jolly' seems to poke fun at those who wallow in melancholy, or take themselves rather too seriously, and so the echo of this song in 'A Winter Night' may also be casting a further glance at the more self-important aspects of 'The Vision' and its holly crown. At the same time, however, the thought of Lear introduces just the kind of 'bleakness' that Seamus Heaney has discerned beneath the sentiment and humour of 'To a Mouse', and thus underlines the darker possibilities already apparent in Burns's opening stanzas.

The contrast between the 'plaintive strain' and the earlier stanzas is therefore less absolute than it might initially seem. For the recollection of *King Lear* links the central passage to both the epigraph and the complicated pattern of allusions and implied parallels that are embedded in the opening section. The introduction of *As You Like It*, on the other hand, points to the less gloomy elements of Burns's poem: the resilience to the elements, the ironic self-image, and the feisty comic closure that is to follow the strange strophic centre. The fusing of Lear's speech and Amiens's song also suggests a balancing of high literature with a more popular, communal form, just as Burns's own poem seems to provide a down-to-earth corrective of the lofty voice of the epigraph. Indeed, the seventh stanza seems to combine elevated diction with a strong rhythm which links it to both Amiens's song and Burns's own characteristic form. In metrical terms, the first line of the supposedly English section, 'Blow, blow, ye Winds, with heavier gust!', is strikingly similar to those of the preceding Scottish verse: 'Dark-muffl'd, view'd the dreary plain'. Although the seventh stanza diverges from Standard Habbie in its fourth line, and then continues with a longer couplet and an alexandrine, the beginning appears to carry on naturally from the Scottish stanzas, suggesting a passage of transition rather than stark contrast.

As a bridge between the regular Scottish form of the opening and the irregular English passages that follow, the stanza perhaps reflects the internal processes of a Scottish poet recalling his English reading. This is not after all a case of the Scottish voice being swept aside by foreign intrusion, but rather of one

tradition engaging with another and adopting a greater pro-
portion of non-native elements as the poem progresses. For, as I
have already suggested, the vernacular opening has exploited
the possibilities offered by the dual awareness of Scots and
English, while the strophes that follow, though largely employ-
ing the English language, nevertheless retain vital Scottish
elements to enrich and complicate the meaning.

Although the movement into the central ode with its abstract
nouns and personifications might indicate an overwhelming
influence from south of the Border, Burns still employs Scottish
vocabulary and idiom in the midst of his echoes of Pope,
Dryden, and Shakespeare. The description of the exploited
farm-worker, for example, employs the Scottish word 'hind',
which refers to a skilled worker whose accommodation is tied
to the estate. He thus capitalizes once again on the prevailing
association between Scots and the lower classes, but only in
order to attack 'pamper'd Luxury' whose 'glitt'ring show' is
sustained by the very people it holds in contempt. 'Hind' also
allows for play on the earlier word 'rear', suggesting not only
bodily associations in the perception of the worker, but also
perhaps a sense of backwardness—of being behind the times—
just as Burns himself was charged with rusticity, archaism, and
grossness in the reviews of his poems. When the 'simple, rustic
Hind' appears, he seems a polar opposite of the personified
female figure of Luxury. However, the word 'hind' also suggests
a female deer and thus anticipates the imagery of sexual
exploitation in the following strophe. The description of the
Hind, 'Plac'd for her lordly use thus far, thus vile, below', refers
primarily to the subordination of the farm-worker to 'Luxury',
but in the light of the second section, it also suggests the notion
of a female servant being used by her master, especially since the
adjective 'lordly' occurs again so soon, and the word 'luxury'
originally meant lechery or lust.

Rather than adopting the rhetoric of the English Pindaric ode
in a merely derivative way, Burns is thus exploring the fluidity
of abstract language and the inversions and pluralities of
meaning it allows.[57] If the odes of Cowley and Dryden were
associated with public statements, Burns experiments with the

---

[57] Cf. Luke Gibbons's reading of allegorical speech and narratives in Irish culture, *Transformations in Irish Culture* (Cork, 1996), 7, 134–48.

form to create a comment equally public, but in critique rather than celebration of the established order. In this, he might be seen to be following Thomas Gray, whose famous ode 'The Bard' has been read as a statement of radical resistance to the expansionist policies of the English king.[58] The difference is also crucial, however, since the voice of Gray's Welsh bard had to be re-created by the English sympathizer, whereas Burns makes his Scots persona adopt standard English. Again, Burns inverts the oppressive tendencies of contemporary primitivist aesthetics by emphasizing the vitality of his own speaker, even when the source of the 'plaintive strain' is somewhat mysterious.

Abstract English nouns are exploited in 'A Winter Night' to expose social injustice, and pave the way to the denunciation of 'lordly Honor' in the following verse. Here, English is again used to convey a radical viewpoint, though the language seems closer to that of more recent sentimental literature. Indeed, James Kinsley points out in his editorial commentary that lines 62–72 are 'an eighteenth-century set piece' comparable to passages in Sterne or to Goldsmith's lament for the fallen young woman in *The Deserted Village*. While Burns is undoubtedly drawing on his immediate predecessors, however, he is again stamping the passage with his own distinctive character, by echoing one of his recently published pieces. 'The Cotter's Saturday Night' had been greeted with enthusiasm by many of the first readers of the Kilmarnock edition, and in 'A Winter Night' Burns seems to be recalling his own success at the same time as developing the more obvious theme of social injustice and the exploitation of lower-class women:

> 'Is there, beneath Love's noble name,
> 'Can harbour, dark, the selfish aim,
>   'To bless himself alone!
> 'Mark Maiden-innocence a prey
>   'To love-pretending snares,
> 'This boasted Honor turns away,
> 'Shunning soft Pity's rising sway,
> 'Regardless of the tears, and unavailing pray'rs!'

---

[58] See e.g. Katie Trumpener, *Bardic Nationalism: The Romantic Novel and the British Empire* (Princeton, 1997), 3–9. Dryden's Odes could also be interpreted as offering not unambiguous support for the established order.

Although quite different in form, the sentiment is very close to that expressed in 'The Cotter's Saturday Night', a similarity highlighted by the echo in the line introducing the passage:

> Is there, in human-form, that bears a heart—
> A wretch! a villain! lost to love and truth!
> That can, with studied, sly, ensnaring art
> Betray sweet *Jenny's* unsuspecting youth?[59]

This is the voice that would later emerge in the far more hard-hitting song 'A Man's a Man for a' That', which begins:

> Is there, for honest Poverty
>   That hings his head, and a' that;
> The coward-slave, we pass him by,
>   We dare be poor for a' that!
> For a' that, and a' that,
>   Our toils obscure, and a' that,
> The rank is but the guinea's stamp,
>   The Man's the gowd for a' that.[60]

The same radical views are being expressed in 'A Winter Night', but in a rather less confident and more surreptitious manner. The voice of the plaintive strain remains unlocated in a single recognizable identity, and the words seem to blow from one source to another. This enables Burns nevertheless to convey radical views through the high literary language familiar to his readers, while at the same time placing his own work in the exalted company of Shakespeare, Dryden, and Johnson. Keen, perhaps, to avoid offending the patrons and landowners on whom he depended, Burns seems to be experimenting with ways of conveying political views that are safely anonymous, and even draw authority from the English voices that are being mimicked. The central stanzas revive not only the language of the epigraph, but also its political charge, as selfishness and social power are overcome by radical sympathy. Although this structural framework was abandoned some years later when the 'English' stanzas were published independently as 'Humanity: An Ode', the recollection of Lear's tragedy that haunts 'A

---

[59] 'The Cotter's Saturday Night', 82–5, *Poems and Songs*, i. 148.
[60] 'A Man's a Man for a' That', 1–8, ibid. ii. 762.

Winter Night' quietly strengthens the caution to tyrannical landowners.[61]

Even as he delivers the radical sentiments at the heart of the poem, however, Burns is also exploring the literary influences on the eighteenth-century Scottish poet. The situation outlined at the opening of 'A Winter Night' depicts the solitary insomniac listening to the storm, and so it is possible to read the 'plaintive strain' as part of the half-waking, half-sleeping thoughts that float across the speaker's confused consciousness. That they should be strongly influenced by his reading seems only too appropriate, and hence the obvious allusiveness of the central passages. As is already clear, Burns is drawing on a host of English authors to construct his own poem within a poem, but perhaps his most significant debts are not to Englishmen, but to Scottish poets who composed their most celebrated work in English. The lines that introduce the description of the rich and powerful, for example, may echo Pope's rejection of 'mad Ambition' in *Windsor Forest*, but contemporary readers are likely to have been reminded even more strongly of James Thomson's enormously popular poem *The Seasons*.[62]

Although Burns's poem seems far removed from the cameo portrait of a happy village in Thomson's *Winter*, his eighteenth-century readers might well assume that the title was taken from *The Seasons*:

> MEAN-TIME the Village rouzes up the Fire;
> While well attested, and as well believ'd,
> Heard solemn, goes the Goblin-story round,
> Till superstitious Horror creeps o'er all.
> Or, frequent in the sounding Hall, they wake
> The rural Gambol. Rustic mirth goes round:
> The simple Joke that takes the Shepherd's Heart,
> Easily pleas'd; the long loud Laugh, sincere;

---

[61] The publication of the central section of 'A Winter Night' as 'Humanity: An Ode' in *The Gentleman's Magazine*, lxiv/2 (Aug. 1794), 748–9, was discovered in 1997 by Patrick Scott Hogg and will be included in the forthcoming edition of Burns's poetry, edited by Andrew Noble and Patrick Scott Hogg. I am greatly indebted to Andrew Noble for drawing my attention to this text.

[62] *Windsor Forest*, 416, *Poems of Alexander Pope*, Vol. I: *Pastoral Poetry and An Essay of Criticism*, ed. E. Audra and Aubrey Williams (London and New Haven, 1961).

The Kiss, snatch'd hasty from the sidelong Maid
On purpose guardless, or pretending Sleep;
The Leap, the Slap, the Haul; and, shook to Notes
Of native Music, the respondent Dance.
Thus jocund fleets with them the Winter-Night.[63]

Despite the discrepancy between this passage and Burns's image of the troubled solitary figure, the most memorable part of Thomson's *Winter* is that describing the death of the poor man caught in a snowstorm. The powerful image of the 'stiffen'd Corse, | Stretch'd out, and bleaching in the northern Blast' leads on to a condemnation of the 'gay, licentious Proud', who remain oblivious to the sufferings of the 'sordid Hut' and 'chearless Poverty'.[64] The narrator's subsequent plea to

> Ye Sons of Mercy! yet resume the Search;
> Drag forth the legal Monsters into Light,
> Wrench from their Hands Oppression's iron Rod,
> And bid the Cruel feel the Pains they give.[65]   (378–81)

finds a clear echo in Burns's 'stern Oppression's iron grip'. In adopting English diction for statements that accord with the radical thrust of the epigraph, then, Burns was not following exclusively English models. For James Thomson, though writing in standard English, was born in the small village of Ednam in Roxburghshire and only settled in London at the age of 24, after completing his education in Edinburgh. His first major poem, *Winter*, which was later revised for inclusion in *The Seasons*, was written soon after his departure from the Borders and, as his biographer James Sambrook has observed, it 'is the most Scottish poem that Thomson wrote in England'.[66] Indeed, the very subject is part of a distinguished Scottish tradition reaching back to poems such as William Dunbar's

---

[63] 'Winter', 617–29, *The Seasons*, ed. James Sambrook (Oxford, 1981). Addison had also written on the 'innocent diversions . . . very proper to pass away a Winter Night for those who do not care to throw away their time at an Opera' in *The Spectator*, 245 (11 Dec. 1711), *Spectator*, ii. 449–54.

[64] 'Winter', 320 ff.

[65] Ibid. 378–81.

[66] James Sambrook, *James Thomson 1700–1748: A Life* (Oxford, 1991), 35. The original version of 'Winter' is included in Thomas Crawford, David Hewitt, and Alexander Law (eds.), *Longer Scottish Poems*, Vol. II: *1650–1830* (Edinburgh, 1987), 57–68, with editorial comment on its Scottish qualities.

'Meditatioun in Wyntir' or the prologue to the seventh book of Gavin Douglas's *Eneados*.[67]

When Burns draws on Thomson for 'A Winter Night', then, his choice is careful and highly appropriate, since 'Winter' offers Scottish landscape and sentiments in language acceptable to English ears. Thomson provides a model of the Scot who excelled in English poetry, demonstrating that it was possible to present original subject matter without being condemned as old-fashioned or 'disgusting'. James Beattie, too, whose hugely successful *The Minstrel* also finds its way into 'A Winter Night', provides a more recent instance of a Scottish poet who had inspired unconditional admiration from English audiences. As James Kinsley points out, the 'plaintive strain' that both 'slow-solemn-stole' and 'rose' in the 'soul' of Burns's speaker is strongly indebted to Beattie's 'visions swarm on Edwin's soul . . . slowly on his ear these moving accents stole'.[68] If Burns's speaker seems to be catching the drifting words of Shakespeare, Pope, Dryden, and Thomson, his reader also hears the echo of Beattie's Minstrel, who epitomized for eighteenth-century readers the figure of the native poet, responding to his surroundings and embodying 'imaginative freedom'.[69] For Burns, still attempting to maintain his equilibrium in the midst of the excitement that had greeted his own poetry, such examples must have held out a certain attraction, not least because they demonstrate that the adoption of English diction does not necessarily mean uncritical submission to an expanding culture. Burns's own use of English is not that of the deeply colonized subject, but of the talented writer equally proficient in more than one language, who thus has a wider range of literary kinds and vocabulary from which to choose.

For the passages that seem to imitate Thomson and Beattie most plainly are sandwiched between the vernacular stanzas of

[67] 'Meditatioun in Wyntir', *The Poems of William Dunbar*, ed. John Small, 2 vols. (Edinburgh and London, 1893), ii. 233–4; Gavin Douglas, *Translation of Virgil's Aeneid*, ed. David Coldwell, 4 vols. (Edinburgh and London, 1957–64).

[68] *Poems and Songs*, iii. 1217. The allusion is to James Beattie, '*The Minstrel; or, The Progress of Genius. A Poem* (London, 1771), II. ix.

[69] As Kathryn Sutherland argues in 'The Native Poet: The Influence of Percy's Minstrel from Beattie to Wordsworth', *Review of English Studies*, NS 33 (Nov. 1982), 414–33. Interestingly, Beattie's inspiration came from Thomas Percy's 'Essay on the Ancient English Minstrels' which prefaced his *Reliques of Ancient English Poetry* (1765).

the opening and the conclusion. If in 'A Winter Night' Burns was attracted to the Anglicized language of these models, he was nevertheless containing it within a strong and more obviously Scottish framework. But just as the transition between the sixth and seventh stanzas turns out to be less absolute formally than it might first appear, so there is considerable internal continuity between the opening stanzas and the central section. For once the opening stanzas are reread in the light of the strophes, the early borrowings from non-vernacular literature emerge with greater force.

As Kinsley's notes make clear, the first stanza of Burns's poem is loaded with references to Thomson's *Winter*, while the epithets used to describe the natural phenomena—'Boreas', 'Phoebus', 'Phoebe'—are derived from Greek. There is nothing incongruous about the appearance of the classical names in the vernacular stanzas, however, because of the ease with which they are absorbed:

> When biting *Boreas*, fell and doure,
> Sharp shivers thro' the leafless bow'r;
> When *Phoebus* gies a short-liv'd glow'r,
> Far south the lift,
> Dim-dark'ning thro' the flaky show'r,
> Or whirling drift.

The reference to the North Wind as 'Boreas' seems perfectly natural because of the alliteration with the familiar word 'biting' and immediate proximity to the emphatically unclassical adjectives 'fell' and 'doure'. 'Doure', in particular, is peculiarly Scottish and thus seems to emphasize the northern origin of the freezing blast. Phoebus is similarly naturalized by the colloquial Scottish 'gies a . . . glow'r', as Burns adapts the classical practice of personifying the natural phenomena in his own locale.

Despite his innovative use of language, however, the adaptation of classical tradition to Scottish poetry was nothing new. The great medieval and Renaissance poets of Scotland had happily appropriated classical ideas and vocabulary to create a rich and highly distinctive literary language. As Kurt Wittig commented in his discussion of Douglas's attempt to expand the literary possibilities of Scots (as opposed to 'Inglis') in his translation of the *Aeneid*, apart 'from a passing reference to Boreas and Eolus the whole of the winter poem (Prol. VII) is founded solely on Scottish experience, and it contains a wealth of sharply-defined sense images drawn from a multiple awareness of nature that was to remain unrivalled until the eighteenth century'.[70] Even in less elevated forms, the presence of classical names in Scottish settings was commonplace, as can be seen in some of the songs collected by Allan Ramsay such as 'Leader Haughs and Yarrow' ('When Phoebus bright the Azure Skies') or 'To Mrs E. C.' (Now Phoebus advances on high').[71] Burns's decision to begin 'A Winter Night' in a vernacular mode that includes classical names is thus indebted to the Scots tradition which could also be seen to include both Beattie and Thomson. But it also underlines the complexity of Scottish poetry, thus countering some of the contemporary prejudice that was only too ready to equate dialect with ignorance.

Eighteenth-century poets writing in Scotland had a large body of classically influenced native literature on which to draw, whether or not they had themselves enjoyed the benefits of an extended classical education. Burns's insertion of an ode into his poem may serve to highlight the classicism of recent English poetry and align his work with that of Gray and Collins, but it also serves to point out the Greek elements in the earlier, vernacular stanzas. 'A Winter Night' may be indebted to James Thomson, but this is not merely a case of imitating a writer whose native voice had been successfully moulded to suit English neoclassical tastes. Instead, Burns seems to deflect the reader from the Anglicized strophes at the centre of his poem towards the vernacular opening and demonstrates in the process that the Scottish stanzas are just as comfortable with the classical tradition. By implication, Thomson's own neo-classicism may be regarded as the natural consequence of his education in the Lowlands, rather than as evidence of his desire to please an English patron.

Burns's poem may be seen, then, at least in part, as an attempt to elevate the status of his own literary language; for

---

[70] Kurt Wittig, *The Scottish Tradition in Literature* (Edinburgh and London, 1958), 85–6. Comparison might also be made with the chilly opening stanzas of Robert Henryson's 'The Testament of Cresseid', *Poems*, ed. Charles Elliott (Oxford, 1963), 90–1.

[71] *The Tea-Table Miscellany, or Allan Ramsay's Collection of Scots Sangs* (London, 1730), 183, 99.

even when restricted to everyday rural life, Scots is capable of highly imaginative adaptations of classical material. Burns is unquestionably writing in the Scots tradition, but it is a tradition that for centuries had been soaking up influences from abroad. Ironically, a poem which seems bent on criticizing those in elevated social positions is also revealing traces of the kind of poetry once composed for the Scottish court. Rather than see this as contradictory, however, it may be also be regarded as a highly rhetorical tactic which wittily reveals the capacity of the down-to-earth man's man to address King Lear in appropriate language.

The juxtaposition of vernacular opening and Anglicized ode may have arisen from the uncertainties that confronted the newly published poet, but the result suggests a renewal of confidence in Scottish poetry. It is as if the very exploration of competing influences has somehow clarified the speaker's cultural position, just as the alternation between different perceptions of poverty has cleared his moral outlook. As he moves into the third part of his ode, the voice of sentiment alights on those whose misfortunes have left them without a proper roof to protect them from the cold:

> 'Oh ye! who, sunk in beds of down,
> 'Feel not a want but what yourselves create,
> 'Think, for a moment, on his wretched fate,
> 'Whom friends and fortune quite disown!
> 'Ill-satisfy'd, keen Nature's clam'rous call,
> 'Stretch'd on his straw he lays himself to sleep,
> 'While thro' the ragged roof and chinky wall,
> 'Chill, o'er his slumbers, piles the drifty heap!'

This passage reinstates the poem's opening images, and echoes the epigraph's call to recognize the difficulties faced by the homeless and outcast. By now, however, the snow has become a metaphor for other kinds of trial, and so the couplet that closes the 'plaintive strain' is not confined to those whose suffering is largely physical or material:

> 'Affliction's sons are brothers in distress;
> 'A Brother to relieve, how exquisite the bliss!'

The more general meanings generated by abstract nouns help to turn the literal idea of homelessness in winter into the larger image of suffering and misery that has been developed through the poem's puns, parallels, and allusions. Burns is able to avoid the more voyeuristic tendencies of contemporary sentimentalism, which often seems to present the misfortunes of others from a somewhat complacent position for the entertainment of readers equally assured of their difference from those depicted. (The subsequent revision of the final line to 'A Brother then relieve, and God the deed shall bless' helps preclude the less attractive possibilities of 'how exquisite the bliss'.[72]) In Burns's poem, those whose lives are such that the snow falls on them as they sleep are not objects to be viewed from a safe distance, but 'brothers in distress'. Just as Lear's experience on the heath provides a metaphor for his mental torture, so miseries like those of the homeless can beset the more comfortable. 'Affliction's sons' share a certain equality, however various their specific woes.

The resolution to the ode is signalled not only by this confident couplet, but also by the most marked shift in form. As the 'plaintive strain' finally comes to a close, the diction shifts again to the broader Scottish dialect of the opening, while the irregular strophes give way to simple, rhythmic quatrains characteristic of the popular ballad:

> I heard nae mair, for *Chanticleer*
> Shook off the pouthery snaw,
> And hail'd the morning with a cheer,
> A cottage-rousing craw.

The bouncing regularity of the new verse comes as quite a relief, as the speaker emerges again as an identifiable voice taking responsibility for his words 'I heard nae mair'. Rather than listening to the words that drift through the darkness, his attention is arrested by the powerful cry of the cockerel as it greets the dawn 'with a cheer'. This is at once a return to the rustic description of the opening stanzas, and a recapitulation of the meanings that are embedded in those stanzas and developed throughout the poem. The positive image of the cockerel's morning routine successfully answers the earlier anxieties concerning the plight of the birds in winter, and thus comments implicitly on the underlying fears about the future of the poet. Birds do not inevitably freeze to death on a winter night, any

---

[72] The line was revised for the poem's republication as 'Humanity: An Ode'.

more than poets necessarily succumb to the pressures they encounter in the wake of their successes. The figure of Chanticleer, whose name recalls the mock-heroic cheerfulness of Chaucer's 'Nun's Priest's Tale' and perhaps the Scottish response of Robert Henryson, suggests that the speaker's confidence returns with the sun.[73] Even as he reaffirms the power of his native literature, however, Burns is still exploiting the additional possibilities offered by the English language since 'pouthery' though meaning only 'powdery', in the vernacular, is able to carry the extra associations of the English 'pother'. The snow, no longer heavy enough to blot out the landscape in a 'whirling drift', nor to block the course of the 'burns', is now reduced to insubstantial powder, a mere nuisance to be swept aside. If Burns retains a degree of self-mockery in his identification with the proud figure of Chanticleer, it is now much more clearly comic than the implied parallels with King Lear.

As Chanticleer shakes off the 'snaw', the poem seems to shed the confusions that have at once impeded and constituted it. In a matter of words, the dominant image of snow and the associated ideas of muffling and covering are removed, allowing the simple truth of the conclusion to stand:

> But deep this truth impress'd my mind—
> Thro' all his works abroad,
> The heart benevolent and kind
> The most resembles GOD.

In the end, it is not the external differences that matter, but the inner character of the individual. It is a form of conclusion that looks back to the 'Moral' favoured by Henryson in the tradition of Aesop, while simultaneously drawing on more contemporary influences from the Moderate Presbyterians and moral philosophers of his own century. But Burns is also returning to the 'moral' introduced by the epigraph, and the levelling image of the ruined king, learning to feel as others feel. If his poem seemed initially to take issue with Shakespeare's representation of the poor, by the end it seems to speak directly to Lear,

[73] Although perhaps better known to most modern readers from Chaucer's 'Nun's Priest's Tale', Chanticleer appears in Henryson's *Fables*, in 'The Taill of Schir Chantecleir and the Foxe'. Allan Ramsay had contributed to the revival of interest in Henryson's *Fables* by including a number in his anthology, *The Ever-Green*, 2 vols. (Edinburgh, 1724).

asserting the common humanity of all members of society. For Burns, the exploration of moral issues is bound up with the linguistic challenges, and so the simple words of the closing stanzas, which draw together Scots and English, rich and poor, is a resolution to all the conflicts that have disrupted 'A Winter Night'.

The final emphasis on the 'heart' in 'A Winter Night' recalls the sentiment of several other pieces in the enlarged edition, thus serving to balance the poem's earlier ironizing of 'The Vision'. The confidence of the closing verses is reminiscent, for example, of the 'Epistle to J. L*****k, An Old Scotch Bard', where Burns had dismissed false learning (despite its power to impress 'your Critic-folk') in favour of 'Nature's fire':

> My Muse, tho' hamely in attire
> May touch the heart.[74]

This is the poem in which Burns had set up a Scottish canon including Allan Ramsay, Robert Fergusson, and Lapraik himself, suggesting that their examples were the only education needed by the 'Scotch bard':

> O for a spunk o' ALLAN's glee
> Or FERGUSON's, the bauld an' slee,
> Or bright L*****K's, my friend to be,
>   If I can hit it!
> That would be *lear* eneugh for me,
>   If I could get it.   (79–84)

In the first edition, this stanza seems a straightforward piece of camaraderie, celebrating the efforts of recent Scottish poets and paying an extravagant compliment to Lapraik. The word 'lear' in this context simply means 'learning', the choice of Scots vocabulary seeming entirely appropriate. Once the collection had been expanded, however, readers would be able to find the 'Epistle to J. L*****k' in the same volume as 'A Winter Night', a conjunction likely to suggest additional associations for the word 'lear'. For when the verse epistle is read after 'A Winter Night', thoughts of Shakespeare's tragedy arise almost inevitably, giving Burns's confident dismissal of 'lear' a double significance.

---

[74] 'Epistle to J. L*****k', *Poems and Songs*, i. 87.

There is a further irony, however, in Burns's rejection of 'lear'. For the very preference for the native was already widely associated with Shakespeare. In the critical discourse of the eighteenth century, Shakespeare was himself regarded by many as the bard of 'nature' rather than learning. As the revolt against neoclassical aesthetics had gained momentum, so too did the celebration of Shakespeare—the original genius, whose natural ability was such that he needed no rules to guide his creative powers. In 1767, Richard Farmer had effectively demolished the concerns of older scholarship about Shakespeare's knowledge of classical texts, with a sparkling essay on Shakespeare's 'Learning'—or rather the lack of it. For Farmer, dependence on classical authority would have diminished the achievement of the great national bard, and so he argues energetically that Shakespeare 'might pick up in the Writers of the time, or the course of his conversation, a familiar phrase or two of French or Italian: but his *Studies* were most demonstratively confined to *Nature and his own Language*'.[75] When Burns claims to reject 'lear' in favour of 'Nature's fire' and the language of Ramsay, Fergusson, and Lapraik, he is thus conforming closely to the new creative ideal epitomized by Shakespeare. If the Kilmarnock edition had appealed to readers because of their new delight in originality and local truth, the second, enlarged edition with its quotation from *King Lear* hints at a parallel between Scotland's new poet and England's bard—a suggestion that has often been made by readers from Burns's day to the present.[76]

Shakespeare is contributing far more to Burns's poem than a portable moral sentiment. It is not just a question of the stricken king haunting the language and situation of Burns's speaker in 'A Winter Night'. When the poem was composed in 1786, Shakespeare had already emerged as the great English bard and

[75] Richard Farmer, *An Essay on the Learning of Shakespeare: Addressed to Joseph Cradock Esq.*', 2nd edn. (1767), in D. Nichol Smith (ed.), *Eighteenth Century Essays on Shakespeare* (Glasgow, 1903), 162–215, 214. For a useful discussion of the controversy over 'Shakespeare's Learning', see Schoenbaum, *Shakespeare's Lives*, 149–53.

[76] Mackenzie compared Burns's 'uncommon penetration' with Shakespeare's 'intuitive glance' in the *Lounger*, 97 (1786), 388, while in 1999 the flotation of the Robert Burns World Federation Ltd., a company aiming to promote Burns over Shakespeare as the world's greatest writer, was widely reported (e.g. in *The Independent*, 7 Sept. 1999, 8).

thus as a model too massive to ignore. Shakespeare represented the new aesthetic of originality which entailed the rejection of examples learned from books in favour of 'nature'—the very ideals set forth in Burns's 'Epistle to Lapraik'. To be 'original', in late eighteenth-century terms, was to reject models and adhere to one's 'own language'. Paradoxically, by so doing, the new Scottish poet was inadvertently following the example of Shakespeare. If some of Burns's contemporaries seemed to hesitate in the face of such difficulties, however, Burns, the self-styled 'David', was ready for the challenge. Rather than ignore the powerful influences from south of the Border, or indeed the literary attitudes fostered in the university cities of the North, Burns's work plays off the very contradictions inherent in contemporary aesthetics, and still manages to conclude 'with a cheer'. Interestingly, in confronting the difficulties, Burns emerged as another poet of originality and as a national bard, as Carlyle's tribute makes plain:

Our literature no longer grows in water, but in mould, and with the true racy virtues of the soil and climate. How much of this change may be due to Burns, or to any other individual, it might be difficult to estimate. Direct literary imitation of Burns was not to be looked for. But his example, in the fearless adoption of domestic subjects, could not but operate from afar; and certainly in no heart did the love of country ever burn with a warmer glow than in that of Burns.[77]

[77] 'The Life of Robert Burns. By J. G. Lockhart', Edinburgh Review, 48 (1828), 289.

3

The Grand Old Ballad in Coleridge's 'Dejection'

Dejection:
An Ode

> Late, late yestreen I saw the new Moon,
> With the old Moon in her arms;
> And I fear, I fear, my Master dear!
> We shall have a deadly storm.
>   Ballad of Sir PATRICK SPENCE.

I

WELL! If the Bard was weather-wise, who made
    The grand old ballad of Sir Patrick Spence,
    This night, so tranquil now, will not go hence
Unrous'd by winds, that ply a busier trade
Than those which mould yon clouds in lazy flakes,
Or the dull sobbing draft, that moans and rakes
        Upon the strings of this Aeolian lute,
        Which better far were mute.
    For lo! the New-moon winter-bright!
    And overspread with phantom-light,
    (With swimming phantom-light o'erspread
    But rimm'd and circled by a silver thread)
I see the old Moon in her lap, foretelling
    The coming on of rain and squally blast.
And oh! that even now the gust were swelling,
    And the slant night-shower driving loud and fast!
Those sounds which oft have raised me, whilst they awed,
        And sent my soul abroad,
Might now perhaps their wonted impulse give,
Might startle this dull pain, and make it move and live!

II

A grief without a pang, void, dark, and drear,
    A stifled, drowsy, unimpassion'd grief,
    Which finds no natural outlet, no relief,

In word, or sigh, or tear—
O Lady! in this wan and heartless mood,
To other thoughts by yonder throstle woo'd,
    All this long eve, so balmy and serene,
Have I been gazing on the western sky,
    And it's peculiar tint of yellow green:
And still I gaze —and with how blank an eye!
And those thin clouds above, in flakes and bars,
That give away their motion to the stars;
Those stars, that glide behind them or between,
Now sparkling, now bedimm'd, but always seen;
Yon crescent Moon, as fix'd as if it grew
In its own cloudless, starless lake of blue;
I see them all so excellently fair,
I see, not feel how beautiful they are!

III

    My genial spirits fail,
    And what can these avail,
To lift the smoth'ring weight from off my breast?
    It were a vain endeavor,
    Though I should gaze for ever
On that green light that lingers in the west:
I may not hope from outward forms to win
The passion and the life, whose fountains are within.

IV

O Lady! we receive but what we give,
And in our life alone does nature live:
Ours is her wedding-garment, ours her shroud!
    And would we aught behold, of higher worth,
Than that inanimate cold world allow'd
To the poor loveless ever-anxious crowd,
    Ah! from the soul itself must issue forth,
A light, a glory, a fair luminous cloud
    Enveloping the Earth—
And from the soul itself must there be sent
    A sweet and potent voice, of its own birth,
Of all sweet sounds the life and element!

V

O pure of heart! thou need'st not ask of me
What this strong music in the soul may be!
What, and wherein it doth exist,
This light, this glory, this fair luminous mist,

This beautiful, and beauty-making power.
　　Joy, virtuous Lady! Joy that ne'er was given,
Save to the pure, and in their purest hour,
Life, and life's effulgence, cloud at once and shower,
Joy, Lady! is the spirit and the power,
Which wedding Nature to us gives in dow'r
　　　A new Earth and new Heaven,
Undreamt of by the sensual and the proud—
Joy is the sweet voice, Joy the luminous cloud—
　　　　We in ourselves rejoice!
And thence flows all that charms or ear or sight,
　　All melodies the echoes of that voice,
All colours a suffusion from that light.

VI

There was a time when, though my path was rough,
　　This joy within me dallied with distress,
And all misfortunes were but as the stuff
　　Whence Fancy made me dreams of happiness:
For hope grew round me, like the twining vine,
And fruits, and foliage, not my own, seem'd mine.
But now afflictions bow me down to earth:
Nor care I that they rob me of my mirth,
　　　But oh! each visitation
Suspends what nature gave me at my birth,
　　My shaping spirit of Imagination.
For not to think of what I needs must feel,
　　But to be still and patient, all I can;
And haply by abstruse research to steal
　　From my own nature all the natural Man—
　　This was my sole resource, my only plan:
Till that which suits a part infects the whole,
And now is almost grown the habit of my Soul.

VII

Hence, viper thoughts, that coil around my mind,
　　　Reality's dark dream!
I turn from you, and listen to the wind,
　　Which long has rav'd unnotic'd. What a scream
Of agony by torture lengthen'd out
That lute sent forth! Thou Wind, that rav'st without,
　　Bare crag, or mountain-tairn, or blasted tree,
Or pine-grove whither woodman never clomb,
Or lonely house, long held the witches' home,
　　Methinks were fitter instruments for thee,

Mad Lutanist! who in this month of show'rs,
Of dark brown gardens, and of peeping flow'rs,
Mak'st Devils' yule, with worse than wint'ry song,
The blossoms, buds, and tim'rous leaves among.
    Thou Actor, perfect in all tragic sounds!
Thou mighty Poet, e'en to Frenzy bold!
        What tell'st thou now about?
        'Tis of the Rushing of an Host in rout,
    With groans of trampled men, with smarting wounds—
At once they groan with pain, and shudder with the cold!
But hush! there is a pause of deepest silence!
    And all that noise, as of a rushing crowd,
With groans, and tremulous shudderings—all is over—
    It tells another tale, with sounds less deep and loud!
        A tale of less affright,
        And temper'd with delight,
As Otway's self had fram'd the tender lay—
        'Tis of a little child
        Upon a lonesome wild,
Not far from home, but she hath lost her way:
And now moans low in bitter grief and fear,
And now screams loud, and hopes to make her mother hear.

VIII

'Tis midnight, but small thoughts have I of sleep:
Full seldom may my friend such vigils keep!
Visit her, gentle Sleep! with wings of healing,
    And may this storm be but a mountain-birth,
May all the stars hang bright above her dwelling,
    Silent as though they watch'd the sleeping Earth!
        With light heart may she rise,
        Gay fancy, cheerful eyes,
Joy lift her spirit, joy attune her voice:
To her may all things live, from Pole to Pole,
Their life the eddying of her living soul!
    O simple spirit, guided from above,
    Dear Lady! friend devoutest of my choice,
Thus may'st thou ever, evermore rejoice.[1]

---

[1] The text is from *Sibylline Leaves: A Collection of Poems. By S. T. Coleridge, Esq.* (London, 1817), 237–43. The major versions of the poem, and the earlier 'Letter to ——' are reproduced with extensive editorial commentary in Stephen M. Parrish (ed.), *Coleridge's* Dejection: *The Earliest Manuscripts and the Earliest Printings* (Ithaca, 1988). See also Stillinger, *Coleridge and Textual Instability*, 91–9; 216–36.

On 19 July 1802 Samuel Taylor Coleridge wrote a long letter to his new friend, the poet and translator William Sotheby. It begins as a progress report on Coleridge's translation of Salomon Gessner's *Der Erste Schiffer* ('The First Navigator'), a fanciful story about the invention of boats, which he had already described at some length in a letter of the previous week. The intervening days had done nothing to improve his opinion of the German poem, and, particularly, of its coy approach to sexuality: 'I am a homebrewed Englishman, and tolerate downright grossness more patiently than this coy and distant Dallying with the Appetites.'[2] Equally unimpressed by its technical qualities, Coleridge observed that, if successful, his 'Translation will be just so much better than the original, as metre is better than prose'.

Had Sotheby read no further than the first paragraph, he might well have concluded that Coleridge was supremely confident of his own abilities, not only as a translator, but also as a poet, a critic, and an Englishman. Nor would this have been an unreasonable assumption, given Coleridge's rapidly increasing list of publications, and the overt patriotism of some of his recent work.[3] And yet, as the letter continues, the self-confidence of the opening gives way first to self-mockery, and then to confessions of depression and failure. The work of translation had not, he admits, been undertaken from any real admiration for Gessner but

---

[2] *The Collected Letters of Samuel Taylor Coleridge*, ed. E. L. Griggs, 6 vols. (Oxford, 1956–71), ii. 813. Coleridge had been influenced by Gessner when composing 'The Wanderings of Cain' in 1798, while 'The Picture, or the Lover's Resolution' of 1802 owes much to Gessner's 'Der Feste Vorsaz': see Bertha Reed, *The Influence of Solomon Gessner upon English Literature* (Philadelphia, 1905), ch. 3. For Wordsworth and Coleridge's reading of Gessner, see Duncan Wu, *Wordsworth's Reading, 1770–1799* (Cambridge, 1993), 62–3. See also John Hibberd, *Salomon Gessner: His Creative Achievement and Influence* (Cambridge, 1976).

[3] In addition to numerous pieces in the *Morning Post*, Coleridge had already published a newspaper called *The Watchman* in 1796; several collections of poetry—*Poems on Various Subjects* (Bristol, 1796) with its second, enlarged, edition the following year, *Fears in Solitude* (London, 1798) and, in collaboration with William Wordsworth, *Lyrical Ballads* (Bristol, 1798); translations from Schiller, *The Piccolomini and the Death of Wallenstein* (London, 1800); his own early play, *The Fall of Robespierre*, written with Robert Southey had been published in Cambridge in 1794. His enthusiasm for Britain is particularly outspoken in 'Fears in Solitude' ('O native Britain! O my Mother Isle!').

because I wished to force myself out of metaphysical trains of Thought—which, when I trusted myself to my own Ideas, came upon me uncalled—& when I wished to write a poem, beat up Game of far other kind—instead of a Covey of poetic Partridges with whirring wings of music, or wild Ducks *shaping* their rapid flight in forms always regular (a still better image of Verse) up came a metaphysical Bustard, urging it's slow, heavy, laborious, earth-skimming Flight, over dreary & level Wastes.

The image of Coleridge's uncontrollable propensity to metaphysical ideas, and the consequent bustard verses, rapidly loses its comic touch as he goes on to explain that such pursuits were in themselves part of a conscious effort to overcome 'Sickness & some other & worse afflictions'.[4] If Sotheby was supposed to accept that Coleridge's more creative powers had been blocked by his philosophical interests, however, the idea was contradicted almost instantly by the subsequent inclusion of lines from a new poem apparently 'written during that dejection to Wordsworth':

> Yes, dearest Poet, yes!
> There was a time when tho' my Path was rough,
> The Joy within me dallied with Distress,
> And all Misfortunes were but as the Stuff
> Whence Fancy made me Dreams of Happiness:
> For Hope grew round me, like the climbing Vine,
> And Fruit and Foliage, not my own, seem'd mine.
> But now Afflictions bow me down to Earth—
> Nor car'd I, that they rob me of my Mirth;
> But O! each Visitation
> Suspends what Nature gave me at my Birth,
> My Shaping Spirit of Imagination!
> – – – – – – – – – – – – – –
> – – – – – – – – – – – – – –
> For not to think of what I needs must feel,
> But to be still & patient all I can;
> And haply by abstruse research to steal
> From my own Nature all the natural Man;
> This was my sole Resource, my wisest Plan—

---

[4] For the image of the bustard, a large, rare bird prone to running rather than flying, Coleridge was probably indebted to Wordsworth's description of its 'thick unwieldy flight', 'Adventures on Salisbury Plain', 154, *The Salisbury Plain Poems*, ed. Stephen Gill (Ithaca, 1975), 127.

> And that which suits a part infects the whole,
> And now is almost grown the Temper of my Soul!

Thank Heaven! My better mind has returned to me—and I trust, I shall go on rejoicing.

Ironically, Coleridge is expressing his inability to write poetry in the form of a poem, and a very good one at that. This is not the doggerel that might be expected from someone who claimed to have lost the muse, but a stunning piece of pentameter verse, highly metaphorical, loaded with literary allusion, and beautifully 'shaped' into rhyme. Perhaps it is the obvious discrepancy between what Coleridge is saying overtly and what actually seems to be going on that leads to the otherwise rather baffling comment that concludes the passage. Why, otherwise, would the articulation of his failing powers induce a state of 'rejoicing'?

Fortunately, many of the puzzles confronting William Sotheby are spared the modern reader who encounters this letter in Earl Leslie Griggs's collected edition of Coleridge's correspondence. The tantalizing passages from the longer poem, chosen especially for Sotheby on account of their 'sufficiently general nature', cannot have the same effect on the reader who has already been privileged a few pages earlier with the verse 'Letter to ——', a poem of over three hundred lines, including these.[5] Anyone with enough interest in Coleridge to be reading his voluminous correspondence is also likely to recognize the lines as part of one of his best-known poems: 'Dejection: An Ode'. The ode had its origins in the long verse letter Coleridge sent to Wordsworth's future sister-in-law, Sara Hutchinson, on 4 April 1802. It was only published in its more familiar form a few months later, however, in the *Morning Post* for 4 October, which was both the day of William Wordsworth's marriage to Mary Hutchinson, and the seventh anniversary of Coleridge's own wedding. Fifteen years later, Coleridge revised his poem again for inclusion in his collected edition, *Sibylline Leaves*, thus providing the version most frequently reprinted and thus familiar to modern readers.

---

[5] Griggs includes the verse letter written on 4 April 1802 in the *Collected Letters* as 'Letter 438. To Sara Hutchinson', ii. 790–8. It is also included in Parrish's edition of *Dejection*, 21–34. A useful reading text is included in Duncan Wu, *Romanticism: An Anthology* (Oxford and Cambridge, Mass., 1994), 544–52.

What must have appeared to Sotheby as an exciting, mystifying fragment is thus regarded by most modern readers as a passage from something more familiar in other forms, or perhaps as a stage in the development of 'Dejection' from verse epistle to ode. (Whether the development is presented in terms of improvement or diminishment varies from critic to critic, but the recovery and publication of the different manuscripts and published texts has given rise to a number of painstaking accounts of the poem's composition, as well as generating puzzles every bit as baffling as those confronting William Sotheby.[6]) What might have appeared to Sotheby as a startling juxtaposition between the lines on the loss of imagination and Coleridge's consequent 'rejoicing' thus seems quite natural to the reader of the complete Ode, with its powerful, but gradual, movement from 'grief' to 'joy'.

Coleridge's awareness of the difficulties facing his correspondent is nevertheless apparent as the letter goes on, and he includes a further 120 lines of the poem, before breaking off at last with an apology for sending 'such a long verse-crammed letter'. It is an extraordinarily self-conscious performance, but fascinating in its controlled revelations, and careful hints on interpretation. His description of the poem as having been written 'to Wordsworth' indicates a desire to disguise the circumstances of composition and to hide his unhappy love for Sara Hutchinson under the more acceptable cover of writer's block, even though the very fact of the verse belies the explanation. Lines in the poem itself which had originally been addressed to 'Sara' and would later refer to a nameless 'Lady', became for Sotheby's benefit apostrophes to Coleridge's former co-writer and still prolific friend: 'O Wordsworth, we receive but what we give', 'Joy, William! Is the spirit and the

___

[6] See e.g. George Dekker, *Coleridge and the Literature of Sensibility* (London, 1978); William Heath, *Wordsworth and Coleridge: A Study of their Literary Relations in 1801–1802* (Oxford, 1970); Lucy Newlyn, *Coleridge, Wordsworth, and the Language of Allusion* (Oxford, 1986); Parrish, *Coleridge's* Dejection; David Pirie, 'A Letter to [Asra]', in Jonathan Wordsworth and Beth Darlington (eds.), *Bicentenary Wordsworth Studies in Memory of John Alban Finch* (Ithaca, 1970), 294–339; Gene Ruoff, *Wordsworth and Coleridge: The Making of the Major Lyrics, 1802–1804* (London, 1989); Luther Tyler, 'Losing "A Letter": The Contexts of Coleridge's "Dejection: An Ode" ', *ELH* 52/2 (1985), 419–45; George Whalley, *Coleridge and Sara Hutchinson and the Asra Poems* (London, 1955).

power', and 'O Wordsworth! Friend of my devoutest choice'. These are among the changes that have led scholars to focus on the dialogue between Coleridge and Wordsworth in the poem, tracing the subtle allusions and the complicated relationship between 'Dejection' and the composition of Wordsworth's 'Resolution and Independence' and 'Immortality Ode'.[7] The letter to Sotheby, however, which represents Coleridge's first attempt to present his new poem to someone beyond his immediate close group of familiar readers, explicitly draws attention to another poet, who may have attracted less critical interest, but whose significance for this study is far greater.[8]

As Coleridge explained to Sotheby, 'the first lines allude to a stanza in the Ballad of Sir Patrick Spence—"Late, late yestreen, I saw the new Moon With the old Moon in her arms; and I fear, I fear, my master dear, There will be a deadly storm"'. Whatever the importance of Wordsworth's great 'Ode' as a creative catalyst for 'Dejection', the poem begins, as Coleridge was at pains to point out, with a much more explicit reference to 'Sir Patrick Spens': 'Well! If the Bard was weatherwise | Who made the dear old Ballad of Sir Patrick Spence'. By spelling out the allusion and including the relevant stanza from the ballad, Coleridge is clearly signalling the need for Sotheby to identify it correctly and to take notice of his opening lines. Whether or not he expected his correspondent to be particularly familiar with the ballad, however, is another matter. He is, after all, very specific about the relevant lines from 'Sir Patrick Spens': those evoking the striking image of the moon and its traditional significance in forecasting the weather. These were the lines that would later be printed with his poem, giving the appearance of a standard epigraph.

Where the significance of Burns's epigraph from *King Lear*

---

[7] See especially Heath, *Wordsworth and Coleridge*; Newlyn, *Coleridge, Wordsworth*; Ruoff, *Wordsworth and Coleridge*; Paul Magnuson, *Coleridge and Wordsworth: A Lyrical Dialogue* (Princeton, 1988).

[8] On the importance of Coleridge's close group of sympathetic readers see Thomas McFarland, *Romanticism and the Forms of Ruin: Wordsworth, Coleridge, and the Modalities of Fragmentation* (Princeton, 1981). On Sotheby as an ideal reader in 1802, see Ruoff, *Wordsworth and Coleridge*, 173, and for Coleridge's later attitude to the reading public, see Lucy Newlyn, 'Coleridge and the Anxiety of Reception', *Romanticism*, I/2 (1995), 206–38.

emerges only gradually, however, Coleridge refers directly to 'Sir Patrick Spens' in the opening line of his poem—'Well! If the Bard was weather-wise'. The earlier verse letter begins with the same opening line as 'Dejection', but Coleridge did not include part of 'Sir Patrick Spens' when writing to Sara Hutchinson. The effect is rather of a conversation in progress, the colloquial 'Well!' seeming a response to an earlier remark, the unexplained allusion suggesting a degree of familiarity too assured to require clarification. This confidence allows Coleridge to play on the sexual connotations of the ballad image ('I see the Old Moon in her Lap, foretelling | The coming-on of Rain & squally Blast— | O! Sara! That the Gust ev'n now were swelling') without needing to gloss his words with quotation. When the poem was revised for William Sotheby in July, the removal of Sara's name and the inclusion of the ballad stanza combined to submerge the original physical longing under a more general expression of melancholy, apparently associated with the poet's inability to write rather than find fulfilment in love.

The growing importance of the lines from 'Sir Patrick Spens', first quoted in the letter to Sotheby, becomes more obvious with the publication of the poem. Readers of the 4 October issue of the *Morning Post* were given the same ballad stanza, printed above the title of the poem:

> 'Late, late yestreen I saw the New Moon
> 'With the Old Moon in her arms;
> 'And I fear, I fear, my master dear,
> 'We shall have a deadly storm.'
> BALLAD OF SIR PATRICK SPENCE

DEJECTION.
AN ODE, WRITTEN APRIL 4, 1802.

WELL! If the Bard was weather-wise, who made
The grand Old Ballad of SIR PATRICK SPENCE,

When the poem was revised for inclusion in *Sibylline Leaves*, the specific date was dropped from the title, and the stanza from the ballad inserted between 'Dejection: An Ode' and the first line of the poem. No longer separate, the lines from 'Sir Patrick Spens' seem, by 1817, to have become an integral part of 'Dejection': an old poem embraced by the new one, and suggesting not disjunction but creative union. The gradual process through which 'Sir Patrick Spens' emerges in the various phases of Coleridge's poem may seem nothing more than an accident of typography, literary fashion, or editorial whim. The development, whether by design or otherwise, is nevertheless entirely appropriate to the movement of the poem itself, with its explicit balancing of isolation and wholeness.

In the poem published in the *Morning Post*, the four lines from 'Sir Patrick Spens' seem to hang above the ode, complete within their inverted commas and traditional form, and apparently unaffected by the irregular movements of Coleridge's verse. Although the stanza appears so complete and self-sufficient, however, all is not quite as it seems. When Coleridge quoted the lines to Sotheby, and later submitted them with the new poem to his editor, he may have been remembering an oral version of the ballad, perhaps familiar from childhood. It is much more likely, however, that his source was Thomas Percy's text of the poem, included in his famous ballad anthology, *Reliques of Ancient English Poetry*, which had enjoyed enormous popularity since its appearance in 1765 and had already reached a fourth edition by the 1790s. Ballads, being essentially oral forms, often exist in a number of different versions, and 'Sir Patrick Spens', despite being much less ancient than late eighteenth-century readers realized, was no exception.[9] Several texts survive, with considerable variations, but only Percy's has the distinctive line 'Late, late, yestreen'. Not only was Coleridge very familiar with the *Reliques*, whose influence on *Lyrical Ballads* is well known, but Percy's volume was also a favourite of Sara Hutchinson. It thus seems much the most likely source for 'Dejection'.[10] Although the lines quoted by Coleridge

---

[9] Nineteen versions of the ballad are included in F. J. Child (ed.), *The English and Scottish Popular Ballads* (1882), facsimile edn., 5 vols. (New York, 1956), ii. 17–32. Percy's is the earliest surviving text; he received two copies of the ballad, one from Lord Hailes, the other probably from John MacGowan—see *The Percy Letters: The Correspondence of Thomas Percy and David Dalrymple, Lord Hailes*, ed. A. F. Falconer (Baton Rouge, 1954), 39. The nineteenth century saw a lively and prolonged controversy over the authenticity of the ballad, but it is now generally regarded as an eighteenth-century poem: see David Buchan, *A Scottish Ballad Book* (London, 1972); id., *The Ballad and the Folk* (London, 1972); David C. Fowler, *A Literary History of the Popular Ballad* (Durham, NC, 1968).

[10] *The Letters of Sara Hutchinson*, ed. Kathleen Coburn (London, 1954), 118,

resemble Percy's text closely, however, there are also some interesting differences, which illuminate Coleridge's attitude to both the ballad and his audience.

Percy's text of 'Sir Patrick Spens' reads as follows:

> The king sits in Dunfermling toune,
>   Drinking the blude-reid wine:
> O quhar will I get guid sailòr,
>   To sail this schip of mine?
>
> Up and spak an eldern knicht,
>   Sat at the kings richt kne:
> Sir Patrick Spence is the best sailòr,
>   That sails upon the se.
>
> The king has written a braid lettèr,
>   And signd it wi' his hand;
> And sent it to sir Patrick Spence,
>   Was walking on the sand.
>
> The first line that Sir Patrick red,
>   A loud lauch lauched he:
> The next line that Sir Patrick red,
>   The teir blinded his ee.
>
> O quha is this has done this deid,
>   This ill deid don to me;
> To send me out this time o'the zeir,
>   To sail upon the se?
>
> Mak haste, mak haste, my mirry men all,
>   Our guid schip sails the morne.
> O say na sae, my master deir
>   For I feir a deadlie storme.
>
> Late late yestreen I saw the new moone
>   Wi' the auld moone in hir arme;
> And I feir, I feir, my deir mastèr,
>   That we will cum to harme.
>
> O our Scots nobles wer richt laith
>   To weet their cork-heild shoone;
> Bot lang owre a' the play wer playd,
>   Thair hats they swam aboone.

139, 148, 221. Coleridge's familiarity with the *Reliques* is obvious from a letter of 23 January 1798 (*Letters*, i. 379) and the volume's importance for *Lyrical Ballads* has often been noted, although Wordsworth's knowledge of Percy increased significantly after his purchase of the *Reliques* in Hamburg in October 1799—see Edwin Stein, *Wordsworth's Art of Allusion* (Pennsylvania, 1988), 176.

> O lang, lang, may thair ladies sit
>   Wi' thair fans into their hand,
> Or eir they se Sir Patrick Spence
>   Cum sailing to the land.
>
> O lang, lang, may the ladies stand
>   Wi' thair gold kems in their hair,
> Waiting for thair ain deir lords,
>   For they'll se thame na mair.
>
> Have owre, have owr to Aberdour,
>   It's fiftie fadom deip:
> And thair lies guid Sir Patrick Spence,
>   Wi' the Scots lords at his feit.[11]

The tale of Sir Patrick Spens, compelled by his King to venture across the North Sea in the depths of winter and shipwrecked with the loss of all life on the homeward voyage, may seem an appropriate choice for the opening of 'Dejection', in that its spare depiction of unjust suffering and needless loss of life creates a mood of wistful melancholy. And yet Coleridge's response to the appearance of the moon and the predicted storm is very different from that dramatized in the ballad. For where Sir Patrick Spens weeps at the state of the sky and dreads his imminent journey, the speaker in 'Dejection' longs for the storm to begin, in the hope that his 'soul' might be 'sent . . . abroad'. The incorporation of the ballad into 'Dejection' is clearly more than a straightforward borrowing based on an incidental similarity of image. Just as Coleridge selected only parts of his own poem for William Sotheby, and adapted the lines specially for his correspondent, so too with 'Sir Patrick Spens' Coleridge extracts only what is necessary for his immediate purposes.

The starting point for Coleridge's poem is the image of the new moon with the darkened side still visible, a meteorological phenomenon that appeared with striking clarity in the spring of 1802, judging by descriptions in Dorothy Wordsworth's Journal. On 8 March, when Coleridge was staying with the Hutchinsons at Gallow Hill in the Yorkshire Moors, she wrote in her diary:

---

[11] *Reliques of Ancient English Poetry*, 3 vols. (London, 1765), i. 72–3; a facsimile edition with a useful introduction by Nick Groom was published in London in 1996. For the longer versions of the ballad, see Child, *English and Scottish Popular Ballads*.

On friday Evening the Moon hung over the Northern side of the highest point of Silver How, like a gold ring snapped in two, & shaven off at the Ends, it was so narrow. Within this Ring lay the Circle of the Round moon, as *distinctly* to be seen as ever the enlightened moon is. William had observed the same appearance at Keswick, perhaps at the very same moment hanging over the Newland Fells. Sent off a letter to Mary H. also to Coleridge & Sara.[12]

The similarity between the appearance of the moon over the fells and that described in 'Sir Patrick Spens' also struck her two months later when she noted on 4 May, 'We had the Crescent moon with the "auld moon in her arms".' But by May, as George Dekker has observed, 'we can reasonably infer that Coleridge was lending Dorothy a mythologizing eye'.[13]

Coleridge's fascination with the moon was already well developed by 1802; but he is likely to have taken a particularly lively interest in its changing appearances during his visit to Gallow Hill because of a recent poem he had composed for Sara Hutchinson. 'A Soliloquy of the full Moon, She being in a Mad Passion' is a humorous diatribe against modern poets ('the Pest of the Nation!') who turn their eyes and metaphors too frequently towards the night sky:

> Ventriloquogusty
> Poets
> With no Hats
> Or Hats that are rusty
> They're my Torment and Curse
> And harass me worse
> And bait me and bay me, far sorer I vow
> Than the Screech of the Owl
> Or the witch-wolf's long howl,
> Or sheep-killing Butcher-dog's inward Bow wow
> For me they all spite—an unfortunate Wight.
> And the very first moment that I came to Light
> A rascal call'd Voss the more to his scandal,
> Turn'd me into a sickle with never a handle.
> A Night or two after a worse Rogue there came,
> The head of a Gang, one Wordsworth by name—

---

[12] Dorothy Wordsworth, *The Grasmere Journals*, ed. Pamela Woof (Oxford, 1991), 76.
[13] Ibid. 95–6. Dekker, *Coleridge and the Literature of Sensibility*, 26. See also Jonathan Livingstone Lowes, *The Road to Xanadu* (London, 1927), 159.

'Ho! What's in the wind?' Tis the voice of a Wizzard!
I saw him look at me most terribly blue!
He was hunting for witch-rhymes from great A to Izzard,
And soon as he'd found them made no more ado
But chang'd me at once to a little Canoe.[14]

The poem goes on in a similar vein, listing Coleridge's own various lunar metaphors before asserting in conclusion

I am I myself I, the jolly full Moon.

Although this comic *tour de force* could hardly be further from the mood of 'Dejection', its vocabulary and self-parodying techniques anticipate the much more serious verse letter that Coleridge was to send Sara in April 1802. The same fascination with the moon, and the idea of poets attempting to transform it, which led in both poems to the affectionate references to Wordsworth's 'sky canoe', was also to inspire the verse letter's evocation of the Bard whose image precedes Coleridge's description of the natural scene apparently before his eyes.[15] The jolly full Moon of the 'Soliloquy' may claim to be herself alone, but it is evident that for the speaker of 'Dejection', the moon was perceived primarily through the lenses of literature. Even though Coleridge almost certainly observed the new moon described by Dorothy Wordsworth, the personal experience was magnified by the memory of the ballad with its powerful folkloric image. To re-create the feelings inspired by the curious new moon, it was therefore necessary to include the lines of the poem that had risen in the mind in unison with the sight that met the eye.

What complicates matters further, however, is that despite Coleridge's insistence that his opening stanza should be read in conjunction with the correct passage from 'Sir Patrick Spens', the lines he quotes are not an accurate transcription. It is plain from Percy's text of the ballad that instead of copying out his source exactly, Coleridge has conflated two separate verses, resulting in a condensed version of the part of the narrative most relevant to his own purposes. Out of a larger whole, and a

---

[14] From Whalley, *Coleridge and Sara Hutchinson*, 5–7.
[15] Wordsworth's 'Canoe' image appeared in the Prologue to *Peter Bell* which, though not published until 1819, was written in 1799: see William Wordsworth, *Peter Bell*, ed. John E. Jordan (Ithaca, 1985), 44–6.

dialogue between the master and his men, Coleridge has extracted the image of the moon and its significance for his own poem. By rolling verses 6 and 7 into one, and accentuating the internal rhyme ('feir . . . feir . . . deir'), Coleridge has created a neat stanza which effectively links the moon's appearance with the oncoming storm. In doing so, he also removes the prediction of 'harme', which in the ballad contributes to the sense of unavoidable disaster, and the equation of the storm with death. Instead, Coleridge weakens the causal link between the state of the moon and the tragic outcome, and thus opens up his own poem to the possibilities of a less pessimistic ending. The predicted storm still occurs, but rather than prove 'deadly', it is animating, and leads not to desolation but imaginative union. Where the moon in the ballad seems to symbolize the inevitability of events and the helplessness of those involved, Coleridge inverts the image, even as he evokes it, closing his poem with images that lead the reader back to the beginning to retrace the narrative. Thus the older text, though apparently fixed and complete, is subtly altered in its encounter with the new poem, and, in the process, gives off a creative charge to make the new verse move and live.

In a sense, Coleridge is following the practice of an oral poet: reciting a familiar poem, while carefully reshaping it according to his own purpose, just as Burns adapted the songs he collected or inherited from local tradition. And yet, the ballad is not entirely amenable to Coleridge's rewriting. The emphasis on the rhymes in the third line of Coleridge's version, 'I fear, I fear, my Master dear', diverts attention from the consequences of his compression of the two separate verses, which has in fact resulted in the loss of the true rhyme between lines 2 and 4. Where Percy's text rhymes 'arme' with 'harm', Coleridge has 'arms' and 'storm', an internal disjunction characteristic of 'Dejection' as a whole. Just as the moon described in the ballad is imaged as two incongruous parts locked together in temporary union, so Coleridge's 'arms' and 'storm' are forced into close proximity when they belong apart. The desire to unite disparate parts and the recognition of the consequent creative power, which is then explored so movingly in the main poem, is thus embodied in the ballad stanza itself.

Coleridge's adaptation of the ballad involves not only the

conflation of adjacent stanzas, however, but also alteration of the language. Although the lines quoted by Coleridge are similar to those in Percy's text, the distinctive Scottish spelling is quietly Anglicized ('Wi' the auld moon in hir arme'/'With the Old Moon in her arms'), and modernized ('moone'/'moon'; 'feir'/ 'fear', 'deir'/'dear', 'mastèr'/'master', 'deadlie storme'/'deadly storm', 'we shall have'). This may suggest nothing more than an attempt to make the ballad more accessible to an early nineteenth-century audience, an attitude influenced perhaps by the unsympathetic responses to the archaic language of 'The Rime of the Ancyent Marinere', as it was originally presented in the 1798 edition of *Lyrical Ballads*.[16] It is not at all clear, however, that such mediation was needed.

'Sir Patrick Spens' may have gained its wide currency through Percy's pages, but the *Reliques* was part of a larger publishing phenomenon which, throughout the eighteenth century, saw the transformation of numerous miscellaneous oral songs and ballads into volumes saleable to a reading public. And many of these collections were Scottish. The efforts of James Watson and Allan Ramsay had been followed by those of later collectors such as David Herd, John Pinkerton, and, most recently, Walter Scott, whose first volumes of *Minstrelsy of the Scottish Border* appeared in February 1802 only a few weeks before the composition of Coleridge's poem.[17] The success of Robert Burns's work over the last two decades had also helped to make Scots familiar as a literary language to anyone with an interest in contemporary verse. Indeed, the evocation of 'Sir Patrick Spens' might have been regarded by the first readers of 'Dejection' as a deliberate attempt to exploit a fashionable trend. It seems odd, then, that Coleridge should have been so careful to erase its distinctive linguistic features and turn the Scots poem into standard English.

Coleridge's treatment of the ballad is of course consistent

---

[16] Wordsworth had removed Coleridge's poem from its prime position at the front of the volume and included a note referring to its 'great defects' when he published the enlarged edition of *Lyrical Ballads* in 1800, as Michael Mason discusses in his introduction, *Lyrical Ballads*, 4–7.

[17] *Ancient and Modern Scottish Songs, Heroic Ballads, etc.*, ed. David Herd, 2 vols. (Edinburgh, 1769); John Pinkerton, *Scottish Poems*, 3 vols. (Edinburgh, 1792); Walter Scott, *Minstrelsy of the Scottish Border*, 2 vols. (Kelso, 1802), 2nd edn., 3 vols. (Edinburgh and London, 1803).

with the obsessive rewriting of his own poetry and may have been inspired by similar aesthetic assumptions. If the verse letter to Sara had to be carved up and the domestic details dropped in an effort to create a poem 'of sufficiently general nature' (or sufficiently impersonal) for Sotheby, then 'Sir Patrick Spens' could also be largely discarded, and only those parts retained which might contribute to a poem of universal significance. The image of the moon could speak directly to a wide audience of sympathetic readers if it were not restricted by its particular manifestation in a medieval ballad.[18] Thus the words had to be smoothed and brought into line with Coleridge's own verse, in the same unifying impetus that gradually came to include the entire stanza within the perimeter of 'Dejection: An Ode'.

To readers from north of the Border, however, Coleridge's attempt to universalize the ballad stanza may seem rather less benign. In the light of Robert Crawford's eloquent plea for greater recognition of 'the differences between Scottish Literature, British Literature, and English Literature', Coleridge's apparent dismissal of the Scottish elements of 'Sir Patrick Spens' might attract accusations of 'naïve cultural imperialism'. In Crawford's eyes, if

we ignore matters of local origin, then we perform an act of naïve cultural imperialism, acting as if books grew not out of particular conditions in Nottingham, Dublin, St Lucia, or Salem, Massachusetts, but out of the bland uniformity of airport departure lounges. The act of inscription is not a simple entry into the delocalized, pure medium of language; it is constantly, often deliberately, an act which speaks of its local origins, of points of departure never fully left behind.[19]

'Sir Patrick Spens' emphasizes its local origin in the very first line, and throughout the ballad the idea of leaving Scotland is portrayed in terms of catastrophe. Coleridge's selection of only the middle stanzas, however, with the universal imagery of moon and storm, and his reshaping of the lines in modern English suggests a rather more cavalier attitude to local origins, or even a positive urge to leave any points of departure far behind.

[18] In the Preface to *Poems on Various Subjects*, Coleridge had written, 'What is the PUBLIC but a term for a number of scattered individuals of whom as many will be interested in these sorrows as have experienced the same or similar?', p. vii.

[19] Crawford, *Devolving English Literature*, 7.

Given Coleridge's national consciousness, heightened through the years of war with France, and during recent work as a translator of German texts, it is possible to interpret his attitude to the ballad as part of a growing sense of his own national identity ('I am a homebrewed Englishman').[20] Delving into his notebooks certainly produces evidence of an attitude that could hardly be less sympathetic to his northern neighbours:

A Scotchman = an HYPANTHROPE, or a Subhuman.[21]

This remarkable piece of xenophobia continues for several lines, before concluding with speculation on 'why the Transtweedians, in defiance of all grammatical analogy, do, one and all, affect to call themselves Scotsmen, instead of Scotchmen . . . Now just cast your eyes on the finals, tch, in Walker's rhyming Dictionary—Bitch, Botch, ⟨Stitch⟩, Blotch, Ditch.' It might seem reasonable to conclude from this that Coleridge's reasons for minimizing the local origins of 'Sir Patrick Spens' were fairly straightforward: he did not like the Scots. He did, nevertheless, admire their poetry and, if he needed to use Scottish material for his own work, he merely made it as English as possible.

If Coleridge's attitude to the ballad seems extraordinarily highhanded, however, he was in a sense following his source more closely than might be immediately obvious. Thomas Percy had after all included 'Sir Patrick Spence', complete with Anglicized title, in the collection entitled *Reliques of Ancient English Poetry*, which was prefaced by an 'Essay on the Ancient English Minstrels'. Percy's own unease over how 'to dispose of the Scotch Pieces' in his miscellany emerges clearly in his correspondence with Shenstone, as he describes his attempts both to fill out the collection with Scottish ballads and yet avoid detracting from its Englishness by scattering 'them promiscuously thro' all

---

[20] *Letters*, ii. 813; cf. ibid. 522. Julie A. Carlson has examined Coleridge's nationalism in *In the Theatre of Romanticism: Coleridge, Nationalism, Women* (Cambridge, 1994). For a broad account of Coleridge's shift from early radicalism to criticism of the French constitution and finally the more conservative Englishness of *On the Constitution of the Church and State*, see John Morrow, *Coleridge's Political Thought* (London, 1990).

[21] *The Notebooks of Samuel Taylor Coleridge,* ed. Kathleen Coburn, 6 vols. (Princeton and London, 1957–), ii. 4134 29.166. The entry dates from early 1812. Cf. ii. 2618, entry for July 1805.

the Volumes'.[22] A similarly contradictory attitude to his sources is evident in the account of his search for materials in Scotland, Wales, the Peak District, Ireland, and even the West Indies, places sufficiently 'remote and obscure' to have preserved 'curiosities of the kind I want'.[23] The language used to describe his antiquarian endeavours is surprisingly violent, however: 'thus shall we ransack the whole British Empire'.[24] Where some eighteenth-century collectors of ancient poetry, especially those working with Gaelic materials in the Scottish Highlands or Ireland, saw their task in terms of a rescue operation—an effort to save the relics of the past before they vanished for ever— Percy casts himself in the role of a conqueror, seizing the treasures of subject lands.[25] Once acquired, too, the precious objects seemed to become the property of the editor, who felt free to present them according to his own tastes. As Shenstone suggested:

suppose then you consider your MS as an hoard of gold, somewhat defac'd by Time; from which however you may be able to draw supplies upon occasion, and with which you may enrich the world hereafter under more current impressions.[26]

The traditional poetry of the British Isles was buried treasure which, once recovered, could be recast to permit its circulation in the contemporary market-place. Unfixed by print, oral poetry was regularly subjected to the polish and refinement of eighteenth-century editors who tended to regard its intrinsic lack of sophistication or defacement through time as an obstacle to the potential readership. Even those collectors primarily concerned with the preservation of a threatened culture were still inclined to transform their materials in honour of the printed

[22] 22 Feb. 1762. *The Percy Letters: The Correspondence of Thomas Percy and William Shenstone*, ed. Cleanth Brooks (New Haven and London, 1977), 140. For an excellent study of Percy's methods, see Nick Groom, *The Makings of Percy's Reliques* (Oxford, 1999).

[23] 19 July 1761, *Percy–Shenstone Correspondence*, 109.

[24] Ibid.

[25] For the texts of the Gaelic ballads collected by a number of antiquarians in the eighteenth century, see J. F. Campbell's invaluable *Leabhar na Féinne* (1872), facsimile edn. (Shannon, 1972). See also James Macpherson, *The Poems of Ossian*, ed. Howard Gaskill (Edinburgh, 1996).

[26] 4 Jan. 1758, *Percy–Shenstone Correspondence*, 5–6.

page, as Jerome Stone's elaborate 'translation' of the traditional Gaelic poem on 'The Death of Fraoch' demonstrates.[27]

Had Coleridge inherited wholesale the antiquarian attitudes of the late eighteenth century, it would thus be unsurprising to find him simultaneously admiring and tinkering with an ancient poem. He had, after all, demonstrated his skills in employing the traditional ballad metre in 'The Ancient Mariner', which revels in its blend of the modern and antique.[28] The opening of 'Dejection', however, gives no sense of the speaker feeling himself superior to the unknown composer of 'the grand old ballad of Sir Patrick Spence'. On the contrary, the words of the balladmaker stand above Coleridge's poem, suggesting authority and precedence—an impression underlined by the opening reference to the 'Bard'.

The very word 'Bard' was heavily laden with associations by 1802, and although Coleridge occasionally used it ironically, he could not have been oblivious to the popular image of the ancient Celtic Bard, singing his inspired lays with his wind harp hanging in a tree above.[29] The Bard embodied very positive ideas of antiquity: of authority within a close community, of inherited wisdom and even divine power.[30] In his 'Essay on the Ancient English Minstrels', Percy describes the 'ancient Bards' of the British Isles, whose 'skill was considered as something divine' and whose 'persons were deemed sacred'.[31] Their work was that of both seer and public orator, and could hardly seem more different from the self-absorbed confessions of the speaker of 'Dejection'. Their very anonymity, too, increased the sense of mysterious strength, by emphasizing that their words were of sufficient importance to be committed to memory and handed down through generations, even if the absence of a named author and definitive text meant that the verses were public

[27] Published in *The Scots Magazine*, xviii (1756), 15–17.

[28] For a helpful account of the importance of the ballad form to Wordsworth and Coleridge, see Mary Jacobus, *Tradition and Experiment in Wordsworth's Lyrical Ballads (1798)* (Oxford, 1976).

[29] For wind harps and their significance for 'Dejection', see Dekker, *Coleridge and the Literature of Sensibility*, ch. 3. Dekker draws attention to Coleridge's earlier poem 'The Eolian Harp', where 'lute' and 'harp' appear to be synonymous.

[30] For a comprehensive discussion of eighteenth-century Bards, see Katie Trumpener, *Bardic Nationalism: The Romantic Novel and the British Empire* (Princeton, 1997).

[31] Percy, 'Essay on the Ancient English Minstrels', *Reliques*, i, p. xv.

property, free to be adapted and reshaped by successive singers. Indeed, Percy's presentation of the medieval minstrels of England as 'the genuine successors of the ancient Bards' shows how eighteenth-century readers reached back to a dim Celtic past as the repository of ancient creative power and happily co-opted the bards as honorary ancestors.[32] The common image of the inspired bard under the oak tree helped to consolidate a general antique Britishness, often smoothing over an early history of conquests and cultural crises. The native poet, planted firmly in his natural environment, seemed to have possessed a visionary power quite different from the urbane, educated verse of classical Rome so admired by writers of the Restoration period, and the contrast proved irresistibly exciting to readers of late eighteenth-century Britain, even if much of the bardic verse had to be reconstructed for the purpose.[33]

These were the associations that perhaps influenced Coleridge's description of the unknown poet as a 'Bard', and empowered the otherworldly qualities of his own poem. The entire poem plays on the realization of the old Bard's prediction, the storm sequence of the conclusion proving that he was in fact 'weatherwise'. His special knowledge is lifted beyond rural tradition of the 'Red sky at night' variety by the presence of supernatural imagery, as the new moon appears remote in a magic circle, the rhythmic couplets and repetition almost suggesting an incantation:

> For lo! the New-moon winter-bright!
> And overspread with phantom-light,
> (With swimming phantom-light o'erspread
> But rimm'd and circled by a silver thread).

The sound of the Bardic wind harp, too, changes from the 'dull sobbing draft' of the opening to the much more disturbing 'scream' that sets off a train of images reminiscent of a Gothic past:

> What a scream
> Of agony by torture lengthen'd out
> That lute sent forth! Thou Wind, that rav'st without,

[32] Percy, 'Essay on the Ancient English Minstrels', *Reliques*, i, p. xv.
[33] The poetry of Macpherson's Ossian, the most famous bard of the period, was as much a case of reconstruction as retrieval: see *The Poems of Ossian*, ed. Gaskill.

> Bare crag, or mountain-tairn, or blasted tree,
> Or pine-grove whither woodman never clomb,
> Or lonely house, long held the witches' home,
>   Methinks were fitter instruments for thee,
> Mad Lutanist! who in this month of show'rs,
> Of dark brown gardens, and of peeping flow'rs,
> Mak'st Devils' yule, with worse than wintry song,
> The blossoms, buds, and tim'rous leaves among.
>   Thou Actor, perfect in all tragic sounds!
> Thou mighty Poet, e'en to Frenzy bold!
>   What tell'st thou now about?
>   'Tis of the Rushing of an Host in rout,
>   With groans of trampled men, with smarting wounds—
> At once they groan with pain, and shudder with the cold!

As the Bard's predicted storm comes into being, so too creative energy seems to flood Coleridge's poem; the modern speaker seems at last to have tapped into an ancient source of power, which can wash away the inertia of the opening.[34]

By the end of 'Dejection', Coleridge's description of the Bard's work as 'grand' seems only too appropriate. It is interesting, therefore, to consider the slight change made in the lines when he sent them to Sotheby. In the verse letter to Sara Hutchinson, Coleridge had described the ballad as 'grand', as he would in the printed version, but for Sotheby he substituted the adjective 'dear'. This might suggest mere experimentation, or perhaps that in correspondence with a relatively new acquaintance, Coleridge preferred to adopt a less reverential epithet for the ballad-maker. It is most likely, however, that when Sotheby read the line, he recalled a letter Coleridge had sent him the week before, lamenting the deficiencies of Gessner's imagination and observing, 'I read a great deal of German; but I do dearly dearly dearly love my own Countrymen of old times, and those of my contemporaries who write in their Spirit.'[35] As Sotheby read the new letter a few days later, he must surely have associated the Bard 'who made the dear old ballad of Sir Patrick Spence' with Coleridge's 'dearly dearly

---

[34] Reeve Parker draws attention to the Miltonic and Wordsworthian echoes in this passage, *Coleridge's Meditative Art* (Ithaca, 1975), 196–200; but see also Lucy Newlyn's emphasis on Coleridge's ironic self-parodying in *Coleridge, Wordsworth, and the Language of Allusion.*

[35] 13 July 1802, *Letters*, ii. 811.

dearly' loved countrymen, whose work so excelled the artificial excesses of Salomon Gessner:

But this is indeed general in the German & French Poets. It is easy to cloathe Imaginary Beings with our own Thoughts & Feelings; but to send ourselves out of ourselves, to *think* ourselves in to the Thoughts and Feelings of Beings in circumstances wholly & strangely different from our own | hoc labor, hoc opus | and who has atchieved it? Perhaps only Shakespere. Metaphisics is a word, that you, my dear Sir! are no great Friend to | but yet you will agree that a great Poet must be, implicitè if not explicitè, a profound Metaphysician. He may not have it in logical coherence, in his Brain & Tongue; but he must have it by *Tact* | for all sounds, & forms of human nature he must have the *ear* of a wild Arab listening in the silent Desart, the eye of a North American Indian tracing the footsteps of an Enemy upon the Leaves that strew the Forest—; the *Touch* of a Blind Man feeling the face of a darling Child— | and do not think me a Bigot, if I say, that I have read no French or German Writer, who appears to me to have had a *heart* sufficiently pure & simple to be capable of this or any thing like it.[36]

The connection between this letter and the next, in which Coleridge sends the lines from 'Dejection' in the account of his own failure to unite poetry and metaphysics, is not difficult to make. For if Coleridge was presenting his own 'abstruse research' as destructive of creative power, the idea gained painful momentum from the implicit comparison with those ideal figures described the previous week, who were both great Poets and profound Metaphysicians by nature. This is also why he emphasized the importance of 'Sir Patrick Spens' to 'Dejection', because the old bard possessed just that capacity for thought and feeling that Coleridge admired so much, and yet felt so lacking in himself. The maker of the ballad seemed to respond immediately to the natural world before him, while at the same time seeing the physical phenomena instinct with life and feelings. His reference to the moon is not a contrived simile, but a natural metaphor deeply appropriate to both the appearance of the moon and the narrative in which it appears. The nameless speaker who is so alarmed by the sight of 'the new moone, | Wi' the auld moone in hir arme' conveys the tragedy of the ballad in his very description, for by the end of the poem all embraces are over:

[36] 13 July 1802, *Letters*, ii. 810.

> O lang, lang, may the ladies stand
>   Wi' thair gold kems in their hair,
> Waiting for thair ain deir lords,
>   For they'll se thame na mair.

The poet who could unite both thought and feeling, physical perception and symbolic meaning, in such simple language seemed far removed from the dejected speaker, gazing at all 'with how blank an eye'. And yet, the subtle rewriting of the ballad stanza and its gradual integration with the ode suggest that, although Coleridge's poem appears to dramatize the difference between the old Bard and the modern poet, they have more in common than the speaker might be prepared to acknowledge at the outset.

Far from suggesting a patronizing attitude, then, Coleridge's reference to the maker of the 'dear old ballad' should be seen in the context of the aesthetic ideal he was developing in 1802, which regarded the greatest poetry as a 'compleat and constant synthesis of Thought & Feeling'.[37] In contrast to the repeated projection of his own development as a poet stunted by philosophy, the idealized poets of the past united passion and reason. And it is this emphasis on the intellect that distinguishes Coleridge's attitude to early poets so fundamentally from the views of many of his immediate aesthetic predecessors. For although he inherited much from the prevailing critical ideas of the late eighteenth century, his admiration of his 'own Countrymen of old times' is quite different from the primitivism of Thomas Percy or the influential Scottish aesthetician, Hugh Blair. For while Percy and Blair were both major proponents of the study of early poetry in Britain, their enthusiasm for the 'energy' or 'sublimity' of the old poets was balanced by a strong distaste for the very different standards of morality and lack of refinement displayed in the productions of 'rude ages'. Percy's encomium on the ancient bards, for example, is somewhat undermined by the subsequent sentence: 'In short, poets and their art were held among them in that rude admiration, which is ever shown by an ignorant people to such as excell them in intellectual accomplishments.'[38] Blair's writings, too, so typical

---

[37] To Richard Sharp, 15 Jan. 1804, *Letters*, ii. 1034.

[38] *Reliques*, i, p. xv. Coleridge would have found similarly contradictory attitudes towards native bards in Edmund Spenser's *A View of the State of Ireland*, which he read in 1801 (*Notebooks*, i. 934 6.18).

of the latter half of the eighteenth century, invariably couple the positive attributes of early poetry ('passion', 'vehemence', 'fire'), with negatives ('irregular', 'unpolished', 'barbarous'), as a consequence of the underlying equations between primitive society and feeling, civilized society and thought.[39] Coleridge, however, unlike Blair or Percy, emphasizes instead an ideal union of the intellectual and the emotional which now seemed largely unattainable, if the 'abstruse research' of modern metaphysicians was able to render the 'natural man' incapable of passion, and thus of poetry. (The notion that thought and feeling had once been united was however, encouraging, since it suggested that the ideal might be attained, whereas primitivist aesthetics maintained a complete opposition between the two.)

Coleridge's later letter to Sotheby, written on 10 September 1802, provides further insights, once again disparaging Gessner, before moving on to criticize the English poet William Lisle Bowles, whose work had been such an influence on his own early poetry:

There reigns thro' all the blank verse poems such a perpetual trick of *moralizing* every thing—which is very well, occasionally—but never to see or describe any interesting appearance in nature, without connecting it by dim analogies with the moral world, proves faintness of Impression. Nature has her proper interest; & he will know what it is, who believes & feels, that every Thing has a Life of it's own, & that we are all *one Life*. A Poet's *Heart & Intellect* should be *combined, intimately* combined and *unified*, with the great appearances in Nature— & not merely held in solution & loose mixture with them, in the shape of formal Similies. I do not mean to *exclude* these formal Similies— there are moods of mind in which they are natural—pleasing moods of mind, & such as a Poet will often have, & sometimes express; but they are not his highest, & most appropriate moods.[40]

[39] Hugh Blair, 'A Critical Dissertation on the Poems of Ossian', *Poems of Ossian*, ed. Gaskill, 345.

[40] *Letters*, ii. 864. Cf. the Preface to *Poems on Various Subjects*: 'I was fearful that the title "Sonnet" might have reminded my reader of the Poems of the Rev. W. L. Bowles—a comparison with whom would have sunk me below that mediocrity, on the surface of which I am at present enabled to float.' Bowles is also celebrated, with Cowper, as the first 'of the then living poets . . . who reconciled the heart with the head' in *Biographia Literaria* (1817), ed. James Engell and W. J. Bate, 2 vols. (Princeton and London, 1984), ii. 25. See Raimonda Modiano, 'Coleridge and Wordsworth: The Ethics of Gift Exchange and Literary Ownership', in Christine Gallant (ed.), *Coleridge's Theory of Imagination Today* (New York, 1989), 243–56.

Unlike the bard of 'Sir Patrick Spens' whose heart and intellect did seem 'combined and *unified*, with the great appearances in Nature', Bowles had to rely on 'formal Similies', owing to inherent shortcomings:

He has not the *Passion* of a great Poet. His latter writings all want *native* Passion—Milton here & there supplies him with an appearance of it—but he has no native Passion, because he is not a Thinker—

The hapless Bowles seems to be emerging in Coleridge's correspondence with Sotheby as the polar opposite of those 'great Poets' who were also 'profound Metaphysicians': he fails where they succeeded because of deficiencies in passion and reason. Just as the intellect and emotions were united in those 'Countrymen of old times', so there is no opposition between the two in the work of Bowles, for the inadequacy of his feelings and his incapacity as a thinker are inseparable. A few ideas may have been borrowed from Milton, but they could only give an illusion of thought, not being 'native' to the poetry.

The sixth stanza of Coleridge's 'Dejection', which was the first passage to be transcribed for Sotheby, seems to describe a similar creative failure, as 'afflictions' combine to obstruct the 'shaping spirit of Imagination'. Except that here, thought and feeling are placed in conscious opposition, the intellect being exerted for the specific purpose of diverting the mind from its painful emotions:

> For not to think of what I needs must feel,
>   But to be still and patient, all I can;
> And haply by abstruse research to steal
>   From my own nature all the natural Man—
> This was my sole resource, my only plan:

Rather than heal the sufferer, however, these mental efforts have led only to further pains:

> Till that which suits a part infects the whole,
> And now is almost grown the habit of my Soul.

In the original verse epistle, and in the July letter to Sotheby, Coleridge had used the word 'temper' instead of 'habit', implying that the infection had been far-reaching enough to alter the mood and natural disposition of the speaker. The later choice, though incorporating this meaning, is less pessimistic because it implies a development that is not irreversible. A 'habit' may be broken by the will to change, while its primary sense of clothing (which also contributes to the pun on 'suits' in the previous line) implies that the new state affects the appearance but not the essence. The theft of the 'natural man' may thus not be irretrievable, a vague hope encouraged by the word 'almost'. Whatever the misfortunes of maturity, the sense of an innate power—'what nature gave me at my birth'—remains, to reassure even in the midst of despondency over its failure.

The 'shaping spirit of Imagination' may have been 'suspended', but this does not mean that it is lost for ever and, once again, the existence of the poem indicates that the condition has been temporary rather than mortal. Where Bowles's poetry was dismissed out of hand because of its fundamental lack of 'native passion', Coleridge's lament for his own decline was revealing the real powers that he had always possessed; as he observed to Sotheby, when bemoaning his pursuit of '*downright metaphysics*': 'I believe that by nature I have more of the Poet in me.'[41] The very exploration of the feelings of dejection led to the recognition of intrinsic abilities, of qualities 'native' to the individual mind. The effort in 'Dejection' is thus one of revival, rather than of discovery: an attempt to recover creative power which had been buried. It is perhaps a kind of internal counterpart to the contemporary attempts to recover the ancient poetry native to the British Isles and bring the creative imagination of early society into the modern world. Just as modern aestheticians had prevented a true revival, by separating feeling from thought and relegating emotion to the rude ages, Coleridge had consciously deadened his feelings in philosophical research. 'Dejection' enacts the highly complicated process of recovery, when thought and feeling are at last brought together again, and 'native passion' permitted to release the imagination of a great poet. The old ballad of 'Sir Patrick Spens' has the power to revive the modern poet from his malaise but, ironically, it is itself dismembered and ingested in the process.

The emphasis on 'native passion' in the September letter to Sotheby reveals Coleridge's developing sense of the importance

41 *Letters*, ii. 814.

of national traditions, which had been heightened by his work as a translator and also by the expansion of French influence under Napoleon. At the same time, however, it reveals his interest in the natural characteristics of the individual: what nature gives to us at birth. This was part of his longstanding interest in the workings of the mind and, though undoubtedly encouraged by his experiences as a father, it had been the subject of 'abstruse research' for many years. In the decade leading up to 1800, he had been fascinated by empirical theories of psychology which, following the work of John Locke and David Hartley in particular, had assumed that the neonate mind was a blank, and that ideas developed as a result of sensory perception.[42] Recently, however, he had begun to see the deficiencies of those philosophies that made the human mind 'a lazy Looker-on on an external world', and seemed to reduce everything to a sequence of impressions on the human nervous system.[43] Through his studies of the work of Berkeley, who demonstrated the difficulties of proving the existence of the physical world independently of the perceiving mind, and of Descartes, who argued that ideas were anterior to physical experience, Coleridge began to embrace a new theory of the mind, privileging the conscious subject over the world of material objects.[44] His visit to Germany in 1799 had also helped him begin to absorb the complicated ideas of Immanuel Kant and his followers, who rejected both Lockean empiricism and Cartesian rationalism in favour of a dynamic theory which saw the mind possessed of

[42] John Locke, *An Essay Concerning Human Understanding* (1690); David Hartley, *Observations on Man* (1749). For Coleridge's response, see e.g. J. A. Appleyard, *Coleridge's Philosophy of Literature* (Cambridge, Mass., 1965); J. Christiansen, *Coleridge's Blessed Machine of Language* (Ithaca and London, 1981); R. Haven, 'Coleridge, Hartley and the Mystics', *Journal of the History of Ideas*, 20 (1959), 477–94; H. W. Piper, *The Active Universe* (London, 1962). For his own account, and useful editorial commentary, see *Biographia Literaria*, i. 89–128.

[43] To Thomas Poole, 23 Mar. 1801, *Letters*, ii. 709.

[44] See the series of philosophical letters to Josiah Wedgwood of February 1801 (*Letters*, ii. 677–703). Coleridge's interest in Berkeley is obvious in his choice of name for his second son, born 14 May 1798 (Hartley Coleridge was born in September 1796). See also J. I. Lindsay, 'Coleridge Marginalia in a Volume of Descartes', *PMLA* 49 (1934), 184–95; Jonathan Wordsworth, 'The Infinite I AM: Coleridge and the Ascent of Being', in R. Gravil, L. Newlyn, and N. Roe (eds.), *Coleridge's Imagination: Essays in Memory of Peter Laver* (Cambridge, 1985), 22–52.

innate faculties, and acquiring knowledge through its active response to the external world.[45]

The importance of Coleridge's interest in the relationship between the human mind and its physical environment has struck many readers of both 'Dejection' and the verse letter that preceded it. David Pirie, for example, has argued that the poem to Sara moves from Cartesian dualism, as expressed in the lines

> I may not hope from outward forms to win
> The Passion & the Life whose Fountains are within

to Kantian synthesis: 'Joy is at once a "beauty-making Power" and itself "beautiful", which perhaps suggests that it is not simply a quality created within the self.'[46] Ironically, the abstruse research which was supposedly stifling Coleridge's creative powers was, according to this reading, offering the very solution to the epistemological crisis articulated at the beginning of the poem. In contrast, George Dekker, while regarding Coleridge's repudiation of mechanistic philosophy as vital to 'Dejection', focuses on the English Neoplatonic tradition rather than on contemporary Continental philosophy. But although consensus over the exact philosophical influences may be lacking, common to such interpretations is the belief that 'Dejection' is largely concerned with the speaker's sense of intense isolation and his inability to find any emotional connection with the outside world:

> I see them all, so excellently fair,
> I see, not feel, how beautiful they are.

Where the Ancient Mariner had been released from despair by a moment of unconscious participation in the natural world— blessing the water snakes 'unaware'—the solipsistic speaker of 'Dejection' is locked in an epistemological prison. When the speaker laments his failure to create:

> I may not hope from outward forms to win
> The passion and the life, whose fountains are within,

[45] For useful discussion, see Paul Hamilton, *Coleridge's Poetics* (Oxford, 1983); G. N. G. Orsini, *Coleridge and German Idealism* (Carbondale, Ill., 1969); Kathleen Wheeler, *The Creative Mind in Coleridge's Poetry* (Cambridge, Mass., 1981).

[46] Pirie, 'A Letter to [Asra]', 303. But see also A. O. Lovejoy, 'Coleridge and Kant's Two Worlds', *ELH* VII (1940), 341–62, 348. Tyler, 'Losing "A Letter"', has a useful survey of critical debate.

he is thus referring to the frustration of not gaining inspiration from the passive perception of the physical beauty before his eyes, an idea strengthened in the verse letter which continues:

> These lifeless shapes, around, below, above—
> Oh dearest Sara, what can they impart?

It is possible, however, to see those elusive 'outward forms' as encompassing more than the natural phenomena and external objects surrounding the speaker, especially as the additional lines on the 'lifeless shapes' were removed from the published ode. For readers of the *Morning Post* and *Sibylline Leaves*, the turbulent night sky with its crescent moon was accompanied from the beginning by the words of an old bard, whose own ballad, excerpted and laid out above Coleridge's poem, could well be perceived as another kind of 'outward form'. As numerous scholars have pointed out, the stanza in which the crucial lines occur is itself heavy with literary allusion:

> My genial spirits fail,
> And what can these avail,
> To lift the smoth'ring weight from off my breast?
> It were a vain endeavor,
> Though I should gaze for ever
> On that green light that lingers in the west:
> I may not hope from outward forms to win
> The passion and the life, whose fountains are within.

Immediately behind Coleridge's failing 'genial spirits' lies Wordsworth's 'Tintern Abbey', with its celebration of the vital interaction between man's mind and the natural world:

> Therefore am I still
> A lover of the meadows and the woods,
> And mountains; and of all that we behold
> From this green earth; of all the mighty world
> Of eye and ear, both what they half create
> And what perceive; well pleased to recognize
> In nature and the language of the sense,
> The anchor of my purest thoughts, the nurse,
> The guide, the guardian of my heart, and soul
> Of all my moral being.
> Nor perchance,
> If I were not thus taught, should I the more

> Suffer my genial spirits to decay:
> For thou art with me, here, upon the banks
> Of this fair river: thou, my dearest Friend
> My dear, dear Friend . . .[47]

The evocation of such an affirmative passage has an obvious irony in this context, as Wordsworth draws joy and creative strength not only from the external world, but also the presence of his 'dearest friend'. Much closer in mood to 'Dejection' is the source to which Wordsworth was also responding in 'Tintern Abbey', Milton's definitive exploration of human despair and psychological imprisonment, *Samson Agonistes*:

> So much I feel my genial spirits droop,
> My hopes all flat, nature within me seems
> In all her functions weary of herself.[48]

Literary allusion extends beyond the 'genial spirits', however, as Lynda Pratt has shown by drawing attention to the similarity between the third stanza of 'Dejection' and a passage in Southey's epic, *Madoc*:

> And when at length the hastening orb hath sunk
> Below the plain, such sinking at the heart
> They feel, as he who hopeless of return
> From his dear home departs. Still on the light,
> The last green light that lingers in the west,
> Their looks are fastened.[49]

Each of these passages is concerned with the relationship between the mind and nature—the obvious 'outward forms' of 'Dejection'. But the larger works from which they are taken can also be regarded as 'outward forms': things external to the poem and which, for various reasons, seem to offer no release from the speaker's 'stifled, drowsy, unimpassioned grief'.

Coleridge's reconstitution of the words of his talented friends

---

[47] 'Lines Written a few miles above Tintern Abbey', 103–16, *Lyrical Ballads (1798)*, ed. James Butler and Karen Green (Ithaca and London, 1992), 119.

[48] John Milton, *Samson Agonistes*, 593–6, *The Complete Shorter Poems*, ed. John Carey (London, 1968).

[49] *Madoc*, xxvi. 256–61, *Poems of Robert Southey*, ed. Maurice Fitzgerald (London and New York, 1909), 600. *Madoc* was published in 1805, but Coleridge appears to have read the manuscript 'some time between autumn 1799 and mid 1801', Lynda Pratt, 'A Coleridge Borrowing from Southey', *Notes and Queries*, NS 42 (1994), 336–8.

and great predecessors may be seen as a symptom of the very loss of power he so laments. Just as Bowles, lacking in 'native passion', had been forced to borrow his ideas from Milton, so Coleridge might be accused of lapsing into a similar dependency. The melancholy of the stanza is thus intensified by its own self-punishing statement of the inadequacy of taking lines from existing works—those 'outward forms' that may be beautiful in themselves, but cannot substitute for original power. As one of Coleridge's notebook entries for 1802 observes, 'he that seeth not by his own light, must in this dangerous Ocean steer by the Lanthorn, which another Vessel hangeth out to him'—a comment also taken, ironically enough, from someone else: the seventeenth-century prose writer Sir Kenelme Digby.[50] The idea of needing to steer by borrowed light rather than one's own also contributes further significance to the presiding image of the moon in Coleridge's poem, whose light may appear to be self-generated but, as a reflection from the sun, is merely borrowed.[51]

Characteristically, however, 'Dejection' seems to contradict the very idea that it appears to express, because far from seeming inadequate, the third stanza is in itself beautiful and deeply moving. For readers unfamiliar with 'Tintern Abbey', *Samson Agonistes*, or *Madoc*, the lines in 'Dejection' still have a power of their own, while those who have enjoyed the other poems find their reading of Coleridge enriched by the additional layers of association. These lines do not read as undigested plagiarisms, but as having been 'modified in the guts of the living' to become an integral part of the new poem.[52] Although the allusions could be read as evidence of failing originality, they seem rather to generate fresh energy, infusing Coleridge's poem with life. 'Dejection' seems to re-enact the sudden access

[50] From the dedication 'To my Sonne Kenelme Digby' of *Two Treatises: In the one of which the Nature of Bodies; In the other, the Nature of Man's Soule, is looked into: in way of discovery of the Immortality of Reasonable Soules* (London, 1645), which Coleridge borrowed from the Carlisle Cathedral Library between 2 April 1801 and 2 July 1802. Notebook entry in Sara Hutchinson's hand, November 1801, *Notebooks*, i. 1004 21.156.

[51] Though Reeve Parker draws attention to I. A. Richards's argument that the phantom-light as 'earthlight' (i.e. reflected on to the moon from the earth) is an image of receiving 'what we give', *Coleridge's Meditative Art*, 185.

[52] W. H. Auden, 'In Memory of W. B. Yeats', 23, *Collected Poems*, ed. Edward Mendelson, rev. edn. (London, 1991), 247.

of bardic power as the speaker is at last able to 'listen to the wind', but it is nourished throughout by the recollection of familiar poems. Coleridge's intense admiration for other writers may have been debilitating in some respects, and certainly increased his personal sense of inadequacy, but it also played an essential part in the development of a kind of poetry so allusive that the poet seems to become almost indistinguishable from his reading.

The 'genial spirits' may not be exclusively Coleridge's any more than is the image of the new moon, but it is the very awareness of the complexity of language and the ways in which associations accumulate through centuries of use that contributes so powerfully to the new poem, not only through additional meanings but also additional voices, all working against the speaker's assertions of isolation. Just as Burns drew instinctively on the poems embedded in his memory, so Coleridge creates much of his own poetry from his reading. Other poems can become as much a part of the mind as experience of the external world; and like the memories of physical sensations they become modified and integrated with what is already there. The reconstitution of familiar poems also invites participation from the reader, who can bring his or her own remembered experience to the new encounter.

For contemporary readers, 'Tintern Abbey' provided an obvious contrast to Coleridge's 'Dejection', made all the more acute by its republication in the expanded editions of *Lyrical Ballads*, a collection now largely regarded as Wordsworth's, and swollen with the new fruit of his apparently unfailingly genial spirits.[53] The misery of Coleridge's speaker is, however, greatly intensified by the evocation of Milton's much older tragedy, with its focus on the mental struggles of a protagonist suddenly bereft of sight, strength, human love, and divine favour. Those who recognize Samson in Coleridge's lines, however, would also remember the latter half of the drama, when the biblical hero begins to rouse himself, before his final, terrifying demonstration of renewed power. The allusion to such a well-known 'outward form' may not stimulate the imagination

---

[53] For the expansion of *Lyrical Ballads* in 1800 and 1802, see the Cornell edition cited in note 47; for the best general account of Wordsworth's activities in this period, see Stephen Gill, *William Wordsworth: A Life* (Oxford, 1989), 176–211.

of the dejected speaker, but it is likely to affect the reader, as it quietly contributes to the sense of impending energy, already suggested by the portentous moon. The reference to *Madoc*, too, though inaccessible to the first readers of 'Dejection', also evokes a moment that represents both departing power as the defeated Aztec priests finish their last hymn, and the prelude to the phenomenal volcanic storm that ushers in the new order. Although the speaker protests that there is nothing to be gained from outward forms, then, the reader may view things rather differently.

The echoes of familiar poems are important not merely as trans-fusions of narrative life into Coleridge's lyric, but also because they emphasize his choice of language, highlighting key words such as the curious adjective 'genial'. For while modern readers might associate it most readily with ideas of cheerfulness and sociability—both very appropriate in the context—it carries further associations which resonate throughout the poem. An older meaning of genial was 'pertaining to natural disposition', which would link the line to the sixth stanza, and its crucial account of the decline of 'the natural man': the failure of the 'genial spirits' thus being virtually synonymous with the diseased 'habit of the soul'. Its primary meaning, however, related to marriage and procreation, which must have had special significance for Coleridge, as he confronted his failing marriage and impossible obsession with the idealized Sara Hutchinson. In the effort to transform the autobiographical verse letter into an ode lamenting the loss of creative power, however, this original meaning was also easy to disguise, because the most obvious connotation of the word in the early nineteenth century was related to that great preoccupation of the aestheticians: genius.[54] When Sotheby read the lines in July, he is thus most likely to have understood 'genial' in this light, as a straightforward acknowledgement of Coleridge's failing genius or creative ability. There is, however, a further, related, and relevant association, which sees 'genial' as being 'conducive to growth', and normally used to describe a climate or physical

[54] For representative texts, see Young, *Conjectures on Original Composition*, William Duff, *An Essay on Original Genius* (London, 1767), Alexander Gerard, *An Essay on Genius* (London, 1774).

environment.[55] This is perhaps the sense in which Coleridge employed the word in the verse letter, when he described 'the conjugal and mother dove | That borrows genial warmth from these she warms' (327–8). Although complicated by the ideas of reciprocal influences, the consciousness of an environment conducive to healthy development is plain. Similar ideas inform 'Tintern Abbey', as Wordsworth refers to 'nature and the language of the sense' as his 'nurse' and 'guardian': these external forces have proved 'genial', enabling the growth of the poet's mind. Indeed, Wordsworth seemed to draw perpetually on the landscape of his youth and, now that he was restored to his native environment, seemed likely to flower into the great English poet of the modern period.

Coleridge, by contrast, was aware of the less promising influences of his own childhood, already acknowledged publicly in 'Frost at Midnight':

> For I was reared
> In the great city, pent 'mid cloisters dim,
> And saw nought lovely but the sky and stars.   (51–3)

The brief and highly creative period which followed Coleridge's marriage and residence in the West Country had ended with the trip to Germany, but the subsequent move to Cumberland, so vital to Wordsworth's creative strength, had proved far from successful for Coleridge. The sense of exile that he had felt so acutely on the Continent did not seem to abate fully when he returned to Britain, and despite his illnesses the years 1802–3 saw constant restless journeying, and a growing admiration for those more rooted in their native environments.[56] At the same time, however, the sense of his own deracination meant that another source of power was needed.

The personal memories and local attachments so nourishing to Wordsworth's imagination were simply not available to Coleridge, any more than was the sense of belonging to a particular part of the country and being able to imbibe from

---

[55] Coleridge's own interest in the meaning of the word 'genial' is explicit in his 1814 essay 'On the Principles of Genial Criticism', *Shorter Works and Fragments* ed. H. J. Jackson and J. de R. Jackson (Princeton and London, 1995).

[56] For details of Coleridge's life, see Rosemary Ashton, *The Life of Samuel Taylor Coleridge* (Oxford and Cambridge, Mass., 1996). On his 'Psychological Homelessness', see Ronald C. Wendling, *Coleridge's Progress to Christianity: Experience and Authority in Religious Faith* (Lewisburg, Pa., and London, 1995), 51–4.

generations of tradition, which poets such as Burns and the old ballad-writers took so much for granted. The growing tendency to link the creation of poetry to particular cultures, which had gained considerable impetus from the various collections of old Scottish songs, and indeed from Percy's *Reliques*, offered little comfort to the rootless Coleridge; hence, perhaps his sense of inferiority to the 'grand old Bard' who was so firmly attached to his native environment. In order to survive as a poet, an alternative approach was necessary.[57] And it was in 'Dejection' that he began to find a possible way forward, from the very recognition of his lack of connection with the external world. If Coleridge's 'genial spirits' hark back to the older, classical meaning of genius as a local, protective deity, albeit mediated through Wordsworthian ideas of nature providing a nurturing environment, their failure might ultimately prove positive. For in 'Dejection', Coleridge's recognition of his own original genius (in the modern sense of extraordinary natural ability) appears to depend on the very realization that the influence of the external world alone is insufficient for the creation of imaginative life.

The stanza following the rather paradoxical expression of the inadequacy of 'outward forms' seems to develop directly from the acknowledgement that the 'fountains are within'. If the external world, or existing literary works, cannot supply the mind with creative impulses, then the sources of the imagination must be internal:

> Ah from the soul itself must issue forth,
> A light, a glory, a fair luminous cloud
>   Enveloping the Earth—
> And from the soul itself must there be sent
>   A sweet and potent voice, of its own birth . . .

This image of inner light anticipates Coleridge's descriptions, the following year, of his son Hartley, 'An utter Visionary! like the Moon among thin Clouds, he moves in a circle of Light of his own making—he alone, in a Light of his own', and his daughter, Sara, 'a remarkably interesting Baby, with the finest possible Skin & large blue eyes—& she smiles, as if she were

---

[57] The association between literature and place was frequently made by Scottish editors and aestheticians, but for influential European theories see also Herder's *Von Deutscher Art und Kunst* (Hamburg, 1773); Germaine de Staël, *La Littérature dans ses rapports avec les institutions sociales* (Paris, 1800).

basking in a sunshine, as mild as moonlight, of her own quiet Happiness'.[58] The innocence of his children, with their self-generated happiness, seems to provide an image of the ideal, creative mind, utterly 'visionary', radiant with joy and, as implied by the imagery of celestial bodies, not dependent on any particular part of the earth.[59]

In 'Dejection', the 'fair luminous mist' of the soul is associated not with the speaker's children, but with his mysterious interlocutor who seems to fulfil a similar ideal of self-sufficiency:

> O pure of heart! Thou need'st not ask of me
> What this strong music in the soul may be!

Although originally part of Coleridge's almost courtly adoration of Sara Hutchinson, the succession of names set up in opposition to the dejected speaker—Sara/William/Edmund/Lady—again shows a conscious projection of the poem from its domestic origins to a wider sphere of reference. Nevertheless, some clue to Coleridge's meaning may still be found in the biographical detail of 1802, and particularly in the reading he enjoyed with Sara Hutchinson.

Among the books they obviously discussed was Kenelme Digby's *Two Treatises: In the One of which, The Nature of Bodies; In the other, The Nature of Man's Soule, is looked into: in way of discovery of the Immortality of Reasonable Soules,* from which Sara had copied the line about having to steer by another's lantern into Coleridge's notebook. Although rather outdated from a medical point of view, Digby's notion that the brain swelled according to the phases of the moon and that, when contracted, its moisture pressed down into the nerves, affecting the heart with grief and heaviness, has an obvious relevance to 'Dejection'.[60] Even more significant, however, was his second *Treatise*, in which the earlier and rather mechanical explanation for the mood and physical well being of the indi-

---

[58] To Thomas Poole, 14 Oct. 1803, *Letters,* ii. 1014. Cf. Wordsworth's to Hartley, 'Who of thy words dost make a mock apparel, | And fittest to unutterable thought | The breeze-like motion and the self-born carol', 'To H.C., Six Years Old', 2–4, *The Oxford Authors: William Wordsworth,* ed Stephen Gill (Oxford, 1984), 246. I am grateful to Lucy Newlyn for pointing out this similarity.

[59] Cf. 'the self-sufficing power of absolute *Genius*' of *Biographia Literaria,* i. 31. Ruoff observes that for Coleridge by 1802, 'true genius is not the genius of place', *Wordsworth and Coleridge,* 194.

[60] Digby, *A Treatise of Bodies,* 352–8.

vidual was balanced by the argument that 'in humane nature there are two different centers, from whence crosse actions doe flow', in other words, the body and the soul.[61] If the passions of the body appeared to be at the mercy of external forces in the first essay, the second described the essential, regulatory power of the human soul:

the soule, being in her owne nature ordered to doe the same thing, which Scholars with much difficulty arrive to know what it is by reflection and study, and then frame rules of that afterwards carry their discourse to a higher pitch, she by an inborne vertue maketh a man doe it orderly, constantly, and certainly.[62]

These ideas must have struck a special chord with Coleridge in 1802, when after grappling with numerous philosophical theories of the mind, he began to recognize, intuitively, his own innate powers. Whether or not Digby's *Treatises* provided a satisfactory explanation for human existence, the language with which the ideas were conveyed seems to have been remarkably congenial. Not only is there repeated emphasis on the 'passions', and especially on the opposition between 'joy' and 'grief', but both the senses and the soul are described in terms of a 'fountaine from whence . . . actions Spring'.[63] The body and the soul are even compared to a 'lutanist', both requiring constant exercise to maintain good health and, crucially, the capacity for action.[64] But it is perhaps the religious dimension of the seventeenth-century treatises that would have appealed most strongly to Coleridge and Sara Hutchinson, and Digby's emphasis on the divine nature of the soul which has 'in her selfe a spring of life; for the which she is not beholding (as Bodies are) to some extrinsecal cause of a nature like unto her; but only to him, who gave her to be what she is'.[65] This accords well with the powerful Christian imagery of the fifth stanza of 'Dejection':

> Joy, virtuous Lady! Joy that ne'er was given,
> Save to the pure, and in their purest hour,
> Life, and life's effulgence, cloud at once and shower,
> Joy, Lady! Is the spirit and the power,

[61] *A Treatise of Man's Soule*, 43.
[62] Ibid. 43–4.
[63] Ibid. 41. See also *Notebooks*, i. 1005.
[64] *A Treatise of Man's Soule*, 104.
[65] Ibid. 85.

> Which wedding Nature to us gives in dow'r
>   A new Earth and new Heaven,
> Undreamt of by the sensual and the proud—
> Joy is the sweet voice, Joy the luminous cloud—
>   We in ourselves rejoice!

The recognition of the divine joy that can illuminate the world, giving rise to visionary moments as remarkable as that experienced by St John, is the revelation at the heart of 'Dejection'. From this moment on, the speaker's personal anguish is contained within a larger sense of possibility, symbolized perhaps by the wind in the seventh stanza.[66] The power of the 'fair luminous mist' issuing from the soul, and ultimately from God, is thus more powerful than the 'swimming phantom light' of the opening lines, which suggests that the new ideal of inner illumination surpasses older ideas of external forces acting on the mind, even if, initially, the speaker remains despondent and passive. This inner illumination is nevertheless articulated through the instantly recognizable allusions to the visions of St John: a correspondence that has not only helped the speaker with his own experience but also facilitated its communication to the reader.

The notion of an inner light enjoyed by the pure was not of course peculiar to Kenelme Digby, and Coleridge would have come across similar ideas in a host of Renaissance writers, especially those influenced by Puritan and Neoplatonic thought. In Milton's *Comus*, for example, the Elder Brother allays fears for the safety of his sister, who is lost in the wood at night:

> Virtue could see to do what Virtue would
> By her own radiant light, though sun and moon
> Were in the flat sea sunk . . .
> He that has light within his own clear breast
> May sit i' the centre, and enjoy bright day,
> But he that hides a dark soul, and foul thoughts
> Benighted walks under the midday sun.[67]   (372–83)

The young man's perception of this self-irradiant virtue in the 'Lady' who forms the central point of Milton's Masque finds a

[66] On the symbolic significance of Romantic wind, see M. H. Abrams, *The Correspondent Breeze: Essays on English Romanticism* (New York, 1984).

[67] Milton, *A Masque presented at Ludlow Castle, 1634* [*Comus*], 372–83, *Complete Shorter Poems*, ed. Carey, 194–5.

strong parallel in 'Dejection', where divine truth seems to be revealed as a result of contemplating the purity of another 'Lady'. In *Comus*, however, the abstract recognition of the Lady's 'unpolluted temple of the mind' does not seem quite sufficient, for the Elder Brother is subsequently given a plant, Haemony, to enable him to see through misleading appearances to the truth:

> Amongst the rest a small unsightly root,
> But of divine effect, he culled me out;
> The leaf was darkish, and had prickles on it,
> But in another country, as he said,
> Bore a bright golden flower, but not in this soil:
> Unknown, and like esteemed, and the dull swain
> Treads on it daily with his clouted shoon:
> And yet more med'cinal is it than that moly
> That Hermes once to wise Ulysses gave;
> He called it haemony, and gave it me,
> And bade me keep it as of sovran use
> 'Gainst all enchantments, mildew blast, or damp
> Or ghastly Furies' apparition.   (628–40)

This is the passage from Milton's poem that fascinated Coleridge, who commented on it at length in his September letter to Sotheby, after the discussion of Bowles's failings as a poet. It is also a passage that he included in *The Statesman's Manual*, published in 1816, at the time when he was preparing *Sibylline Leaves*, with the revised version of 'Dejection', for the press.[68] According to Coleridge (whose views have in fact been developed by a number of subsequent Miltonists) the lines are an extended allegory, and demonstrate 'Milton's platonizing spirit—who wrote nothing without an interior meaning'.[69] As he explained to Sotheby:

Do look at the passage—apply it as an Allegory of Christianity, or to speak more precisely of the Redemption by the Cross—every syllable is full of Light!—['] a small unsightly Root [']—to the Greeks Folly, to the

---

[68] *The Statesman's Manual* included in *Lay Sermons*, ed. R. J. White (Princeton and London, 1972), 88.

[69] *Letters*, ii. 866. Lucy Newlyn comments on the passage as evidence of Coleridge's preoccupation with 'symbolic vision' in ' "Radical Difference": Wordsworth and Coleridge in 1802', in Gravil, Newlyn, and Roe (eds.), *Coleridge's Imagination*, 125.

Jews a stumbling Block—[']The leaf was darkish & had prickles on it[']—If in this Life only we have hope, we are of all men the most miserable / & [a] score of other Texts—[']But in another country, as he said, Bore a bright golden Flower'—the exceeding weight of Glory prepared for us hereafter / —[' but [not] in this soil, unknown, & like esteem'd & the dull Swain treads on it daily with his clouted shoon['] / The Promises of Redemption offered daily & hourly & to all, but accepted scarcely by any—[']He called it Haemony[']—Now what is Haemony? Αἷμα—οἶνος—Blood-wine.—And he took the wine & blessed it, & said—This is my Blood— / the great Symbol of the Death on the Cross.

What was needed in addition to the recognition of virtue's intrinsic power was the greater protection afforded by Christ's sacrifice, which held out the hope of redemption even to those whose souls seemed blemished by sin. For the speaker of 'Dejection', racked by the sense of his own inadequacy, the purity of the Lady might seem an unattainable ideal, but hope remains through Christ, whose promise of 'a new earth and new heaven' is at the heart of the poem's 'Joy'. With the recollection of the Revelation, Coleridge's imagery of weddings and light assumes a much more positive aspect, since the new Jerusalem, which appears to St John as 'a bride adorned for her husband', has 'no need of the sun, neither of the moon, to shine in it: for the glory of God did lighten it, and the Lamb is the light thereof'.[70] At last, the 'rejoicing' that attends Coleridge's exploration of dejection begins to make sense.

That Coleridge should have been contemplating the suffering of Christ on 4 April 1802 is hardly surprising, given that it was Lent, and exactly two weeks until Easter Sunday. Indeed, the verse letter shows a strange mixing of the sacred and the personal in its allusion to Milton's unfinished poem, 'The Passion'. Coleridge looks back, as he did in 'Frost at Midnight' on the 'first dawn of youth', to describe how

> At eve, sky-gazing in 'ecstatic fit'
> (Alas far-cloistered in a city school,
> The sky was all I knew of beautiful),
> At the barred window often did I sit,
> And often on the leaded school-roof lay,
>   And to myself would say,

[70] Revelation 21: 23.

'There does not live the man so stripped of good affections
As not to love to see a maiden's quiet eyes
Upraised and linking on sweet dreams by dim connections
To moon, or evening star, or glorious western skies!'
While yet a boy, this thought would so pursue me,
That often it became a kind of vision to me.   (62–73)

It is a curious play on Milton's meditation on the cross:

> There doth my soul in holy vision sit
> In pensive trance, and anguish, and ecstatic fit.[71]

Although Coleridge wisely abandoned the lines when he rewrote his poem, the associations between his image of the maiden gazing at the night sky and the ideas of religious vision still infuse the later 'Dejection'. Milton's 'The Passion' is an Easter poem, depicting the poet alone at night, invoking the lute as his accompaniment, but ultimately unable to compose his poem. Coleridge, on the other hand, though asserting that his creative powers have failed, nevertheless produces first a substantial verse epistle and later a complete ode. Milton's failure is said to have resulted from his ambitious choice of subject—the direct confrontation of Christ's Passion. In Coleridge's poem, however, the acknowledgement of Christianity comes in the midst of his confessions of personal suffering, in the sudden recognition of inner light: 'the passions and the life, whose fountains are within'. It is this discovery that seems to startle the dull pain and, echoing St Paul, makes it 'move and live'.[72]

In his September letter to Sotheby, Coleridge emphasizes the religious dimension of his developing conception of the creative imagination, finding the faculty primarily in the Hebrew Poets, but 'next to them the English':

In the Hebrew Poets each Thing has a Life of it's own, & yet they are all one Life. In God they move & live, & *have* their Being—not *had* as the cold system of Newtonian Theology represents | but *have*.[73]

These were ideas that were subsequently to be developed and published as Coleridge tried to convey his view of the imagination as a redemptive 'living power', uniting the intellect and the

---

[71] Milton, 'The Passion', 41–2, *Complete Shorter Poems*, ed. Carey, 121.
[72] Acts 17: 28.
[73] *Letters*, ii. 866.

passions, and not only derived from God, but also the means through which God could be perceived in the world.[74]

For Coleridge, as he grappled with his ideas in 1802, Milton's description of 'haemony' seemed to demonstrate the astonishing capacity of English poetry not so much through the technical quality of the verse, but because it had the power to convey divine truth. As he explained to Sotheby, and later to the reading public, the entire passage could be interpreted as an account of Christianity and its assurance of salvation. It is also likely to have attracted Coleridge's attention because of the issue that had preoccupied him throughout the year: the importance to the individual of place and culture. His interpretation of the haemony passage suggests, yet once more, the influence of St Paul, whose epistle to the Hebrews describes the passage of the faithful to 'a better country, that is, an heavenly'.[75] Milton's account of the plant that 'in another country | Bore a bright golden flower' suggests to Coleridge the 'Glory prepared for us hereafter', just as the epistle to the Hebrews assures those who live in faith of their heavenly salvation.[76]

As Coleridge began to recognize that, unlike Wordsworth, his imagination could not be sustained adequately by his physical surroundings, and that rather than finding a satisfactory 'Home at Grasmere' he seemed destined to remain a wanderer, he is likely to have been strongly attracted to St Paul's celebration of the 'strangers and pilgrims on the earth' who sought the 'better country' of God. Discovery of the divine was not dependent on 'that *country* from whence they came out', but on faith.[77] Indeed, Coleridge's renewed sense of the superiority of inner experience to physical circumstances can be seen in the same remarkable letter of 10 September, when he describes the composition of 'Hymn in the manner of the Psalms' when climbing Sca Fell, but then, deciding the ideas were 'disproportionate to our humble mountains', transferred

---

[74] *Biographia Literaria*, i. 304. See also J. Robert Barth, SJ, 'Theological Implications of Coleridge's Theory of Imagination', in Gallant (ed.), *Coleridge's Theory of Imagination*, 3–13; id., *Coleridge and Christian Doctrine* (Cambridge, Mass., 1969).

[75] Hebrews 11: 16.

[76] Cf. the emphasis on Hebrews 10: 13 in *The Statesman's Manual*, *Lay Sermons*, 18.

[77] Heb. 11: 15.

the scene to the Vale of Chamounix.[78] The facts of physical experience were far less important than their symbolic potential, in the imaginative expression of God's vital power.

Coleridge's interest in the lines from *Comus* is enormously helpful to a reading of 'Dejection' but, even more surprisingly perhaps, to an understanding of the possible significance of 'Sir Patrick Spens' for the poem. His somewhat idiosyncratic translation of haemony as 'blood-wine' finds a curious correspondence in the first verse of the ballad: 'The king sits in Dunfermling toune | Drinking the blude-reid wine'. This might seem merely coincidental, especially as Coleridge extracts only the later part of the poem for 'Dejection'. These very lines, however, form part of his correspondence with Sara Hutchinson in the summer of 1802. As he sat in Keswick on the evening of 10 August, he evoked a situation very similar to that of his earlier verse letter, gazing at a strange green light in the western sky, and anticipating a storm:

More Rain coming! I broke off writing to look at the Sky | it was exactly 35 minutes after 7, which [was] 4 minutes after the real Sunset, and long long after the apparent sun-set behind our Vales—& I saw such a sight as I never before saw. Beyond Bassenthwaite at the end of the view was a Sky of bright yellow-green; but over that & extending all over Bassenthwaite, & almost up to Keswick church a Cloud-Sky of the deepest most fiery Orange—Bassenthwaite Lake look'd like a Lake of 'blood-red Wine'.[79]

'Sir Patrick Spens' is again functioning as a special language for Coleridge and Sara Hutchinson, as he attempts to convey his experience before the landscape, describing the lake through allusion to the ballad.

In the light of the letter written to Sotheby a few weeks later, however, it is possible to see Christian symbolism in the ballad as well as in the lines from *Comus*. For if 'haemony' could be interpreted as 'blood-wine' through its possible Greek etymology, it is hard to see how Coleridge could have overlooked similar possibilities in the more straightforward 'blude-reid

[78] *Letters*, ii. 864–5. Other explanations have been suggested for the change of location, e.g. Coleridge's unacknowledged debt to Friederika Brun's 'Chamouny Beim Sonnenaufgange': see Norman Fruman, *Coleridge: The Damaged Archangel* (New York, 1971), 29–30.

[79] *Letters*, ii. 848–9.

wine' of 'Sir Patrick Spens'. If Milton's account of haemony had an allegorical dimension, 'Sir Patrick Spens' could as easily be read in terms of the Christian sacrament, and the obligation of the faithful to leave their homes in search of the 'better country'. The apparently tragic story of Sir Patrick Spens is thus transformed into a divine comedy, through which the departure from the native land is the route to salvation. With this interpretation in mind, it is thus understandable that Coleridge should have reworked the verses to erase the original, more historical, notion of 'harm' being the consequence of the storm.

Coleridge's rewriting of the old ballad may thus involve more than a mere tidying up of the language and rearrangement of the verses. If his own poem initially seems dependent on the older one for its existence, the encounter of the old and new has a transformative effect on both. The presence of 'Sir Patrick Spens' sheds light on 'Dejection', but the new poem also encourages a radical reinterpretation of the familiar. This is not so much a question of invention, but of seeing in a new light what has been there all the time, just as Coleridge depicts the speaker of 'Dejection' discovering the truth not from external forms, but from within. And yet, as 'Dejection' suggests, and as Coleridge was later to develop more explicitly in *The Statesman's Manual*, what is within is not always obvious, and often needs to be startled into life by the recognition of some corresponding external object. In 'Dejection', it is the correspondence between the physical scene outside and the recollected image from 'Sir Patrick Spens' that seems to provide the creative catalyst for the new poem. The sudden, surprising glimpse of similarity reveals a correspondence between things apparently separate. Indeed, the moon of both the poems is itself a symbol of Coleridgean oneness, since it appears to the eye as two separate things, but the mind knows it to be one.[80]

Between the publication of 'Dejection' in the *Morning Post* and *Sibylline Leaves*, Coleridge's ballad source underwent a surprising development. After the appearance of the third volume of Scott's *Minstrelsy of the Scottish Border* in 1803, a longer version of 'Sir Patrick Spens' became widely known, and

---

[80] For an excellent discussion of Coleridge's fascination with 'the one and the many', see Seamus Perry, *Coleridge and the Uses of Division* (Oxford, 1999).

with it the conjectural context which placed the ballad in the thirteenth century. Scott suggests that Sir Patrick's voyage was based on that of the Scots nobles who were sent to bring home the 'Maid of Norway' (Margaret, granddaughter to Alexander III) to marry Edward, Prince of Wales, and succeed to the Scottish throne, an embassy defeated by the untimely death of the infant princess. Scott's purpose was partly political, as he describes the Scottish nobility who 'patriotically looked forward to the important advantage of uniting the island of Britain into one kingdom', but it was also part of his general strategy to ground the ballads he had assembled in historical fact and specific geographical detail.[81]

None of this seems to have had much impact on Coleridge's use of 'Sir Patrick Spens', though the additional associations of the proposed wedding and its disappointment may have increased the poignancy of the dejected speaker's predicament for readers familiar with the expanded ballad. It becomes harder to read 'Sir Patrick Spens' as a Christian allegory, however, once the narrative has been enlarged and augmented by historical detail, since its meaning in Scott's edition seems to be determined by history rather than any transcendent truth that might be discernible. As editorial practice became more concerned with the factual aspects of poetry, however, Coleridge appears increasingly to have sought the symbolic: 'all the puzzle is to find out what Plant Haemony is—which they discover to be the English Spleenwort . . . They thought little of Milton's platonizing spirit—who wrote nothing without an interior meaning'.[82] The ideas with which he bombarded Sotheby in 1802 were gradually to develop into explicit public statements on the importance of symbolic, rather than factual, meaning: 'A Symbol . . . is characterized by a translucence of the Special in the Individual or of the General in the Especial or of the Universal in the General. Above all by the translucence of the Eternal through and in the Temporal.'[83] Divine truth was to be glimpsed through symbols, and thus Coleridge came to regard the Bible as a better guide for statesmen than histories and political economies, with their lifeless facts and statistics.

---

[81] Scott, *Minstrelsy of the Scottish Border*, iii. 64.
[82] *Letters*, ii. 866.
[83] *The Statesman's Manual*, 30.

The recognition of Coleridge's growing belief in the superiority of the eternal and universal over the temporal and particular also helps to illuminate his somewhat high-handed treatment of 'Sir Patrick Spens'. For if, as he argued in *Biographia Literaria*, '*facts* are valuable to a wiseman, chiefly as they lead to the discovery of an indwelling *law*, which is the true *being* of things, the sole solution of their modes of existence, and in the knowledge of which consists our dignity and power', the specific details that tied the old ballad to time and place were of no consequence in comparison to the inner meaning of the poem.[84] The recasting of the chosen lines and rejection of the rest of the poem are not so much an act of 'naïve cultural imperialism', then, as an attempt to extract and purify the essential part. And here his attitude to *Der Erste Schiffer* makes an interesting parallel. For although Coleridge appears to have been so contemptuous of Gessner's poem in 1802, he nevertheless proposed the story to Godwin, as a possible English children's book, some ten years later:

I told dear Miss Lamb that I had formed a complete plan of a Poem with little plates for children, the *first* thought, but that alone, taken from Gesner's First Mariner: and this thought I have reason to believe was not an invention of Gesner's—It is this—that in the early times in some island or part of the continent the Ocean had rushed in, overflowing a vast plain of 20 or 30 miles, & thereby *insulating* one small promontory or Cape of high Land—on which was a Cottage, containing a man & his wife & an infant Daughter—This is the *one* thought—all that Gesner has made of it (for I once translated into blank verse about half of the poem, but gave it up under the influence of a double disgust, moral & poetical) I have rejected—& strictly speaking, the tale in all it's parts, that one idea excepted, would be original—the tale will contain the cause, the occasions, the process, with all it's failures & ultimate success, of the construction of the first Boat, and of the undertaking of the first naval expedition.[85]

Although Coleridge was unimpressed by Gessner's handling of the narrative, and especially the prurient fascination with a stranded 16-year-old girl, he was obviously strongly drawn to the 'first thought', which may have been his reason for beginning the translation in 1802. For the *Erste Schiffer* could be

---

[84] *Biographia Literaria*, ii. 53. Cf. i. 16.
[85] To William Godwin, 26 Mar. 1811, *Letters*, iii. 313.

read as a parable of the human imagination, which springs into creativity in response to the perception of likeness in something physically separate. The boat is the solution to the predicament of being cut off from the rest of the world, and so the tale might demonstrate the ways in which isolation and a consequent desire for union can set in motion the powers of invention. For Coleridge, there is 'one thought' in Gessner's poem that is valuable and of universal significance, and thus he proposes to extract it and remake the work according to his own principles.

It is hardly surprising that Coleridge's handling of his sources has attracted so much critical interest, both from those anxious to trace the sources of his extraordinary ideas, and those who regard his unacknowledged debts as plagiarisms. In the case of 'Dejection', the source of the epigraph is located clearly, but objections might still be made to his inaccurate representation of the lines from the poem. For the argument that Coleridge's practice results from a highly idiosyncratic Christian theory of literature, which seeks transcendent meanings in the particular, is itself open to attack. As Luke Gibbons has observed in relation to the universalizing tendencies of the late eighteenth-century emphasis on sympathy and fellow feeling, 'the theory of sympathy . . . helped to dispel some of the intense English prejudice against Scottish culture. But in so doing, it also cemented the Union, laying the foundation for a unity of hearts and minds as well as trade and politics.'[86] The late eighteenth-century search for the universal, which rendered meaning accessible to otherwise disparate readers, could also be interpreted as a means to impose a certain set of values on others, whether or not they were willing recipients. Coleridge's absorption of 'Sir Patrick Spens' according to his own purposes would, in this light, seem distinctly imperialistic.

And yet, as I have suggested with regard to the tension between the speaker of 'Dejection' and the Bard who made the grand old ballad, the balance of power is complicated and unstable. The poem seems to emphasize the protagonist's sense of inadequacy, thus directing the reader's sympathy towards the modern English voice rather than to the ballad-maker who appears to be possessed of a wisdom quite beyond the reach of

[86] Luke Gibbons, 'The Sympathetic Bond: Ossian, Celticism and Colonialism', in Terence Brown (ed.), *Celticism* (Amsterdam and Atlanta, Ga., 1996), 273–91, 289.

the speaker. This effectively inverts the normal dynamics of sentimental and primitivist literature, which tends to position the member of a non-literate or superseded community as an object of sympathy for the modern reader. And so, with Coleridge's curious attitude to other writings, sympathy for his overtly stated sense of impotence may be as appropriate as annoyance over his seizing of others' treasures. As *Biographia Literaria* makes plain, Coleridge needed constant encounters with books and writers to enable his own intellectual and imaginative activity, and hence, perhaps, his intense admiration for those great figures, Shakespeare, Milton, and Wordsworth, whom he regarded as entirely self-sufficient. The problem here, though, is an obvious one: Coleridge's own abilities are so abundantly clear that it is hard to take his self-deprecation entirely at face value, just as 'Dejection' disproves its own apparent lament for the muse. Indeed, it is worth noting in this context that later nineteenth-century editors of Percy's *Reliques* would gloss 'Sir Patrick Spens' with a reference to Coleridge's by then more famous poem.

When he described the use of quotations in an essay written for *The Friend*, Coleridge revealed his admiration for the detached citations of Johnson's *Dictionary*: 'it is the beauty and independent worth of the citations far more than their appropriateness which have made Johnson's Dictionary popular even as a reading book—and the mottos with translations of them are known to add considerably to the value of the Spectator'.[87] Johnson's quotations were valuable not because they helped to define a particular word, but because of their own 'independent beauty and worth'. Rather than being seen as incomplete fragments of a larger whole, Coleridge saw that they possessed a value in their own right. Respect for these isolated sentences is, however, almost immediately balanced by the reference to his own pursuit of epigraphs:

I have taken more than common pains in the selection of mottos for the Friend: and of two mottos equally appropriate prefer always that from the book which is least likely to have come into my Readers' hands. For I often please myself with the fancy, now that I may have saved from oblivion the only striking passage in a whole volume,

---

[87] 'Essay vii', *The Friend*, ed. Barbara E. Rooke, 2 vols. (Princeton and London, 1969), i. 52–3.

and now that I may have attracted notice to a writer undeservedly forgotten.

Despite their 'independent beauty and worth', it seems, quotations must still rely on the good offices of the transcriber for their survival.

4

James Clarence Mangan and Percy Bysshe Shelley

The Dying Enthusiast to His Friend

Life—like a dome of many-colored glass—
Stains the white radiance of Eternity,
Until Death tramples it to fragments.——SHELLEY

Speak no more of life—
   What can life bestow
In this amphitheatre of strife,
   All times dark with tragedy and woe?
Knowest thou not how care and pain
Build their lampless dwelling in the brain,
Ever as the stern intrusion
   Of our teachers, Time and Truth,
Turns to gloom the bright illusion
   Rainbowed on the soul of youth?
Wouldst thou have me live when this is so?
            Oh! no—no!

As the flood of Time
   Sluggishly doth flow,
Look how all of beaming and sublime
   Sinks into the black abysm below!
Yea, the loftiest intellect
Earliest on the strand of death is wrecked.
Nought of lovely—nothing glorious
   Lives to triumph o'er decay;
Desolation reigns victorious—
   Mind is dungeon-walled by clay.
Could I bear to feel mine own laid low?
            Oh! no—no!

O'er the troubled earth
   Thronging millions go—

But, behold how Genius, Love, and Worth,
    Move like lonely phantoms, to and fro.
Suns are quenched, and kingdoms fall,
But the doom of these outdarkens all!
Die they, then? Yes, Love's devotion,
    Stricken, withers in its bloom;
Fond affections, deep as ocean,
    In their cradle find their tomb.
Shall I linger but to count each throe?
        Oh! no—no!

Prison-bursting Death!
    Welcome, then, thy blow!
Thine is but the forfeit of my breath,
    Not the Spirit—not the Spirit's glow!
Spheres of Beauty! hallowed Spheres,
Undefaced by time, undimmed by tears,
Henceforth hail! Oh! who would grovel
    In a world impure as this,
Who would dwell in cell or hovel
    When a palace might be his?
Dare I longer the bright lot forego?
        Oh! no—no![1]

The idea of native poetry provided various challenges to late eighteenth- and early nineteenth-century writers, depending partly on their own backgrounds, homes, and education. For Burns to command admiration for the 'simple strains' apparently flowing from 'the native feelings of his heart', he had to adopt a kind of Scottish dialect which could nevertheless incorporate elements of standard English and literary influences from south of the Border. Coleridge, on the other hand, being less firmly rooted in a particular area, expressed his restless modernity through admiration for traditional bards and ballad-makers, while simultaneously developing a sense of the fundamental importance of internal rather than external resources. For both poets, as for many of their readers, an awareness of local origins and the peculiarities of certain regions was pronounced. As Linda Colley has argued influentially, the period

[1] 'The Dying Enthusiast to his Friend', *Dublin Penny Journal*, I (5 Jan. 1833); *The Collected Works of James Clarence Mangan: Poems 1818–1837*, ed. Jacques Chuto, Rudolf Patrick Holzapfel, Peter Mac Mahon, Pádraig Ó Snodaigh, Ellen Shannon-Mangan, Peter Van de Kamp (Blackrock and Portland, Oreg., 1996). All references to Mangan's poetry will be to this edition.

when Burns and Coleridge were publishing their work also saw
the emergence of a new national consciousness, accentuated by
the massive war which seemed to provide the final evidence of
France's irredeemable difference from 'Britain'.[2] Individual
responses to the events of the 1790s varied widely and con-
tinued to shift throughout the decade, of course; but the start-
ling nature of the French Revolution and its aftermath, together
with the scale of Napoleon's campaign, combined to raise
British consciousness of a fundamental Gallic 'otherness'.[3] While
the writings of Burns and Coleridge both reveal a clear sense of
the differences between Scotland and England, then, they also
belong to neighbouring countries whose ninety-year-old Union
was in the process of being strengthened by the conflict with a
common enemy.

In Ireland, the situation was not quite the same. Here the Act
of Union with England became law only in January 1801, in the
middle of the great war with France. As with the Scottish
response to the 1707 Union, attitudes in Ireland varied con-
siderably according to personal values, economic considera-
tions, and political and religious allegiances.[4] Within the new
United Kingdom, however, a strong sense of Ireland's difference
from England and Scotland was widely felt, on both sides of the
Irish Sea. Detailed exploration of the contemporary adjustment
or resistance to the political Union is not possible within the
scope of this chapter, but some sense of the larger context is
important nevertheless to any understanding of Irish poetry in
the first decades of the nineteenth century. Since my focus is on
the way in which a rather individual Irish writer engaged with a
distinctly unusual English model, it is particularly necessary to
keep the wider historical moment and the complicated internal

---

[2] Linda Colley, *Britons*, 297–337.

[3] Burns's death in 1796 prevented him from witnessing key events, such as the
invasion of Switzerland, that caused so many British radicals, including Coleridge,
to lose their early sympathy with France. For helpful discussion of British responses
to the revolution and Napoleonic wars, see Ronald Paulson, *Representations of
Revolution 1780–1820* (New Haven, 1983), Marilyn Butler (ed)., *Burke, Paine,
Godwin and the Revolution Controversy* (Cambridge, 1984), Stephen Prickett,
England and the French Revolution (London, 1989), Simon Bainbridge, *Napoleon
and English Romanticism* (Cambridge, 1995).

[4] It is nevertheless a mistake to impose similarities on the two events, as Ron
Weir has argued forthrightly in 'The Scottish and Irish Unions: the Victorian View
in Perspective', in S. J. Connolly (ed.), *Kingdoms United? Great Britain and Ireland
since 1500: Integration and Diversity* (Dublin and Portland, Oreg., 1999), 56–66.

politics of the islands broadly in mind as a framework for the more specific analysis.

Although there is some debate over the significance of the Union to Irish history and cultural development, there seems little doubt that it gave considerable impetus to interests that had already begun to gather force in the eighteenth century.[5] Antiquarian efforts to recover traditional Irish poetry, songs, and historical materials continued in the nineteenth century with renewed energy, stimulated by a certain urgency which transformed an academic pursuit into an act of rescue. At the same time, creative writers began to pour out new versions of Irish Melodies, albeit in purest English diction. In the decade immediately after the Union, the tendency to look back is understandably prevalent, as Vivien Mercier has remarked in relation to Thomas Moore's famous collection: 'Memory . . . is the main, if not the only, theme of the *Melodies*. It is as if Irish history had ended on 1 January, 1801, or at least on the day of Emmet's execution. Only the vaguest aspirations towards a better future are entertained, in a very few poems: otherwise we hear of nothing but "a nation's eclipse".'[6] An elegiac note is similarly discernible in collections such as Lady Morgan's *The Lay of an Irish Harp*, with its evocations of the sentimental lamentations of Macpherson's old Celtic bard, Ossian.[7]

By the 1830s, however, in the wake of the momentous Act of Catholic Emancipation of 1829, a more confident spirit seemed to be abroad. When Samuel Ferguson reviewed James Hardiman's important collection of traditional songs, *Irish Minstrelsy*, published in 1831, for example, he struck a much more optimistic note: 'far, then, from yielding to despair, we rejoice in all auspicious hopes for our country'.[8] Although, as Joep Leerssen

---

[5] Joep Leerssen, *Remembrance and Imagination: Patterns in the Historical and Literary Representation of Ireland in the Nineteenth Century* (Cork, 1996), 8–111.

[6] Vivien Mercier, *Modern Irish Literature: Sources and Founders*, ed. Eilis Dillon (Oxford, 1994), 42. Thomas Moore's series of *Irish Melodies* were published between 1808 and 1834. For details see M. J. MacManus, *First Editions of Thomas Moore* (Dublin, 1934).

[7] Sydney Owenson, Lady Morgan, *The Lay of an Irish Harp* (London, 1807). For discussion of the symbolic harp, see Leerssen, *Remembrance and Imagination*, 59, and Mary Thuente, *The Harp Re-strung: The United Irishmen and the Rise of Irish Literary Nationalism* (Syracuse, 1994). See also Trumpener's introduction to *Bardic Nationalism* 'Harps hung upon the Willow', 1–34.

[8] Samuel Ferguson, 'Hardiman's Irish Minstrelsy No. III', *Dublin University*

has pointed out, Ferguson was taking issue with what he seems to have perceived as an attempt to annex ancient Ireland for the Catholic, nationalist population, the tone of his review is generally progressive and forward-looking.[9] While acknowledging the damaging effects of both 'the violence of an oppressive conquest' and what he regarded as 'the lingering tyranny of a debasing priestcraft', he nevertheless seizes on the publication of Hardiman's book as a sign of better times to come: 'sooner or later, Ireland must rise into importance, perhaps as an emulator, perhaps as an equal, perhaps as a superior to the other members of our imperial confederacy'.[10] Ireland is being presented here primarily in relation to the other countries of the Union; but whatever its past or present position, the future painted by Ferguson is relatively bright and open.

Ferguson's perception of Ireland's possible future within the United Kingdom offers an interesting glimpse of the literary and intellectual attitudes current in Dublin in the early 1830s. For his reading of Hardiman's collection leads not to nostalgia or resentment, but rather to a mood of hope. Crucial to this optimism was the growing awareness of Ireland's national history, antiquities, and literature, which seemed not necessarily confined to a lost past, but to provide the foundations for new generations. The *Irish Minstrelsy* provided evidence of the abundant native talent which had flowered in the past and should, therefore, be able to flourish once again. Although the national heritage might prove rather more fragmentary and open to contesting narratives than Ferguson's rhetoric is prepared to allow, his desire to look forward rather than remaining preoccupied exclusively with the past is significant. The anticipated recovery seemed to require some form of measure nevertheless, and so Ferguson assesses the future of Ireland according to relations with England and Scotland—as 'emulator', 'equal', or 'perhaps as a superior'.

Even those with most confidence in Ireland's cultural pros-

Magazine, IV (1834), 447. The substantial review was published in four parts: *Dublin University Magazine*, III (1834), 465–78; IV (1834), 152–67, 447–67, 514–30.

[9] Leerssen, *Remembrance and Imagination*, 181. See also Michael Cronin, *Translating Ireland: Translation, Languages, Cultures* (Cork, 1996), 108–13.

[10] *Dublin University Magazine*, IV (1834), 447.

perity were apparently unable to conceive of the nation's progress without some reference to the neighbouring island; the future of Irish literature was thus seen to lie in English. At the same time, the advance of English in the poorer, Catholic areas of Ireland had also accelerated, as the Irish language was increasingly perceived as an obstacle to individual progress. From 1831, the national schools were attempting to improve their pupils' prospects through English lessons while, as Oliver MacDonagh has commented, 'the politicization of the masses (O'Connell's marvellous achievement of 1825–45) implied linguistic anglicisation upon a massive scale, for the language of agitation was almost invariably English'.[11] The 1820s and 1830s also saw the launch of numerous journals and newspapers in Dublin, which not only fostered interest in Irish culture but also contributed to the spread of English words, styles, and publishing practices.[12] Young writers who wanted to take advantage of the new outlets, and in so doing might be contributing to the realization of Ferguson's cultural vision, were thus writing in English for an English-speaking readership.

When the young Dublin poet James Clarence Mangan submitted a short lyric to the editors of the *Dublin Penny Journal* in the winter of 1832, it is not surprising therefore to find him employing an epigraph from an English poem and writing in a literary language that seems in keeping with his chosen quotation. Unlike Burns, whose epigraphs so often ensure that his readers experience something of a jolt when the poem begins, or Coleridge, whose evocation of 'Sir Patrick Spens' emphasized the remoteness of his source, Mangan's choice of three lines from Shelley offers a much smoother introduction to his poem. There is no immediate sense of disjunction, nor of the earlier poem being part of a culture fundamentally alien to that of the new composition. Instead, the abstract nouns, elegant assonance, and striking imagery of the epigraph continue almost uninterrupted in the body of the poem. Whether this apparent harmony renders Mangan an 'emulator', 'equal', or

---

[11] Oliver MacDonagh, *States of Mind: A Study of the Anglo-Irish Conflict 1780–1980* (London, 1983), 104.

[12] For a fascinating discussion of the development of the Irish 'literary journal', see Richard Kearney, 'Between Politics and Literature: The Irish Cultural Journal, *The Crane Bag*, 7/2 (1983), 160–71. See also Barbara Hayley, 'Irish Periodicals from the Union to the Nation', *Anglo-Irish Studies*, II (1976), 83–103.

'superior' in relation to Shelley, however, is a matter for further investigation.

James Clarence Mangan's 'The Dying Enthusiast to his Friend' makes an interesting focus for this book because it is the only poem of those chosen for detailed analysis that was initially published without a starting line from another text. For although his poem appeared in the *Dublin Penny Journal* on 5 January 1833 accompanied by the lines from *Adonais*, it had originally been published without an epigraph in the satirical political paper *The Comet* the previous August.[13] The congruity between the language of the poem and that of the epigraph is thus particularly intriguing, since Mangan's poem appears to have been composed independently of the lines that would later become its companion. Rather than acting as an accelerator to kick-start Mangan's composition, Shelley's words have been added subsequently, and thus seem to serve as a traditional poetic motto, embodying an essential theme and adding authority to the new work.

Why this was felt necessary so soon after the initial, unadorned publication is not known and may reflect nothing more than a chance discovery by Mangan of lines that seemed to accord with the sentiments of his recent poem. Another possible explanation would be the different style of the two journals. For although the *Dublin Penny Journal* was explicitly aimed at a popular market, its contents were less topical and overtly political than those of the anti-tithe paper, *The Comet*. Shelley's memorable statement on death has an air of universality that might be thought to lift Mangan's poem from its immediate circumstances and make it easier to accommodate in the pages of a journal packed with history and antiquarian interest. The presence of an epigraph also draws attention to the poem's status as a written text, whereas the first line, 'Speak no more of life', might otherwise suggest the conditions of orality—powerful, emotive, but also, perhaps, transient. What might seem in the pages of a radical newspaper to represent an urgent contemporary voice, or a song lyric, subsequently assumes the status of a lyrical poem whose formal qualities are quietly emphasized by the presence of the quotation. Perhaps the initial publication

[13] 'The Dying Enthusiast to his Friend' was published in *The Comet*, 5 Aug. 1832, and in the *Dublin Penny Journal*, I (5 Jan. 1833), 224.

threatened to prove too ephemeral, and unable to offer any pro-
longed life to the 'Dying Enthusiast'.

Before assuming too rapidly that the republication of
Mangan's poem in the *Dublin Penny Journal* neutralized any
political dimension, however, it is worth bearing in mind
that despite an overt claim to exclude 'politics and sectarian
religion', the magazine's editorial emphasis on national history
and biography was not entirely detached from the affairs of the
state.[14] Nor was the name 'Shelley' (which on account of
Mangan's anonymity was the only name visibly connected to
'The Dying Enthusiast to his Friend') without a certain political
association in Ireland. For Percy Bysshe Shelley, who died
exactly ten years before the first publication of Mangan's poem,
had been an active campaigner for both Catholic Emancipation
and the Repeal of the Union.

It is possible to see the first flickerings of a new Irish critical
interest in Shelley in an article published in 1830 in the first
volume of the explicitly non-sectarian *The National Magazine
and Dublin Literary Gazette*.[15] Although the emphasis is largely
literary and the poems featured include some of Shelley's less
inflammatory pieces—'A Hymn to Intellectual Beauty', 'The
Cloud', 'To a Skylark', or 'The Sensitive Plant'—the plea for a
more tolerant attitude towards the English poet, and indeed
for a readership of any kind, is significant. For Shelley's free-
thinking views and rather scandalous personal life were not
easily forgotten, whatever his political ideals. As late as the
1840s, Denis MacCarthy's essays on Shelley in *The Nation* were
to cause a minor furore in Dublin, where even MacCarthy's
close friends and political allies saw any reference to the notori-
ous poet as 'plain proof' of a certain 'sympathy with infidelity'.[16]

---

[14] Preface (written at the end of the first year of publication), *Dublin Penny
Journal*.

[15] 'The Works of Percy Bysshe Shelley', *The National Magazine and Dublin
Literary Gazette*, I/3 (Sept. 1830), 285–300. On the politics of this journal and
others in the period, see Kearney, 'Between Politics and Literature', 163.

[16] Charles Gavan Duffy, *Four Years of Irish History, 1845–1849* (London,
1880), 104–5. Denis Florence MacCarthy, 'Recent English Poets: John Keats', *The
Nation*, III/157 (11 Oct. 1845), 858–9; IV/159 (25 Oct. 1845), 27; 'Recent English
Poets: Percy Bysshe Shelley', *The Nation*, IV/167 (20 Dec. 1845), 154; 168 (27 Dec.
1845), 171–2. See also the earlier debate in the *Dublin Evening Post*, of November
and December 1842.

Fifteen years earlier, the essay in *The National Magazine and Dublin Literary Gazette* provoked a predictably indignant response from *The Christian Examiner and Church of Ireland Magazine*, but its very existence demonstrates that an early appreciation of Shelley's work was not confined to England.[17]

The sense of momentous political change which characterizes British public feeling in the early 1830s and undoubtedly influenced the shifting critical attitudes towards Shelley was perhaps even more acute in Ireland because of the Catholic Emancipation Act.[18] For the Irish, the Reform Act was only another significant step on the path of progress and a further encouragement to continuing improvement. From the perspective of an Irish Catholic, Emancipation and the Reform of the House of Commons meant that the abolition of tithes and even the Repeal of the Union might one day be realized. Since Percy Bysshe Shelley had campaigned for these very goals, the more liberal circles in Ireland were likely to greet his reviving reputation with a degree of approval, or at least with interest. For Shelley was known increasingly not merely as an 'infidel', but also as a 'passionate sympathiser with Irish nationality'.[19] Even *Queen Mab*, though seeming shockingly irreligious to many, expressed an appealing egalitarianism which had particular significance in Dublin, since much of it had been composed in the wake of Shelley's visit to the Irish capital in 1812.[20]

The effect of Shelley's own experiences in Dublin had been profound, as is obvious from a letter he wrote to William Godwin in March 1812:

I had no conception of the depth of human misery until now.—The poor of Dublin are assuredly the meanest & most miserable of all.—In their narrow streets thousands seem huddled together—one mass of animated filth! With what eagerness do such scenes as these inspire me, how self confident too, do I feel in my assumption to teach the lessons

---

[17] *The Christian Examiner and Church of Ireland Magazine*, X/65 (Nov. 1830), 880. On the politics of *The Christian Examiner*, see Mercier, *Modern Irish Literature*, 44–5.

[18] For a helpful account see Fergus O'Ferrall, *Catholic Emancipation: Daniel O'Connell and the Birth of Irish Democracy* (Dublin, 1985).

[19] Duffy, *Four Years of Irish History*, 104.

[20] For details of the composition, see *The Poems of Shelley*, Vol. I: 1804–1817, ed. G. M. Matthews and Kelvin Everest (London, 1989), 265–9.

of virtue to those who grind their fellow beings into worse than annihi-
lation.[21]

Though rather too distant from those he observed to be
described as sympathetic, Shelley's horror at the mass poverty
he witnessed in Ireland seems to have translated almost
instantly into reforming zeal. His eagerness 'to teach the lessons
of virtue' to those responsible must have fed directly into *Queen
Mab*, which he began in earnest within days of returning from
his trip. However unpalatable some of the poem's metaphysical
speculation, there can be no doubt about the intrinsic interest of
Queen Mab to an Irish audience.

Shelley's visit to Dublin, too, though featuring little in the
memoirs of his English friends, had attracted considerable
interest in Ireland in 1812. The methods used by Shelley and his
first wife, Harriet, to distribute his *Address to the Irish People*,
which ranged from handing out the pamphlets in pubs to
popping them into the hats and bags of unsuspecting passers-by,
were not likely to guarantee the survival of many copies. That
some did reach the hands of those who would respond posi-
tively to Shelley's intentions 'to awaken in the minds of the Irish
poor a knowledge of their real state . . . and suggesting rational
means of remedy—Catholic Emancipation, and a Repeal of the
Union Act', is clear, nevertheless, from Denis MacCarthy's sub-
sequent description of the pamphlet he had treasured 'for forty
years'.[22] The publicity surrounding Shelley's visit was inspired
not so much by the little political pamphlet, however, as by the
speech he made at the Aggregate Meeting of the Catholics of
Ireland, where he had the good fortune to appear on the same
platform as Daniel O'Connell. Shelley had arrived in Ireland
with an introduction from Godwin to the prominent lawyer and
politician John Philpot Curran, and had managed to secure an

[21] To Godwin, 8 Mar. 1812, *The Letters of Percy Bysshe Shelley*, ed. Frederick
L. Jones, 2 vols. (Oxford, 1964), i. 268.

[22] Percy Bysshe Shelley, *An Address to the Irish People* (1812), *The Prose Works
of Percy Bysshe Shelley*, Vol. I, ed. E. B. Murray (Oxford, 1993), 8; Denis Florence
MacCarthy, *Shelley's Early Life from Original Sources* (London, 1872), p. xii.
MacCarthy's volume is an invaluable source of information on Shelley's activities in
Ireland. See also P. M. S. Dawson, *The Unacknowledged Legislator: Shelley and
Politics* (Oxford, 1980); Timothy Webb, ' "A Noble Field": Shelley's Irish Expedi-
tion and the Lessons of the French Revolution', in Nadia Minerva (ed.), *Robespierre
and Co.*, 3 vols. (Bologna, 1990), 553–76.

opportunity to address the important assembly on 28 February. After O'Connell had made his speech and departed, Shelley was able to hold the stage for over an hour. His performance was widely reported in the Dublin newspapers, which describe with various degrees of enthusiasm the 'English gentleman (very young)' who had admitted that 'when he reflected on the outrages that his countrymen had committed here for the last twenty years . . . he blushed for them'.[23] Although it was recognized that his father was 'a Member of the Imperial Parliament', his own unequivocal support for the 'liberties of Ireland' and the 'perfectibility of human society' won him admiration from several of those reporting on the meeting.[24]

James Clarence Mangan was only nine when Shelley visited Dublin, so it is unlikely that he would have attended the historic meeting. However, as the assembly took place in the theatre in Fishamble Street, where Mangan had lived since his birth in 1803, he is likely to have been at least dimly aware of the event, and may even have glimpsed the pale-faced, auburn-haired young Englishman on his way down the street. Whether this early coincidence could have had any bearing on Mangan's later interest in Shelley is open to doubt, but it might well have made his name familiar, and thus increased the younger poet's interest in the reports of Shelley's early death in 1822 and the subsequent publications of his poetry. Mangan's biographer, Ellen Shannon-Mangan, has pointed to a strong Shelleyan influence on one of his earliest publications, the enigma in *Grant's Almanack* for 1823, which Mangan wrote at the age of twenty:

> In the unbeginning first ere earth arose
> From chaos old,
> Thy lovely empire, Spirit of Repose!
> Thou didst uphold!
> The splendid firmament is vast to view—
> Can Fancy roam
> That wilderness of silver and of blue!
> It is thy home![25]

---

[23] *Freeman's Journal*, 29 Feb. 1812, *Saunders's News-Letter*, 29 Feb. 1812; included in *Prose Works of Shelley*, App. 1, 293, 295. Murray includes all surviving reports of Shelley's speech, together with a useful editorial.

[24] *Dublin Weekly Messenger*, 7 Mar. 1812, *Prose Works of Shelley*, 297–8.

[25] Ellen Shannon-Mangan, *James Clarence Mangan: A Biography* (Blackrock and Portland, Oreg., 1996), 67. Keats also seems to have some bearing on the poem: cf.

If Mangan was already an admirer of Shelley's poetry in the early 1820s, he is likely to have read the biographical accounts that appeared in the years following Shelley's death with great interest.

Although the poor sales of Shelley's works during his lifetime might lead to the assumption that his name was largely unknown before the publication of the substantial four-volume edition of his poetry in 1839, this was far from being the case. The public interest generated by the boating tragedy continued to be fostered for years afterwards by influential friends such as Leigh Hunt, whose tireless efforts did much to counter popular prejudices and establish Shelley as a major literary figure.[26] Shelley's own work, too, continued to appear, as Mary Shelley laboured to produce her edition of the *Posthumous Poems*, in 1824, and then assisted the Galignani brothers with their substantial collection, *The Poems of Coleridge, Shelley and Keats*, which included a sympathetic memoir of Shelley. The Galignani edition came out in Paris in 1829, but within a year British readers were able to acquire a reasonably priced volume of *The Beauties of Percy Bysshe Shelley, Consisting of Miscellaneous Selections from his Poetical Works: The Entire Poems of Adonais and Alastor, and a revised Edition of Queen Mab Free from all Objectionable Passages*. In Cambridge, Shelley also became fashionable with the brilliant circle of undergraduates surrounding Arthur Hallam, who was the driving force behind a new edition of *Adonais* in 1829.

The success of these various volumes, not to mention the popular pirated editions of *Queen Mab* that began to circulate in the 1820s, demonstrates that whatever the notoriety of his life and opinions, Shelley had attracted an enthusiastic following by 1830. The review of the Cambridge edition of *Adonais*

'Ever let the Fancy roam, | Pleasure never is at home', 'Fancy', 1–2, published in *Lamia, Isabella, The Eve of St Agnes, and Other Poems* (1820).

[26] Leigh Hunt, *Lord Byron and Some of his Contemporaries*, 2 vols. (London, 1828) contained a sympathetic representation of Shelley, while Hunt continued to publish Shelley's work posthumously. Tim Webb's 'Religion of the Heart: Leigh Hunt's Unpublished Tribute to Shelley', *Keats–Shelley Review*, 7 (1992), 1–61, provides an invaluable account. For details of Shelley's posthumous reception, see also Karsten Klejs Engelberg, *The Making of the Shelley Myth: An Annotated Bibliography of Criticism of Percy Bysshe Shelley, 1822–1860* (London, 1988); Newman Ivey White, *Shelley*, 2 vols. (London, 1947), ii. 389–418.

which appeared in the *Athenaeum* gives a good indication of the changing state of opinion:

few such occurrences are more interesting than the gradual and steady rise of Shelley's fame. The present reprint of one of his most beautiful poems is a single evidence, among many others, that he is beginning to be estimated as a great poet. We rejoice of this, for we believe him to have been one.[27]

The rehabilitation of Shelley was part of the larger change in public mood that accompanied the accession of William IV in 1830 and the subsequent defeat of the old Tory government, culminating in the passing of the Reform Act in 1832. As Shelley's visions for the improvement of mankind seemed to be turning into realities, at last the public seemed ready for poems such as *The Masque of Anarchy*, brought out by Hunt in 1832, or 'Lines written during the Castlereagh Administration', which appeared in the *Athenaeum* the same year.[28] Edward Dowden was to comment half a century later that these poems could only be published some years after Shelley's death, 'when the first great battle for reform had been fought and won'.[29]

Even before the appearance of some of Shelley's more radical works, however, the editor of the *Athenaeum* evidently decided that July 1832 was a suitable moment to run a series of articles by Shelley's 'relative, school-fellow, and friend', Thomas Medwin. Although these essays were only part of the larger endeavour by Shelley's surviving friends and followers, they provide in accessible form much that would have been of particular interest to Shelley's Irish admirer, Mangan. From the first article, which appeared within a day of the tenth anniversary of Shelley's death, Medwin's emphasis was not on his friend's more controversial opinions and behaviour, but rather on his 'active benevolence' and hatred of 'tyranny'.[30] Though neither

[27] 'Adonais. An Elegy on the Death of John Keats, Author of "Endymion", "Hyperion" etc.', *Athenaeum*, 97 (1829), 544–5.
[28] Percy Bysshe Shelley, *The Masque of Anarchy*, ed. Leigh Hunt (London, 1832); 'Lines written during the Castlereagh Administration', *Athenaeum*, 267 (8 Dec. 1832), 794, which includes the comment that 'these lines . . . may . . . now be published without the chance of exciting either personal or party feeling'.
[29] Edward Dowden, *The Life of Percy Bysshe Shelley*, new edn. (London, 1896), 438.
[30] Thomas Medwin, 'Memoir of Shelley', *Athenaeum*, 247 (21 July 1832), 472–4; 248 (28 July 1832), 488–9; 249 (4 Aug. 1832), 502–4; 250 (11 Aug. 1832), 522–4; 251 (18 Aug. 1832), 535–7; 252 (25 Aug. 1832), 554–5.

the notorious expulsion from Oxford after the publication of *The Necessity of Atheism* nor the death of Harriet Shelley was entirely glossed over, Medwin's stress throughout is on Shelley's desire to 'promote liberty' and his belief in the ultimate 'perfectibility of the human race'. Medwin also commented on the beauty of Shelley's poetry, and the lines singled out as 'among the sublimest in any language' were these:

> Life—like a dome of many-coloured glass—
> Stains the white radiance of Eternity,
> Until Death tramples it into fragments.

These lines appeared in the essay published on 11 August, just a week after Mangan had published 'The Dying Enthusiast to his Friend' in *The Comet*. It is tempting, therefore, to imagine the young poet reading Medwin's piece and seizing on the sublime lines as a suitable epigraph for his own poem.

If biographical information is to be taken into account, Mangan's severe depression in the summer of 1832 might well have meant that the lines singled out by Medwin struck a special chord, for, as his biographer John McCall records, 'even at that early period, from his unsettled habits and mysterious mode of concealing himself for whole weeks at a time, his life appears to have become a burthen to him'.[31] However, it is also possible that as a poet, struggling to escape the drudgery of his early working life, Mangan admired the literary qualities of Shelley's lines rather than merely responding to their content. It is likely that Medwin's portrayal of the young poet, committed to his principles despite personal misfortune, would have appealed to the troubled figure who emerges from the various accounts of Mangan's early life, but so would the representation of Shelley's intellectual pursuits. Shelley's interest in German literature, for example, and especially the notion that Gottfried Bürger's 'Leonora' was 'the wild ballad' that had inspired him to become a poet, would have fascinated Mangan, whose own translation of 'Leonora' dates from 1834.[32] Shelley had been similarly

---

[31] *The Life of James Clarence Mangan*, by John McCall, ed. Thomas Wall, facsimile edn. (Blackrock, 1975), 19. See also Ellen Shannon-Mangan's account of the genesis of 'The Dying Enthusiast to his Friend', *James Clarence Mangan*, 111, which draws on D. J. O'Donoghue's *The Life and Writings of James Clarence Mangan* (Dublin, 1897), 32–4.

[32] Medwin, 'Memoir of Shelley', *Athenaeum*, 247 (21 July 1832) 472; *Poems 1818–1837*, 88–95.

excited by the legend of the Wandering Jew, a figure who also preoccupied Mangan, influencing his strange story, 'Extraordinary Adventures in the Shades', of 1833, and a later poem, 'The Wandering Jew'.[33] Goethe's *Faust*, too, which Shelley had tackled in 1822, inspired Mangan's 'Faust and Other Minor poems of Goethe' for his *Anthologia Germanica* series in the *Dublin University Magazine*, though, in the case of *Faust*, both poets were indebted to the work of the Irish professor of law, John Anster.[34] Even more appealing, perhaps, would have been Shelley's interest in the poetry and philosophy of the East, given Mangan's own extensive work on Oriental literature.[35]

Whether Mangan identified consciously with Shelley, or merely warmed to the idea of the brilliant young writer whose interests were so similar to his own, is difficult to ascertain, but parallels between the two poets have been drawn by others. James Joyce, for example, saw Mangan achieving 'the changing harmonies of Shelley's verse', while Charles Gavan Duffy regarded him as having been 'as truly born to sing deathless songs as Keats or Shelley'.[36] In his later critical writings, Mangan would quote Shelley with the relaxed tone that comes through deep familiarity. Although his early acquaintance with Shelley can only be guessed at, it is clear that his use of *Adonais*

[33] 'Extraordinary Adventures in the Shades', *The Comet*, 20 and 27 Jan. 1833, 'The Wandering Jew', 1837, *Poems 1818–1837*, 377–80. Shelley's 'The Wandering Jew' was published in parts in the *Edinburgh Literary Journal*, 33 (27 June 1829), 43–5; 34 (4 July 1829), 56–60; 59 (26 Dec. 1829), 425–6; and in a different form in *Fraser's Magazine for Town and Country*, III/17 (June 1831), 529–36; 18 (July 1831), 666–77. See *Poems of Shelley*, 41.

[34] Shelley was inspired to translate *Faust* partly by the article by John Anster and J. G. Lockhart, 'The Faustus of Goethe', *Blackwood's Edinburgh Magazine*, VII (1820), 235–8; his unfinished translation was included in *Posthumous Poems*, 1824. Mangan's 'Faust and Other Minor Poems of Goethe' appeared in the *Dublin University Magazine*, VII (1836), 278–302; he also wrote in praise of Anster in *The Irishman* in 1849, as discussed by Michael Cronin, *Translating Ireland*, 122–3. I am grateful to Tim Webb for drawing my attention to the significance of Anster in this context.

[35] Mangan's substantial series of articles, *Literae Orientales*, were published in the *Dublin University Magazine* X (1837), 274–92; XI (1838), 291–312; XII (1838), 328–46; XV (1840), 377–94; XXIII (1844), 535–50; XXVII (1846), 43–57.

[36] James Joyce, 'James Clarence Mangan', *St Stephen's* (May 1902), 117, cited in Ellen Shannon-Mangan, *James Clarence Mangan*, 324; Charles Gavan Duffy, *Young Ireland: A Fragment of Irish History, 1840–1850* (London, 1880), 297. In *Four Years of History*, too, Duffy's discussion of the Shelley controversy in Dublin leads directly to recollections of Mangan (104–6), while his preface to *The Ballad Poetry of Ireland* (Dublin, 1845) includes reference to both Shelley and Mangan.

as an epigraph for 'The Dying Enthusiast' was by no means a serendipitous choice, but part of a much larger interest, which may also explain the congruity between the epigraph and a poem composed independently.

The first readers of Mangan's 'The Dying Enthusiast to his Friend', who read the poem without its epigraph, are likely to have been influenced to some extent by the general political thrust of *The Comet*, which had been founded as an anti-tithe paper in 1831. Those familiar with the paper's trick of using biblical quotations to satirize the contemporary Church might well have seen in the opening line of Mangan's poem a reference not to Shelley but to Deuteronomy 3: 26 ('speak no more unto me of this matter'), where Moses is refused fulfilment of his ambition to reach the Promised Land.[37] Since it appeared surrounded by articles on political issues, Mangan's poem may well have struck its original readers less as a personal expression of despair than as a poem charged with political meaning. Even when it reappeared in the *Dublin Penny Journal*, which was less committed to commentary on the tithe issue, Parliamentary debates, or Repeal of the Union, Mangan's poem was placed immediately after an article on 'Machinery' which warned against the dangers of rapid mechanization: 'as Ireland is yet comparatively *guiltless* of machinery, let it be introduced cautiously and deliberately, lest in breaking up the soil for her future improvement, we hastily and wantonly plough through the hopes, the prospects, and the interests of her working classes'.[38] The *Dublin Penny Journal* may generally have avoided direct political comment, but its target audience—'the poorer classes of society'—also suggests an inherent radicalism. Even the attribution of the added epigraph to Shelley is likely to have encouraged readers to look not merely for a straightforward personal expression in Mangan's poem but also for a political dimension, because of Shelley's own political activities in Ireland.

For Mangan's presentation of human life as a perplexing experience of gradual disillusionment and deepening gloom is

---

[37] *The Comet* ran a series of 'Ecclesiastical Melodies' based on Byron's popular *Hebrew Melodies*, through which biblical texts were liberally scattered—see Ch. 1, above.

[38] 'Machinery', *Dublin Penny Journal*, I (25 June 1833), 223.

not hard to translate into a political arena. The frustration of the idealist faced with the dawning recognition of the world as it is, rather than as it should be, has always been a powerful force behind radical movements, but seems to have been especially widespread in late eighteenth- and early nineteenth-century Europe. The 'Enthusiast's' solution to his disenchantment with the world, too, greeting death with fortitude 'Henceforth hail!') is an expression of a kind of heroism not dependent on social status or public renown. The imagery of the closing stanza is brimming with radical possibility as Death is rescued from its associations with the 'dungeon-walled' physicality of stanza two, to become 'Prison-bursting'.

The violent escape from prison brings a palace within the grasp of the enthusiast who, until now, has had to 'grovel . . . in cell or hovel'. Although obviously metaphorical, the choice of language leads easily to a radical interpretation, especially in the context of an overtly political newspaper such as *The Comet*. The publication of 'The Dying Enthusiast' in the *Dublin Penny Journal*, which regularly featured biographical articles on national figures, might also have encouraged the assumption that the poem was intended to evoke the voice of a political enthusiast rather than a melancholy poet. Memories of the 1790s had inevitably been stirred during the year of Reform, so it would not be difficult to read into Mangan's poem an expression of the kind of feeling once characterized as 'enthusiasm defying punishment'. This is the phrase, first used by the Under-Secretary at Dublin Castle in 1795, which the modern historian of Ireland, Roy Foster, has adopted for the title of his chapter on the radical movements of the 1790s.[39] Although Foster distinguishes carefully between 'middle class radicalism and Defender "enthusiasm" ', those for whom the risings were more immediate tended to be less precise and absolute in their terminology. The thirty years which elapsed between the deaths of the leaders of the United Irishmen and the renewed agitation for Reform did much to enhance their memories, and to fix them in many minds as models of heroic enthusiasm.

[39] Roy Foster, *Modern Ireland, 1600–1972* (Harmondsworth, 1988), 273. On the more widespread associations between 'enthusiasm' and radical movements, see Jon Mee's 'Anxieties of Enthusiasm: Coleridge, Prophecy, and Popular Politics in the 1790s', *Huntington Library Quarterly*, 60/1, 2 (1998), 179–203.

Thomas Moore's portrait of Lord Edward Fitzgerald, for example, which was published in 1831, depicts a man of high ideals, driven to action by his republican sympathies and anger at the repressive policies of the Pitt government. The emphasis throughout is on his natural nobility, his strong attachment to family and friends, his unmatched courage and the frank, guileless character that left him ultimately defenceless against the deceit and treachery that brought his downfall. Although Moore did not know Fitzgerald personally, the biography gave him an opportunity to vent his own feelings about the movement, and those whose lives had been wrecked in its cause:

Though then but a youth in college, and so many years have since gone by, the impression of horror and indignation which the acts of the government of that day left upon my mind is, I confess, at this moment, far too freshly alive to allow me the due calmness of a historian in speaking of them. Not only had I myself, from early childhood, taken a passionate interest in that struggle which, however darkly it ended, began under the bright auspices of Grattan, but among those young men whom, after my entrance into college, I looked up to with the most admiration and regard, the same enthusiasm of national feeling prevailed. Some of them, too, at the time of terror and torture I am now speaking of, were found to have implicated themselves far more deeply in the popular league against power than I could ever have suspected; and these I was now doomed to see, in their several ways, victims,—victims of that very ardour of patriotism which had been one of the sources of my affection for them, and in which, through almost every step but the last, my sympathies had gone along with them.[40]

The 'victim' whose fate Moore probably regretted most was Robert Emmet. *The Life of Fitzgerald* includes a passionate memorial to Moore's close friend, whom he describes as a 'martyr', driven to forfeit his life by his unquenchable 'enthusiasm for Irish freedom'.[41] Emmet is openly described as a 'friend', and in a footnote expanding on the description of the 'dying entreaty' made by Emmet at his trial, Moore acknowledges the speech as the inspiration for his own popular Irish melody, 'Oh breathe not his name'.[42]

---

[40] Thomas Moore, *The Life and Death of Lord Edward Fitzgerald*, 2 vols. (London, 1831), i. 300–1. Moore describes his one glimpse of Fitzgerald in 1797, i. 306.   [41] Ibid. 304.

[42] Ibid. 303. On the political dimensions of the *Irish Melodies*, see Thuente, *The Harp Re-strung*, 117–92.

As an image of the enthusiast, whose dying speech has been transformed into a lyric poem by his close friend, Moore's account of Emmet makes an intriguing parallel for Mangan's poem, and one which might well have occurred to readers who came to *The Comet* or *Dublin Penny Journal* fresh from the *Life of Fitzgerald*. Indeed, the language of Mangan's poem might almost seem to evoke the *Irish Melodies*, since the poem immediately preceding 'Oh breathe not his name' in Moore's collection takes as its central image the rainbow:

> Erin! The tear and the smile in thine eyes,
> Blend like the rainbow that hangs in thy skies!
>   Shining through sorrow's stream,
>   Sadd'ning through pleasure's beam,
>   Thy suns, with doubtful gleam,
>   Weep while they rise![43]

The next verse, however, transforms the rainbow into a biblical 'arch of peace', and thus introduces an implicit faith in the future, despite the sorrow caused by Emmet's untimely death:

> Erin! thy silent tear shall never cease,
> Erin! thy languid smile ne'er shall encrease,
>   Till, like the rainbow's light,
>   Thy various tints unite,
>   And form, in heaven's sight
>   One arch of peace!

Although the possibility of peace still seems far in the future, and dependent on social and political change, the very use of the biblical image recalls God's covenant with mankind and related ideas of a new world. The religious imagery also prepares the reader for the Christian ideal of self-sacrifice which is skilfully deployed in 'When he who adores thee', a poem supposedly spoken by Emmet:

> Oh! blest are the lovers and friends who shall live
>   The days of thy glory to see;
> But the next dearest blessing that heaven can give
>   Is the pride of thus dying for thee![44]

---

[43] Thomas Moore, *Irish Melodies, and a Melalogue upon National Music* (Dublin, 1820), 6.

[44] 'When he who adores thee', ibid. 9.

If Mangan's poem catches some of this enthusiasm for death in its final lines, however, his image of the rainbow in the first stanza seems not to suggest smiles and tears so much as a false illusion. Where Moore deployed his image to suggest hope in adversity, Mangan's rainbow seems unable to withstand the forces of care, pain, Time, and, most depressingly, Truth. His Dying Enthusiast may have been indebted to images of Emmet, or, indeed, any of the other republican leaders, but Mangan's perception of their feelings prior to death is very different from that presented by Thomas Moore.

In his stimulating study of Mangan, David Lloyd has considered the image of Robert Emmet not in relation to any particular poem by Mangan, but rather as part of his more general discussion of Irish cultural nationalism:

Robert Emmet's famous appeal for the suspension of his epitaph until his country 'takes her place among the nations of the earth' stands as the classic statement of the Romantic Irish nationalist insofar as the question of the individual's true meaning is bound up with the nation's assumption of its own identity and both are cast in the future tense. It is exactly in becoming—in the strictly Coleridgean sense of the term—a symbol, which 'while it enunciates the whole, abides as itself as a living part of the Unity, of which it is the representative', that the martyr is transformed simultaneously into a 'confessor': by his absolute identity with the fullness of meaning that the spiritual nation embodies he invokes the realization of that identity by the members of a nation that is yet to be.[45]

He goes on to argue that, as a result, the martyr figure becomes crucial to narratives of nationalism. The martyr's significance is not as an individual, but as a symbolic embodiment of the spirit of the emerging nation:

Through his association in the continual labour of creating the nation to which he is bound and called, the nationalist transcends the potentially divisive effects of his presence as an individual subject and re-enters the continuous stream which . . . provides Romantic thought with the analogy by which it can produce a method that is unifying in

---

[45] David Lloyd, *Nationalism and Minor Literature: James Clarence Mangan and the Emergence of Irish Cultural Nationalism* (Berkeley and Los Angeles, 1987), 71. The quotation from Coleridge is from the *Statesman's Manual*, 30. For the complicated afterlife of Emmet's speech, see the editorial commentary in Seamus Deane (ed.) *The Field Day Anthology of Irish Writing*, 3 vols. (Derry, 1991), i. 933–5.

effect at all its stages . . . .The figure of the martyr, his identity totally immersed in the spirit of the nation, forms the ideal paradigm of the individual's relation to the nation.[46]

According to Lloyd, however, this kind of nationalist thought, which he sees in relation to the Romantic aesthetics developed by Schiller and Coleridge, cannot accommodate James Clarence Mangan. Despite the attempts of biographers to absorb Mangan into Irish cultural nationalism, Lloyd argues persuasively that Mangan's work remains resistant to its unifying tendencies: 'most generally, this entails his rejection of any metaphysics of the identification of the individual with the whole that, presented as a solution to the individual's dread of mortality, in fact imposes on the individual the ethical injunction of dying into the whole'.[47]

The contrast between Mangan's 'The Dying Enthusiast to his Friend' and Moore's tribute to Emmet is quite telling in this respect. Moore represents Emmet embracing death willingly ('the next dearest blessing that Heaven can give | Is the pride of thus dying for thee'), apparently unwavering in his belief that one day, however distant, the true significance of his death will be recognized: 'When my country takes her place among the nations of the earth, *then, and not till then*, let my epitaph be written. I have done.'[48] Mangan's Enthusiast, on the other hand, is more equivocal altogether. His desire to abandon life seems to stem from a growing conviction that it offers nothing but misery, and that even the brightest ideals are doomed to rapid dissolution. Indeed, the force of the poem comes largely from the vacillation of stanza two, when the speaker pauses to consider the physical consequences of death:

> Nought of lovely—nothing glorious
>   Lives to triumph o'er decay;
> Desolation reigns victorious—
>   Mind is dungeon-walled by clay.
> Could I bear to feel mine own laid low?
>   Oh! no—no!

[46] Lloyd, *Nationalism*, 71–2.
[47] Ibid. 189.
[48] Moore, *Life of Fitzgerald*, i. 303. But see also Norman Vance, 'Text and Tradition: Robert Emmet's Speech from the Dock', *Studies*, lxxi (Summer 1982), 185–91.

This hesitation is answered by the pessimistic perception that witnessing the disappearance of 'Genius, Love, and Worth' is even less attractive, and therefore death is to be welcomed as the preferable alternative. The speaker seems to swing from one extreme of despair to another, before propelling himself towards death. There is little sense here that future years will bring consolation, nor that subsequent generations will look back on this death and applaud. Unlike the forward-looking nationalist ideology described by David Lloyd, the Dying Enthusiast's image of time is hardly that of a 'continuous stream', in which the individual is happily submerged:

> As the flood of Time
>   Sluggishly doth flow,
> Look how all of beaming and sublime
>   Sinks into the black abysm below!
> Yea, the loftiest intellect
> Earliest on the strand of death is wrecked.

Far from being immersed in the whole, the speaker in Mangan's poem is 'wrecked' on the shore, while the central flood continues on its destructive path. What appears to fortify him in the final stanza is not a nationalist faith in the spirit of the nation, but a rather more individual sense of personal salvation:

> Prison-bursting Death!
>   Welcome, then, thy blow!
> Thine is but the forfeit of my breath,
>   Not the Spirit—not the Spirit's glow!

While this does not preclude a reading of the poem which assumes the speaker to be a political figure, it suggests that the focus is on the feelings of the individual rather than on his significance in relation to the nation. Others might well read Mangan's speaker into a nationalist narrative, but the poem itself seems to insist on the difficulties posed by death and time to the individual consciousness.

In Mangan's writing of this period, 'enthusiasm' does not exclude politics, but it appears to refer to a quality that may also inspire other forms of action and characterize a variety of human beings.[49] His poem on the subject, published in the

---

[49] On the complicated connotations of the word 'enthusiasm' in the period, see Susie Tucker, *Enthusiasm: A Study in Semantic Change* (Cambridge, 1972).

Dublin Penny Journal a few months after 'The Dying Enthusiast', includes an explicit invocation to the mysterious power of 'Enthusiasm':

> Sacred flame—which art eternal
>   O, bright Essence!
>   Thou, Enthusiasm!—forsake me not.
> Oh! though life be reft of all her vernal
>   Beauty, ever let thy magic presence
>   Shed its glory round my clouded lot.[50]

Here, too, a political speaker could be envisaged, especially in lines 17–19:

> Shall I, dare I, shame the bright example
>   Beaming, burning in the deeds and struggles
>   Of the consecrated few of old?

There is no real sense, however, that this enthusiasm is fired by a particular political cause, nor that the speaker's enthusiasm is a collective energy, or an embodiment of the spirit of the nation. Mangan's contemplation of the subject seems very different from Moore's apparently straightforward and specific recollection of the 'enthusiasm of national feeling' that had prevailed among his fellow students at Trinity College Dublin in the 1790s.

In the fragmentary autobiography Mangan left unfinished at his death, he actually defined 'enthusiasm' in a curious footnote attacking Voltaire:

Strange that a man of such an analytical mind as the philosopher of Ferney should not have perceived that Fanaticism, so called, is but another name for Enthusiasm: the spirit that has always governed, and to eternity will govern the Universe. Its proper name is Activity. It

> '—makes the madmen who have made men mad
>   By their contagion,—conquerors and Kings,
>   Founders of sects and systems'*   *Byron.

But with the vast amount of Evil which it has unquestionably generated is intermingled a still vaster amount of Good,—and if 'a little leaven leaveneth the whole lump', what may we anticipate from an abundance of it?[51]

---

[50] 'Enthusiasm', *Poems 1818–1837*, 73–4. First published in the *Dublin Penny Journal*, II (13 July 1833), 10.

[51] 'The Autobiography of James Clarence Mangan', Royal Irish Academy

Enthusiasm, for Mangan, appears to have meant a kind of energy and will to action which, though dangerous when misdirected, was essential to combat the more oppressive aspects of existence. In his earlier poem 'Enthusiasm', the second stanza concludes, 'But, cold world! I will not die thy slave!', which recalls the end of Shelley's poetic exploration of idealistic and cynical attitudes embodied in 'Julian and Maddalo', with its tantalizing 'she told me how | All happened—but the cold world shall not know'.[52] If the speaker of 'Enthusiasm' is implicitly aligned with the idealistic, Shelleyan figure of Julian, however, the lines quoted in the 'Autobiography' are from the third canto of Byron's *Childe Harold*. It is the very passage where Byron describes the strange power that distinguishes not only 'Conquerors, Kings, Founders of Sects and Systems' but also 'Sophists, Bards, Statesmen, all unquiet things':

> There is a fire
> And motion of the soul which will not dwell
> In its own narrow being, but aspire
> Beyond the fitting medium of desire;
> And, but once kindled, quenchless evermore,
> Preys upon high adventure, nor can tire
> Of aught but rest; a fever at the core,
> Fatal to him who bears, to all who ever bore.
>
> 43
> This makes the madmen who have made men mad
> By their contagion; Conquerors and Kings,
> Founders of sects and systems, to whom add
> Sophists, Bards, Statesmen, all unquiet things
> Which stir too strongly the soul's secret springs,
> And are themselves the fools to those they fool;
> Envied, yet how unenviable! What stings

Library, MS 12/P/18, 74–5. The footnote is substantial and, by its position in the little notebook, actually stands as the last words of the unfinished memoir. The text has been published as *The Autobiography of James Clarence Mangan*, ed. James Kilroy (Dublin, 1968), but all further references are to the manuscript source.

[52] 'Julian and Maddalo', 616–17. First published in *Posthumous Poems*, 1824. The two protagonists are generally seen to represent Shelley and Byron. All references to poems not included in *Poems of Shelley*, Vol. I: *1804–1817*, are from *Shelley: The Poetical Works*, ed. Thomas Hutchinson, rev. edn. G. M. Matthews (Oxford, 1970).

> Are theirs! One breast laid open were a school
> Which would unteach mankind the lust to shine or rule.[53]

The destructive and isolating effects of the 'fire' which Mangan names 'enthusiasm' are then passionately articulated by Childe Harold:

> Their breath is agitation, and their life
> A storm whereon they ride, to sink at last,
> And yet so nurs'd and bigotted to strife,
> That should their days, surviving perils past,
> Melt to calm twilight, they feel overcast
> With sorrow and supineness, and so die;
> Even as a flame unfed, which runs to waste
> With its own flickering, or a sword laid by
> Which eats into itself and rusts ingloriously.   (III. 388–96)

Despite Byron's eloquent expression of the miseries that afflict great men, the self-referential qualities of the passage point to consolatory satisfactions none the less. For underlying the complaint is a Romantic conception of genius—a fascination with the exceptional individual destined for greatness by his extraordinary ability:

> He who ascends to mountain-tops, shall find
> The loftiest peaks most wrapt in clouds and snow;
> He who surpasses or subdues mankind,
> Must look down on the hate of those below.   (III. 399–400)

Despite the imagery of fevers and fatal illness, those afflicted with enthusiasm also have a power denied more ordinary men and women: an energy that is predatory and adventurous, and infinitely more attractive than the dull peace of normal existence. Whatever the sufferings endured by the enthusiast, his condition is clearly preferable to that of the undistinguished mass of 'those below'.

A similar sense of the importance of imaginative action, even when apparently misplaced or deceptive in its effects, emerges in Mangan's first essay on Oriental poetry, published in the *Dublin University Magazine* in 1837. His account of the human Mind, 'restless, rebellious—a vagrant . . . a Cain that can build

---

[53] Lord Byron, *Childe Harold's Pilgrimage*, III. 371–87, *The Complete Poetical Works*, ed. Jerome J. McGann, Vol. II (Oxford, 1980), 91–2.

cities, but can abide in none of them',[54] is strongly Byronic, and, once again, developed through explicit reference to *Childe Harold*. As he describes the mind's capacity to convince its possessor of the reality of its own creations, Mangan observes:

We do confess that the Mind, with all its indifferentism, looks rather Eastward than Northward; do acknowledge, are proud to acknowledge, that, whatever the human sympathies that it has, they are with the East, or with its conceptions of the East, that shadowy species of affinity which the Mind in its complacent moods delights to assume as subsisting between the Orient and its own images of Genii-land possesses rich and irresistible charms for human contemplation. Imagination feels averse to surrender the paramount jewel in the diadem of its prerogatives—a faith, to wit, in the practicability of at some time or other realising the Unreal. If the East is already accessible, so may be at last—the reverse also who dares prophesy?—'the unreached paradise of our despair'; and so long as the Wonderful Lamp, the dazzler of our boyhood, can be dreamed of as still lying perdu in some corner of the land of Wonders, so long must we continue captives to the hope that a lovelier light than any now diffused over the dusky pathway of our existence will yet be borne to us across the blue Mediterranean.

Once again, Mangan is quoting *Childe Harold*, evoking a passage in which Byron had also pondered the misleading tendencies of the youthful imagination:

Of its own beauty is the mind diseased,
And fevers into false creation:—where,
Where are the forms the sculptor's soul hath seized?
In him alone. Can Nature show so fair?
Where are the charms and virtues which we dare
Conceive in boyhood and pursue as men,
The unreach'd Paradise of our despair,
Which o'er-informs the pencil and the pen,
And overpowers the page where it would bloom again? (IV. 1090–8)

This is the very passage singled out more recently by Michael O'Neill as the best example of the inseparability of the 'fake' and the 'genuine' in *Childe Harold's Pilgrimage*, and the way in which Byron uses 'self-consciousness about "creation"' to undermine the poem's idealism.[55] Mangan, who was influenced

[54] 'Literae Orientales', *Dublin University Magazine*, X (1837), 274.
[55] Michael O'Neill, *Romanticism and the Self-Conscious Poem* (Oxford, 1997), 104.

by German conceptions of the mind as well as by Byron's self-consciousness, continues his essay with an acknowledgement of the falseness of early hopes and imaginings: 'Alas! wanting that which we have not, cannot have, never shall have, we mould that which we already have into an ill-defined counterfeit of that which we want; and then, casting a veil over it, we contemplate the creature of our own fancy.'[56] Even in the face of this pessimistic observation, however, Mangan refuses to dismiss the imagination entirely as an agent of deceit. Instead, he answers his own recognition of the mind's self-delusions with an assertion of the crucial psychological role of the imagination: 'it is on the whole fortunate that Speculation can fall back on such slender resources. Slender and shifting though they seem, they serve as barriers against Insanity.' Whatever the ironies of his defence, Mangan is clearly rebutting Byron's vocabulary of mental 'disease' and 'madness', and arguing that illusions are vital to the 'healthier volition and energy of the spirit'.

The vacillations of Mangan's essay on Oriental poetry are reminiscent of the Dying Enthusiast, whose recognition that the hopes of youth were merely 'bright illusions' is nevertheless combated by a renewal of enthusiastic fervour, albeit directed towards death. In the poem, 'care and pain' may build a 'lampless dwelling', effectively extinguishing any hope of discovering the 'Wonderful Lamp, the dazzler of our boyhood', but by the final stanza the speaker still chooses to strive for the 'bright lot'. In answer to the problem of being misled by false hopes, it seems that the Enthusiast comes at last to recognize that spiritual light ('the Spirit's glow') cannot be put out.[57]

Byron's perceptions of the mind's capacity to make what it desires, only to discover that the image is merely fantasy, seem to have found some degree of support in Mangan. And yet his work also demonstrates an opposing tendency to resist the pessimism, and embrace what might still 'be borne . . . across the blue Mediterranean'. Just as he had evoked Shelley in his own poem on 'Enthusiasm', here it is Shelley rather than Byron who seems to underline the appeal of optimism. The echo from

[56] 'Literae Orientales', 275. David Lloyd has examined the influence of the image of the statue of Sais, as developed by Novalis and Schiller, in relation to this passage, *Nationalism and Minor Literature*, 125.

[57] Cf. Mangan's 'Enthusiasm', 3, where enthusiasm is described as the 'spirit's flickering lamp'.

Shelley's stirring 'Ode to the West Wind' ('Thou who didst waken from his summer dreams | The blue Mediterranean', 29–30) directs the reader to an altogether less gloomy response to the possibility of creative failure, which ends with the celebratory 'Be thou, Spirit fierce, | My spirit'.[58] In 'The Dying Enthusiast to his Friend', too, Mangan acknowledges the misleading tendencies of the imaginative mind, but nevertheless looks in the end to the possibility of spiritual redemption. Although Mangan's work frequently demonstrates an irony that seems closer to Byron than Shelley, it also displays a fascination with the idealism embodied in much of Shelley's work. As he observed in the note to his 'Autobiography', enthusiasm may have generated a 'vast amount of evil', but with it was 'intermingled a still vaster amount of Good'. And no one was more outspoken about the positive aspects of enthusiasm than Shelley, even if, in his darker moments, he recognized its potential to deceive.

In his emphasis on the broader implications of enthusiasm Mangan, despite his obvious doubts, seems even closer to Shelley than to Byron—a point that becomes obvious if we return to the image of 'the flood of time' in 'The Dying Enthusiast'. For while the notion of time flowing on like water is a Romantic commonplace, Mangan's phrase is virtually a quotation from Shelley. Since Mangan's substitution of the word 'flood' for 'stream' is one of the few changes he made to the poem when he submitted it to the *Dublin Penny Journal*, it is hard to believe that the similarity can be accidental, even if the reference is to a much earlier poem than *Adonais*. It is almost as if, having chosen his epigraph, Mangan wished to underline further debts to Shelley, and even to suggest the possibility of conscious allusion within his poem.

Shelley's original poem 'To Harriet', which contains the image of the 'flood of time', was not published until 1886, but the lines had originally been included among the extensive notes to *Queen Mab*. The relevance of Shelley's poem to Mangan's lyric is striking:

[58] Shelley, 'Ode to the West Wind', 29–30, 61–2. First published with *Prometheus Unbound* in 1820.

> Dark flood of time!
> Roll as it listeth thee—I measure not
> By months or moments thy ambiguous course.
> Another may stand by me on the brink
> And watch the bubble whirled beyond his ken
> That passes at my feet. The sense of love,
> The thirst for action, and the impassioned thought
> Prolong my being: if I wake no more,
> My life more actual living will contain
> Than some grey veteran's of the world's cold school,
> Whose listless hours unprofitably roll,
> By one enthusiast feeling unredeemed.[59]

Shelley's celebration of the young 'enthusiast' suggests an unqualified optimism about the possessor of 'the sense of love, the thirst for action, the impassioned thought' and thus contrasts sharply with the gloomy observations of Childe Harold. It also makes an interesting comparison with Mangan's treatment of the enthusiast contemplating death. For in both Shelley's note and 'The Dying Enthusiast' the 'flood of time' is dark and threatening, but the speaker finds a way of defying the gathering gloom and, at the same time, overcoming the fear of death. Shelley's response to the dilemma is spelled out even more clearly in the prose note which he appended to the passage above:

the life of a man of virtue and talent, who should die in his thirtieth year, is, with regard to his own feelings, longer than that of a miserable priest-ridden slave, who dreams out a century of dulness. The one has perpetually cultivated his mental faculties, has rendered himself master of his thoughts, can abstract and generalize amid the lethargy of every day business;—the other can slumber over the brightest moments of his being, and is unable to remember the happiest hour of his life. Perhaps the perishing ephemeron enjoys a longer life than the tortoise.[60]

Life, according to Shelley, should not be measured by conventional years and dates, but rather by the intensity of experience, and degree of mental development. The young enthusiast who dies before he reaches thirty may thus enjoy a longer life than the unenquiring centenarian. Like Childe Harold, the poet of *Queen Mab* is associating enthusiasm with

[59] *Poems of Shelley*, 406.   [60] Ibid.

early death, but his tone is one of jubilant defiance rather than disdainful dismay.

Although the echo of Shelley's poem and the similarity of subject matter might lead to the assumption that Mangan was merely imitating an established master, important distinctions should still be made between 'The Dying Enthusiast' and the note on *Queen Mab*. For apart from the obvious difference of form, the responses to the dilemma posed by death are quite dissimilar. While Shelley argues that time is a relative concept, created by the individual in response to mental experience, Mangan's Enthusiast appears to assume a more traditional notion of time as an all-powerful external force capable of wrecking the 'lovely', the 'glorious', and the 'loftiest'. Far from finding his being prolonged by the 'sense of love', Mangan's speaker pictures love as a 'lonely phantom', its initial power withering as it flowers. And yet, despite this pessimistic portrayal of the ideals that Shelley's poem upholds as life-giving, Mangan's closing stanza still looks forward to a state in which time's power will be rendered meaningless. It is a completely different way of answering the fear acknowledged in the 'flood of time' image, and demonstrates that Mangan's fascination with Shelley was by no means that of the passive admirer. Instead, the engagement with the question explored in *Queen Mab*, and the profoundly different solution that is offered, points to an independence of mind and a capacity to debate and disagree. This is not a master–subject relationship, but suggests rather an imaginary dialogue between literary friends.

It is also, of course, a dialogue between a living poet and one whose creative life was over (even though new pieces continued to appear throughout the nineteenth century as editors and biographers recovered the scattered remains from the manuscripts). Writing in 1832, Mangan could turn not only to the notes on *Queen Mab*, but also to the much later contemplation of early death in *Adonais*, his own poem thus being able to reflect different moments of Shelley's poetic career. Indeed, 'The Dying Enthusiast' is full of fleeting echoes of different poems, to which the reader has been alerted by the presence of the epigraph. Just as 'Adonais' itself is soaked in reminiscences of Keats's poetry so 'The Dying Enthusiast', published ten years after Shelley's death, evokes Shelley in many of its individual words and phrases. 'Lampless', for example, one of Mangan's more distinctive adjectives, is also found in a number of Shelley's poems, but occurs rarely in the work of other writers.[61] The poem's other adjectives, 'beaming', 'sublime', 'lovely', 'lonely', 'bright', though far less unusual, are nevertheless common in Shelley's poetry. The general use of abstract nouns in a short lyric is also characteristic, as are the particular examples: 'Desolation', 'Love', 'Time', 'Truth', 'Beauty', 'Genius'.

It is of course unwise to point to specific allusions on the basis of any one of these far from uncommon words, but their use nevertheless contributes to a sense of continuity between the epigraph and the poem. Images are equally hard to attach to a particular source, especially since Shelley reused his favourites in different contexts. The rainbow, for example, which occurs in many of his poems, conveys a wistful sense of transience in 'A Hymn to Intellectual Beauty':

> Ask why the sunlight not for ever
> Weaves rainbows o'er yon mountain river
> Why aught should fail and fade that once is shewn.[62]

Before isolating this as a source for Mangan's 'bright illusion | Rainbowed on the soul of youth', however, it is worth recalling that in 'The Cloud' Shelley described his rainbow as a 'triumphal arch', which, though perhaps also encompassing a sense of passing time, is a rather more solid construction. This instance may seem remote from the mood of 'The Dying Enthusiast', but the closing lines of 'The Cloud' contain a further set of images that may echo in the background of Mangan's poem:

> Like a child from the womb, like a ghost from the tomb,
>   I arise, and unbuild it again.[63]

The bouncing rhyme of 'womb' and 'tomb' is different in tone from the Dying Enthusiast's gloomy perception of 'Fond affections, deep as ocean | In their cradle find their tomb', but the similarity of the images clustered in the last stanza of Shelley's

---

[61] The Chadwyck-Healey English Poetry database records 12 uses of 'lampless' in Mangan's work, and 9 in Shelley's.

[62] 'A Hymn to Intellectual Beauty', 18–20. First published in full in *Posthumous Poems*, 1824.

[63] 'The Cloud', 84–5. First published with *Prometheus Unbound*, 1820.

poem may indicate that Mangan was remembering 'The Cloud' ironically, rather than merely poaching Shelley's images:

> The triumphal arch, through which I march
>   With hurricane, fire, and snow,
> When the Powers of the Air, are chained to my chair,
>   Is the million-coloured Bow;
> The sphere-fire above its soft colours wove
>   While the moist Earth was laughing below,
> I am the daughter of Earth and Water,
>   And the nursling of the Sky;
> I pass through the pores, of the ocean and shores;
>   I change, but I cannot die—
> For after the rain, when with never a stain
>   The pavilion of Heaven is bare,
> And the winds and sunbeams, with their convex gleams,
>   Build up the blue dome of Air—
> I silently laugh at my own cenotaph,
>   And out of the caverns of rain,
> Like a child from the womb, like a ghost from the tomb,
>   I arise, and unbuild it again.   (67–84)

By echoing Shelley's favourite images, Mangan effectively draws attention to Shelley's practice of reusing metaphors and similes in different contexts for radically different purposes. In this stanza, for example, the image of the dome is associated with the sky and with death, just as it is in *Adonais*, but the response of the Cloud is to 'laugh' at its 'cenotaph'; rather than suggesting a glassy structure vulnerable to being trampled, this dome seems a more fluid image, that can apparently be built or unbuilt at will. Mangan's attraction to the mobility of Shelley's imagery, which tends in itself towards the rather insubstantial— water, rainbows, clouds, light—may also reflect his resistance to the symbolizing ideals of Coleridge. For where Coleridge sought to affirm the vital connections between an individual object and the larger whole, Shelley's poetic practice suggests a perpetual deflection from one image to another, and an approach to meaning that avoids the consistent and symbolic. To echo a line from Shelley is thus fraught with complications, because of Shelley's own habit of recycling material into new forms, with only precarious recollection of the earlier context.

At the same time, however, since similar images occur else- where in Shelley's work, it is also possible that 'The Cloud' has no significant influence on Mangan's poem. The juxtaposition of the cradle and tomb images, for example, occurs in 'When the Lamp is shattered', which may provide a more straight-forward source image for 'The Dying Enthusiast':

> O Love! who bewailest
> The frailty of all things here
> Why choose you the frailest
> For your cradle, your home and your bier?[64]

But again, the location of a specific source is problematic, for the idea that love 'withers in its bloom' is as typical of Shelley as it is of Mangan. In 'Marenghi', for example, Shelley makes the point explicitly: 'Love and freedom blossom but to wither.'[65] It is perhaps in *Adonais*, however, when he turned his attention to the early death of John Keats, that Shelley explored the problems of transience, untimely destruction, and the para-doxical identity of birth and death most eloquently and influen-tially:

> Go thou to Rome,—at once the Paradise,
> The grave, the city, and the wilderness;
> And where its wrecks like shattered mountains rise,
> And flowering weeds, and fragrant copses dress
> The bones of Desolation's nakedness.[66]

Even here, however, the cluster of associated images is not per-forming in exactly the same way as in the earlier poems. This is not the traditional *carpe diem* motif of 'Marenghi', for these flowers are not withering in themselves, but rather growing from the wreckage of human life. In the context of *Adonais*, this recalls the striking self-portrait of Shelley that occurs several stanzas earlier:

> A pardlike Spirit beautiful and swift—
> A Love in desolation masked;—a Power
> Girt round with weakness;—it can scarce uplift
> The weight of the superincumbent hour;
> It is a dying lamp, a falling shower,

---

[64] 'When the Lamp is Shattered', 21–4. First published in *Posthumous Poems*, 1824.

[65] 'Marenghi', 48. Stanzas 7–15, which include this line, were first published in *Posthumous Poems*, 1824.

[66] *Adonais. An Elegy on the Death of John Keats*, 433–6. First published in 1821.

A breaking billow;—even whilst we speak
Is it not broken? On the withering flower
The killing sun smiles brightly: on a cheek
The life can burn in blood, even while the heart may break.   (279–88)

Shelley's striking antitheses, the yoking of 'Love' with 'Desolation', 'Power' with 'weakness', 'lamp' with 'dying', 'flower' with 'withering', form a telling background to Mangan's poem and its acknowledgement that enthusiasm is doomed by its very nature, especially when exposed to the material processes of time. For a reader such as Mangan, contemplating this stanza ten years after its original publication, the imagery of dying, falling, and withering must have acquired additional force, even if the emphatic recognition of physical fragility made the creative power of Shelley, the 'pardlike Spirit', seem even greater. For the images of Rome, which perhaps find an echo in Mangan's 'amphitheatre of strife', were all the more poignant for readers who knew that not only John Keats and little William Shelley were buried there, but also Shelley himself.

Although the language of the stanza describing Shelley among the parade of mourners has a beauty that seems to counter the pessimism of the sentiment, there are subsequent passages in *Adonais* in which mortality is confronted more directly. Mangan, who was to paint the Dying Enthusiast contemplating the human mind 'dungeon-walled by clay', is likely to have been struck by Shelley's uncompromising emphasis on physical decomposition:

> *We* decay,
> Like corpses in a charnel; fear and grief
> Convulse us and consume us day by day,
> And cold hopes swarm like worms within our living clay.   (348–51)

What is particularly significant, in relation to Mangan's poem, is that these lines develop directly from a somewhat Byronic acknowledgement of the human capacity to be misled by visions:

> 'Tis we, who lost in stormy visions, keep
> With phantoms an unprofitable strife,
> And in mad trance, strike with our spirit's knife
> Invulnerable nothings.   (345–8)

Although the subject matter is similar to that discussed by Mangan in his essay on Oriental poetry and the language has much in common with that of 'The Dying Enthusiast', the point being made in *Adonais* is rather different. For while Shelley seems to suggest here that life itself is largely illusory, Mangan's essay on Oriental poetry moves on from the Byronic exposure of illusions to defend the visionary, ironically through the evocation of Shelley's own 'Ode to the West Wind'. The Dying Enthusiast, too, moves on from his meditation on clay to lament the loss of Genius, Love, and Worth: the 'phantoms' haunting him disturb through their bodiless absence, not through their misleading presence. And here again it is possible to see Mangan playing with Shelley's own favourite, but not symbolic, words. For while the 'phantoms' of line 346 in *Adonais* are dismissed as 'invulnerable nothings', misleading human beings during their 'dream of life', the same term has been used earlier to refer to the image of Shelley himself, who is not only a 'pardlike Spirit', but also a 'frail Form, | A phantom among men; companionless | As the last cloud of an expiring storm' (271–3). Mangan's image of 'Genius, Love, and Worth' moving 'like lonely phantoms' can be seen as an echo of *Adonais*, but not as a straightforward imitation of Shelley's usage. Instead, by evoking the companionless 'phantom among men', Mangan is able to pay his own tribute to Shelley, whose memory has in fact been magnified by his shocking death. Through the loss of the young elegist, the words of *Adonais* have taken on additional levels of meaning, enabling Mangan to challenge the poem even as he appears to submerge himself in its beauty. Shelley might represent the living striking out at 'phantoms', but Mangan laments the loss of 'Genius, Love, and Worth' and, in the process, emphasizes that these 'lonely phantoms' represent true spiritual values in the face of universal desolation. It is almost as if Mangan's poem, by choosing words which reveal Shelley's own equivocations, attempts to redeem the poet of *Adonais* from his moments of despair.

If Shelley's emphasis on the illusory nature of life is, as some critics have argued, part of a Platonic view of the world as a 'shadow of a transcendent and eternal reality', the stanza describing the human beings 'lost in stormy visions' paves the way to the subsequent repudiation of the individual body, and the consolatory assertions of Adonais's escape from 'the contagion of the world's slow stain' (356) and translation to the abode of the Eternal. Whether this involves a material reintegration into the atomic structures of the natural world, a spiritual reunion with the One Spirit, or a metaphorical rebirth through the immortal quality of his poetry is open to debate, but the elegiac movement from lament, 'He will awake no more, oh, never more!' (190), to consolation, 'He lives, he wakes—'tis Death is dead, not he' (361), leads to the conclusion that in some ways, death is a state superior to life.[67] While this anticipates the general movement of Mangan's poem, however, there is a profound contrast between the closing lines of *Adonais*, in which the speaker is 'borne darkly, fearfully, afar', and those of 'The Dying Enthusiast', who has decided at last to embrace 'the bright lot'.

In *Adonais*, the speaker is an elegist, coming to terms with the early death of a young poet, and writing in a distinguished literary tradition. Unlike his predecessors, however, whose poems tended to move towards conclusions in which the survivor looked forward to 'fresh woods and pastures new', Shelley can be seen to break with the traditions of elegy and, as Peter Sacks has argued, 'concludes on a suicidal note'.[68] In this reading, *Adonais* is offering no consolation in this life to those who have experienced loss, while its striking image of life as 'a dome of many-coloured glass' leaves little room for posthumous reconstruction. Indeed, the presence of Keats in the poem might seem to confirm this sense of utter destruction, for although Shelley echoes moments of the dead poet's works, the reminiscences seem rather fragmentary. They have, in a sense, been absorbed into the texture of the elegy, just as Adonais has been 'made one with Nature', his voice heard 'in all her music'; although this is a kind of life, it is very different in form from the original existence. Anyone unfamiliar with Keats's poetry would find little of the lost poet in *Adonais* and even those readers who do discover Keatsian images are likely to find them dissolving and being reconstituted in the new verse. Although the subsequent description of Chatterton, Sidney, and Lucan, 'whose transmitted effluence cannot die', might suggest that

[67] For different interpretations of 'Adonais', see A. D. Knerr (ed.), *Shelley's Adonais: A Critical Edition* (New York, 1984).

[68] Peter Sacks, 'Last Clouds: A Reading of "Adonais"', *Studies in Romanticism*, 23 (1984), 380–400, reprinted in Michael O'Neill (ed.), *Shelley* (London, 1993), 194.

Keats (and, by implication, Shelley too) will continue to live through his own poetry, this traditional consolation is somewhat undermined by the poem's pessimistic view of the world and the emphasis on the impersonal 'one Spirit's plastic stress' which is said to sweep 'through the dull dense world, compelling there, | All new successions to the forms they wear' (381–3). For if the 'world' is not fit to appreciate the great, their secular immortality must be rather limited, while the notion of an impersonal power dictating new creations renders individual poets mere passive agents of larger forces. It is not surprising, in the light of this, that the conclusion of the elegist is to anticipate death, 'darkly' and 'fearfully'. For although the very beauty of *Adonais* goes some way to counter its more pessimistic tendencies, the absence of traditional consolations is emphasized through the clear evocation of earlier pastoral elegies: unlike Milton's Lycidas, there is little sense that Adonais has 'mounted high | Through the dear might of him who walked the waves', nor indeed that Shelley's lost poet has become a more classical 'genius of the shore'.[69]

For Mangan, the perception of the world's shortcomings seems to have led to metaphysical (and political) conclusions of a slightly different kind from Shelley's. Just as David Lloyd has pointed to Mangan's resistance to Romantic nationalism on the grounds that it denies individuality, so it is possible to discern a similar tendency in Mangan's engagement with the English poet. Indeed, the structure of 'The Dying Enthusiast' can almost be seen as a dialogue, with Shelley's opening observation on life being firmly refuted by the speaker: 'Speak no more of life.' Mangan's image of the rainbow may seem to accord well with the dome of many-coloured glass, especially given Shelley's own use of 'many-coloured' to describe the rainbows in 'Mont Blanc', but the very preponderance of rainbows in Shelley's verse, not to mention in other poetry of the period, renders such firm associations unsafe, as we have seen. Mangan's careful revision of 'Stream' to 'Flood', however, suggests a possible reminiscence not only of Shelley, but also of the Bible. Indeed, by juxtaposing two apparently Shelleyan images—of the rain-

[69] 'Lycidas', 172–3, 183.

bow and the 'flood of time', Mangan effectively points to an earlier and much more universally acknowledged authority.

On a first reading, the biblical association may seem as ironic as the use of 'apt quotations' in other poems in *The Comet*, but in retrospect it can be seen as a sign of hope in the face of quenching suns and falling kingdoms. The rainbow may have disappeared, the loftiest intellect been wrecked by time, but in spite of this the speaker looks forward at last to 'Spheres of Beauty' which, being described explicitly as 'hallowed', seem to offer hope of everlasting life. While the speaker of *Adonais* envisages the dome of many-coloured glass being smashed, the dying Enthusiast employs the image of heavenly spheres as a solution to the power of time and death:

> Spheres of Beauty! hallowed Spheres,
> Undefaced by time, undimmed by tears,
> Henceforth hail!

The wiping away of tears has powerful biblical precedence, being an image used by Isaiah to demonstrate God's power over death, 'He will swallow up death in victory; and the Lord God will wipe away tears from off all faces', and echoed by St John, 'And God shall wipe away all tears from their eyes; and there shall be no more death.'[70] It is as if death itself has been eclipsed, the flood of time rendered insignificant, and the beautiful but insubstantial images of the dome and rainbow replaced by the complete perfection of the 'spheres'.

The troubling physicality of the human body, conveyed in Mangan's last stanza through the metonymous 'breath', is redeemed at last through the much less tangible idea of 'Spirit':

> Thine is but the forfeit of my breath,
> Not the Spirit—not the Spirit's glow!

Rather than suggesting the 'one Spirit' of *Adonais* with its all encompassing 'plastic stress', or, indeed, the 'Spirit of the Nation' into which the political enthusiast might be absorbed, this seems a more personal concept. Though individual, it also suggests traditional Christian ideas of God's creative breath, the Holy Spirit, and the 'Spirit' who welcomes the visionary in through the bright gates of the new Jerusalem.[71]

---

[70] Isa. 25: 8; Rev. 21: 4.   [71] Rev. 22: 17.

Far from embracing the ideas embodied in *Adonais*, then, Mangan adopts Shelleyan language but seems to refute elements of his philosophy. The epigraph thus stands not as a summary of the central theme of Mangan's poem, but as a challenge to be answered. And where Shelley's poem seems to point to the possible suicide of the speaker, Mangan's seems rather to lead to traditional Christian consolation in the face of a death that is unavoidable. For the short lyric entitled 'The Dying Enthusiast to his Friend' suggests the last words of a dying man, whose contemplation of death is inspired by its imminence. *Adonais*, on the other hand, is a meditation on the death of another, the speaker's gradual turn towards his own demise resulting from the very process which traditionally brings about healing. It is almost as if in his poem Mangan is giving the dying John Keats the opportunity to answer his friend's lofty but deeply pessimistic thoughts about his early death. For in addition to the Shelleyan echoes in 'The Dying Enthusiast', there are a number of reminiscences of Keats's poetry, which might indicate an interest in recovering something of the lost poet submerged in Shelley's elegy.[72] As an image of the dying Keats responding pre-emptively to *Adonais*, Mangan's poem would exhibit a similar kind of ventriloquism to that practised in many of his Oriental poems, where an original poem appears in the guise of a translation from the Persian or Turkish.

Keats, however, was no more inclined than Shelley to seek comfort from the Bible in the face of death, and so in order to shed more light on Mangan's departure from the Shelleyan model, it is perhaps more fruitful to consider his own writings and recollections of the same period. In 'The One Mystery', published in the *Dublin Penny Journal* in May 1833, for example, Mangan confronts the problem of death directly, employing language similar to that of 'The Dying Enthusiast':

> The flood of life runs dark—dark clouds
>   Make lampless night around its shore:
> The dead, where are they? In their shrouds—
>   Man knows no more![73]

[72] Compare e.g. the notion of care and pain building in the brain with Keats's 'Ode to Psyche', the meditation on the physicality of death and the role of 'thronging millions' with 'Ode to a Nightingale', or the use of distinctive words such as 'abysm' with *Endymion*, II. 379, III. 28.

[73] 'The One Mystery', 5–8, *Poems 1818–1837*, 68.

The poem reflects on the possibilities of redemption beyond the grave before concluding that such speculation is largely futile:

> And all philosophy, all faith,
>   All earthly, all celestial lore,
> Have but ONE voice, which only saith,
>   Endure,—adore!   (36–40)

While this may seem more resigned in tone than the closing lines of 'The Dying Enthusiast', it nevertheless shares the tendency, when faced with troubling uncertainties, to turn to God. It could hardly be further removed from the conclusion to *Adonais*, with its alarming acceleration towards death.

Mangan's religious convictions, like so many aspects of his life and personality, are difficult to ascertain with any confidence. Despite his attraction to Eastern philosophy and spiritualism, however, he remained a Catholic throughout his life and, according to Ellen Shannon-Mangan, 'never seems to have questioned the existence of God or the "large tenets" of his faith'.[74] In the brief autobiography composed shortly before his death, Mangan drew attention to his deep preoccupation with religious matters: 'my readers will pardon the frequent allusions to GOD and Providence which occur in the course of these Memoirs. But, as Malebranche saw all things in GOD, so I see GOD in all things. GOD is *the* idea of my mind.'[75] Scholars have long regarded the memoir as a somewhat dubious biographical source; and Seamus Deane has gone so far as to call it 'one of the most obvious Gothic fictions of the century in Ireland'.[76] Whatever the factual basis of Mangan's account, however, as a literary text it is extremely interesting. At the beginning, Mangan consciously distinguishes his aims from those of Godwin, Byron, St Augustine, Rousseau, and Lamb, but still confesses a desire to leave an autobiography 'that may not merely inform but instruct—that may be adapted to all capacities and grades of intellect—and that, while it seeks to develope for the thinking the more hidden springs of human frailty, shall also operate, simply in virtue of its statements, as a warning to the uneducated votary of Vice'.[77] As he approached death,

---

[74] Ellen Shannon-Mangan, *James Clarence Mangan*, 309.
[75] 'Autobiography', 18–19, n.
[76] Deane, *Strange Country*, 126.
[77] 'Autobiography', 9.

Mangan turned to review his life, and chose to present it in a context primarily religious. The account of his early years is inevitably coloured by the moment of composition and his conception of his text as a spiritual autobiography, but it nevertheless provides intriguing clues to the period around 1830, immediately prior to the publication of 'The Dying Enthusiast'.

One of the more striking memories is that of the year-long period when Mangan felt most distant from God:

> I derived no consolation from prayer. I felt none of that confidence in God then, which, thanks to His Almighty power and grace, I have since so frequently known. The gates of Heaven seemed barred against me: its floors and walls of brass and triple adamant, repelled my cries; and I appeared to myself to be sending a voice of agony into some interminable chasm.[78]

This 'deplorable interior state' sets the scene for the new phase of Mangan's life that begins in 1831. Exactly what constitutes the new phase is unfortunately unclear, since the memoir breaks off within a couple of pages, but that some kind of further Fall is imminent seems evident from the introductory comments:

> Years of so much mingled pleasure and sorrow! whither have you departed, or rather, why were you allotted me? You delivered me from sufferings which, at least, were of a guiltless order, and would shortly in a better world have been exchanged for joys, to give me up to others, the bitter fruits of late repentance, and which await no recompense, and know no change, save change from severe to severer. But, alas! thus it was, is, and must be. My plaint is chorussed by millions. Generation preaches to generation in vain. It is ever and everywhere the same old immemorial tale. From the days of Adam in Eden to our own we purchase Knowledge at the price of Innocence. Like Aladdin in the Enchanted subterranean Garden, we are permitted to heap together and gather up as much hard bright gold and diamonds as we will—but we are forever there entombed from the fresh natural green pastures and the healthful daylight.[79]

Even as he prepares the reader for his Fall, however, Mangan's choice of imagery indicates a simultaneous recognition of consolation or redemption. Adam may lose his innocence, but it is through his Fall that Christ comes into the world to save mankind, while Aladdin is rescued from his underground

---

[78] 'Autobiography', 61–2.   [79] Ibid. 66–8.

sojourn by the discovery of the magic lamp. Just as the rainbow in 'The Dying Enthusiast' conveys hope as well as despair, so the images recalling the period of life beginning in 1831 are balanced by the reader's familiarity with the larger narratives from which they are derived. This is not the beginning of the 'lampless' reign of 'care and pain', but a time of 'mingled pleasure and sorrow' which is itself conveyed in prose built up of carefully paired ideas. At the same time, the layering of ideas is once again resistant to fixed meaning, since the end of the narrative is left open, just as the fragments of allusion may remain unrestored to the consoling stories from which they are derived. Mangan's analogies remain at the level of passing parallel, and it is not clear whether they will develop into re-assuring wholes, or retain the intriguing mystery of unexplained sherds.

The balancing of opposites continues in the ensuing anec-dote, which unfortunately breaks off with the memoir. As Mangan reflects on the period of life beginning in 1831, he recalls a meeting with 'a fashionably dressed and intelligent looking young man', whom Ellen Shannon-Mangan has tenta-tively identified as John Sheehan.[80] When the young man dis-covers Mangan reading *Les Pensées de Pascal*, he tries to persuade him that the work is 'unhealthy' and depressing. Looking back on the incident from 1849, however, Mangan acknowledges the impact of the 'sublime truths contained in this celebrated work'; and it is in the context of the reported dia-logue with the young stranger that his note on 'enthusiasm', discussed above, occurs.[81] Mangan's account of 'the spirit that has always governed, and to eternity will govern the Universe' is appended to a description of the young man reading out 'that passage in which Pascal compares the world to a dungeon, and its inhabitants to condemned criminals, awaiting the hour that shall summon them to execution'. Just as Voltaire had regarded this as 'la pensée d'un fanatique', so it seems the fashionably dressed young man selects this as the epitome of Pascal's unhealthy view of the world. But Mangan's own defence of 'that Fanaticism, so-called', which 'is but another name for Enthusiasm', lines him up with Pascal, against the scepticism of

---

[80] 'Autobiography', 69; *James Clarence Mangan*, 105.
[81] 'Autobiography', 73–5.

Voltaire and his new friend. Given the striking passage that forms the centre of the dispute, it is thus worth considering a possible connection between Pascal's conception of the world as a 'dungeon' and Mangan's poem of the following summer, 'The Dying Enthusiast to his Friend'. For despite the unverifiable nature of much of the memoir, it seems likely that Mangan had been reading Pascal in the summer of 1831. The carefully dated anecdote has a specificity uncharacteristic of the more rhetorical passages, while the concern with 'Enthusiasm' accords with the poetry he published in the years immediately following. The emphasis on conversation in the recollection, which is paralleled by the footnoted dispute between Pascal and Voltaire, may also be related to the suggestion of dialogue in 'The Dying Enthusiast to his Friend'.

The internal dynamic of the poem, however, suggests that the Enthusiast's disputant is not a fashionably dressed young Irishman, but Shelley. Given Mangan's obvious sympathy with Pascal's outlook, the opposition to Shelley implicitly places the latter in the company of the sceptics who are critical of Pascal's 'fanaticism'. This is a view in keeping with the influential current of contemporary opinion that labelled Shelley an 'infidel', and remembered him for the materialism of *Queen Mab* and *The Necessity of Atheism* or, by September 1832, the scepticism of the 'Essay on Life' and 'Essay on a Future State'.[82] Mangan's echoes of Shelley both in 'The Dying Enthusiast' and the later essay on Oriental poetry, however, indicate an awareness of Shelley's own capacity for 'enthusiasm', which makes the opposition rather less neat and clear cut. For although the echo from the note on *Queen Mab* points to a passage in which the underlying philosophy is materialist, Shelley is arguing for the possibility of combining such a position with 'enthusiasm'. Mangan's poem, therefore, despite its differences from *Adonais*, is not presenting a straightforward debate between a Christian and an atheist, but rather exploring the more complicated relationship between enthusiasm and scepticism. Indeed, the energy that propels it towards a religious conclusion seems to be generated by the very oscillation between these opposing forces.

It is thus not surprising to learn of Mangan's interest in

[82] Both essays were published for the first time in the *Athenaeum*, 29 Sept. 1832, though the 'Essay on a Future State' only appeared complete in 1840.

Pascal, whose work was heavily influenced by the sceptical logic of Montaigne and yet still constituted a powerful defence of religious belief. The seventeenth-century French scientist had no comforting illusions about the human condition, but his image of the world as a dungeon, which struck both Voltaire and Mangan's friend as unhealthy, is to be found in the midst of reflections on the promise of salvation embodied in Jesus Christ. Taken out of context, Pascal's meditation may indeed sound intolerably gloomy:

434 Imagine a number of men in chains, all under sentence of death, some of whom are each day butchered in the sight of the others; those remaining see their own condition in that of their fellows, and looking at each other with grief and despair await their turn. This is an image of the human condition.[83]

In the *Pensées*, however, this perception of man's predicament is juxtaposed with observations on the radical strength of Christianity, and the saving power of Christ's spirit. Pascal's gloomy image of the human condition thus has much in common with the Dying Enthusiast's perception of his own situation. For while the imprisoning facts of physical existence are confronted with uncompromising clarity, such disturbing thoughts are more than countered by the emphasis on the power of Christ.

Pascal's appeal for Mangan, especially in a period of religious crisis, is easy to comprehend, for much of his work dwells on the difficulties of maintaining faith. In the *Pensées*, Pascal laments his own inability either to enjoy an unquestioning faith or to accept a resigned scepticism ('If I saw no sign . . . of a Divinity I should decide on a negative solution: if I saw signs of a Creator everywhere I should peacefully settle down in the faith. But, seeing too much to deny and not enough to affirm, I am in a pitiful state'[84]). This swinging between possibilities resembles the opening stanzas of 'The Dying Enthusiast', as they dwell alternately on the pains of life and death. It is Pascal's famous 'Wager', however, that is most interesting to consider in relation to Mangan's poem, and especially its closing stanzas. For in the section where Pascal puts forward his central

[83] Blaise Pascal, *Pensées*, transl. by A. J. Krailsheimer, rev. edn. (Harmondsworth, 1995), 137.
[84] No. 429, ibid. 135.

argument for Christianity, he adopts the language of gambling to reason with a fictional interlocutor over the existence of God. According to Pascal, all human beings are faced with the choice of whether or not to believe in God. Their passions may render belief impossible but Pascal maintains that the rational choice is faith. Since there are no more reasonable grounds for disbelief than for belief, it is obviously better to choose the possibility of eternal happiness:

Yes, but you must wager. There is no choice, you are already committed. Which will you choose then? Let us see: since a choice must be made, let us see which offers you the least interest. You have two things to lose: the true and the good; and two things to stake: your reason and your will, your knowledge and your happiness; and your nature has two things to avoid: error and wretchedness. Since you must necessarily choose, your reason is no more affronted by choosing the one rather than the other. That is one point cleared up. But your happiness? Let us weigh up the gain and the loss involved in calling heads that God exists. Let us assess the two cases: if you win, you win everything, if you lose, you lose nothing. Do not hesitate then; wager that he does exist.[85]

Faced with a similar dilemma, Mangan's Enthusiast, who is dying either through some cause unknown to the reader or, in Pascal's view, simply by virtue of being alive and human, resolves at last to choose infinite gain. According to Pascal's reasoning, it is folly to choose unbelief and so, too, the Dying Enthusiast comes to see that he dare not forego 'the bright lot'.

The presence of Pascal in the background of the poem helps to illuminate the curious language of the closing stanzas. For while the term 'bright lot' may suggest a group of heavenly beings reminiscent, perhaps, of 'the Eternals' in *Adonais*, or of a more orthodox band of departed spirits, it might also suggest an illustrious destiny, a 'lot' in the sense of something that is allotted to the individual. In either case the speaker's decision not to forgo it seems wise. The latter sense of 'lot', however, is the more interesting, since it is derived from the ancient process of arriving at decisions through the casting of lots, which in turn recalls Pascal's cool recognition of the human condition: 'Yes,

---

[85] No. 418, ibid. 123. See also Lucien Goldmann, 'The Wager: The Christian Religion', in Harold Bloom (ed.), *Blaise Pascal* (New York and Philadelphia, 1989), 53–80.

but you must wager.' The origin of the word 'lot', as R. and G. Brenner have explained in their study, *Gambling and Speculation*, is found in the Teutonic *hleut*—the pebble cast to decide disputes—but they go on to emphasize the religious tradition of casting lots to reveal the will of God:

Perusal of the Bible reveals that drawing lots was regularly used to discover God's will in decisions on a number of issues, ranging from the election of a king (I Sam. 10: 20–1) to that of cult functionaries (I Chron. 24–6), to the selection of the 'scapegoat' for the atonement ritual (Lev. 16: 8–10), to the identification of a party guilty of some sacrilege (Josh. 7: 10–26), and to the selection of a date for some future action (Esther 3: 7; 9: 24).[86]

Man's 'lot' was traditionally seen to be determined by the will of God, while the practice of casting lots did not acquire associations of gambling and chance until the late seventeenth century. Although Mangan, like Pascal, was fully aware of more sceptical attitudes to lot-casting, the religious associations of the word provide an interesting context for the Dying Enthusiast's decision to take the 'bright lot'.

Biblical traditions of lot-casting may also lie in the background of the previous stanza, where Mangan's speaker ponders the experience of observing the disappearance of 'Love': 'Shall I linger but to count each throe?' The primary meaning of 'throe' is the violent pang accompanying birth or death, which leads to the subsequent identification of the cradle and tomb. When linked to the idea of counting, however, the word 'throe' might also conjure up thoughts of playing dice—of counting each *throw*. This in turn connects to the 'bright lot', for one interpretation of Urim and Thummin, worn by Aaron in Exodus 28, is that they were two dice, or lots cast to determine the will of God.[87] Even without the scriptural associations, the suggestion of throwing dice includes the possibility of gain even in the face of apparently unfavourable odds. And thus the poem moves towards the more optimistic conclusion in which the Enthusiast, having given up on the passions, makes the rational choice of the 'bright lot'.

[86] R. Brenner and G. Brenner, *Gambling and Speculation: A Theory, A History, and a Future of Some Human Decisions* (Cambridge, 1990), 2.
[87] Ibid.

As a response to Shelley's observations on life and death in *Adonais*, then, Mangan's poem can be seen not as an imitation, but as a challenge. Instead of accepting the suicidal tendencies of the elegy, Mangan's Enthusiast moves through the contemplation of the human existence to make the apparently rational choice of Christian consolation. In adopting the epigraph from Shelley, he is not after all selecting a beautifully phrased summary of his own theme, but rather taking issue with its more pessimistic sentiments.

There may even be a further dimension to Mangan's dialogue with Shelley, in that his use of Shelleyan language and careful selection from *Adonais* might contribute to the larger critical effort to recover the poet from the damaging associations of infidelity. Several contemporary readers had detected an underlying orthodoxy in Shelley's mature poetry ('whatever was positive in his mind, is an essential part of Christianity; in all in which he had faith, a Christian must have faith'[88]) and so it seems quite possible that Mangan too shared this desire to restore Shelley to the Christian fold. Such an attitude would be entirely consistent with that expressed in a poem he wrote in 1835:

> Come, Byron, thou, and wile new magic from its tone!
> For God created Genius for the Truth alone:
> Why must the Powers of Ill monopolise thy praise,
> Till Heaven half envies Hell the music of thy lays?
> Look to thy God![89]

Mangan's admiration for Byron's powers as a poet seems to have been mingled with dismay at the sceptical tendencies of his verse, so his response to Shelley may have been similarly complicated, especially since this was the very dilemma voiced by so many of Shelley's most sympathetic readers.

Whatever the attraction of Shelley's political ideals, his concern for the condition of Ireland, or his skills as a lyric poet, the unacceptable nature of his religious opinions remained a stumbling block. But it is characteristic of Mangan, who would later create idiosyncratic representations of Oriental verse, and produce somewhat creative 'translations' of Gaelic poetry, that his response to the problems posed by Shelley was to absorb

[88] 'Adonais', *Athenaeum*, 97 (1829), 544.
[89] 'Man: Addressed to Lord Byron', 255–9, *Poems 1818–1837*, 197.

them into a poem in which the ultimate thrust is Christian and idealist. Mangan's later praise of John Anster's work is reveal-ing in this context: 'Dr Anster has not merely translated *Faust*: he has done much more—he has translated Goethe—or rather he has translated that part of the mind of Goethe which was unknown to Goethe himself . . . he has actually made of Goethe the man whom his German worshippers claim him to be.'[90] Similarly, perhaps, though in an act of inverted translation, Mangan retains Shelley's language, but transforms the contents for his own poem. Shelley's own diction is redeployed to create an image of a Shelleyan poem, but in this very adaptation, un-appealing philosophical views are overwhelmed by an alterna-tive perspective.

To many present-day readers, Mangan's response to Shelley may seem profoundly conservative in that he appears to be recasting Shelley into a form suitable to more orthodox tastes—much as the 1830 collection of the *Beauties of Shelley* reprinted *Queen Mab* 'free from all objectionable passages'. Since these more orthodox tastes were probably shared by the majority of Irish Catholic readers, however, the definition of 'conservative' becomes problematic. For if Daniel O'Connell, the great Liberator, was appalled by his friend Denis MacCarthy's interest in Shelley, 'the author of Queen Mab', then it is clear that Shelley's particular brand of radicalism was not entirely welcome to the Catholics of Ireland. Just as Shelley had attracted both applause and hisses when he spoke at Fishamble Street in 1812, so his work continued to provoke a mixed response from Irish readers after his death.

Mangan's attempt to use Shelleyan material for his own poetry, while challenging the associated religious opinions, can be seen as an early form of the 'antithesis of plagiarism' sub-sequently developed in his translation work.[91] As Terry Eagleton has commented, this practice involves 'writing a work modelled on an existing one and declaring the latter to be filched from the former, thus reducing the source text to deriva-tive status'.[92] Although Eagleton's discussion focuses on the politics of translation, Mangan's later treatment of Gaelic texts

[90] *The Irishman* (1849), cited by Cronin, *Translating Ireland*, 123.

[91] Lloyd, *Nationalism and Minor Literature*, 103.

[92] Terry Eagleton, *Crazy John and the Bishop and Other Essays on Irish Culture* (Cork, 1998), 187.

makes an interesting comparison with his earlier handling of Shelley. For while *Adonais* has clearly not been 'filched' from 'The Dying Enthusiast', Mangan's use of Shelleyan echoes, in a poem that follows the very Christian traditions that Shelley himself had reacted against, suggests a similar desire to reach a state anterior to that of the source poem. (The notion of a dying man in dialogue with his elegist indicates a similar interest in playing with the interdependence of past and present.) According to Eagleton, such strategies are 'subversive' rather than conservative, because they offer a means through which Irish writers can deny their imposed secondary status and claim an antiquity superior to that of the colonial power. If applied to the dynamic of 'The Dying Enthusiast', it could be argued that Mangan avoids seeming dependent on Shelley despite his obvious indebtedness, because the thrust of his poem is towards the older traditions that Shelley himself fought to shed. It might also explain Mangan's decision to highlight a literary influence that had been less apparent on first publication.

Whether Mangan himself would have viewed his relationship with Shelley in terms of a colonial power struggle is, however, open to doubt. For what emerges explicitly from his poem, as from his broken memoir, is the idea of dialogue between friends. And there is surely a stronger sense of affection and admiration in Mangan's references to Shelley than of resentment or unwilling subjugation. It must after all have been difficult to see the rebellious Shelley as representative of 'Britain', or, indeed, of 'English Literature', when both these concepts were still in the making, and Shelley had done his best to avoid being an ingredient of either. Shelley's wilful rejection of his country and inheritance in favour of intellectual exile in Italy may strike modern readers as a sign of his privileged background and education but, in the 1830s, when his widow was still struggling to support herself and their surviving child, Shelley's actions appeared rather differently. So while it may be tempting to regard Mangan's treatment of Shelley as subversive and anti-colonial, it is perhaps more accurate to see their relationship as a unique engagement between two very untypical writers.

Mangan's alienation is attested not only in his own memoir, but in the recollections of almost all his friends and acquaintances, including Charles Gavan Duffy:

The man most essentially a poet among the writers of the *Nation* was Clarence Mangan. He was as truly born to sing deathless songs as Keats or Shelley; but he lived and died in a provincialised city and his voice was drowned for a time in the roar of popular clamour. He was so purely a poet that he shrank from all other exercise of his intellect. He cared nothing for political projects. He could never be induced to attend the weekly suppers and knew many of his fellow labourers only by name. He lived a secluded unwholesome life, and when he emerged into daylight he was dressed in a blue cloak, midsummer or midwinter, and a hat of a fantastic shape, under which golden hair as fine and silky as a woman's hung in unkempt tangles, and deep blue eyes lighted a face colourless as parchment. He looked like the spectre of some German romance, rather than a living creature.[93]

Although the account is retrospective, and informed by the knowledge of Mangan's early death, it is clear that Duffy at least saw Mangan not as a typical Irishman, but as a Romantic poet. It is thus perhaps as risky for modern readers to seize on Mangan as a representative Irish Catholic as it is to regard Shelley as a straightforward member of the English canon. Both writers were, in their very individual ways, strongly influenced by their own cultural situations, making Mangan's interest in Shelley an interesting example of cross-cultural exchange. To see it as a paradigm for early nineteenth-century British–Irish relationships, however, would be misleading and inappropriate.

'The Dying Enthusiast to his Friend' is a minor poem by a writer who apparently resisted absorption into the cultural mainstream, while *Adonais* is a major work by a writer long since deemed one of the principal figures of the Romantic period. As Mangan's poetry continues to appear in scholarly editions, his status as a 'minor poet' is nevetherless becoming open to question. At the same time, the critical onslaught on the canons of Romanticism has begun to change decisively the ways in which those traditionally regarded as the 'major poets' of the period are being read. It will be interesting to see, in time, whether the relationship between the 'Dying Enthusiast' and *Adonais* appears radically altered, and whether Mangan's literary standing will be seen to have fulfilled Samuel Ferguson's optimistic forecast for Irish literature, moving from a position as 'emulator' to 'equal', or 'even superior'. Or perhaps his work

---

[93] Duffy, *Young Ireland*, 297.

will move more stealthily into the cultural mainstream, coming to rest at a position closer to the original equality of the two young and far from established poets.

5

The Homes of England

The Homes of England

> Where's the coward that would not dare
> To fight for such a land?
>
> *Marmion*

The stately Homes of England,
  How beautiful they stand!
Amidst their tall ancestral trees,
  O'er all the pleasant land.
The deer across their greensward bound
  Thro' shade and sunny gleam,
And the swan glides past them with the sound
  Of some rejoicing stream.

The merry Homes of England!
  Around their hearths by night,
What gladsome looks of household love
  Meet in the ruddy light!
There woman's voice flows forth in song,
  Or childhood's tale is told,
Or lips move tunefully along
  Some glorious page of old.

The blessed Homes of England!
  How softly on their bowers
Is laid the holy quietness
  That breathes from Sabbath-hours!
Solemn, yet sweet, the church-bell's chime
  Floats through their woods at morn;
All other sounds in that still time,
  Of breeze and leaf are born.

The Cottage Homes of England!
  By thousands on her plains,
They are smiling o'er the silvery brooks,
  And round the hamlet-fanes.

Thro' glowing orchards forth they peep,
    Each from its nook of leaves,
And fearless there the lowly sleep,
    As the bird beneath their eaves.

The free, fair Homes of England!
    Long, long, in hut and hall,
May hearts of native proof be rear'd
    To guard each hallow'd wall!
And green for ever be the groves,
    And bright the flowery sod,
Where first the child's glad spirit loves
    Its country and its God!

                       Felicia Hemans[1]

The Stately Homes of England

Verse 1

Lord Elderley, Lord Borrowmere,
Lord Sickert and Lord Camp
With every virtue, every grace
Are what avails the sceptr'd race.
Here you see—the four of us,
And there are so many more of us,
Eldest sons that must succeed.
We know how Caesar conquered Gaul
And how to whack a cricket ball;
Apart from this, our education
Lacks co-ordination.
Tho' we're young and tentative
And rather rip-representative,
Scions of a noble breed,
We are the products of those homes serene and stately
Which only lately
Seem to have run to seed!

Refrain 1

The Stately Homes of England
How beautiful they stand,
To prove the upper classes
Have still the upper hand;
Tho' the fact that they have to be rebuilt

---

[1] Felicia Hemans, *Records of Woman, with Other Poems*, 2nd edn. (Edinburgh, 1828), 169–71.

And frequently mortgaged to the hilt
Is inclined to take the gilt
Off the gingerbread,
And certainly damps the fun
Of the eldest son—
But still we won't be beaten,
We'll scrimp and screw and save,
The playing fields of Eton
Have made us frightfully brave—
And tho' if the Van Dycks have to go
And we pawn the Bechstein Grand,
We'll stand by the Stately Homes of England.

Verse 2

Here you see
The pick of us
You may be heartily sick of us
Still with sense
We're all imbued.
Our homes command extensive views,
And with the assistance from the Jews
We have been able to dispose of
Rows and rows and rows of
Gainsboroughs and Lawrences,
Some sporting prints of Aunt Florence's,
Some of which were rather rude.
Although we sometimes flaunt our family conventions,
Our good intentions
Mustn't be misconstrued.

Refrain 2

The Stately Homes of England
We proudly represent,
We only keep them up for
Americans to rent.
Tho' the pipes that supply the bathroom burst,
And the lavatory makes you fear the worst,
It was used by Charles the First
Quite informally,
And later by George the Fourth
On a journey north.
The State Apartments keep their
Historical renown,
It's wiser not to sleep there

In case they tumble down;
But still if they ever catch on fire
Which, with any luck, they might,
We'll fight for the Stately Homes of England.

Refrain 3

The Stately Homes of England,
Tho' rather in the lurch,
Provide a lot of chances
For Psychical Research—
There's the ghost of a crazy younger son
Who murdered, in Thirteen Fifty-One,
An extremely rowdy Nun
Who resented it,
And people who come to call
Meet her in the hall.
The baby in the guest wing,
Who crouches by the grate,
Was walled up in the west wing
In Fourteen Twenty-Eight.
If anyone spots
The Queen of Scots
In a hand-embroidered shroud,
We're proud
Of the Stately Homes of England.

Verse 3

Lord Elderley—Lord Borrowmere,
Lord Sickert and Lord Camp
Behold us in our hours of ease
Uncertain, coy and hard to please.
Reading in Debrett of us
This fine Patrician quartette of us
We can feel extremely proud
Our ancient lineage we trace
Back to the cradle of the Race
Before those beastly Roman bow-men
Bitched our local Yeomen.
Tho' the new democracy
May pain the old Aristocracy
We've not winced nor cried aloud
Under the bludgeonings of chance what will be—will be.
Our heads will still be
Bloody but quite unbowed!

The Stately Homes of England
In valley, dale and glen
Produce a race of charming,
Innocuous young men.
Tho' our mental equipment may be slight
And we barely distinguish left from right,
We are quite prepared to fight—for our principles,
Tho' none of us know so far
What they really are.
Our duty to the nation
It's only fair to state,
Lies not in pro-creation
But what we pro-create;
And so we can cry
With kindling eye
As to married life we go,
What ho! for the Stately Homes of England!

The Stately Homes of England
Altho' a trifle bleak,
Historically speaking,
Are more or less unique.
We've a cousin who won the Golden Fleece
And a very peculiar fowling-piece
Which was sent to Cromwell's niece,
Who detested it,
And rapidly sent it back
With a dirty crack.
A note we have from Chaucer
Contains a bawdy joke.
We also have a saucer—that Bloody Mary broke.
We've two pairs of tights—that King Arthur's Knights
Had completely worn away
Sing Hey! for the Stately Homes of England.

Noel Coward[2]

When Noel Coward published his handsome *Song Book* in
1953, he reflected on the success of his various productions, and
on the growth of his musical talent. The introduction is charac-
teristically concise; and yet, in its brisk assessments of popular
music in the first half of the twentieth century, it manages to
convey a sense of massive dislocations, and of longstanding

---

[2] Noel Coward, *Operette* (London, 1938), I. vii (verse 1 to Refrain 3); II. v (verse
3 to the end), 53–6; 119–20.

traditions wrecked beyond recognition. From the opening sentence, 'I was born into a generation that still took light music seriously', to the concluding images of 'the cheaper outpourings of Tin Pan Alley . . . dinned into [the public's] ears interminably by the B.B.C.', the sense of the larger change beyond the personal detail is only too apparent.[3] The modest assertions of the essay are infused neither with outrage, sentiment, nor nostalgia, however, and strike the reader more with an air of detached observation. Coward presents himself as part of the generation who witnessed the virtual annihilation of English culture during the First World War and were afterwards simply 'too tired' to do much about it.[4] But despite this unpromising context, the songs which follow are remarkably jaunty, and so the volume as a whole suggests the same determination to entertain in the face of utter exhaustion that also characterizes Coward's record of his troop concerts in the Second World War.[5]

Among the few pieces mentioned individually in the introduction to the *Song Book* is 'The Stately Homes of England', which he singles out as one of the redeeming features of the 'sadly meagre' musical, *Operette*. The song was a 'showstopper' at its first performance in 1938, but went on to reach a wider audience through becoming a record and part of Coward's concert repertoire. It rapidly became one of his best-known songs, apparently 'popular with everyone with the exception of a Mayoress in New Zealand who said that it let down the British Empire'.[6] Though rather different in character from the poems so far discussed, the very success of 'The Stately Homes of England' makes it an interesting subject for this book. As with the poems in the preceding chapters, its title and the opening line of the refrain are drawn from an earlier text (which also begins with an epigraph from an existing poem), but the relationship between the works is very different. While *King Lear*, 'Sir Patrick Spens', and *Adonais* have all maintained an independent life quite apart from the poems to which they

---

[3] *The Noel Coward Song Book* (London, 1953), 9, 16.

[4] Ibid. 11.

[5] Coward's daily diary covering July to October 1943 was published as *Middle East Diary* (London and Toronto, 1944).

[6] *Noel Coward Song Book*, 76. On the failure of *Operette* as a whole, however, see Clive Fisher, *Noel Coward* (London, 1992), 129.

unwittingly contributed, Felicia Hemans's 'The Homes of England' seems destined to remain under the shadow of a subsequent work. The twentieth-century audiences who have laughed their way through 'The Stately Homes of England' may well have been aware that its title, like that of his earlier hit 'A Room with a View', was 'unblushingly pinched';[7] but the fame of the later song has largely eclipsed that of its poetic predecessor. Anyone who has heard Coward's catchy lyric must find it difficult to run through Hemans's 'The Homes of England' without being mentally accompanied by the memorable tune and an equally striking image of the composer, or perhaps a 'fine Patrician quartette'. In making so much of Hemans's opening line, it seems, Coward effectively made it his own, consigning the rest of the poem to an oblivion so complete that even those who have recently attempted to revisit her poem in its original context cannot entirely escape its twentieth-century descendant.[8] For although new editions of Hemans's work may enable readers to encounter the poem on its own terms, it still seems likely that on hearing a rendition of Coward's song, the original would instantly undergo a radical transformation in their minds. This has not been true of the other textual encounters explored so far. There may well be readers who discover 'Sir Patrick Spens' in the wake of 'Dejection', but it is most unlikely that their reading of the ballad would be effectively destroyed by familiarity with Coleridge's poem: on the contrary, the ballad has a power of its own, as Coleridge was acutely aware, and his own Ode is in part a homage to the earlier, simpler text. Readings of *Adonais*, too, are only likely to be enhanced by James Clarence Mangan's 'Dying Enthusiast', while *King Lear* remains sublimely indifferent to Burns's response.

Why, then, should Noel Coward's lighthearted encounter with Mrs Hemans have proved so devastating? Various possible reasons might be floated to account for this difference, such as

---

[7] 'A Room with a View', of 1928, was composed in Honolulu: 'the title, unblushingly pinched from E. M. Forster's novel, came into my mind together with a musical phrase to fit it and I splashed up and down in the shallows, searching for shells and rhymes at the same time', *Noel Coward Song Book*, 21.

[8] See e.g. Jerome J. McGann, writing in three persons as Anne Mack, J. J. Rome, and Georg Mannejc, 'Literary History, Romanticism, and Felicia Hemans', *MLQ*, 54/2 (1993), 215–35, n. 20.

the perennial power of musical rhythm in the human memory, which renders the unsung 'Homes of England' instantly less indelible than the catchy 'Stately Homes'. If Bakhtin's theories of literary forms and historic processes were to be brought to bear on the question, it would be possible to point to the effects of the 'parodic-travestying word' on more direct, straight-forward kinds of discourse, and suggest that Felicia Hemans's verse has a monolithic quality, incapable of representing the contradictions of 'reality'; Coward's mischievous lyric could then be seen as her poem's 'parodying and travestying double', which instantly became more influential than its elevated model.[9] To apply Bakhtin's observations, however, is to take them out of the context of his discussion of late antiquity and, while interesting parallels may be drawn, there are crucial differences between the forms and culture of early nineteenth-century England and those of classical Rome. Indeed, if more emphasis were to be placed on the cultural environments that produced the two texts, the shift from Hemans's stately homes to those of Noel Coward could be seen as symptomatic of the movement from Victorian to Modern—from a period in which high seriousness inspired admiration, to one in which embarrassment and irony are perhaps more likely responses.[10] Such explanations, however, are hardly adequate, since they imply not only a rather generalized view of the two periods, but also the inevitable eclipse of any nineteenth-century poem by a later parody, a conclusion hardly borne out by the evi-dence.

It is also rather doubtful whether Coward's 'The Stately Homes of England' is really a parody, in any case. There may be parodic elements in his lyric, but the nature of his response does not entirely correspond with the standard analyses of parody. For despite certain difficulties of definition, most critics seem to agree that a literary parody is largely aimed at an earlier text. The purpose of the encounter may vary—parody having been defended as a means of exposing absurdity, falseness, narrow-ness, or pomposity, and more recently as a vital means to

---

[9] M. M. Bakhtin, *The Dialogic Imagination*, ed. Michael Holquist, trans. by Caryl Emerson and Michael Holquist (Austin, Tex., 1981), 53.

[10] For a stimulating discussion of parody in the twentieth century, see Linda Hutcheon, *A Theory of Parody: The Teachings of Twentieth-Century Art Forms* (New York and London, 1985).

'refunction' weary literary genres—but whatever the motivation behind the parodic text, there seems little doubt about the existence of a 'target text' which has given rise to the new work, and which is generally made risible in the process.[11]

The amusement of twentieth-century audiences who have listened to 'The Stately Homes of England', however, is probably unconnected with any specific ridicule of Mrs Hemans. Even those familiar with her poem, which was after all very popular in the nineteenth century, are more likely to respond to the intrinsic humour of Coward's lyrics than to any perceived contrast with the earlier text. There may have been an initial laugh deriving from the incongruity of the music and the thwarted expectation following the familiar opening lines, but the concentration required by the unfolding lyrics would quickly dispatch the original poem from the stage. In the context of the original musical especially, the presence of Lord Elderley, Lord Borrowmere, Lord Sickert, and Lord Camp would direct the audience's attention to the subject of their song rather than to the text from which it had grown, while the jokes they so eloquently sing against themselves are far more obvious than the literary dimensions of their act. The reference to Hemans is also complicated by the discovery that her poem is not the only one to be evoked, and the entire lyric is filled with fleeting echoes of familiar verses. Coward's lyric can hardly seem a parody of a specific text, when it is saturated with quotations from a diverse selection of authors. Indeed, Hemans's poem might almost seem irrelevant to Coward's, since he apparently took only the bits he wanted and left the rest. As the term 'stately homes of England' had long since acquired a life independent of Hemans's original coinage, it might almost seem possible that Coward was merely adopting a familiar phrase for his musical.

The reference to 'The Stately Homes of England' is extraordinarily loud and clear, however, while the inclusion of the qualifying 'How beautiful they stand!' underlines the presence of Felicia Hemans. Even if Coward's primary purpose was to entertain, and secondarily to make witty comment on the English upper classes in the twentieth century, he was neverthe-

[11] On refunctioning, and other uses of parody, see Margaret Rose, *Parody, Ancient, Modern, and Post-Modern* (Cambridge, 1993), 5–53.

less reliant on Hemans's un-ironic verse for the structure of his own. She provides the framework for his comedy—a phrase sufficiently powerful to open her own poem and also to allow him inside, to work within the grand façade and reveal to a twentieth-century audience the cracks that had now begun to show. And this is perhaps the real reason for the eventual dominance of Coward's lyric—not because it represents a satiric attack on the earlier poem, but because it is a logical successor. In a pair of poems concerned with inheritance, the twentieth-century piece fulfils the role of a natural heir, fully conscious of both the past it perpetuates and the increasing incongruities between its own traditions and the world into which they must be borne. It is, in a sense, an eldest son which must succeed—but one acutely conscious that the two meanings of 'succeed' are no longer necessarily compatible.

For the relationship between Hemans's poem and Coward's is difficult to disentangle, not just because of the borrowed phrasing, but because both grow from the same cultural legacy that had been so badly fractured by the First World War. Felicia Hemans's image of a stable community symbolized by its ideal homes belongs to the very Victorian schoolrooms that produced such upright young men as Lords Elderley, Borrowmere, Sickert, and Camp. When it was published in *Records of Woman* in 1828, the patriotic sentiments had been qualified by its position as part of a series of verses representing different countries— 'The Bride of the Greek Isle', 'The Peasant Girl of the Rhone', 'The Queen of Prussia's Tomb', 'The Sicilian Captive'. In such company, the 'woman's voice' of 'The Homes of England' is more obvious, while the feelings that radiate from the domestic hearth to warm the entire land seem only the local counterpart of those being expressed by different women all over the world.

While England's song is only one among many, there seems nothing particularly competitive or xenophobic about it, especially in the wake of verses such as that of 'The Switzer's Wife', who displays her 'free Alpine Spirit' with a rousing call to her despondent husband: 'And man must arm, and woman call on God!' It was, however, 'The Homes of England' even more than 'The Switzer's Wife' or any of the other passionate pieces that was to find a life beyond *Records of Woman*, being reprinted and quoted in numerous Victorian contexts and thus shedding its earlier restraining companion pieces.[12] Once removed from its position in the original volume, 'The Homes of England' seemed designed to foster the unquestioning patriotism that would eventually send the country's young men to their deaths in Flanders, as readily as they had defended the honour of the home team on the playing fields of Eton. From his retrospective vantage point in 1938, with the prospect of another massive war looming, Noel Coward would have been fully alert to the historical ironies of his patrician quartette's confidence. *Operette* is set in 1906, and so a 1930s audience would have seen only too clearly the discrepancy between the four Lords' assumptions about their future and the actual course of history. With this in mind, the jingling jingoism of 'The Homes of England' takes on a distinctly chilling tone.

The poignant shadows cast by historical knowledge, however, seem to have little place in the song itself, which hardly seems conceived for the purpose of inspiring pity or indignation. It is much too full of bone-headed self-confidence, and much too funny. If there is a sense in which Felicia Hemans is being taken to task for the same kind of 'facile patriotism' Coward deplored among certain American politicians,[13] the criticism is submerged under a kind of humour that seems to stem more from affection than animosity. Indeed, her poem seems to be just one more treasure in the massive inheritance of the English aristocrats, almost a part of their birthright and certainly so familiar as to seem woven into the very texture of their existence. 'The Homes of England', whether taken as the descriptive title of the poem, or as a direct reference to country houses, or as a free-standing phrase, represents a set of values apparently rooted in the English landscape.

Hemans's poem presents an image of social and physical harmony, where there is a place for everyone, and everyone is happy in their place. The very organization of her verse reflects the unquestioned supremacy of the aristocracy, who appear first in the list and at the top of the page, while the train of adjectives, 'stately', 'beautiful', 'tall', 'ancestral', 'pleasant',

---

[12] On the popularity of 'The Switzer's Wife', see Tricia Lootens, 'Hemans and Home: Victorianism, Feminine "Internal Enemies", and the Domestication of National Identity', *PMLA* 109 (1994), 238–53, 244.

[13] *Middle East Diary*, 25.

'rejoicing', leaves no openings for an alternative view. When the 'Cottage Homes' finally appear in the parade, they are 'smiling' from their positions of obscurity, and seem quite content to be united with the huts and halls of the final celebratory verse. It is a shining image of a green and pleasant land, which the future curators of the country might feel proud to inherit.

The emphasis on the Homes of England as places of continuity, reaching into the past and looking forward to safeguard the future, is central to Hemans's poem. The landscape she celebrates is not a wild mountainside or Romantic seashore, but cultivated parkland and well-managed orchards, where even the trees have been planted hundreds of years ago by the ancestors of the current inhabitants. Nor is this continuity exclusive to a particular class; for although her poem moves from stately homes to cottages, at the heart of her ideal community is the domestic unit. Each evening, families gather together to sing traditional songs and read from 'the glorious page of old', thus imbibing and nurturing the inseparable love of God and country which seems essential to the well-being of their own descendants. The poem is a proclamation of the native, and underlines the connection between birth and homeland at every turn. These homes are not the goal or long-lost departure point of the restless exile, but the originating idyll, where maternal love is all-powerful. If Pope had sought the regreening of the vanished Groves of Eden in the Royal domain of Windsor Forest, Hemans suggests that it should be looked for in the rural homes of England. Her Paradise is a domestic one, that links classes by revealing their similarities rather than differences, and smooths away any jarring notes by emphasizing the traditional and therefore eternal.

The past is evoked at every turn, but it is never a lost or unattainable past. The very language of the poem has the air of an old country, mixing the archaic, the simple and familiar with a reassuring sense that this is how things have always been and how they must continue to be. The 'deer', like the 'hut and hall', seem to hark right back to Anglo-Saxon society, when the English countryside—and language—were originally being settled. The 'greensward' is deliberately archaic, reaching back not only to Old English but also deepening its antique resonance through the fleeting echo of Pope's translation of Chaucer: 'The

Knights so nimbly o'er the Greensword bound.'[14] Hemans explicitly emphasizes the continuity of the generations who have lived through the centuries in these homes, using and reusing the same country houses, cottages, orchards, and churches, and thus her own language partakes of the past, delving down to the oldest remains, but at the same time absorbing the layers of association that have built up to the nineteenth century. This is not so much an attempt to mimic the style of the medieval past as an affirmation of the continuing presence of the earliest English society in the contemporary world. The fact that 'greensward' derives from Pope rather than Chaucer—from an eighteenth-century idea of Middle England rather than directly from fourteenth-century usage—is thus appropriate, since the poem is concerned to present not only a particular image of the past, but also a sense of origins and gradual development. Like the tall ancestral trees and glowing orchards of England, the language not only has deep roots, but has also been strengthened by the layers of meaning that have grown over the years. That the celebrated continuities were perhaps less continuous than the poem implies, that the image of eternal harmony is achieved only through careful selection and skilful reconstitution, and that the discrepancy between the glowing scene and the hard facts of history were to become painfully apparent in the ensuing century was as much the foundation of Coward's ironic song as the specific opening lines of Hemans's poem.

Despite the smoothness of her diction, the sugar-coating of the imagery, and the careful blending of literary echoes, however, Hemans's highly selective approach is signalled before her poem has even begun—by her epigraph. Jerome McGann has expended considerable energy and ingenuity on an argument for Hemans's work being the 'poetry of quotation, a conscious elevation of various inherited and signifying signs',[15] but this must always have been apparent to readers of 'The Homes of England', since it begins with a motto from *Marmion*. Indeed, Scott's lines stand out not only through their physical contrast with the neat stanzas that follow, but also because the rousing rhetorical question seems somewhat at odds with the

[14] Pope, 'January and May; or, the Merchant's Tale from Chaucer', 621.
[15] McGann, 'Literary History, Romanticism, and Felicia Hemans', 230.

tranquillity of the first four verses. Neither the 'stately', 'merry', 'blessed', or 'cottage' homes seem to have much to do with fighting, and it is not until the concluding lines that the martial spirit of the epigraph rings out again, suddenly transforming the preceding domestic scenes into military training centres. The homes of England are revealed at last as nurseries of stout-hearted soldiers, ready to guard their sacred hearths and therefore English liberty. The coward that dare not fight for such a land is certainly not to be found among the homes of England, it seems.

Further consideration of the epigraph, however, suggests a rather less straightforward relationship. Its stirring patriotism may appear to chime with the sentiments of the closing stanza, and thus complete the frame for Hemans's picture, but the acknowledgement that the lines come from Scott's *Marmion: A Tale of Flodden Field* raises potentially uncomfortable questions. That a Scottish writer, and particularly Sir Walter Scott, should furnish Hemans with an expression of patriotic pride is not surprising, especially in the early nineteenth century when notions of British unity were probably as strong and prevalent as they have ever been.[16] Scott's own efforts to welcome George IV to Edinburgh in 1822 are well known, as are the numerous examples of the symbolic union of Scotland and England in his novels.[17] And yet, in *Marmion*, he chose to focus on one of the most emotive moments in the history of the two countries, and approached it through a figure not only English but also characterized by a 'general rottenness'.[18]

Lord Marmion's physical courage is never in doubt, but much of the poem's narrative interest turns on the consequences of his treacherous behaviour towards Lady Clara, Constance de Beverley, and his rival, the wronged De Wilton. Byron's summary of Marmion's character,

[16] Colley, *Britons: Forging the Nation 1707–1837*; but see also Murray Pittock's alternative emphasis on ' "four nations" literary history', *Poetry and Jacobite Politics in Eighteenth-Century Britain and Ireland* (Cambridge, 1994).

[17] Pittock, *Poetry and Jacobite Politics*, 231–6; Crawford, *Devolving English Literature*, 130–2. For recent debate over whether Scott was 'centrist' or 'nationalist', see Jane Stevenson, 'Scott, Scotland and the Roman Past', *Scotlands*, 4/2 (1997), 21–40, and the reply by P. H. Scott, 'The Distortions of Unionism', *Scotlands*, 5/1 (1998), 114–22.

[18] J. H. Alexander, *Marmion: Studies in Interpretation and Composition*, Salzburg Studies in English Literature: Romantic Reassessment, 30 (Salzburg, 1981), 50.

Not quite a Felon, yet but half a Knight,
The gibbet or the field prepared to grace;
A mighty mixture of the great and base,[19]

reveals that for contemporary readers, too, Marmion was hardly the epitome of English chivalry. Scott's representation of Flodden Field is thus coloured by imaginative involvement with a nobleman who may be on the winning side but whose character no one finds admirable. His death in the battle may go some way to transform his tale into a tragedy, but the weight of the historical disaster makes the demise of Marmion himself seem less significant than it might have done, had the setting been fictional. Although Scott does not make the point explicitly, knowledge of the massive losses suffered by King James's army in 1513 seems all the more shocking when juxtaposed with the figure of Lord Marmion.

Although the Battle of Flodden does not dominate the entire narrative, the lines selected by Hemans as an epigraph for her own poem come from the latter half of *Marmion*, when military preparations are in full flow. The words are uttered by Marmion's page, Fitz-Eustace, but, significantly, it is neither the army nor the landscape of England that inspires his exclamation. The scene is rather the Blackford Hills, south of Edinburgh, where the English party and their escort, Sir David Lindesay, Lord Lion King-at-Arms, chief Herald of Scotland and well-known poet, are looking across the panoramic scene at the army of King James. The dynamics are thus curiously complicated, as the reader's experience comes partly through the eyes of Marmion, partly Fitz-Eustace, partly Lindesay, and partly the narrator. The tone of the responses differs, but there is nevertheless a common sense of deep admiration for the Scottish soldiers and their surroundings. For although Marmion characteristically displays aggression, it emerges through his profound respect for the military power he beholds:

'Oh! well, Lord-Lion, hast thou said,
Thy King from warfare to dissuade
     Were but a vain essay;
For, by St George, were that host mine,

[19] *English Bards and Scotch Reviewers* (1809), 168–70, *Complete Poetical Works of Lord Byron*, i. 234.

> Not power infernal nor divine,
> Should once to peace my soul incline,
> Till I had dimm'd their armour's shine,
>   In glorious battle-fray!'[20]

Through this curious sleight-of hand Scott manages to convey a celebration of Scottish martial prowess, while at the same time using the voice of the poet, David Lindesay, to respond to Marmion's militaristic excitement by emphasizing the superiority of 'peace and wealth' to war. By placing the admiration of the Scottish army on the lips of the English nobleman whose character the reader already despises, he evokes the overwhelming magnificence of the Scots, while also indicating that battle lust is undesirable. In the charged exchange between Marmion and Lindesay, the Scots thus emerge not only as a powerful fighting force, but also as the representatives of peace, restraint, prosperity, and good sense—an unlikely combination for the sixteenth century perhaps, but one that would appeal strongly to Scott's post-Enlightenment readers.

The distinctive landscape, which is also crucial to this key moment in the poem, works similarly to fuse Romantic ideals and medieval pageantry. The voice of the narrator conveys an authenticating and affectionate familiarity with the land which seems almost Wordsworthian: 'And I could trace each step they trode: | Hill, brook, nor dell, nor rock, nor stone, | Lies on the path to me unknown.'[21] These very hills and stones, however, also function as a spectacular counterpart to the colourful banners of King James's army:

> The wandering eye could o'er it go,
> And mark the distant city glow
>   With gloomy splendour red;
> For on the smoke-wreaths, huge and slow,
> That round her sable turrets flow,
>   The morning beams were shed,
> And ting'd them with a lustre proud,
> Like that which streaks a thunder-cloud.
> Such dusky grandeur cloth'd the height,
> Where the huge Castle holds its state,

[20] *Marmion*, IV. xxix, *Scott: Poetical Works*, ed. J. Logie Robertson (Oxford, 1904), 134.

[21] *Marmion*, IV. xxiii.

And all the steep slope down,
Whose ridgy back heaves to the sky,
Pil'd deep and massy, close and high,
    Mine own romantic town!
But northward far, with purer blaze,
On Ochil mountains fell the rays.
And as each heathy top they kiss'd,
It gleam'd a purple amethyst.
Yonder the shores of Fife you saw;
Here Preston Bay and Berwick-Law:
    And, broad between them roll'd,
The gallant Frith the eye might note,
Whose islands on its bosom float,
    Like emeralds chas'd in gold.[22]

It is this bejewelled, and almost heraldic, scenery that inspires Fitz-Eustace's comment:

Fitz-Eustace' heart felt closely pent;
As if to give his rapture vent,
The spur he to his charger lent,
    And rais'd his bridle hand,
And, making demi-volte in air,
Cried, 'Where's the coward that would not dare
    To fight for such a land!'
The Lindesay smil'd his joy to see;
Nor Marmion's frown repress'd his glee.

The moment of unity poised on this passionate exclamation is also a moment of deep irony. For the English page is deeply moved by the breathtaking beauty of the land and the corresponding energies of those raised there, but historical knowledge enables the reader to see beyond this charged moment to the forthcoming battle, when those now inspiring admiration would be struck down by the forces of the spectators.

Once seen in context, Fitz-Eustace's words seem a rather odd starting point for a poem celebrating 'The Homes of England'. Although the creation of Great Britain during the three centuries that had intervened between Flodden Field and the post-Napoleonic *Records of Woman* led many to regard Scotland and England as part of a United Kingdom, Hemans's poem does not seem intent on evoking the former in its domestic

[22] *Marmion*, IV. xxx.

celebration. By the nineteenth century, Scotland had acquired an easily recognizable shorthand of symbolic attributes and distinctive vocabulary, but mists, mountains, and glens have no place in 'The Homes of England' (a point made subtly by Noel Coward's 'stately homes of England | In valley, dale, and glen'). Scott's lines thus seem a strange choice, especially as his continuing popularity meant that readers were quite likely to recall their original context: the sight of Edinburgh and its stunning surroundings, and the sound of the Scottish army preparing to march south.

Scott's wide acclaim, of course, might also account for the apparent inappropriateness of the epigraph, since his work had acquired the status of a modern classic and could therefore be regarded as a common resource—a source of beautiful lines to be borrowed by subsequent writers, almost as a *Dictionary of Quotations* might furnish elegant expressions unconfined by their contexts. Hemans's own admiration for his poetry was longstanding, emerging naturally in the easy references that are scattered through her writings. When she visited Scotland in 1829, the highlight of her exciting trip was the visit to Abbotsford, when she walked with Scott along the Yarrow to Newark Castle, and spent a number of days listening to his tales of local people, discussing the trees on his estate, and entertaining him with her own poems and songs.[23] It is also clear from this visit that her poem had given no offence to Scottish readers, since she was welcomed not only by Scott himself, but also the leading literary figures in Edinburgh, including Mrs Grant of Laggan, Captain Hall, and, most memorably, Francis Jeffrey, whose conversation she described as '*mental champagne*'.[24]

When he reviewed *Records of Woman* and *The Forest Sanctuary*, Jeffrey lavished high praise on Hemans as 'beyond all comparison, the most touching and accomplished writer of occasional verses that our literature has yet to boast of', which does not suggest any sensitivity about either her appropriation of Scott's lines or her celebration of Englishness.[25] Indeed, his reference to 'our literature' is clearly the literature of Great

[23] 'Memoir of the Life and Writings of Mrs Hemans, by her Sister', *The Works of Mrs Hemans, with a Memoir by her Sister*, 7 vols. (Edinburgh, 1839), i. 178–91.
[24] Ibid. 193.
[25] *Edinburgh Review*, 50 (Oct. 1829), 32–47, 47.

Britain, since in the same paragraph he ranges through the work of Scott, Byron, Wordsworth, Campbell, and Keats. In the light of this, Hemans's use of Scott might be regarded as a celebration of the Union, an evocation of Scottish courage by an English writer whom Jeffrey regarded as 'a fine exemplification of Female Poetry'. Since he saw her work as 'sweet, elegant, and tender', it was more likely to inspire feelings that were protective and patronizing than those of indignation or anger.

Of course, Jeffrey was not expecting to discover 'political investigations' in the poetry of a fair writer such as Mrs Hemans.[26] But although his review is likely to irritate twenty-first-century readers into scouring the volume for social issues and philosophy, it is actually possible that Hemans herself was largely oblivious to the political ironies of her epigraph for 'The Homes of England'. Consciousness of national identity is nevertheless abundantly obvious in *Records of Woman*, as well as being much to the fore in the account of Hemans's trip to Scotland. One of the things that apparently struck her most about Sir Walter Scott, for example, was his fondness for 'any air which possesses a national character, or has a story, or strong feeling connected with it'.[27] It is important to recognize, however, that this interest was by no means an exclusively Scottish matter, for among her own contributions to their discussion was a rendition of various Spanish songs, while she later compared Scott's 'chivalric loyalty' to that of the Paladins. Nor did her interest in the songs of different countries originate with Scott, for her sister's 'Memoir' records that, from an early age, 'what she loved best were national airs, whether martial or melancholy, (amongst these the Welsh and Spanish were her favourites), and whatever might be called suggestive music, as awakening associations either traditional, local, or imaginary'.[28]

This enthusiasm seems to have been fostered from childhood by the girls' awareness of their own cosmopolitan ancestry, their father being Irish, their mother of Italian and German descent. Hemans came from a multilingual family and grew up

---

[26] *Edinburgh Review*, 32 ('women . . . perhaps . . . are incapable of long moral or political investigations'). Jonathan Wordsworth discusses the contemporary perception of Hemans as 'both feminine and unpolitical' in *The Bright Work Grows: Women Writers of the Romantic Age* (Poole and Washington, DC, 1997), 174.

[27] 'Memoir of Mrs Hemans', *Works*, i. 186.

[28] Ibid. 14–15.

with a sense of difference from her Welsh neighbours, but, perhaps as a result of this, she seems to have regarded local traditions of all kinds as something admirable and deeply sustaining.[29] Her admiration for Scott is thus part of a long-standing fascination with the relationship between cultures and countries, which also emerges in an account of Wordsworth's poetry sent to her friend Maria Jane Jewsbury the year before her visit to Abbotsford:

This author is the true poet of home, and of all the lofty feelings which have their root in the soil of home affections. His fine sonnets to Liberty, and indeed all his pieces which have any reference to political interest, remind me of the spirit in which Schiller has conceived the character of William Tell, a calm, single-hearted herdsman of the hills, breaking forth in fiery and indignant eloquence, when the sanctity of his hearth is invaded.[30]

Wordsworth is the poet of both home and liberty—ideals that seem almost inseparable in the work of Felicia Hemans. Wordsworth, like William Tell, seems possessed of a heart of native proof and ready to guard his hallowed walls should an external threat appear. Just as 'The Switzer's Wife' (who appeared in *Records of Woman* adorned with epigraphs from both Jewsbury and 'Wilhelm Tell') is goaded into action by tyranny and oppression, so Hemans presents anyone who has been reared in a traditional community as being ready to stand and fight should the sacred hearth be invaded. Her characterization of Scott's 'chivalric loyalty' is part of the same warm admiration for local heroes who form the basis of a country's strength.

Paradoxically, Hemans's exploration of different national cultures seems to have been driven by a desire to find similarities. What appears to be a Romantic delight in the individual and the local is perhaps not very far removed from the earlier eighteenth-century interest in a universal human nature, albeit discovered through suffering and sympathy rather than reason. If Hemans could discern the same essential feelings in Sicily or Greece, in Switzerland or Spain, she would not have found it

---

[29] Her sister's 'Memoir' records that their father was an Irish merchant and their mother the daughter of the Imperial and Tuscan Consul in Liverpool. The family moved to Wales when Felicia was 6.

[30] 'Memoir of Mrs Hemans', *Works*, i. 146.

difficult to sympathize with the emotions stirred by the sight of a Scottish army on its home territory, irrespective of its subsequent destination. For Fitz-Eustace's exclamation on the Blackford Hills in *Marmion* has much in common with Hemans's representations of Wordsworth, William Tell, or 'The Switzer's Wife', being a form of spontaneous applause at the ideal of fighting for the homeland. Tricia Lootens has commented on Hemans's capacity to glorify 'the courage both of Crusaders and of their Arab opponents',[31] but this apparent contradiction is perfectly consistent if it is the relationship between an individual and home that is the object of admiration, rather than a particular nation. Similarly, as a reader of *Marmion*, Hemans could be moved, just as Fitz-Eustace is within the text, by the image of the Scots and Scotland, and thus feel able to borrow the lines that epitomize the warm feeling for her own purposes. Her emphasis on essential emotions is part of the cultural legacy of *Lyrical Ballads*, where Wordsworth had argued for a new kind of poetry in which 'the feeling therein developed gives importance to the action and situation, and not the action and situation to the feeling'.[32]

Since the feelings that moved Hemans most deeply were associated with the home, however, and especially the idea of a home under threat, her poems frequently represent moments of trial or conflict in which 'action and situation' inevitably begin to dominate.[33] Even 'The Homes of England', which seems almost assertively tranquil at first, turns defensive and muscle-flexing in the end. Indeed, the contradictory impulses towards essential feelings on the one hand, and 'action and situation' on the other, are epitomized by 'The Homes of England' and its epigraph. For although Scott's lines introduce the feelings of patriotic loyalty that form a vital strand of the poem, the insistent Englishness of the verses that follow and, in particular, the obsession with landscape work against the universalizing

---

[31] 'Hemans and Home', 239.
[32] Preface to *Lyrical Ballads* (1800), *Lyrical Ballads*, ed. Mason, 64. See also Marlon Ross's discussion of the influence on Hemans of Joanna Baillie's Introduction to *Plays on the Passions* (1798), in which similar ideas are developed, *The Contours of Masculine Desire: Romanticism and the Rise of Women's Poetry* (New York and London, 1989), 285–9.
[33] Anne K. Mellor explores Hemans's preoccupation with the home in *Romanticism and Gender*, 124–43.

tendencies of shared emotion. If the epigraph asserts that feeling gives importance to a poem, the poem itself seems to reply that in fact situation is equally important. Strong feelings, indeed, seem dependent on physical locations for healthy growth and maturity. By attaching Scott's lines to a poem in which passion and place are indivisible, Hemans makes it hard to ignore the origins of her epigraph and, in doing so, points to the tendency of patriotic loyalty to lead to military action. With this in mind, the epigraph begins to seem less like a formal device to introduce a major theme or to frame the poem by corresponding to its conclusion, and more like an external threat. Perhaps the challenge issued by Scott finds an opponent rather than a follower in Hemans's poem, as the nurseries of England prepare for an invasion from beyond the Border.

Even if the epigraph suggests a more straightforward piece of jingoism, with Scott being evoked in the context of a nineteenth-century United Kingdom, its very emphasis on the connections between local loyalties and military action makes it a somewhat ironic tag for the images of blessed domesticity. 'The Homes of England' and their Scottish epigraph form a slightly uneasy Union, which is at once on the defensive against the world, while also registering a history of violent opposition. This uncomfortable dynamic is nevertheless typical of the entire poem, which appears to present happy balances and harmonies, but in fact strikes many readers as an unconvincing series of sentimental scenes, or a stucco façade attempting to disguise serious structural problems. Huts and halls may be momentarily brought to order through alliteration and syntax, but their differences, like those between past and present, male and female, rich and poor, North and South, are never entirely erased. Hence perhaps the need for the final evocation of an external threat which might divert attention from the difficulties within. Since this merely recalls the epigraph, however, and the ambiguities inherent from the start, the strategy seems evasive and circular, rather than the means to find a satisfactory resolution.

Despite the tensions introduced by the epigraph, it was clearly a careful choice, because when 'The Homes of England' was first published in 1827, it was not accompanied by Sir Walter Scott.

Instead, when the poem appeared in *Blackwood's Edinburgh Magazine*, the epigraph was taken from the work of another Scottish writer, Joanna Baillie:

> ——A land of peace,
> Where yellow fields unspoil'd, and pastures green,
> Mottled with herds and flocks, who crop secure
> Their native herbage, nor have ever known
> A stranger's stall, smile gladly.
> See through its tufted alleys to Heaven's roof
> The curling smoke of quiet dwellings rise.[34]

This extended passage from one of Hemans's favourite plays, *Ethwald*, is very different in tone from the swashbuckling lines from *Marmion*. In the original play, it is part of a longer speech by the 'noble thane', Ethelbert, who is trying to dissuade the ambitious Saxon leader, Ethwald, from plunging his land into renewed warfare with the 'damned Britons' from Wales. Although it is another Romantic treatment of the bloody internal history of the British Isles, when removed from its context the lines do not carry any obvious reference to battles or civil strife. The change of epigraph from Baillie to Scott may thus indicate a conscious attempt to emphasize the martial undercurrents of 'The Homes of England' and also the notion of peace under threat, which is apparent in Baillie's play, but not in the excerpted lines. For even if the rest of *Marmion* were unfamiliar to Hemans's readers, the impulse to fight is quite explicit in the lines chosen, which provide a tone very different from the earlier, pastoral image of 'a land of peace'.

The shift from rural description to rhetorical question is also striking. Fitz-Eustace's words obviously demand an answer in the negative, but the very structure of his speech implies participation from the reader. It is perhaps unsurprising that Noel Coward should have found the challenge irresistible, given his own unlucky surname, but what is equally interesting is the discovery that a host of earlier writers had already risen in reply to Hemans's poem. Over a century before the opening night of

---

[34] *Blackwood's Edinburgh Magazine*, 21 (Apr. 1827), 392. The passage is from *Ethwald*, Part II, I. ii. *The Dramatic and Poetical Works of Joanna Baillie* (London, 1851), 170. Her sister recalls the young Felicia Hemans's memorable first encounter with *Ethwald* in the ruins of Conway Castle, 'Memoir of Mrs Hemans', *Works*, i. 17.

Operette, the Dublin newspaper *The Comet*, which was soon to publish James Clarence Mangan's 'Dying Enthusiast to his Friend', printed the following:

The Contrast

'The stately homes of England,
  'How beautiful they stand,
'Amidst their tall ancestral trees,
  'O'er all the pleasant land'
MRS HEMANS

The stately homes of Ireland,
  How desolate they stand
Amidst the forests, groves, and trees,
  Of this deserted land.
The deer no more o'er meadows bound,
  Or bask in summer's beam;
The swan her song in plaintive sound
  Is wailing on the stream.

The mournful homes of Ireland!
  Around the turf by night,
There looks of famine—not of love—
  Meet in the dismal light.
No woman's voice is heard in song;
  No childhood's tale is told;
The calls of hunger are among
  The youthful and the old.

The wretched homes of Ireland!
  The demon discord lowers;
Banished the holy quietness
  Of sacred Sabbath hours.
Solemn, yet sad, the Church bell's chime
  Floats o'er the wilds at morn;—
Fierce passions rise in that still time,
  Engendering hate and scorn.

The Cottage homes of Ireland,
  By thousands on her plains;
The cabin and the smoking hut
  No comfort now contains.
Through bog and rushes forth they peep,
  O'erwhelmed with rankling weeds;

In deep despair their inmates sleep,
    And dream of desperate deeds.

The free, fair homes of Ireland
    Ere long, in hut and hall,
May hearts of native proof return,
    And guard each hallowed wall,
And green for ever be the groves,
    And bright the flowery sod,
Where true the patriot spirit loves
    Its country and its God.[35]

In its careful imitation and selective alteration of Hemans's verses, the new poem emphasizes the extraordinary discrepancy between the glossy image of England she had presented to the world, and the writer's perception of the state of Ireland. The adjectives which are such a substantial part of Hemans's literary technique are systematically transformed, as 'beautiful' becomes 'desolate', 'pleasant' is now 'deserted', 'merry' turns to 'mournful', 'ruddy' to 'dismal', 'blessed' to 'wretched', and 'sweet' to 'sad'. With each change, the superficiality of the original seems more apparent—a thin veneer that cannot withstand the shocks of poverty and discontent.

Far from using Hemans's opening lines as a springboard for fresh composition, this is a sustained attack which retains particular elements of the earlier poem in order to expose its weaknesses. The swan which had been gliding along a rejoicing stream in the English country estate now becomes a symbol of death, wailing her song to the desolate houses of Ireland, while the sounds issuing from the less stately homes are cries of starvation. As in the homes of England, the experience of rural life in Ireland seems bound up with physical action, but the essential feelings that have grown up in the domestic unit are those of 'hate and scorn'. It is only the patriotic conclusion of Hemans's poem that seems to be transferred without major adjustment to the language, but by now the greatest irony is obvious—that from this writer's point of view, the recovery of 'free, fair homes' in Ireland means independence from the very land whose portrait is being borrowed to make the point. If the potential ambiguities of Hemans's enthusiasm for both local

---

[35] *The Comet* (22 April 1832). The poem is attributed to 'K.H', whose identity I have so far been unable to discover.

attachments and military valour are partially submerged in 'The Homes of England', they are forced into direct light by the hard-hitting parody that her poem provoked in Ireland.

Not all Irish readers were nettled in quite the same way, however, by Hemans's poem. When Denis MacCarthy was promoting the Spirit of the Nation in the following decade, he too responded to 'The Homes of England', but avoided the parodic approach of the Cometeers. His own poem is indebted to Hemans for both form and tone, but rather than remaining in the thrall of the earlier, already very famous English text, he used it to produce what Joep Leerssen has described as 'still the most anthologised of MacCarthy's poems':[36]

The Pillar Towers of Ireland

The pillar towers of Ireland, how wondrously they stand
By the lakes and rushing rivers through the valleys of our land;
In mystic file, through the isle, they lift their heads sublime,
These grey old pillar temples—these conquerors of time!

Beside these grey old pillars, how perishing and weak
The Roman's arch of triumph, and the temple of the Greek,
And the gold domes of Byzantium, and the pointed Gothic spires—
All are gone, one by one, but the temples of our sires!

The column, with its capital, is level with the dust,
And the proud halls of the mighty and the calm homes of the just;
For the proudest works of man, as certainly, but slower,
Pass like the grass at the sharp scythe of the mower!

But the grass grows again when in majesty and mirth,
On the wing of the Spring comes the Goddess of the Earth;
But for man in this world no springtide e'er returns
To the labours of his hands or the ashes of his urns!

Two favourites hath Time—the pyramids of Nile,
And the old mystic temples of our own dear isle—
As the breeze o'er the seas, where the halcyon has its nest,
Thus Time o'er Egypt's tombs and the temples of the West!

The names of their founders have vanished in the gloom,
Like the dry branch in the fire or the body in the tomb;
But to-day, in the ray, their shadows still they cast—
These temples of forgotten Gods—these relics of the past!

---

[36] Leerssen, *Remembrance and Imagination*, 110.

Around these walls have wandered the Briton and the Dane—
The captives of Armorica, the cavaliers of Spain—
Phoenician and Milesian, and the plundering Norman Peers—
And the swordsmen of brave Brian, and the Chiefs of later years!

How many different rites have these grey old temples known?
To the mind what dreams are written in these chronicles of stone!
What terror and what error, what gleams of love and truth,
Have flashed from these walls since the world was in its youth?

Here blazed the sacred fire—and, when the sun was gone,
As a star from afar to the traveller it shone;
And the warm blood of the victim have these grey old temples drunk,
And the death-song of the Druid and the matin of the Monk.

Here was placed the holy chalice that held the sacred wine,
And the gold cross from the altar, and the relics from the shrine,
And the mitre shining brighter with its diamonds than the East,
And the crozier of the Pontiff and the vestments of the Priest!

Where blazed the sacred fire, rung out the vesper bell,
Where the fugitive found shelter became the hermit's cell;
And Hope hung out its symbol to the innocent and good,
For the cross o'er the moss of the pointed summit stood!

There may it stand for ever, while this symbol doth impart
To the mind one glorious vision, or one proud throb to the heart;
While the breast needeth rest may these grey old temples last,
Bright prophets of the future, as preachers of the past![37]

Although 'The Homes of England' is obviously the starting point for MacCarthy's poem, by allowing it to fade into the background as his own celebration of Irish Round Towers unfolds, he appears to have liberated himself from the English model. While the earlier parody in *The Comet* remains obsessed and oppressed by Mrs Hemans's verses, MacCarthy's 'Pillar Towers' seem to rise above existing works, claiming superiority on the grounds of antiquity. Indeed, this strategy has something in common with Mangan's response to Shelley, in that it again avoids the condition of secondariness or imitation by emphasizing a tradition older than that of the earlier poem with which it engages. If Mrs Hemans sought to emphasize the eternal continuity of England by reaching back to its Saxon foundations, MacCarthy responds by asserting that 'the old mystic temples'

---

[37] Denis Florence MacCarthy, 'The Pillar Towers of Ireland', *The Spirit of the Nation: Ballads and Songs by the Writers of 'The Nation'* (1845), facsimile edn., with introduction by John Kelly (Poole and Washington, DC, 1998), 279–80.

of Ireland dwarf such claims by going back to the time of the pyramids. Her poem is in a sense entirely subsumed in his longer meditation, her reassuring references to halls and homes dismissed in the *carpe diem* of MacCarthy's third verse. The sweeping European perspective, which includes Rome, Greece, Egypt, and Byzantium, underlines the parochial and defensive character of Hemans's lyric, while pointing to its misplaced pride and disproportionate sense of English importance in either time or space. The use of Christian imagery, too, and explicit emphasis on the towers as religious sites is a further part of his answer to 'The Homes of England', where children seem to discover God and their own country simultaneously.

Rather than respond to Hemans's poem through parody, MacCarthy preferred to answer boast with boast. Instead of employing irony, his rhetorical strategy is to establish primacy through extreme longevity, effectively countering any English claims to calmness or continuity. Whatever the historical accuracy of MacCarthy's poem, he turns the Irish towers into symbols of permanence and, by demonstrating the bloody history they have witnessed and survived, implies that recent Irish difficulties may also pass away, while the towers continue unmoved and unshakeable. The debate over the Irish Round Towers has been admirably explored by Joep Leerssen and so need not concern us here.[38] What is important from the perspective of this book is the different ways in which Hemans's poem was read and reused in Ireland in the years after its initial publication. For if Scottish readers welcomed Mrs Hemans to Edinburgh after the publication of 'The Homes of England' in *Blackwood's* and *Records of Woman*, her reception in Ireland was perhaps a little less warm. Indeed, when she moved there in 1831, she expressed surprise at the degree of anti-English feeling in a comment that seems to anticipate the feelings that would be expressed in 'The Contrast' only a few months later: 'It is scarcely possible to conceive bitterness and hatred existing in the human heart, when one sees nature smiling so brightly and so peacefully all around; and yet those dark feelings *do* here exist to a degree which I could not have credited.'[39]

---

[38] *Remembrance and Imagination*, 108–43.
[39] 'Memoir of Mrs Hemans', *Works*, i. 243. See also Henry Chorley, *Memorials of Mrs Hemans*, 2 vols. (London, 1836), ii. 206.

If Edinburgh literary figures welcomed Hemans's work in the context of a United Kingdom, Irish readers were likely to feel excluded from the partnership that enabled a 'British poetess' to evoke a Scottish poet in a celebration of England.[40] Despite the Act of Union which had come into effect in 1801, the sense of Ireland as an unwelcome poor relation was still prevalent in certain influential quarters. The very volume of *Blackwood's Magazine* that had published 'The Homes of England' for the first time, for example, placed the poem directly after an outrageous Malthusian article on 'The Surplus Population of the United Kingdom', which argued for a systematic programme of emigration from Ireland and suggested that 'a large dash of English and Scottish blood would greatly improve the Irish character'.[41] It is perhaps not surprising, in the face of such publicly paraded attitudes, that Irish readers were less impressed by the happy imagery of 'The Homes of England' than those who lived in Scotland or England. The very currents of British feeling that were to carry Mrs Hemans's poem away from its original context and into the great tide of Victorian Imperialism helped to provoke less enthusiastic responses from those who regarded her domestic Paradise as alien or simply unattainable.

To assume that all readers living in England were uncritically delighted by Hemans's poem, however, would also be wide of the mark. Her scenes of communal harmony may have been particularly galling to writers conscious of the plight of the contemporary Irish rural poor, but they also had the capacity to provoke comment from a number of writers who perceived certain discrepancies between these and their own perceptions. Four years after 'The Contrast' had emphasized the differences between Hemans's merry homes and their mournful Irish counterparts, Caroline Norton published a poem in London in which the new industrial towns of England were exposed as places unredeemed by domestic bliss. In *A Voice from the Factories*, no objection is made to the ideals of Hemans's poem,

[40] Hemans described herself as a 'British poetess' in one of her last letters, 'Memoir of Mrs Hemans', *Works*, i. 297.
[41] *Blackwood's Edinburgh Magazine*, 21 (Apr. 1827), 388. Hemans herself made a rather more sympathetic comment on the issue in her 'Song of Emigration', published in the July issue of *Blackwood's*, 22 (1827), 32.

which seem to stem from the same tradition of rural celebration as Gray's equally well-known 'Elegy written in a Country Churchyard':

> 'The happy homes of England!'—they have been
> A source of triumph, and a theme for song;
> And surely if there be a hope serene
> And beautiful, which may to Earth belong,
> 'Tis when (shut out the world's associate throng,
> And closed the busy day's fatiguing hum),
> Still waited for with expectation strong,
> Welcomed with joy, and overjoyed to come,
> The good man goes to seek the twilight rest of home.[42]

The very ideal epitomized by Mrs Hemans's familiar lyric, however, is then shown to be sadly removed from the experience of the child forced to work in the mills and factories of nineteenth-century England:

> But the day hath its End. Forth then he hies
> With jaded, faltering step, and brow of pain;
> Creeps to that shed,—his HOME, where happy lies
> The sleeping babe that cannot toil for Gain;
> Where his remorseful Mother tempts in vain
> With the best portion of their frugal fare:
> Too sick to eat—too weary to complain—
> He turns him idly from the untasted share,
> Slumbering sinks down unfed, and mocks her useless care.[43]

Norton's image of the exhausted child labourer and his desperate mother seems a far cry from the songs and stories of Hemans's happy family circle. And yet, unlike that of her Dublin contemporary, Norton's contrast does not attack 'The Homes of England' itself, but rather the new social conditions that exclude so many English children from the kinds of happiness represented in the poem.

If readers of the mid-1830s were ready to be moved by Norton's approach to the exploitation of children just as they were by *Oliver Twist*, they were to find the Condition of England provoking far more militant responses in the Hungry Forties. Less sentimental in its approach than *A Voice from the*

---

[42] Caroline Norton, *A Voice from the Factories*, xxxii (London, 1836), 27.
[43] Ibid. xlix.

Factories, but similarly alert to the limitations of the old, rural ideal of 'Home' for a newly industrialized nation was Charles Mackay's radical poem 'The Wants of the People'. In an overtly un-nostalgic collection entitled *Voices from the Crowd*, Mackay's ballad 'The Wants of the People' also evoked Hemans's English Homes. Since the entire thrust of his volume was progressive, with 'The Days that are gone' being depicted as the 'days when the gallows stood black in the way', the outdated image of feudal harmony clearly had no appeal.[44] Nevertheless, the notion of a happy, stable background for those at all levels of society is still upheld. Mackay is not invoking 'free, fair homes' as the basis of defence against external threats to the country: his militancy is directed at the problems within. Nor does he present the ideal home as the eternal continuing birthright of every Englishman, but rather as an ideal still to be realized:

> What do we want? Our daily bread:—
>   Grant it:—make our efforts free;
> Let us work and let us prosper;
>   You shall prosper more than we;
> And the humblest homes of England
>   Shall, in proper time, give birth
> To better men than we have been,
>   To live upon a better earth.[45]

Neither Norton nor Mackay, though of Irish and Scottish descent respectively, are objecting here to the patriotic sentiments of Hemans's poem. What their own poems do reveal is an acute consciousness that nineteenth-century England included levels of existence that had found no representation in her apparently inclusive rhetoric.

As the century progressed, and the need for better housing became more and more urgent, so Mrs Hemans's poem, which seemed to epitomize the Victorian ideal of home and hearth, began to sound more and more hollow. Even in the most progressive circles, however, the notion of the 'homes of England' survived as a model against which to measure the woeful shortcomings of contemporary society; and when Octavia Hill

[44] Charles Mackay, 'The Days that are Gone', *Voices from the Crowd*, 3rd edn. (London, 1846), 26.
[45] 'The Wants of the People', ibid. 5.

published her exposure of the appalling conditions in the London slums, for example, she called her pamphlet *Homes of the London Poor*.[46] Even after Parliament had finally begun to address the issue, the memory of Mrs Hemans's rhetoric continued to float behind the title of essays on the housing problem. As late as the 1920s, Averil Sanderson Furniss chose the now loaded title *The Homes of the People* to draw attention to the acute housing shortage, and concluded the essay by contrasting the life of the slum child with the experience of a child brought up in a spacious residence. The succession of parallel homes made famous by Mrs Hemans had by now become a device for emphasizing the discrepancy between the old ideals and the perceived realities of modern Britain.[47]

For every reader who felt moved by the contrasts between 'The Homes of England' and the conditions they perceived with their own eyes, however, there must have been many who merely warmed to the reassuring images and found their own optimistic views confirmed. When Hemans's friend Bernard Barton was recording fond thoughts about his native Suffolk in the 1840s, for example, there is little sign of the need for a better earth where everyone might get their daily bread. When he quotes from the first stanza of Hemans's poem as an epigraph for his own 'Helmingham Hall', it is quite without irony or radical intent. 'This ancient moated Hall' is one of the very stately homes celebrated in the earlier poem, and thus Mrs Hemans seems more of a presiding deity than an uncomfortable spectre rebuking the age with a lost ideal.[48]

Thirty years later, Llewellynn Jewitt and Samuel Carter Hall decided to produce a series of illustrated articles on English country houses for the *Art Journal*, which they subsequently collected and published in volumes explicitly indebted to Felicia Hemans's poem:

---

[46] Octavia Hill, *Homes of the London Poor (1875)* and *The Bitter Cry of Outcast London: An Inquiry into the Condition of the Abject Poor (1883)*, facsimile edn., ed. A. Mearns (London, 1970); in the second pamphlet, Hill refers to 'THE CONDITION IN WHICH THEY LIVE—We do not say the condition of their homes, for how can those places be called homes, compared with which the lair of a wild beast would be a comfortable and healthy spot', 6. See also Gillian Darley, *Octavia Hill: A Life* (London, 1990).

[47] Averil Sanderson Furniss, *The Homes of the People* (Oxford, 1925).

[48] Bernard Barton, *Household Verses* (London, 1845), 198–200.

Beautifully has the gifted poet, Mrs Hemans, sung of English 'Homes,' and charmingly has she said—

> 'The Stately Homes of England,
>   How beautiful they stand
>   Amidst their tall ancestral trees
>   O'er all the pleasant land!'

and thus given to us a title for our present work.[49]

Although it was clearly Hemans's first class of home that had attracted his interest, Jewitt's introduction nevertheless reveals a new awareness of the possible objections to privilege, as he explains the rationale behind their selection of subjects: 'Of these "Stately Homes" of our "pleasant land" we have chosen some few for illustration, not for their stateliness alone, but because the true nobility of their owners allows their beauties, their splendour, their picturesque surroundings, and their treasures of art to be seen and enjoyed by all.' By the 1870s, it seems, 'stateliness' was not enough. Conscious, perhaps, of their own potential market ('we have accomplished [the task of illustration] with a sincere desire to make our work acceptable to a large number of readers'), Jewitt and Hall's emphasis is not only on the great homes of England, but also on public access. It is fitting from a later perspective, then, that they should have begun with Alton Towers.

This picturesque Staffordshire seat is presented not only as 'one of the most interesting of the many stately Homes of England that dignify and glorify the Kingdom', but also as a place for 'the people' to visit.[50] And here Hemans's influence is obvious on both the language and the attitudes, for the description of the great house thrown open to the public has much in common with the earlier nineteenth-century image of peaceful class cohesion. There is no sense that 'the people' might feel anything other than admiration for the treasure houses into which they were occasionally allowed to peep, any more than the old 'cottage homes' ever stopped 'smiling':

on fixed days, the chief rooms, such as are highly decorated or contain pictures—the STATE APARTMENTS—are open also; and all that wealth

---

[49] 'Introduction', L. Jewitt and S. C. Hall, *The Stately Homes of England* (London, 1874).
[50] Ibid. 1.

has procured, as far as the eye is concerned, is as much the property of the humblest artisan as it is of the lord of the soil.

And what a boon it is to the sons and daughters of toil—the hard-handed men—with their wives and children—workers at the forge, the wheel, and the loom,—who thus make holiday, obtain enjoyment, and gain health, under the shadows of 'tall ancestral trees' planted centuries ago by men whose names are histories . . .

The good that hence arises is incalculable: it removes the barriers that separate the rich from the poor, the peer from the peasant, the magnate from the labourer; and contributes to propagate and confirm the true patriotism that arises from holy love of country.[51]

Although the eagerness of the landed 'to share their acquisitions with the people' is seen entirely in terms of benevolent patronage—evidence indeed of the very nobility that had been rewarded with such establishments in the first place—the very defensiveness of the description points to an underlying sense of unease about the subject matter. Though clearly infused with deep admiration for the families, architecture, scenery, opulent interiors, and historical associations that combine to make a home 'stately', Jewitt and Hall's volume also demonstrates a growing awareness that the old social structures were changing and that not everyone shared their enthusiasm for English country houses. The fact that many great families now opened their homes to the public on a regular basis was as much a sign of economic instability as of any noble desire to propagate patriotism; the apparently widespread inclination to remove the barriers between rich and poor, too, was probably driven largely by self-preservation. For the idea that the 'humblest artisan' possessed 'all that wealth procured' merely by being allowed to look at the hoard from time to time was not a very persuasive argument even though it follows logically enough from the opening celebration of the common ownership of England's true fortune :

---

[51] Jewitt and Hall, *The Stately Homes of England*, 1–3. Although from the 1760s onwards, some country houses allowed carefully vetted visitors to admire the collections and even produced guide books for the purpose, 'mass visiting' was a mid-nineteenth-century development, facilitated by railways, paid holidays, and better relations between the classes, according to Peter Mandler, *The Fall and Rise of the Stately Home* (New Haven and London, 1997), 8–10, 71–6.

England is rich—immeasurably richer than any other country under the sun—in its 'Homes;' and these homes, whether of the sovereign or of the high nobility, of the country squire or the merchant-prince, of the artisan or the labourer, whether, in fact, they are palace or cottage, or of any immediate grade, have a character possessed by none other.[52]

Despite the slightly unconvincing nature of these assertions, however, the emphasis on the equivalence of 'palace or cottage' reveals the continuing appeal of modest rural communities to Victorian readers. Although many were concerned by the plight of the urban poor, the imaginative appeal of village England had by no means diminished since Hemans's celebration of church bells and glowing orchards. Indeed, it was probably enhanced by the increasing awareness of the very different conditions that marred the large industrial cities. By the end of the century, the 'Cottage Homes of England' were attracting as much attention from artists and writers as their stately neighbours, and when Helen Allingham and Stewart Dick's beautiful volume appeared under this title, it extolled the virtues of English cottages in preference to much grander establishments:

The mansions of the great, 'the stately homes of England' as they are called, hardly deserve their title. They are not homely enough. They are the show-places of the country, standing aloof with impressive dignity amid their acres of green grass and groves of noble trees, but they seem more like museums or picture-galleries than English homes. On stated days the great gates are thrown open and throngs of visitors pour in, and are led from room to room and down the long corridors, viewing the ancestral portraits to a garrulous accompaniment of parochial history. It is magnificent, no doubt, and we ought to feel the spell of the old feudal grandeur, but it is very wearisome and seems strangely unreal. Did anyone really live amid all this icy splendour? Had it always this look of emptiness, or did it once form a living picture? Anyhow the memory we carry away is of the caretakers living among the half-forgotten ancestors, the shrouded furniture; and the streams of visitors, blatant or timid, but obviously out of place in either case, passing in and out of the great doors.[53]

Once again Felicia Hemans's poem echoes in the background, but her stately homes are no longer the point from which all

[52] Jewitt and Hall, *The Stately Homes of England*, 'Introduction'.
[53] Helen Allingham and Stewart Dick, *The Cottage Homes of England* (London, 1909), 4–5.

inferior forms of life take their bearings. The groves may still be green and the trees tall, but the ancestors are 'half-forgotten' now, while the rejoicing streams have turned into 'streams of visitors', out of place in the dusty museum of the feudal past. Instead of remaining quietly in the shadow of their wealthy neighbours, the Cottage Homes have now become the true centre of the country: the places through which 'the deep, main current of English life has flowed'.[54]

The cottage is no longer exalted as the soil from which loyal soldiers will be raised, but in its celebration of Englishness this volume is far more nationalistic than Hemans's original praise of patriotism. Like the earlier poem, Dick argues that 'through all changes the home and the family circle have always been the real centre of English life', but his interest in the physical architecture rather than the mere idea of home reflects a new kind of interest in 'the national character'.[55] It is an interest that excludes not only the foreign and the wealthy, but also the urban and suburban, seeking 'the typical English home' only in the country: 'Varying slightly in different localities by dint of local custom, or from the use of materials peculiar to the district, old English cottages have yet a common character, thoroughly English.' If earlier Irish readers had felt excluded from the happy 'Homes of England', and right-minded Victorians were concerned by its under-representation of the urban poor, how would they have reacted to this later narrowing of Hemans's vision to the fourth verse alone?

On the complicated route from Mrs Hemans to Noel Coward, this is an important juncture, nevertheless. Stewart Dick's warm account of English cottages and Helen Allingham's sunny, flower-sprinkled paintings seem far away from those Victorian writings that had evoked 'The Homes of England' in protest against the conditions of the London poor, but the turn of even conservative observers in search of 'the most typical thing in England' against stately homes was perhaps a clearer indication of the decline of the great house than any radical response could be. By 1909 when *The Cottage Homes of England*

---

[54] Allingham and Dick, *The Cottage Homes of England*, 9.
[55] Ibid. 4.

appeared, the situation of English landowners was completely different from 1827 when Felicia Hemans had coined the phrase. The severe agricultural depression of the late nineteenth century had reduced income from big estates very significantly, causing real difficulties to their owners and tenants. Sir William Harcourt's introduction of death duties in 1894 had created further anxiety for the old landed families—not only in practical terms, but also by providing an alarming symbol of a different attitude to class structures that seemed to establish itself with the new century. In the very year that Stewart Dick was exalting cottage rather than stately homes, Lloyd George introduced four new land taxes to ensure that some degree of social levelling might actually take place. If Felicia Hemans's original readers had sensed that her rosy vision of England was perhaps based on somewhat shaky foundations, by the beginnings of the twentieth century the internal divisions were only too apparent.[56]

In this context, Andrew Lang's use of the now very familiar poem is particularly interesting:

The Haunted Homes of England

The haunted homes of England
  How eerily they stand,
While through them flit their ghosts—to wit,
  The Monk with the Red Hand;
The Eyeless Girl—an awful spook—
  To stop the boldest breath,
The boy that inked his copybook,
  And so got 'wopped' to death!

Call them not shams—from haunted Glamis
  To haunted Woodhouselea,
I mark in hosts the grisly ghosts
  I hear the fell Banshie!
I know the spectral dog that howls
  Before the death of squires;

---

[56] On the situation facing English landowners at the beginning of the twentieth century, see Madeleine Beard, *English Landed Society in the Twentieth Century* (London, 1989), 1–54; Mark Girouard, *Life in the English Country House* (New Haven and London, 1978), 300–18; Mandler, *Fall and Rise of the Stately Home*, 153–91; Merlin Waterson (ed.), *The Country House Remembered* (London, Melbourne, and Henley, 1985).

In my 'Ghosts'-guide' addresses hide
  For Podmore and for Myers!
I see the vampire climb the stairs
  From vaults below the church;
And hark! the pirate's spectre swears!
  O psychical research,
Canst *thou* not hear what meets my ear,
  The viewless wheels that come?
The wild Banshie that wails to thee?
  The Drummer with his drum?

O haunted homes of England,
  Though tenantless ye stand,
With none content to pay the rent,
  Through all the shadowy land,
Now, science true will find in you
  A sympathetic perch,
And take you all, both grange and hall,
  For psychical research![57]

Perhaps not surprisingly for a writer who became the President for the Society of Psychical Research in 1911, Lang's poem focuses primarily on the ghostly inhabitants rather than the residences themselves. Indeed, the interest of the 'Homes of England' in his poem seems to stem entirely from their reputations for being haunted. And yet, as the light-hearted verses unfold, it becomes obvious that Lang is not exploring the cottage homes of the country in his pursuit of paranormal tales.

The royal castle of Glamis is probably as stately a home as one could wish for, so by naming it in the second verse an association develops between the highest level of society and the supernatural. While this is not particularly remarkable given the numerous legends that have accumulated around the country houses and castles of Britain over the centuries, it acquires

[57] *The Poetical Works of Andrew Lang*, ed. Mrs Lang, 4 vols. (London, 1923), ii. 95–6. The poem is undated but internal references indicate that it belongs to *c.*1900, when Lang's interest in Psychical Research was at its height. 'Podmore and Myers' refers to two of the founders of the Society for Psychical Research, Frank Podmore (1855–1910), whose *Apparitions and Thought-Transference* had appeared in 1894, and F. W. H. Myers (1843–1901), whose *Human Personality and its Survival of Bodily Death* was published posthumously in 1903. Lang's poem may be partly a retort to Podmore's sceptical attitude to spiritualism. On 'Lang as a Psycho-Folklorist', see Richard M. Dorson, *The British Folklorists: A History* (Chicago and London, 1968), 212–16.

additional significance in the context. For although the poem appears to play on the turn-of-the-century vogue for psychical research, it also registers a parallel consciousness of the contemporary decline of many landed families. The homes are filled with ghosts not merely because of grisly events in the past, but because the families that had always lived there are now gone. They have been 'tenantless' since the old families had had to retrench, and no one else is 'content to pay the rent'. In the light of this, the image of the spectral dog howling 'Before the death of squires' or the vampire emerging from the vault takes on additional meaning, as the ghost stories originally told by the inhabitants turn into prophecies of the fate of the family itself.[58] When the Liberals came to power in December 1905, Sir Henry Campbell-Bannerman made their policy for the new century clear: 'we wish to make the land less of a pleasure-ground for the rich and more of a treasure-house for the nation'.[59] And it is at just this point in the long history of the stately homes of England that Noel Coward cast his four Lords in *Operette*.

Although *Operette* belongs to the 1930s, its setting is 1906— a point made clearly in the prologue when the chorus of Ladies and Gentlemen announces that

> We represent those carefree days
> That still retained a bland hypocrisy
> And looked upon Democracy
> As quaint.

Before assuming that this evocation of the 'Edwardian era' was merely an opportunity for ironic humour, however, it is worth bearing in mind that this was the very period that Coward would look back on so admiringly when he introduced his *Song Book*:

The whole Edwardian era was saturated with operetta and musical comedy: in addition to popular foreign importations by Franz Lehar, Leo Fall, André Messager, etc., our own native composers were writing musical scores of a quality that has never been equalled since the 1914–18 war . . . Their famous and easily remembered melodies can still be heard on the radio and elsewhere, but it was in the

---

[58] The Lang family also had a traditional 'death omen' in the shape of a black cat, which Lang saw in January 1912, a few months before he died—see Roger Lancelyn Green, *Andrew Lang: A Critical Biography* (Leicester, 1946), 207.

[59] Mandler, *Fall and Rise of the Stately Home*, 174.

completeness of their scores that their real strength lay: opening choruses, finales, trios, quartettes and concerted numbers—all musicianly, all well balanced and all beautifully constructed.[60]

Here, the first decade of the twentieth century is presented as a halcyon era in which native English music flourished, and everything seemed 'well balanced' and 'complete'—a golden age dimly remembered before the cataclysm of the First World War. *Operette*, too, is at least in part a lament for the lost world of Edwardian England, whose music is evoked in 'The Model Maid', the play within the play. Nostalgia is nevertheless checked by the plot of the larger drama, since the heroine, Rozanne, who at last takes on the star role in 'The Model Maid', still loses her beloved Nigel Vaynham to the army, because she is persuaded that their marriage would ruin his social standing, career, and, implicitly, his inheritance. The piece thus seems to pull in rather contrary directions, as sympathy for the lovers who are thwarted by the class-based arguments of Nigel's formidable mother Lady Messiter ('It has been a tradition in our family for several hundred years that the eldest son should always be a soldier'[61]) is balanced by the obvious attraction to the 'carefree' world in which aristocrats and actresses knew their places and knew that they could never be the same.

The same fascination with upper-class attitudes, coupled with an awareness that they are no longer tenable, or even particularly admirable, is epitomized by the show's most successful song: 'The Stately Homes of England'. Whatever the audience of *Operette* may have thought about the central story of class-crossed love, the spotlighting of the Stately Homes is likely to have stirred a degree of sympathy, because by 1938 their fate was only too apparent. The unremitting cheerfulness of the patrician quartette becomes heavily ironic once it is clear that many of 'the Stately Homes of England' had altogether ceased to stand.

Andrew Lang had registered the growing difficulties of ancient families in his playful imitation of Felicia Hemans's poem, but by the time Coward revisited the 'Stately Homes', it had become obvious that the problems encountered by late

---

[60] *Song Book*, 9–10.   [61] *Operette*, II. iv, 116.

Victorian landowners were only omens of a much greater disaster. If the agricultural depression of the 1880s and 1890s and the introduction of new taxes had combined to rock the stability of the aristocracy, forcing them to rent out or even sell their estates, these difficulties were as nothing to the situation in the 1920s and 1930s, when loss of money during the war paled into insignificance beside the catastrophic loss of young men. The natural grief of bereavement was made even more unbearable by crippling death duties, a broken succession, and often the consequent disappearance of the family seat. As John Harris has put it, 'The holocaust of 1914–18 was to herald the death of over four hundred houses', giving as the main cause the loss of the sons who should have succeeded: 'All those heirs who sipped their gin and lime on lawns bathed in sunshine were to be mown down like blades of grass on the fields of Picardy or the beaches of Gallipoli.'[62] With the heirs to the estate gone, the houses soon had to be mown down too. In 1925 Lady Newton concluded her *Lyme Letters* with a virtual *ubi sunt* for the country house:

And what of the stately homes of England? How many of these will survive the cruel and ruthless taxation? Why are we not allowed the right to live? Why should it be a crime that we should have succeeded to places too large for present-day requirements? Why, also, should we be prevented from enjoying our homes that have come down to us from our forefathers? We only demand the right to live in them, without the amenities of former days, but this is to be denied us. What are we to do? We cannot sell, there are no buyers. We cannot afford to live in our homes, what is to become of them?[63]

The idea of Lady Newton asserting the right to live in her home would have seemed extraordinary to the radical campaigners of the previous century, but by the 1920s the notion of class equality had been inscribed for ever on the ubiquitous War Memorials. As Merlin Waterson has commented, 'the roll of honour in innumerable parish churches lists the dead in alphabetical order, with only their rank to distinguish the sons of the country house, half-hidden by cedars across the churchyard,

---

[62] John Harris, 'Gone to Ground', in Roy Strong, Marcus Binney, and John Harris, *The Destruction of the Country House 1875–1975* (London, 1974), 15–100, 16.
[63] Cited in Waterson (ed.), *The Country House Remembered*, 22.

from the poorest agricultural labourer'.[64] If Felicia Hemans had looked for common ground among the classes in England's homes, survivors of the Great War were to see it in her graves.

Like John Harris's image of heirs sipping gin and lime on sunny lawns, Coward's four Lords are blithely unaware of what was to confront them in the following decade. So while an audience of 1938 might have watched *Operette* with the knowledge that houses and heirs were tragically interconnected, those on stage are brimming with humour and high spirits. Though obviously oblivious to the Great War, which was still eight years away, the young men are nevertheless aware of the difficulties faced by their generation, making their comedy seem part of a generally ebullient attitude to life. By allowing voices to the owners of the Stately Homes, Coward, unlike his many predecessors, pre-empts hostile or servile responses from the audience. His four Lords seem to be laughing at themselves, and so the jokes become an act of sharing, among the speakers and, crucially, between stage and audience. Ironically, then, despite being a comment on the decline of aristocratic power, Lords Elderley, Borrowmere, Sickert, and Camp seem more in charge of 'The Stately Homes of England' than their ancestors, who were largely invisible in the insistently external approaches of Hemans and her many imitators. Paradoxically, the acknowledgement that the Homes of England are now 'rather in the lurch' seems to give the landed class a vitality denied by previous visitors to the poem. Coward's exposure of interior problems underlines the outwardness of Hemans's effusive representation, while simultaneously giving life to those who have inherited the cracks. Far from minimizing the predicament of the old houses and their owners, the song emphasizes the difficulties; but in doing so it also reveals the fighting spirit and ingenuity of the generation born into this moment of economic misfortune. It is laden with references to recent changes in the estate income, which have led to the pawning of pianos, sale of sporting prints, and mortgaging of estates.

The continuity that seemed such a current of strength, flowing through the generations in Mrs Hemans's Homes, is now shown to be a somewhat mixed blessing, threatening to

---

[64] Waterson (ed.), *The Country House Remembered*, 22.

overwhelm the latest successor with objects inappropriately venerated and ludicrously inescapable. The very antiquity of the houses is as much a burden as a benefit, for while Georgian provenance might enhance the value of the silver, it is less of an asset when it comes to the lavatory. No longer is unchanging domesticity upheld as an ideal—the need for renewal and adaptation seems urgent, while the future seems endangered rather than ensured by the past. At the same time, however, a little rethinking can turn even the antique plumbing to the advantage of the current owners. For although by the turn of the century (as Oscar Wilde had observed in *The Canterville Ghost*) Americans might have had the money, they were still lacking in old buildings and History. Rather than being abandoned entirely to the ghosts, like Andrew Lang's 'Haunted Homes', the ancestral mansions in Coward's song are thus rented out to those who might regard the shades of crazy younger sons and extremely rowdy nuns as a positive attraction.[65]

If Jewitt and Hall had applauded the generosity of the great nineteenth-century landowners who opened their doors from time to time to lesser beings, Noel Coward took a rather more irreverent view of the Stately Homes of England, recognizing that their future was far from secure. Although his speakers present their inheritance with a degree of irony, however, there is no admission of defeat. On the contrary. The burdens they are now bearing seem just the kind of challenge for which they were all born, and for which their early years at Public School have been the perfect preparation:

> But still we won't be beaten,
> We'll scrimp and screw and save,
> The playing fields of Eton
> Have made us frightfully brave.

For a post First World War audience, the allusion to Wellington's well-known (if inauthentic) attribution of the British victory at Waterloo to the playing fields of Eton might seem a grim reminder of the future of England's stately homes. It embodies just the kind of bracing equation between school

---

[65] *The Canterville Ghost* was published in 1887. On this and subsequent appearances of 'the country-house ghost', see Mandler, *Fall and Rise of the Stately Home*, 259–61.

sports and military prowess that had come to seem so desperately inappropriate in the face of trench warfare and machine guns.[66] In the Edwardian context of *Operette*, however, the reference is part of the song's humorous exposure of an underlying confidence that derives not only from inheritance but also from consolidating experiences at England's foremost public school. As with the title, the phrase is doubly allusive: the fields of Eton evoking attitudes inherited from Victorian parents and grandparents, while also recalling the four Lords' schooldays. For these speakers there is no division between the ancestral and the personal, even if precise details of the former are now somewhat hazy. The present is almost entirely constituted from earlier generations, whose varied traces are everywhere. The military language that seems to come so naturally to these speakers not only reaches back through the centuries, but also blends with twentieth-century phrases and concerns. Being 'mortgaged to the hilt', for example, carries memories of a sword-wielding past just as much as Hemans's 'greensward' or 'bowers', but the colloquial tone and less than idealized meaning give Coward's speakers an appealing immediacy which is altogether absent from the original poem.

This is partly perhaps because Coward's song responds not only to 'The Homes of England' but also to the intervening century of accumulating associations and massive social change. Hemans's composition was a christening present to the embryonic Victorian age, her call for 'hearts of native proof . . . | To guard each hallow'd wall' according perfectly with the later nineteenth-century emphasis on physical courage and patriotic pride. The values she articulated were just the kind of muscular Christian ideals that would later be drilled into young aristocrats such as Lords Elderley, Borrowmere, Sickert, and Camp—hence their willingness to 'fight for the Stately Homes of England', whether or not any specific enemy could be identified. At the same time, their situation in *Operette*, and in the social moment that the play depicts, demands a very distinctive, tongue-in-cheek manner utterly different from Hemans's

---

[66] Mark Girouard examines the connections between school sport and military action, and the resistance of the Great War to these conventional metaphors in *The Return to Camelot: Chivalry and the English Gentleman* (New Haven and London, 1981), 276–93.

external representation of England's Stately Homes. Their atti-
tude is in part a reflection of the very real economic difficulties
confronting the aristocracy at the turn of the century, which are
signalled so clearly in the second verse. But the tone is also a
brilliant evocation of what Ian Hay had described in 1914 as
'the Public School Attitude':

Among the higher English castes it is not good form to appear deeply
interested in anything, or to hold any serious views about anything, or
to possess any special knowledge about anything. In fact, the more you
know, the less you say, and the more passionately you are interested in
a matter, the less you 'enthuse' about it. That is the Public School
Attitude in a nutshell. It is a pose which entirely misleads foreigners,
and causes them to regard the English as an incredibly stupid or
indifferent nation.[67]

When Coward's patrician quartette admit to knowing little
more than 'how Caesar conquered Gaul | And how to whack a
cricket ball', they correspond closely to Hay's light-hearted pen
portrait. If the juxtaposition of the Gallic Wars and school sport
initially seems nothing more than an accidental conjunction for
the sake of a bouncy rhyme, however, it also draws on the wide-
spread awareness that the same breed of men were responsible
for bringing large areas of the world under British rule, and for
teaching the natives to play cricket in the process.

Coward's quartette may exhibit just the embarrassment
about 'brains' that Ian Hay discusses in his essay, but their song
nevertheless demonstrates a capacity to make very good use of
the scraps of knowledge that have somehow been acquired.
Walter Savage Landor's lament for Rose Aylmer ('Ah what
avails the sceptred race, | Ah what the form divine! What, every
virtue, every grace! | For, Aylmer, all were thine'), for example,
is cheerfully evoked and inverted in the opening lines, as the
four speakers show that they are at once representative of the
'sceptred race' and very much alive.[68] The prime reason for
adapting the quotation may be purely comic, as the familiar is
invoked in an unfamiliar context, with a striking disparity

---

[67] 'The Lighter Side of School Life: VII. The Father of the Man', *Blackwood's
Magazine*, cxcvi (Oct. 1914), 458–66, 458.
[68] 'Rose Aylmer' (1806), 1–4, *The Poetical Works of Walter Savage Landor*, ed.
Stephen Wheeler, 3 vols. (Oxford, 1937), ii. 77. The poem was revised in 1831 and
1846, and was finally inscribed on a monument to Rose Aylmer in 1909 at the site
of her grave in Calcutta.

between the tones of the original and its imitation. Beneath the immediate joke, however, is a quiet assertion of power, as the elegiac 'ah' becomes the emphatic 'are'. Landor's well-known articulation of the vanity of human riches may seem an ominous starting point for a song about the stately homes of England in 1906; Coward's adaptation nevertheless asserts the continuing possession of sceptres, whatever spectres might be lined up to appear in subsequent verses.

The curious echoes and juxtapositions of the first verse are indicative of not only an education lacking in coordination, but also an eclectic power, which absorbs and draws strength from the fragments amassed. Like Hemans's 'Homes of England', Coward's song is a virtual mosaic of old and new, of anecdotal reference, buried quotation and colloquial phrase. Its surface unity is achieved, however, not through a rhetorical deflection of any alternative viewpoint, but rather through the engagingly ironic and self-deprecating tone. Lines from diverse poems, like the strange acquisitions listed towards the end, acquire a new identity through being set side by side in the 'Stately Homes', their value enhanced by the curious new situation. Poems that display particular kinds of attitude, such as W. E. Henley's elegy on R. T. Hamilton Bruce, make ideal material, being at once evocative of a childhood strong on stiff upper lips and self-sacrifice and also memorable enough to be recognizable in the new, and entirely unmelodramatic context:

> In the fell clutch of circumstance
> I have not winced nor cried aloud.
> Under the bludgeonings of chance
> My head is bloody, but unbowed.[69]

The adaptation of Henley's somewhat extravagant portrayal of the isolated sufferer, who combats misfortune with stoic self-control, to Coward's set of 'charming | Innocuous young men' has a comic incongruity that brings out the absurd qualities of both. Nevertheless a certain heroic dimension emerges through the surface mockery, as the four Lords knock for six the very real threats to their position by blithely refusing to acknowledge the seriousness of their current predicament. Their comic self-

---

[69] 'Out of the night that covers me' (1875), *Echoes*, IV, *The Works of W. E. Henley*, 7 vols. (London, 1908), i. 125.

presentation reveals not only the inadequacies of their upbringing, but also a capacity to resist social change and disarm the opposition through charm.[70]

It is a careful balancing act, and one that threatens to tip out of control at any moment. For if, as Ian Hay points out, the English patrician pose is so easily misinterpreted, its power must also be precarious. Indeed, there are moments in the song when the deceptions of 'the Public School Attitude' can easily be mistaken for damaging revelations, such as the admission that 'our mental equipment may be slight | And we barely distinguish left from right'. On one level this is merely Etonian unwillingness to admit to cleverness, exaggerated for comic effect. For a 1930s audience, however, for whom 'left and right' were highly charged political terms, the suggestion that such matters were irrelevant, boring, or merely *beyond* the 'old Aristocracy' has more serious implications. In such lines it is possible to see Coward using his speakers ironically to make a stronger satirical comment on contemporary society, and to emphasize the gap between his immediate audience and the Edwardian setting of his play. What might have seemed charmingly disingenuous in 1906 was no longer appropriate in the late 1930s, just as Lord Newton's joke about the Grinling Gibbons at Lyme being fake began to seem less amusing after the First World War, when his house and entire way of life were under threat.[71] At other points in the song, it is internal inconsistency that seems to betray the surface *savoir faire*. The off-hand reference to Caesar's Conquest of Gaul, for example, gives way in Verse 3 to the rather more vigorous description of 'those beastly Roman bow-men', who 'Bitched our local Yeomen'. What appeared at the outset to be a casual endorsement of the successful expansion of Empire is thus checked suddenly by the portrayal of the Romans as a hostile invading army. The warmth of the language, here, and the identification with the victims rather than the victors, may suggest that 'the new Democracy' poses rather more of a threat than the speakers care to admit.

Whether such moments really invite meditations on the decline and fall of the old order, however, is doubtful, not only

---

[70] Cf. Anthony Blanche's observation that 'Of course those who have charm don't really need brains', Evelyn Waugh, *Brideshead Revisited* (London, 1945), 48.
[71] Waterson (ed.), *The Country House Remembered*, 23.

because of the song's capacity to turn the most incongruous scraps and allusions to comic contexts, but also because of its pace. Where Hemans had diverted attention from the tensions within her own poem by pointing to external threats, Coward's speakers are saved by the rapidity of their song, which always leaves its audience a step or two behind, unable to ponder underlying problems for fear of missing the next joke.

Coward's song is in many ways a celebration of incongruity, and the capacity to conquer through humour. He answers Hemans's somewhat unconvincing certainties by revealing the surprising power of uncertainty. For it is not only the audience who feels unsure about the implications of the various striking lines in the song—the speakers themselves are shown to revel in their ignorance ('We are quite prepared to fight—for our principles, | Tho' none of us know so far | What they really are'). This explicit foregrounding of uncertainty not only evokes Hemans's ideals ironically, but also exposes her tendency to disguise potential difficulties with empty rhetorical gestures. It is thus particularly interesting that when Coward alludes to Scott's *Marmion*, which had furnished the stirring epigraph for 'The Homes of England', he should choose the line 'Uncertain, coy and hard to please'. Where Hemans had evoked Fitz-Eustace's exclamatory 'Where's the coward that would not dare | To fight for such a land?', Coward prefers to recall Lord Marmion's observations on the fair sex: 'O Woman! in our hours of ease, | Uncertain, coy, and hard to please.'[72] By putting the second line of the couplet into the mouths of his speakers, Coward is again using the joke of defamiliarizing the familiar, and emphasizing the present's dependency on reconstituting the past. The obvious shift in gender, however, also serves to reveal the gulf between Victorian Public School ideals of manliness and his own 'rip-representative' aristocrats. The allusion follows immediately from the repetition of the speakers' names, which reach its mini-crescendo with 'Lord Camp', a title whose military *and* rather less masculine associations are underlined by the adaptation of Scott's memorable line.

This playful attitude to gender is perhaps the most mischievous aspect of Coward's response to Hemans's 'Homes', since it sends up the sexual stereotyping that is so fundamental

[72] *Marmion*, VI. xxx.

to her vision of England's future. In her image of domestic happiness, it is woman's voice that flows forth in song, while in Coward's revisiting the singers are male (but not very). The challenge to traditional assumptions about gender is a key element in Coward's encounter with Hemans since it rocks her poem from within. Though constrained in some ways by their inheritance, the heirs to the 'Stately Homes' are not confined to any straightforward repetition of the glorious page of old. The precious possessions of earlier generations do not command the care and veneration of a museum curator, but are there to be enjoyed or adapted to new purposes. Hemans's image of a 'flower, with some fine sense imbued', which belongs to 'The Home of Love' rather than 'The Homes of England', is as much part of her legacy as the 'Stately Homes of England' and so it too can be reused for the creation of a new image that will gently flaunt both family and literary convention, even as it ensures their continuity.[73] The more subversive tendencies of Coward's humour are carefully controlled nevertheless, so the main flow of the song continues undiverted by the implications of fleeting allusion and submerged innuendo.

It is the very capacity to pick the gems from their setting and fix them in new sequences, however, that so engages the audience, while at the same time rendering the old contexts dull and outworn. Indeed, the revivification of the tired and apparently redundant is perhaps the essential survival strategy of 'The Stately Homes of England', uniting literary allusions and colloquial clichés with lists of miscellaneous curiosities. Just as elderly drains can become objects of desire when presented in the right light, so too can all the broken debris of earlier genera- tions. Cromwell's niece may have been unimpressed by the 'very peculiar fowling piece', but it has survived to become a part of the family treasure none the less. Rather than destroy its value, the 'dirty crack' serves to link it ironically to both the saucer broken by Bloody Mary and, through linguistic play, to Chaucer's 'bawdy joke'. Though initially little more than a catalogue of bric-à-brac, the bits and pieces come together, cemented by rhymes, puns and alliteration, to form a new unity which is as fascinating as it is unpredictable.

If Hemans's juxtapositions of 'hut and hall' seem somewhat

[73] 'The Home of Love', 61, *Works*, vi. 200–3.

contrived, Coward's have an energy which derives from the foregrounding of incongruity. There is no pretence that these objects have any intrinsic relationship in the external world, but their new context gives them a peculiar value, setting them off creatively against each other. In 'The Stately Homes of England' these curious items belong unquestionably together, drawing on each other in ways resistant to conventional methods of classification or evaluation. To worry over their authenticity or historical contiguity is to misunderstand their special situation—just as Waugh's Charles Ryder has to be rebuked by Sebastian for enquiring about the dome at Brideshead ('O Charles, don't be such a tourist. What does it matter when it was built, if it's pretty?[74]).

The image of 'two pairs of tights—that King Arthur's Knights | Had completely worn away' is the perfect conclusion to 'The Stately Homes of England' in that it is wonderfully inconclusive. The tights follow naturally from the extraordinary list of possessions on display in country houses, while at the same time seeming to vanish before the audience's eyes and ears through being 'completely worn away'. As 'two pairs' they are almost a counterpart to the four speakers, who seem similarly proud and precious, and yet threatened with disappearance through the combined pressures of earlier generations and the end of the show. The blend of romance and mundaneness, as Arthurian legend is domesticated into an image of tired hosiery, epitomizes both the bathetic comedy of the entire song and its capacity to bring to life things normally remote or unreal. Knights in tights make an extravagantly irreverent image, playing up the gender joke and collapsing boundaries not only between romance and history, past and present, male and female, but also the aristocracy and the stage. This self-reflexivity is in itself a theatrical convention, often used to bring a play to an end, but in the context of *Operette* it has particular resonance. For in the play which originally brought Lords Elderley, Borrowmere, Sickert, and Camp into the limelight, Lady Messiter prevents her son from marrying an actress on the grounds that it would ruin his career in the army. The 1930s audience would nevertheless have seen that her unbending adherence to class distinctions was likely to have fatal consequences for her eldest son with the out-

[74] Waugh, *Brideshead Revisited*, 72.

break of the First World War. The survival of the tights rather than the Knights themselves has a certain dark irony in this context, despite the exuberant comedy of the image itself. The failure of *Operette*, too, meant that Lady Messiter and her family were rapidly forgotten, while the only characters to survive the play were those whose posterity has depended on the very medium she so despised.

Although this is an irony of theatrical history rather than an intrinsic part of the play itself, Coward's song does in fact leave listeners with a sense of inconclusiveness and doubt about the future. The quartette has already appeared, disappeared, and reappeared, so it is not clear at the end of their last refrain whether or not there is more to come. We simply arrive at the pair of tights and stop. The audience is thus left wondering whether this is the most cherished part of the great collection, or whether things have completely fallen apart. Has the accumulative weight of heirlooms become too much to manage, or has the stock now run dry leaving only a few miscellaneous items that have no interest for rich purchasers or businesslike creditors? There is no final indication as to whether the fragments are being shored against ruin on a grand scale, or whether they represent a mere taste of a massive collection that will continue to reconstitute itself through adapting past to present. The ironic poise of the song is sustained to the very end, leaving the audience to guess at what might now succeed. Where Felicia Hemans had concluded her celebration of England's Homes with a benedictory appeal to the future, Noel Coward brings his song to a close with a moment of uncertainty in keeping with the ironies of the entire piece. Like Hemans, he has confronted the question of inheritance, but rather than merely accepting it as a permanent, protective force, he has presented its ambivalent aspects, and the challenges posed to later generations. 'The Stately Homes of England' is a direct descendant of 'The Homes of England', but rather than being inspired to imitation, provoked into antagonism, or intimidated into silence, the new poem takes familiar materials and breathes new life into them, before returning its ancestor politely but firmly to its nineteenth-century shelf.

6

'The Irish for No'

The Irish for No

Was it a vision, or a waking dream? I heard her voice before I saw
What looked like the balcony scene in *Romeo and Juliet*, except
    Romeo
Seemed to have shinned up a pipe and was inside arguing with her. The
    casements
Were wide open and I could see some Japanese-style wall-hangings, the
    dangling
Quotation marks of a yin-yang mobile. *It's got nothing*, she was
    snarling, *nothing*
To do with politics, and, before the bamboo curtain came down,
That goes for you too!

It was time to turn into the dog's-leg short-cut from Chlorine Gardens
Into Cloreen Park, where you might see an *Ulster Says No* scrawled on
    the side
Of the power-block—which immediately reminds me of the Eglantine
    Inn
Just on the corner: on the missing *h* of Cloreen, you might say. We
    were debating,
Bacchus and the pards and me, how to render *The Ulster Bank—the
    Bank*
That likes to Say Yes into Irish, and whether eglantine was alien to
    Ireland.
I cannot see what flowers are at my feet, when yes is the verb repeated,
Not exactly yes, but phatic nods and whispers. *The Bank That
    Answers All*
Your Questions, maybe? That Greek portico of Mourne granite,
    dazzling
With promises and feldspar, mirrors you in the Delphic black of its
    windows.

And the bruised pansies of the funeral parlour are dying in reversed
gold letters,
The long sigh of the afternoon is not yet complete on the promontory
where the victim,
A corporal in the UDR from Lisbellaw, was last seen having driven over
half
Of Ulster, a legally-held gun was found and the incidence of stress
came up
On the headland which shadows Larne Harbour and the black pitch of
warehouses.
There is a melancholy blast of diesel, a puff of smoke which might be
black or white.
So the harbour slips away to perilous seas as things remain unsolved;
we listen
To the *ex cathedra* of the fog-horn, and *drink and leave the world
unseen*—
What's all this to the Belfast business-man who drilled
Thirteen holes in his head with a Black & Decker? It was just a normal
morning
When they came. The tennis-court shone with dew or frost, a little
before dawn.
The border, it seemed, was not yet crossed: the Milky Way trailed
snowy brambles,
The stars clustered thick as blackberries. They opened the door into
the dark:
The murmurous haunt of flies on summer eves. Empty jam-jars.
Mish-mash. Hotch-potch. And now you rub your eyes and get
acquainted with the light
A dust of something reminiscent drowses over the garage smell of
creosote,
The concrete: blue clouds in porcelain, a paint-brush steeped in a
chipped cup;
Staples hyphenate a wet cardboard box as the upturned can of oil still
spills
And the unfed cat toys with the yin-yang of a tennis-ball, debating
whether *yes* is *no*.[1]

First encounters with Felicia Hemans's 'Homes of England' or
James Clarence Mangan's 'The Dying Enthusiast to his Friend'
are unlikely to prove particularly unsettling to the reader. The
sentiments expressed in the two poems may not be entirely

---

[1] 'The Irish for No' is the title-poem of Ciaran Carson's collection, *The Irish for
No*, published in July 1987 by The Gallery Press in Dublin. It first appeared in *The
Honest Ulsterman*, 82 (Winter 1986), 3–4, together with 'Serial'.

congenial, but they are immediately accessible, at least on one level. Their forms are regular, their diction clear, and their epigraphs, distinguished from the rest of the text, seem formal devices in keeping with the conventions of the time. There is no immediate indication that the quotations are anything other than traditional mottoes—appropriate introductions to new compositions.

Scott's rhetorical question seems to be addressed by the patriotic poem that unfolds beneath it, while Shelley's eloquent musing on death finds an appropriate counterpart in the words of Mangan's Enthusiast. That the relationship between these poems and their borrowed lines turns out to be rather less smooth than is apparent initially should by now be evident, but in each case the possibility of simply reading a straightforward text, complete with title and epigraph, remains. Very different, then, is the signal sent out to readers by Ciaran Carson's 'The Irish for No', a poem which also begins with another poem, but which from the first exudes irony, discord, and conflict.

Like his predecessor, James Clarence Mangan, Carson chooses a starting line from a great English Romantic poem—not *Adonais*, but rather the best-known composition of its subject, John Keats's 'Ode to a Nightingale'. Like Felicia Hemans's choice from *Marmion*, too, the opening line takes the form of a question: '*Was it a vision, or a waking dream?*' But where Mangan evoked Shelley in a dialogue between friends, and Scott's challenge implies an obvious response, the quotation from Keats appears in a context of rejection and anger, its lyrical musing transformed into painful uncertainty. Ironically, Keats's text is more obviously woven into Carson's poem than the neatly rolled epigraphs of the nineteenth century. Mangan seems to have welcomed Shelley into his composition, consciously highlighting traces of the English poet. Carson's lines, however, lock uncomfortably with those of Keats, their differences marked out by the typographical shifts. Mrs Hemans may have been content to place Scott's verse in an authoritative position above her own work, but Carson's poem seems bent on dismembering Keats's Ode, nullifying its question with a pre-emptive title. Whatever the English poem might be offering or pursuing, the answer seems to be a resounding 'No'.

To see such a beautiful, familiar poem broken to bits and

crammed into a new, disturbing context is an experience quite unlike those examined so far. The strategy is very different from Noel Coward's mischievous play on 'The Homes of England', for the context largely blacks out the humour. In Northern Ireland in the mid-1980s, the survival of things of beauty was precarious and may even have seemed strangely inappropriate; here Keats's lines are almost submerged in the streets of Belfast. In a conflict at once inherited and self-perpetuating, forms from the past appear precious but at the same time oddly culpable, desirable and repellent, unignorable and yet, irrelevant. Carson accordingly seizes on Keats's 'Nightingale' not with the high-spirited irreverence of Noel Coward encountering Hemans, but more in the manner of his own 'unfed cat', toying 'with the yin-yang of a tennis-ball, debating whether yes is no'.

Yin-yang, black-white, mish-mash—even the poem's imagery seems to challenge its own neat binaries, as words and referents pull apart, posing the question of whether any encounters in modern Belfast can find adequate expression. For although the poem begins with Keats, it is also beginning with an image of what appears and, almost simultaneously, does not appear to be a meeting between lovers. The 'vision, or waking dream' (if 'it' is either) has not after all been triggered by thoughts of Keats, but rather by the sight of a couple at a window—by the immediate world of Belfast:

Was it a vision or a waking dream? I heard her voice before I saw
What looked like the balcony scene in Romeo and Juliet, except
  Romeo
Seemed to have shinned up a pipe and was inside arguing with her. The
  casements
Were wide open . . .

The speaker's attempt to express his encounter with their encounter leads to a string of ironic allusions, to 'Ode to a Nightingale', 'Ode to Psyche', and to *Romeo and Juliet,* the very proliferation serving to derail the parallels that are apparently being suggested. The English literary tradition seems fragmented and impotent in the context of Northern Ireland, evoked only to demonstrate its inability to mediate in these circumstances. For rather than declare love in heady Shakespearian blank verse, the Irish 'Romeo' is silenced by the 'snarling' resistance of his unnamed Juliet. In a matter of lines, moments of high poetry are similarly resisted by the insistence of colloquial speech, which leaves the familiar allusions dangling as helplessly as the 'Quotation marks' of the yin-yang mobile.[2]

Carson's poem seems to be saying 'No' not only to Keats and Shakespeare but also, perhaps, to the kinds of approach that seek for affirmative meanings in the wreckage of torn communities. If this is the case, then 'The Irish for No' would be consistent with Carson's earlier review of *North*, where Heaney is taken to task for putting on 'an Ulster '75 Exhibition of the Good that can come out of Troubled Times'.[3] Carson's objection to 'applying wrong notions of history instead of seeing what's before your eyes' might be seen in the background of his own work, which deals unflinchingly with the sectarian killings that were taking place as the poem was written. If Heaney had been criticized for including not only Viking heroes, but also 'Shakespeare, Hercules and Raleigh (to name but a few who figure in the Madame Tussaud's Gallery of Greats)', then it would seem rather contradictory for Carson to be invoking Shakespeare, some ten years on, in an affirmation of human values over violence.

The evocation of *Romeo and Juliet* in response to scenes of bloodshed and intense civil conflict is by no means unusual, however. One of the documentaries on the Bosnian crisis of the early 1990s, for example, homed in on the individual tragedy of a young couple from either side of the ethnic divide and chose as its title 'Romeo and Juliet in Sarajevo'. When he reviewed the programme for *The New York Times*, Bob Herbert praised its strategy of focusing 'on the thoroughly human individuals caught up in a horror that, from afar, can seem abstract and

---

[2] Cf. Carson's review of Christopher Reid's 'Katerina Brac' (which appeared in the same volume of *The Honest Ulsterman*, 82 (Winter, 1986) as 'The Irish for No'), 'Cannot poetry speak for itself? Must everything appear in quotation marks?', 86. See also 'Queen's Gambit', *Belfast Confetti* (Dublin, 1989), whose reference to 'quotation marks' is discussed by Richard Kirkland in *Literature and Culture in Northern Ireland since 1965: Moments of Danger* (London, 1996), 45.

[3] Carson, 'Escaped from the Massacre? *North* by Seamus Heaney', *The Honest Ulsterman*, 50 (1975), 183–6, 186. For discussion of the review in relation to *The Irish for No*, see Neil Corcoran, 'One Step Forward, Two Steps Back: Ciaran Carson's *The Irish for No*', in Neil Corcoran (ed.), *The Chosen Ground: Essays on the Contemporary Poetry of Northern Ireland* (Chester Springs and Bridgend, 1992), 213–33.

almost unimaginable', before going on to draw broader conclusions: 'only the times and places change, Bosnia today, Rwanda and Burundi tomorrow. Jews versus Arabs, Chinese versus Japanese, blacks versus whites. There are various ostensible reasons for the endless conflicts—ideological differences, border disputes, oil—but dig just a little and you will uncover the ruinous ethnic or religious origins of the clash.'[4] While such sentiments may offer some consolation to distant observers, however, they are not perhaps the most helpful to those in the midst of a particular conflict, with specific political and historical dimensions and where the casualties include friends.

Belfast has also produced its lovers crossed by their affiliations to opposing communities, but Carson's poem is not prepared to represent individual passions as redemptive or transcendent. It makes no concessions to the desires of its readers for hope, inspiration, or even catharsis. What the speaker sees and hears is really nothing like *Romeo and Juliet*, though the recollection of such an archetypal love scene may serve to darken metaphorically what is now being experienced, even if physically the window is lit up against a black night. But if the allusion is not meant to suggest the importance of individual relationships in a larger conflict, neither is Shakespeare's work set up as an unreachable ideal against which the present is being found horribly wanting. This is not tragedy, but neither is it mock-heroic or satire, where great literature of the past towers over modern life to emphasize its littleness. Instead, *Romeo and Juliet* is being dismissed, along with Keats's Odes, as inadequate to the matter in hand.

In his literary references Carson thus seems to be employing strategies quite different from those examined in previous chapters. He is clearly not engaged in the reverential activity of imitation, nor does he seem bent on deepening his own poem through allusion to kindred pieces from the past. His opening quotation is not a motto, standing above the text to signal an essential theme. But neither is he creating a parody, since this, like the mock heroic, suggests a greater interest in an earlier text than this poem seems prepared to acknowledge. To read 'The

---

[4] Herbert's review of 'Romeo and Juliet in Sarajevo', *New York Times* (8 May 1994), 17, is reprinted in Alan Hager (ed.), *Understanding Romeo and Juliet* (London, 1999), 204–5.

Irish for No' as any kind of wrestle with past masters imbues the older texts with a power that is not readily conceded by the deeply ironic voice of the opening lines. Just as the form defies easy categorization according to familiar genres, so the use of quotation is teasingly enigmatic.[5] The recent tendency to see Irish literature in terms of postcolonial ideas may encourage a similar approach to Carson's work, and afford some fresh insight into his deployment of Keats's Ode.[6] Homi Bhabha's ideas on mimicry, for example, offer an analysis of cultural exchange that is rather different from the more submissive attitudes towards a dominant culture that have often been assumed to prevail in a colonized country: 'Under cover of camouflage, mimicry, like the fetish, is a part-object that radically revalues the normative knowledges of the priority of race, writing, history. For the fetish mimes the forms of authority at the point at which it deauthorizes them.'[7] According to Bhabha, in the 'ambivalent world of "not quite/not white" ', it is the *founding objects* of the Western world' which become 'erratic, eccentric, accidental *objets trouvés*', as the centre is displaced and the margins become central. A Bible distributed by an early nineteenth-century evangelist to the bemused of Bengal then becomes 'strangely dismembered': losing its status as an object of reverence and embodiment of the divine, it is just something to be bartered in the markets or used for wrapping paper. Bhabha's brief but provocative essay explicitly challenges the kind of view that sees the colonized subject being immobilized by his unrealizable desire to imitate the forms of an imposed power. Rather than remaining passive and incapable, the colonized subject emerges from Bhabha's account as a potentially threatening figure, while the colony acquires the power to

[5] To suggest, as Neil Corcoran does, that 'this is a poem which, throughout, almost uninterpretably plays Keats's "Ode to a Nightingale" across its own wayward surface' ('One Step Forward, Two Steps Back', 214) is perhaps a little defeatist nevertheless. In the same essay, Corcoran points more helpfully to the influences of C. K. Williams, Irish story-telling, and traditional music on Carson's 'very long line', 217.

[6] *The Star Factory* contains numerous thoughts on twentieth-century Irish history, such as the fascinating meditation on 'The General Post Office', 30–40.

[7] Bhabha, 'Of Mimicry and Man', *The Location of Culture*, 91. For a stimulating and postcolonially influenced exploration of the relationship between Ireland and England, see Declan Kiberd, *Inventing Ireland: The Literature of the Modern Nation* (London, 1995).

challenge assumptions which may have been an essential part of the dominant nation's stable identity.

Although the relationship between Ireland and England is perhaps too singular to be easily accommodated by postcolonial theories of discourse, Bhabha's ideas on mimicry may provide an interesting opening into a poem which seems to treat another partly as a foreign object available for dismemberment. For just as a Bible might have been oddly out of place in early nineteenth-century Bengal, so the works of Keats may not have seemed appropriate reading matter for everyone in late twentieth-century Belfast. Until very recently, Keats's poetry was widely regarded as being deliberately apolitical: a position especially hard to justify among those encountering bombs and bullets on a daily basis. When Richard Kearney addressed the ethical responsibilities of poets in his Field Day pamphlet of 1984, for example, it was Keats who seemed to embody the dangerous tendency to revere imagination and myth, 'divorced from the challenge of reality':

Keats once remarked that imagination is amoral and apolitical, transcending all considerations of good and evil. 'The poetical character,' he wrote, has no ethical commitments and takes 'as much delight in conceiving an Iago as an Imogen.' 'What shocks the virtuous philosopher', he concluded, 'delights the chameleon Poet.' Keats was no doubt right—up to a point. And that point, I suggest, is often signalled when literary myth spills over into political myth. So that while a poet may be exempt from moral intentions—we all prefer poetry without propaganda—he or she can never be wholly exempt from moral consequences.[8]

In the context of Northern Ireland, Keats seemed an example of the kind of aesthetic that allowed for a false separation between art and life and a worrying abnegation of moral responsibilities. The very perfection of Keats's greatest poetry seemed to draw 'a magic circle' around itself and thus exclude dialogue with 'all that is other'. Kearney's essay, on the other hand, is arguing for the counter-demands of history and the power of circumstance to prevent literature from ascending into the realms of transcendent truth.

---

[8] Richard Kearney, *Myth and Motherland*, in *Ireland's Field Day* (London, 1985), 61–82, 78. He quotes Keats's letter to Richard Woodhouse of 27 October 1818, *Letters*, i. 387.

Nor was it merely Keats's subject matter, as traditionally perceived, that belonged to a different world: the very form and language of his poems, especially the Odes, have a completeness and, crucially, an Englishness that seems far removed from modern Ireland. When Declan Kiberd composed his own pamphlet on the English invention of 'an idea of Ireland', the first English writer to be cited in the case was Keats, describing the Irish in 1818 as 'cunning blusterers and gallous fellows'.[9] Here Keats emerges as a dubious pioneer, contributing to the creation of a disastrous English attitude to Ireland:

The Scotchman will never give a decision on any point—he will never commit himself in a sentence which may be referred to as a meridian in his notions of things—so that you do not know him—and yet you may come in nigher neighbourhood to him than to the irishman who commits himself in so many places that it dazes your head—A Scotchman's motive is more easily discovered than an irishman's. A Scotchman will go wisely about to deceive you, an irishman cunningly. An Irishman would bluster out of any discovery to his disadvantage— A Scotchman would retire perhaps without much desire of revenge— An Irishman likes to be thought a gallous fellow—A scotchman is contented with himself—It seems to me they are both sensible of the Character they hold in England and act accordingly to Englishmen.

In this somewhat unfortunate letter, evidently designed to amuse his younger brother, Keats strikes the modern Irish critic as a quintessentially English poet, representative of the problematic attitudes encountered by the Irish over so many years.

Even Seamus Heaney, whose early poetry was strongly influenced by Keats and other English writers, has still confessed to feelings rather akin to social unease, when confronted at school by *The Ambleside Book of Verse*, an anthology of English Romantic writing: 'we expected that the language on the written page would take us out of our unofficial speaking selves and transport us to a land of formal words where we would have to be constantly on our best verbal behaviour'.[10]

---

[9] Declan Kiberd, *Anglo-Irish Attitudes*, in *Ireland's Field Day*, 83–105. The reference is to Keats's letter to Tom Keats of 11 July 1818, *Letters*, i. 330–31. For a useful discussion of the Field Day pamphlets, see Marilynn Richtarik, *Acting Between the Lines: The Field Day Theatre Company and Irish Cultural Politics 1980–1984* (Oxford, 1994).

[10] Heaney, 'Burns's Art Speech', in Crawford (ed.), *Robert Burns and Cultural Authority*, 218. See also Ch. 2.

Although Heaney does not specifically mention Keats in this passage, the contrast he draws between the lofty language of English poetry, exemplified by Shelley's 'Hail to thee blithe spirit', and the reassuring demotic vocabulary that he stumbled across with such relief in Burns's 'To a Mouse' reveals the sense of a great gulf between the spoken and the written, standard English and its provincial variations. Indeed, he had expressed a more acute sense of difference some years earlier, in *North*:

> I tried to write about the sycamores
> And innovated a South Derry rhyme
> With *hushed* and *lulled* full chimes for *pushed* and *pulled*.
> Those hobnailed boots from beyond the mountain
> Were walking, by God, all over the fine
> Lawns of elocution.
>   Have our accents
> Changed? 'Catholics, in general, don't speak
> As well as students from the Protestant schools.'
> Remember that stuff? Inferiority
> Complexes, stuff that dreams were made on.[11]

Despite the ironies of the passage, with its echoes of *The Tempest* and *A Portrait of the Artist as a Young Man* (not to mention the difficulty so neatly pointed out by Bernard O'Donoghue of determining the pronunciation of '*hushed*' and '*lulled*'), it demonstrates only too clearly the sense of distance between the people of Northern Ireland and the English tradition.[12] As Heaney observes in the same poem:

> Ulster was British, but with no rights on
> The English lyric.

His own attitudes have undergone a number of modifications in the quarter-century since *North* was published, but the need to distinguish his poetry from the English tradition has been a recurrent preoccupation. As he observed in *An Open Letter*, for

---

[11] 'The Ministry of Fear', *North* (London, 1975), 64. See also Ciaran Carson's 'The New Estate', with its reference to 'Rusty | Iambics that escaped your discipline | Of shorn lawns', *The New Estate* (Belfast, 1976), 41.

[12] *The Tempest*, IV. i. 156–7, is played against the representations of Catholic education in *A Portrait of the Artist as a Young Man*. The continuing importance to Heaney of Joyce is discussed in Ch. 7, below. For Bernard O'Donoghue's perceptive reading of Heaney's language and the phonetic implications of the passage in *North*, see *Seamus Heaney and the Language of Poetry* (Hemel Hempstead, 1994), 73.

which he adopted the Standard Habbie stanza characteristically used by Burns, 'My passport's green.'[13]

For Heaney's contemporary, Brendan Kennelly, it is not so much the diction of English Romantic verse that makes it seem inappropriate to those still in school, but rather the inherent difficulty of the meaning: 'to expect a 17 year old to understand and give an account of the subtle complexity of "Ode to a Nightingale" is truly stupid. I don't think you should ask any body at any stage of his or her life to understand more than what his or her experience has given.'[14] Though Kennelly's objection to letting Keats loose among schoolchildren is of a slightly different kind from Heaney's recollection of his polite encounters with *The Ambleside Book of Verse*, it reveals a similar sense of a somewhat unmanageable obstacle set up between the text and the reader. While part of the barrier has been built from the unhappy history of Irish–British relations, which has turned questions of language, education, and the teaching of literature in Ireland into issues of acute political sensitivity, the remarks by Heaney and Kennelly also suggest a more basic sense of alienation: of a natural awkwardness in the face of the unfamiliar. Since the birds known as nightingales in England are migrants who do not travel as far as Ireland, the 'Ode to a Nightingale' can be seen almost as a symbol of an essentially foreign culture.[15]

The difficulty with English traditions and especially with language is not, of course, confined to the Catholic community. Tom Paulin, for example, has expressed a similar sense of disjunction between standard English and the language of Northern Ireland, even though his tone is less ironic and remains characteristically unabashed. When he pondered the 'language question' in the early 1980s, the differences perceived led more readily to a celebration of the vernacular than to respect for the standard. According to Paulin, the writer who

[13] 'An Open Letter' was published as a Field Day pamphlet in response to Heaney's inclusion in Blake Morrison and Andrew Motion's anthology, *The Penguin Book of Contemporary British Poetry* (Harmondsworth, 1982), *Ireland's Field Day*, 23–32.

[14] Reported in Siobhan McSweeney's 'The Poet's Picture of Education', *The Crane Bag*, 7/2 (1983), 134–42, 139.

[15] Cf. Seamus Heaney, 'The Irish Nightingale | Is a sedge-warbler', 'Serenades', *Wintering Out* (London, 1972), 50.

employs words peculiar to his local community 'will express something very near to a familial relationship because every family has its hoard of relished words which express its members' sense of kinship. These words act as a kind of secret sign and serve to exclude the outside world.'[16] The corollary of this may, nevertheless, be a sense of distance from the language used by those outside the family. The very next paragraph turns to the notion of an ideal 'Standard British English', but only to argue that 'such an aspiration must always be impossible for any Irish writer'. Although this remark might be read in isolation as a confession of failure, the essay as a whole makes it clear that this is far from the case. Paulin's attitude towards Standard English here is quite different in tone from the rather apologetic frustration voiced two centuries earlier by James Beattie when he was faced with a similar recognition of the difference between his own speech and the words of the printed pages emanating from South of the Border. *A New Look at the Language Question* may acknowledge some doubts about the possibility of 'good critical prose' in Ireland, but there is no touch of contempt in Paulin's account of 'Irish English', the language that 'lives lithely on the tongue'. Instead it seems instinct with energy, 'a language which lives a type of romantic, unfettered existence—no dictionary accommodates it, no academy regulates it, no common legislative body speaks it, and no national newspaper guards it'. The language that has evolved in the North of Ireland is emphatically different from that which holds sway in England, but this does not lead inevitably to the kind of collective inferiority complex so often associated with Scottish intellectuals in the decades following the 1707 Union. For Tom Paulin at least, its very lack of discipline symbolizes a spirit of independence and originality.

The history of Ireland is, of course, quite different from that of Scotland, and the issue of language perhaps even more politically charged. Nevertheless, the contrast between the acknowledgement by some contemporary Irish poets and some Enlightenment Scots that standard written English is fundamentally different from their own spoken language is instructive. For if a recognition of cultural difference leads not to

---

[16] Tom Paulin, *A New Look at the Language Question* (1983), reprinted in *Ireland's Field Day*, 3–22, 16.

self-denigration but rather to a rejection of the alien, then the engagement with particular artefacts or texts is likely to provoke a stance more combative than deferential. And hence, perhaps, the relevance of Bhabha's ideas of mimicry to contemporary Irish culture rather than any notion of paralysing imitation or, to recall the distinctions attempted in the first chapter of this study, the forensic rather than the devotional model of eloquence, which adopts an opening quotation in order to demolish the case of the previous speaker.

If the relationship between writings from different parts of these islands is to be explored, then a sense of prevailing attitudes towards the local and the national, the familial and the standard, is of the utmost significance. The very diversity of languages even in a single locale, however, makes it difficult to gather individual writers under one umbrella, however capacious and inviting it might seem. And, as the elegant literature of the Scottish Enlightenment demonstrates, self-depreciatory statements made by writers are not always borne out by the evidence of their own work, so caution is advisable when exploring such areas. Poems especially are capable of reflecting a number of conscious and unconscious attitudes, and of employing wit and irony to render meaning complicated and often uncertain. Rather than attempting to fit poets and poems into a single theory of interpretation, then, it is perhaps more satisfactory to venture tentatively on the particular, and especially in the context of Northern Ireland.

For Ciaran Carson, whose own familial language is not 'Irish English', 'Ulster English', 'Ulster Lallans', or even 'Ullans' but rather Irish, the 'language question' poses a slightly different problem from that discussed by Paulin. Here the difference is not merely between the written and spoken word, but between different oral discourses, too. In one of the autobiographical passages of his fascinating prose work, *The Star Factory*, he recalls Hans Christian Andersen's 'Constant Tin Soldier', a story familiar since childhood:

I cannot tell if I received this story first from reading or from listening, for my father used to cull such stories from *The Arabian Nights*, Grimm, Robert Louis Stevenson, Arthur Conan Doyle, and the like, and re-tell them to us children in Irish, which was the language of the home (the world beyond its vestibule was densely terraced with the English language, which I remember learning or lisping on the street, whose populations looked on us with fear and pity; yet we strange bilingual creatures, self-segregated from the mêlée, sometimes felt we had an edge on it, as we used our first language as a private code, in the way that the US intelligence services, in the Second World War, employed speakers of dwindling Native American languages. As English words and constructs seeped into our speech, our gradually bastardized Irish stood in daily correction by my father, and to this day I have a deep uncertainty about prepositions, those important little syntactical bolts which English uses in such confusing abundance). I can hear the smoky grain of my father's voice in the dark as I enter the colour of the world described by him.[17]

In Carson's recollection, there is no clearly defined opposition between reading and listening, written and spoken. Tales which have begun in distant oral communities, have then been fixed on the page by master story-tellers, whose own words have been translated into English books, only to be retold in Irish by Carson's father, whose command of narrative is a recurrent pre-occupation of his son's strange text.[18] The recollection of early childhood, however, where magical stories were imported and turned into Irish, is set against the experience of the world out-side, where English words 'seeped' into his speech, and in doing so, turned the 'language of home' into a 'bastardized' language, in need of regulation. English seems an external force, and part of 'the densely terraced' surroundings, but nevertheless it has the power to intrude and transform the very heart of Carson's existence.

Despite the use of Irish in his childhood, the language of his own poetry is English, as he explained to Niall McGrath in an interview conducted soon after the publication of his later volume, *First Language*: 'I write in English because the Irish that I spoke was the Irish of home and I wouldn't be able to write in the same way in Irish as I can in the English I have. If I were to write in Irish I'd have to go back and learn it all over again very well.'[19] The remark is not made in a tone of indignation or

---

[17] *The Star Factory*, 269–70.
[18] *The Star Factory* opens with the memorable image of Carson's father, who worked as a postman, telling a story while 'seated on the "throne" of the out-house', 1.
[19] 'Ciaran Carson: Interview with Niall McGrath', 64–5.

regret, however, for he continues, 'I feel at times that the idea that I should write in Irish because it's the language of the Irish soul or something like this is a bit off, anyway.' Carson's sympathy with Irish culture does not mean an unquestioning adherence to the Irish language as a medium inherently superior to English. Indeed, in *The Star Factory*, his emphasis is on the creative potential of a bilingual upbringing, rather than an exclusively Irish-speaking background. For if some moments in the text suggest the sense of a Fall from a magical bilingual world of colour into a linguistically disciplined adolescence, the volume also demonstrates that memories of his earliest years continue to provide a sustaining current. Reminiscences of the Falls Road may seem a far cry from Wordsworth's recollections of the English Lakes or indeed of Heaney's fond returns to Anahorish, but in the middle of Carson's insistently urban and changing landscape comes a deep sense of continuity centred on the figure of his father and his great hoard of stories. If his childhood home rendered much of the surrounding neighbourhood unfamiliar territory, it also afforded imaginative resources that were to prove both liberating and deeply sustaining:

I used to lull myself to sleep with language, mentally repeating, for example, the word *capall*, the Irish for horse, which seemed to be more onomatopoeically equine than its English counterpart; gradually, its trochaic foot would summon up a ghostly echo of 'cobble', till, wavering between languages, I would allow my disembodied self to drift out the window and glide through the silent dark gas-lit streets above the mussel-coloured cobblestones. I was bound for the Star Factory, where words were melted down and like tallow cast into new moulds.[20]

Although his approach is rather different, Carson is no more apologetic here than Tom Paulin about the use of his own 'language of home'. If being bilingual set him apart, it was also quietly empowering, and opened doors inaccessible to others. The condition of 'wavering between languages' was to prove highly creative, not merely through offering an opportunity to engage with linguistic puzzles and associations far more mercurial than a single language might allow, but also by encouraging imaginative freedoms that explode any sense of being limited to or by 'what's before your eyes'. It has also left

[20] *The Star Factory*, 234.

Carson with a fundamental sense of alternatives rather than absolutes:

I was brought up with Irish at home, so at an early age I was aware that there was the English and the Irish language. And at the end of the day if something is said in Irish it's not the same as if it is said in the English language. So there's no final way of saying **here is how it is**. There isn't finally an answer to the objective structure of the world. So that what is going on here, in terms of how things are expressed and things are said with absolutes, that there's only one way, it has to be this way or that way; from a very early age I understood that it's not like that. It depends on the language.[21]

This equivocation seems very different from Tom Paulin's forth-right approach to the 'language question'; and yet Carson's sense of his first language being 'a private code' seems strikingly similar to Paulin's view of local vocabulary as a 'secret sign' powerful enough to exclude outsiders. Ironically, however, those excluded by the 'strange bilingual creatures' of Carson's immediate family were those so at home with Paulin's 'Irish English'.

The 'language question' in the North of Ireland is by no means a straightforward confrontation with standard English, but remains complicated by internal differences between Irish (complete with regional variations), the Scots-influenced language of Ulster, spoken English, and the great variety of words and constructions that have evolved from these rather tangled roots. In some ways, the situation seems similar to that facing Burns two centuries earlier, as he explored the creative possibilities of standard English and the Scots dialect, while also developing an interest in Highland culture, perhaps influenced by his father's roots in the North-East, perhaps by the softening of attitudes towards the *Gaeltachd* in the later eighteenth century. Hence perhaps the affinities with Burns that have been expressed by both Heaney and Paulin, as they each recognize in his vocabulary terms familiar from their own local areas.[22] Despite similarities in the linguistic complexion, however, there are crucial differences between rural Ayrshire and modern

---

[21] 'Ciaran Carson: Interview with Niall McGrath', 64.
[22] See Heaney, 'Burns's Art Speech' for explicit comment; Paulin has also analysed the Scots elements in Heaney's 'Broagh' in *The English Review*, 2/3 (1992), 28–9.

Ulster. Eighteenth-century Scotland may have possessed an equally rich linguistic diversity, but those most exercised by their embarrassment over Scots were generally happy to see the old Celtic language recede. Although the deliberate policy of erosion which was put into force in response to the Jacobite Risings eventually relaxed and the latter part of the century even saw the creation of the Highland Society, Scottish ideas of nationhood have never centred on the Gaelic. Gaelic poetry enjoyed an astonishing revival in the eighteenth century, while symbols of Highland culture were absorbed into a distinctively Scottish identity, but Scottish nationalism has always been driven by the energies of those in the Lowlands. In twentieth-century Ireland, however, the Gaelic language has been a key political issue since before the establishment of the Free State, and continues to complicate senses of identity North and South of the Border.

In Ireland, the Gaelic League was set up in 1893 to address the issues raised by Douglas Hyde in his famous lecture of November 1892, 'On the Necessity for De-Anglicising the Irish People'. Hyde had taken as his theme the 'anomalous position' of the Irish who were 'imitating England and yet apparently hating it'.[23] His solution to this demoralizing situation was to urge the revival of the Irish language, the loss of which over the previous century was the 'greatest blow and the sorest stroke' inflicted by the 'rapid Anglicisation of Ireland'. Although Hyde resigned from the Gaelic League in 1915, as it became a more overtly political body, his ideas continued to inspire later nationalists; Padraic Pearse, one of the leaders of the Easter Rising, had been a prominent member of the Gaelic League from the 1890s and his vision of an independent Ireland was bound up with his commitment to fostering the native language and culture. After the foundation of the Free State in 1922, Irish was made a compulsory subject at school, while the policy of Gaelicizing Ireland continued to gain momentum in the 1930s under the government of de Valera.

Although the initial interest in reviving Irish was largely antiquarian and many of the earliest scholars were Protestant,

[23] Douglas Hyde, 'The Necessity for De-Anglicising Ireland', *The Revival of Irish Literature: Addresses by Sir Charles Gavan Duffy, KCMG, Dr George Sigerson, and Dr Douglas Hyde* (London, 1894), 117–61.

by the twentieth century, as Oliver MacDonagh has argued, 'Gaelic was conterminous with Catholic, and Catholic with Gaelic, in Irish circumstances.'[24] This was to prove particularly problematic in the North after the Civil War, where nationalism was increasingly understood in terms of cultural considerations. The ideals of the Gaelic League echo clearly in the background of Cahir Healy's argument, for example:

the true national ideal means far more than an Ireland governing herself without interference from any outside source. It means an Ireland true to herself, true to her past, therefore living her own life, thinking her own thoughts, preserving and proud of her own distinctive characteristics that have come down through the centuries. This is the Ireland that the true nationalist loves, honours, and is prepared to defend with his life. In a word, it means an Irish-Ireland—not an anglicised Ireland.[25]

Central to the nationalist cause in the twentieth century has been the question of the Irish language and its survival. At the same time, this very emphasis on 'de-Anglicizing' has not always been entirely congenial to the largely English-speaking population of Ireland. In the North, especially, the Protestant community has been uneasy about Ireland's 'language, her traditions, her music, her games and amusements' and, as Thomas Hennessy suggests, the 'Gaelicisation of the Free State' contributed to a 'process of alienation by Ulster Unionists from their sense of Irishness and a greater reliance on their sense of Britishness'.[26] This has in turn created difficulties of various kinds both for those who are Irish but not Irish-speakers, and for those whose first language is Irish.[27]

Although in the early decades of the nineteenth century, writers such as Denis Florence MacCarthy and others in the Young Ireland movement saw no real difficulty in promoting the national culture through collections of poetry in English, the situation in the succeeding century has been very different. The

---

[24] MacDonagh, *States of Mind*, 116. But see also Risteárd Ó Glaisne, 'Irish and the Protestant Tradition', *The Crane Bag*, 5/2 (1981), 33–44, for a vigorous account of the use of Irish by Protestants in Ireland.

[25] *Fermanagh Herald*, 7 Oct. 1933; quoted by Thomas Hennessy, *A History of Northern Ireland, 1920–1996* (London, 1997), 74.

[26] Ibid.

[27] For a brief but revealing account, see George Watson, 'Celticism and the Annulment of History', in Terence Brown (ed.), *Celticism*, 207–20.

legacy of Ireland's relationship with Britain since the Famine and the complicated interlacing of language and literature with political developments has meant that no Irish writer in the twentieth century can engage with English poetry without a consciousness of the past and its implications. As Sean Golden observed in 1979, 'the colonized native *cannot* have the same relationship with the English tradition that the native Englishman has (without deluding himself into thinking he is English)'.[28] What appears to be a representation of the Irish dilemma as it appeared to Golden in the late 1970s, however, also contains a veiled warning to contemporary writers: 'When the colonized writer attempts to deal impartially with the colonizer's tradition, problems develop. Having no native culture left, he internalizes the culture of his oppressor.' In the face of this kind of anxiety, it is not surprising to find that quotations from English canonical authors are not easily integrated into modern Irish poetry. There is a self-consciousness about the colonial past that renders the private collection of favourite English lines, an activity so vital to Robert Burns, difficult and undesirable to many Irish writers. Though Golden's view of the English tradition as 'historical, not living' is slightly different from Kearney's emphasis on the importance of history to maintain the ethical responsibilities of the imaginative writer, both demonstrate the preoccupation with the past that marks so much Irish writing of the 1970s and 1980s.

Carson's apparent resistance to, and fascination with, Keats is inevitably and overtly political. It is thus tempting to read the dismemberment of the 'Ode to a Nightingale' as an act of mimicry, disturbing to the old Imperial power. But if 'The Irish for No' sets out to dismiss the English tradition as its title may suggest, then the absorption of Keats's poem is deeply problematic. Mimicry may be a liberating response in that it has the power to marginalize or, in Bhabha's terms, 'deauthorize' the forms of power, but its own potential threat is still dependent on the visibility of its appropriating tactics. To put it more simply, unless the reader recognizes what is being mimicked, the

---

[28] Golden, 'Post-Traditional English Literature: A Polemic', 13–14.

purpose of the mime is lost. In 'The Irish for No', there are obvious borrowings from Keats which stand out clearly from Carson's lines and which might, therefore, be read as mimicry: '*Was it a vision or a waking dream?*', '*I cannot see what flowers are at my feet*', '*drink and leave the world unseen*', '*the murmurous haunt of flies on summer eves*'. These are in a sense, scattered limbs, or broken sherds, reset in a new context. The transitions are marked out in italics: the scraps of material may be stitched into a new pattern, but never entirely absorbed, their former existence still traceable from the distinctive texture. In amongst the more eye-catching patches, however, are less obvious allusions to Keats—'perilous seas', 'casements', 'eglantine', the 'clustered' stars, and the pervasive darkness. If these suggest a less dismissive attitude towards the Ode, then the exchange becomes rather more complicated.

When W. K. Wimsatt was pondering the 'meaning of poetry' in *The Verbal Icon*, he emphasized the difference 'between a quotation or an allusion, something which has its full literary value only when it is recognised as such, and a simple borrowing, something which when recognised helps only to explain how a work came about'.[29] Although his distinction may be somewhat limited, the hierarchical ordering of the quotation or allusion (whose value depends on recognition) over the 'simple borrowing' (which reveals nothing more than its source) has interesting implications for the idea of mimicry. For if the obvious allusion possesses intrinsic value, while the borrowing merely confesses to dependency on an earlier text, this may mean in a postcolonial context that quotation symbolizes an independent voice in charge of the material, while an echo is a sign of still unexorcized influences. While the former suggests a threatening attitude towards the old Imperial power, the latter may be quietly undermining the new-found confidence by unwittingly exposing 'how the work came about'.

From the point of view of the poet and reader, however, the question is further complicated since unobtrusive borrowing is often so much more satisfying than undigested quotation. The single word 'casements', for example, perhaps contributes more to the reading experience than some of the obvious, block,

[29] W. K. Wimsatt, *The Verbal Icon: Studies in the Meaning of Poetry* (Lexington, Ky., 1954), 261.

quotations because of its uncertain status. Is it an allusion to the 'Ode to a Nightingale', where the song charms 'magic case-ments, opening on the foam | Of perilous seas, in faery lands forlorn'? Or to the 'Ode to Psyche', with its closing image of the 'casement ope at night, | To let the warm Love in!'? Or is it rather a more straightforward reference to the kind of window generally found in terraced houses in Belfast? Since one of Carson's childhood homes was in Mooreland Drive, 'a cul-de-sac which abutted on the side wall of Roger Casement Park, the main G.A.A. (Gaelic Athletic Association) ground in County Antrim', there is also the possibility of a more personal reson-ance.[30] A word used by Keats and reused by Carson is thus charged with additional possibilities which derive from the various contexts, and while there is a danger in overplaying what may be arbitrary or misleading associations (the ghost of Roger Casement is not necessarily knocking on the door), the sense of proliferating meanings is a vital aspect of the poem. This awareness of meanings that are not singular and easily grasped, but seem rather constituted of multiple, and almost transparent, layers, is also directly related to the poem's fore-grounding of alternative traditions. Rather than developing into a political statement, evoking English lines only in order to reject them, 'The Irish for No' is formed from the very con-ditions of cultural cross-over, and takes as its subject the experience of multiplicity.

When Carson's poem muses on 'whether eglantine was alien to Ireland', for example, it is exploring the complex relationship between England and Ireland and revealing the inseparability of the 'alien' and the 'native', even while acknowledging profound differences. The word 'eglantine' first appears in the poem as the name of a pub. The monologue opens with a late evening walk in the University area of Belfast, through Chlorine Gardens, pre-sumably turning right along Malone Road and into Cloreen Park, in the neighbourhood of the Eglantine Inn. And yet, the 'pastoral eglantine' also features in the 'Ode to a Nightingale'. Since Carson's poem begins with such a clear recollection of Keats, the sardonic voice of the opening stanza rapidly gives way to tipsier speculation in the second, for which has come

[30] Carson, *Last Night's Fun*, 79.

first—the eglantine or the Eglantine?[31] If the opening lines had seemed to assert the strangeness and irrelevance of the 'Ode to a Nightingale' in comparison to the commanding power of immediate, local experience, the second stanza is more equivocal altogether. Thoughts of the 'Eglantine Inn, | Just on the corner' appear to arise naturally and inevitably from the sight of Unionist graffiti, 'an *Ulster says No* scrawled on the side | Of the power-block'. The earlier presence of Keats's Ode signals the possibility of a more complicated process, however, in which English influences are deep at work in the Irish poet. Where 'casements' had simply been allowed to stand, its possible associations left to the reader's imagination, 'eglantine' poses a more explicit question about the sources of contemporary Irish poetry. The issue is presented in a speculative and self-ironizing manner, as if to reveal genuine uncertainty:

We were debating,
Bacchus and the pards and me, how to render *The Ulster Bank—the Bank*
That likes to Say Yes into Irish, and whether eglantine was alien to
    Ireland.
I cannot see what flowers are at my feet, when yes is the verb repeated,
Not exactly yes, but phatic nods and whispers. *The Bank That Answers All*
Your Questions, maybe?

The parenthetical query over whether 'eglantine was alien to Ireland' unsettles the speculation on translation. It is an uncertainty that seems to result from spending the evening in the Eglantine Inn, and not merely from what has been consumed there. The subsequent italicized '*I cannot see what flowers are at my feet*' may suggest a reassertion of the more dismissive tone, but at the same time the overt reintroduction of Keats is pointing to the possible literary origin of the word 'Eglantine'. In a poem entitled 'The Irish for No', the notion that the imagery may derive not just from the immediate Irish context but rather from the lingering residue of an English-influenced education is a matter for further exploration. Since the very word 'alien' could also be read as a quotation from the 'Ode to a Nightingale', with its haunting image of Ruth 'in tears amid the alien corn', the possibility of establishing origins becomes even

[31] The Eglantine Inn, 332 Malone Street, known locally as 'the Egg'.

more remote. And this troubling thought remains at the heart of the puzzle over language, its sources, relationships, and resting places.[32]

What may seem clearly distinguished at first is rapidly shown to be deeply intertwined, as the language of Belfast and the literature of England jostle together in an all-encompassing chaos of political, sexual, and economic transactions. Indeed, if a distinction is set up initially between Carson's speaker and the Keats quotation it is upset at once by the other emphatic voice of the first stanza, whose italicized words also stand out from the text to proclaim that *'it has nothing to do with politics'*. But if the defiant female speaker appears to challenge the idealizing language of English Romanticism and the male observer who is telling the tale, her own resistance is in turn ironized by the poem's acknowledgement that whatever 'it' may be, it has everything to do with politics. As nothing turns inside out, so 'no' begins to mean 'yes'. 'The Irish for No' thus experiences a series of internal depth charges from the very first, as it reveals the uncertainties beneath the apparent confidence of the opening snatches. Echoing from the title is another slogan of the period, from the feminist anti-rape campaign, 'No means no'. But the apparent overturning of stereotypical sexual power relations at the beginning of the poem is undermined by the linguistic puzzles of the second stanza. The 'snarling' Juliet may not after all mean 'No', any more than Molly Bloom's negatives withstood the pressure to give way to a very memorable 'Yes'. For the irony inherent in the title, the 'private code' for those familiar with the Irish language, lies in the knowledge that there is no Irish for 'no'.[33]

The Gaelic language is constructed on very different principles from English and so, in place of the direct affirmative and negative, 'yes' and 'no', the verb that has been used to form the question is repeated in the answer. In his *English–Irish Dictionary*, Tomás de Bhaldraithe translates the word 'yes' in the following way:

---

[32] The eglantine rose, or sweetbriar, is native to Ireland. I am indebted to Timothy Walker of the Botanic Gardens, Oxford, for this helpful information.

[33] A point made by Neil Corcoran in 'One Step Forward, Two Steps Back', 216, 232, and by Declan Kiberd when he included the poem in the section on 'Contemporary Irish Poetry' which he edited for *The Field Day Anthology of Irish Literature*, iii. 1405.

yes, adv. (a) (*Verb repeated in appropriate person*) Will you come?—
Yes, an dtiocfaidh tú?—Tiocfad.

(b) Interrogatively. (*Verb repeated* or an ea). Michael has been
arrested—**Yes**? Tógadh Mícheál—(Ar) tógadh? An ea?

Hence part of the difficulty in attempting to render '*The Ulster
Bank—the Bank | That likes to Say Yes* into Irish . . . when yes is
the verb repeated'. It is partly a technical problem of translating
from one language to another, but may also be read as a symbol
of the larger differences between Ireland and England.[34] The
English marketing slogan seems to assert its autonomy, making
its position clear and its articulation unproblematic. In Irish,
however, it is impossible to say 'yes' without a specific question
to frame the affirmative answer. As phrasebooks continue to
warn the would-be Irish speaker, 'questions make up a large
part of conversation and are very often followed by answers
that would be meaningless but for their association with the
questions. It is therefore important to ask the right questions.'[35]

P. W. Joyce attempted to explain these fundamental differ-
ences to an English-speaking audience many years ago in his
splendid *English as we Speak it in Ireland*, whose second
chapter begins: 'The various Irish modes of affirming, denying
&c., will be understood from the examples given in this short
chapter better than from any general observations.'[36] He then
continues with numerous examples of the different kinds of
common affirmative and negative constructions:

An emphatic 'yes' to a statement is often expressed in the following
way:—'This is a real wet day.' Answer, 'I believe you.' 'I think you
made a good bargain with Tim about that field.' 'I believe you I did.'

[34] In his analysis of *Ireland's English Question: Anglo-Irish Relations 1534–1970*
(London, 1971), Patrick O'Farrell emphasized the fundamental barriers to construc-
tive dialogue: 'To say that English and Irish were ignorant of each other, misunder-
stood each other, is to say not nearly enough, though these things are true. Ireland
and England were divided by differing views of reality, understandings so divergent
that what was precious and meaningful to the one, was worthless and incomprehen-
sible to the other', 4.

[35] Diarmuid Ó Donnchadha, *An Ráleabhar Gaeilge: The Irish Phrase Book*
(Boulder, Col., n.d.), 9. Ciaran Carson's interrogative mode emerges clearly in his
review of Christopher Reid's 'Katerina Brac', which is entirely made up of
questions, and also in the famous review of *North*, 'Escaped from the Massacre?',
which frames its title from Heaney's poem 'Exposure', and concludes that 'No one
really escapes from the massacre, of course', *The Honest Ulsterman*, 50 (1975), 186.

[36] P. W. Joyce, *English as we Speak it in Ireland*, 2nd edn. (London and Dublin,
1910), 13.

A person who is offered anything he is very willing to take, or asked to do anything he is anxious to do, often answers this way:—'James, would you take a glass of punch?' or, 'Tom, will you dance with my sister in the next round?' In either case the answer is 'Would a duck swim?'

Although the examples now seem rather dated, the point about the difference between Irish and English is made very clearly. What is perhaps particularly striking to English readers is the essentially dialogic nature of Irish, and the way in which questions and answers relate to each other. Negatives, it seems, are inseparable from their opposites. With this in mind, Carson's poem then takes on a different tone from the very beginning, but it is a tone difficult to detect for readers unfamiliar with Irish. What may seem to an English reader to be a clear and emphatic title capable of directing responses to the poem is likely to seem rather more ambiguous and ironic to those who know Irish.

'The Irish for No' is not after all a straightforward repudiation, for as Irish speakers would recognize at once, any answer depends on the question. Since no obvious question precedes this title, it is, in a sense, meaningless. However, both the title and the poem that follows are in English, a language which does allow for 'No' and 'Yes' to be phrased in independent constructions. Carson's irony is thus cutting in a number of directions. If it signals to an Irish-speaking audience the private double meaning, it is also playing to English prejudices about the 'question' of Northern Ireland, since the title could be seen as an exercise in self-caricature—the knee-jerk response of a people unwilling to negotiate.[37] Entrenched positions are certainly displayed in the poem, not only in the striking Unionist slogan, 'Ulster says No', but also perhaps in the unarticulated action which has led to the death of the 'victim: | A corporal in the UDR from Lisbellaw'. Set against the linguistic puzzles in the poem are images of violence which on one hand seem to render problems of translation irrelevant pedantry, while on the other revealing the appalling consequences of the collective failure to communicate. The potential humour of the title is thus crushed by the uncompromising images of the third and fourth stanzas, which

---

[37] O'Farrell describes Northern Ireland as 'The Continuing Question' in his study of *Ireland's English Question*, 300.

imply that the late evening musings of the individual have far-reaching implications for the community at large.

If the title possesses a degree of absurdity in that there appears to be no question being posed, this assumption is also checked through the insistent location of the text in a particular place at a particular moment. The poem is set in central Belfast, in an area identified precisely by its named streets, while its mid-1980s setting is signalled equally loudly by the contemporary slogans on display there. If the joke in the title depends on the answer being uttered in a vacuum—dangling like the quotation marks of the mobile—it is a joke that turns inside out almost immediately as the poem points to its context. This poem is emphatically not in a vacuum—on the contrary, everything seems to be outside the text. And as soon as the context is recognized, the title acquires yet another layer of meaning. It is not merely a reference to the so-called 'Irish Question', or in O'Farrell's version, 'Ireland's English Question', for details in Carson's poem point to very specific political circumstances. When Neil Corcoran pointed out that 'there is no Irish for no', he went on to add, 'there is nevertheless, an Ulster English for no: *Ulster Says No* is scrawled in huge letters on the side of a power-block'.[38] This is the detail that immediately counters the words being shouted from the casement window, by introducing a specific political reference.

'Ulster Says No' was the rallying call of the Unionist MPs who resigned their seats in protest at the signing of the Anglo-Irish Agreement by the British and Irish Governments on 15 November 1985.[39] Hence the further irony of Carson's title, since many Unionists saw the Treaty as a symbol of Britain and Ireland saying 'Yes' to each other and, in the process, jeopardizing British sovereignty over the Province. Since many Protestants in the North considered themselves to be Irish as well as British, however, the matter was even more complicated, for in that sense some of 'the Irish' at least were expressing a very firm 'No'. The 'no' in question is not, however, a sign of resistance to Britain, but to the perceived alliance between

---

[38] Corcoran, 'One Step Forward, Two Steps Back', 216.
[39] Hennessy, *A History of Northern Ireland*, 273–4. All fifteen Unionist MPs resigned after a huge demonstration against the Treaty at Belfast City Hall on 23 November.

Britain and the Republic of Ireland. 'Ulster says No' is thus a direct consequence of the continuing assent by many Protestants in the North to the Union with Great Britain. Since British sovereignty was also widely associated with economic prosperity in the Province, the Unionists' negative slogan was closely related to the Ulster Bank's positive one. Saying 'no' and saying 'yes' may be antithetical linguistically, but, as so often in this poem, words seem to slip their ostensible meanings as a result of the particular context.

The simple words of Carson's brief title seem, on closer inspection, to be riddled with possible avenues of interpretation, which the reader may or may not wish to hurry down. What may appear to be a local clue, leading into areas of experience peculiar to the people of Northern Ireland, will also turn out to be a path through history. In Belfast, the spatial and temporal cannot be separated: 'space is a function of time and vice versa', as Carson points out in *The Star Factory*.[40] Political allegiances are written into the very fabric of the city, on the 'power-block', which is itself both physical and metaphorical. But if the political moment seems reified by the monumental graffiti, often the events represented in Carson's work seem more secure than the buildings themselves. The strange story of the 'tin-can ghost of the Lower Falls', for example, which is also part of *The Star Factory*, demonstrates the rapid metamorphosis of happenings into history, of bricks and mortar to rubble: 'It was first heard in the twenties, when a policeman was shot dead outside the National Bank on the corner of Balaclava Street; since its habitat has been demolished, it has not been heard, but its memory lives on, even within the minds of those who'd never heard it, since it acquired the status of a story.'[41] The recollection of Balaclava Street concludes with images of destruction and reconstruction, as a new housing estate is instantly absorbed into the larger landscape:

I used to watch the bricklayers ply their trade, as they deployed masonic tools of plumb-line, try-square and spirit-level, setting up taut

---

[40] *The Star Factory*, 209.
[41] Ibid. 124. For an interesting discussion of Carson's 'fusing of geography and communal perceptions of the past', see Kirkland, *Literature and Culture in Northern Ireland since 1965*, 44–6.

parallels of pegs and string, before throwing down neatly gauged dollops of mortar, laying bricks in practised, quick monotony, clinking each into its matrix with skilled dints of the trowel. Had their basic modules been alphabet bricks, I could have seen them building lapidary sentences and paragraphs, as the storeyed houses became emboldened by their hyphenated, skyward narrative, and entered the ongoing, fractious epic that is Belfast.[42]

Every building is part of the continuing narrative, every team of builders constructs another scene. The 'storeyed houses' of Belfast rapidly accumulate their additional layers, through which new audiences will one day climb. The city emerges from Carson's work not as a mere place, but as a 'fractious epic', a huge rambling system of interwoven stories and streets. His readers, too, are constantly surprised by the 'dog's-leg short cuts' which lead suddenly from one narrative strand to another, following Carson's 'non linear dictates' like the bookworm he imagines working through the *Belfast Street Directory*.[43] For this writer, space is 'riddled with the swarming worm holes of . . . past and present', and so every detail of the local landscape is seething with association and narrative possibility. The mind of the Irish story-teller, too, is perceived as a 'terrain . . . honeycombed with oxymoron and diversion', where 'the tiny ancillary moments of your life assume an almost legendary status. There are holes within holes, and the main protagonists are wont to disappear at any time.'[44] The tales are there, waiting to be told; but in the very process of recital, they are apt to re-animate other half-dormant stories which may in turn send them back underground.

Ironically, the metaphors of mental travelling coalesce most conveniently in one of the many extended quotations that are laid like manhole covers in *The Star Factory*, enabling readers to cross safely from one part of the text to another. But the excerpt from Christian Barman's account of Renaissance towns is really another avenue linking different paths through the text: a passage which invites the reader to enter and explore:

during the preceding centuries the street had been so far overlooked that it could hardly be said to exist at all. It was just a hole in the town . . . The churches and surrounding houses were observed, and between

---

[42] *The Star Factory*, 126.   [43] Ibid. 8.   [44] Ibid. 62, 69–70.

them there was just space, straight or crooked inlets from that greater Space that lapped the sun and stars. In architecture the movement known as the Renaissance is principally the discovery of the walls of these inlets. In its way it was at least as great a discovery in architecture as the discovery of the unconscious mind in modern psychology.[45]

Streets, holes, surprising discoveries, and the workings of the unconscious mind mesh in this passage, which in turn finds itself stitched into the fabric of Carson's text. The key words cluster together, suggesting links to earlier parts of the text and signalling possible ways forward. That the explicit equation of 'streets' and 'holes' comes from a book on architecture is characteristic of Carson's careful approach, for it demonstrates not only that things apparently unrelated can nevertheless be found swarming with significance, but also that reading is itself an active, creative process, capable of furnishing material for new texts. Just as the urban landscape is in a state of perpetual flux, so the stories that make up the 'fractious epic' are constantly being remade as listeners and readers turn into new story-tellers.

The sudden meshing together of words and ideas that have been acquiring life throughout the text is peculiarly satisfying to the reader but, paradoxically, each additional illumination also increases the sense of remaining partially in the dark. The idiosyncratic and personal nature of so many of the emerging connections hints always at tricks being missed, at holes still unplumbed. The writer may seem to be inviting readers inside his mind but always there is a consciousness that he is ultimately inaccessible, that full meaning of the text will remain out of reach. Holes do not necessarily lead to the whole.

This very awareness, however, encourages the partial discoveries that are afforded by Carson's elusive writings. For it is through recognizing the existence of 'diverse personal narratives and many-layered timescales' that the reader is able to catch 'glimpses of an underlying structure, like a traffic flow-chart with its arteries and veins and capillaries'.[46] Or so it seems in *The Star Factory*. Ten years earlier, however, in 'The Irish for No', which seems to demonstrate the same 'hook-and-eye

---

[45] *The Star Factory*, 198, quoting from Christian Barman, *Architecture* (London, 1928), 50.
[46] *The Star Factory*, 62.

principle' of composition, the sense of an underlying structure is perhaps less secure.[47] Although the poem is built up of similar juxtapositions, apparently accidental but also charged with curious potential—Chlorine/Cloreen; eglantine/Eglantine; 'Ulster says No'/'the Ulster Bank: the Bank that likes to say Yes'—there is less sense of an organic unity beneath the surface. The speaker's nocturnal wanderings lead not to revelation or imaginative flight or even home to bed, but seem to stop abruptly at the ominous black windows of the Bank. Unlike the later *Star Factory*, the connections being made in the streets of Belfast in 1986 lead to disjunction and destruction. The 'holes' are not those swarming trails of experience from which stories are perpetually being manufactured, but have the capacity, rather, to stop the reader dead in his tracks:

> What's all this to the Belfast business-man who drilled
> Thirteen holes in his head with a Black & Decker?

It is a moment when the protagonist disappears, but not on an intriguing journey into another narrative world. The reader cannot even make out the source of these 'holes': are they the work of unknown enemies, or self-inflicted? For the syntax is strangely at odds with the imagery, the subject of 'his' unclear. Is it the Belfast businessman committing suicide or another sectarian murder, perhaps in retaliation for the death of the corporal in the previous stanza? Since the death of the corporal could also have been suicide, it is impossible to determine the relationship (if any) between the two events, even though the possibility of a parallel seems implicit in the structure of the poem.

The startling image provokes a defensive grappling for connection, but the holes are too sudden and too numerous for sense. The metaphor of drilling, with its relentless, rapid power, and associations of shooting, violent sex, and modern industry, pulls together the threads of the poem with an unexpected force that threatens to snap them completely. If this image is offering the reader a glimpse of arteries and veins and capillaries, it is more like being put in the position of a police pathologist than of an audience gradually recognizing the inner life of a work of art. (If the poem is to be seen in relation to Carson's earlier

[47] *The Star Factory*, 226. See also Ch. 1, above.

objection to Heaney's mythologizing of the Troubles, then the power drill may also be a rather heavy-handed retort to the latter's well-known 'artesian' techniques.[48])

The 'Black & Decker' produces multiple shock waves, for in addition to its obvious graphic horror, and its capacity to yank together the different linguistic threads of the poem, it also delivers the final blow to the already wavering binary opposition between black and white. The strong contrasts of the first stanza, with its yin-yang symbol and the chiaroscuro of the bedroom window against the night sky, had already begun to seem less certain in the second, where the façade of the Bank is both dazzling and black. The third stanza, which sees a shift of tense and letters reversing, also presents the 'black pitch of warehouses' as harder to distinguish from the 'shadows' of the headland, and the diesel smoke 'which might be black or white'. By the end of the poem, the inversion is almost complete, with 'snowy brambles' and stars 'thick as blackberries'; but rather than turn full circle, the images seem unstable, the yin-yang tennis ball an ironic reminder of ideal balances smashed. Once black and white has become 'Black & Decker', any attempt to explain human behaviour according to the dynamic logic of eternal cosmic principles seems very wide of the mark.[49]

In the last stanza, the sense of aftermath is reflected in the forlorn attempt to establish an earlier normality, and the re-creation of a lost pastoral world of clear skies and brambles. But even here, the grass is shining with 'dew or frost', while neat distinctions of space or time, private or public, are unattainable: 'The border, it seemed, was not yet crossed'. The passive construction adds to the confusion, since no subject is identified and could therefore be singular or plural, personal or impersonal. The connection between 'the Belfast business-man' and 'they' remains frustratingly obscure. But it is the horrific action at the centre of the stanza that seems beyond the power of words, and hence perhaps the recourse to quotation, as bits of Heaney and Keats are plucked out and placed side by side :

[48] Blake Morrison, *Seamus Heaney* (London, 1982), 53.

[49] The light/dark, male/female associations of the *Yin* and *Yang* theory can be seen playing ironically throughout the poem. For a succinct explanation of the principles, see Fung Yu-Lan, *A Short History of Chinese Philosophy*, ed. Derk Bodde (New York and London, 1948), ch. 12, 'The *Yin-Yang* school and Early Chinese Cosmogony'.

The stars clustered thick as blackberries. They opened the door into
the dark:
The murmurous haunt of flies on summer eves. Empty jam-jars.
Mish-mash. Hotch-potch.

Rather than being balanced opposites, the two poets, English
and Irish, are confused in the general hotch-potch, Keats's line
sandwiched within Heaney's 'Blackberry-picking' with its 'jam-
pots', the 'blackberries' themselves involved in Keats's 'Queen-
Moon . . . Clustered around by all her starry Fays'. The 'flies on
summer eves' also recall 'At Ardboe Point', a poem published in
Heaney's *Door into the Dark*, almost as readily as the 'Ode to a
Nightingale'.[50] Nothing here is capable of disentanglement, for
as daylight breaks all that really becomes visible is the darkness.

This is a poem in which 'things remain unsolved', 'unseen',
and 'unfed'. The very adjectives point to their antonyms but in
so doing assert their own lack of resolution. Like the negative
constructions of the Irish language, these English words are
dependent on a pre-existing verb, on the certainties of solving,
seeing, feeding. As such they pose another quiet challenge to the
poem's title, and to the assumption that Irish and English are
completely different. Like all the other clear oppositions that at
first seemed so fixed in the Northern Irish context, this distinc-
tion too eventually fragments in the larger kaleidoscope of shift-
ing pieces. In 'The Irish for No', the looking-glass is not so
much cracked as shattered.[51] Where in the later *Star Factory* the
debris is cemented by recurrent ideas and images of creativity,
craftsmanship, and continuity, the reader of 'The Irish for No'
seems much closer to the moment of devastation.[52]

It is not merely the deaths that assault the reader of the poem,
but also the way in which its imagery re-enacts the shattering,
scattering effects of the conflict. Just as binary oppositions
break down, so single words seem to split and split again,

[50] Keats's 'Queen-Moon' and 'flies on summer-eves' are both from the 'Ode to a
Nightingale'; 'Blackberry-Picking' appeared in *Death of a Naturalist* (London,
1966), 8; 'At Ardboe Point' in *Door into the Dark* (London, 1969), 23–4. Both
these poems by Heaney are indebted to Keats's 'Ode to Autumn'.

[51] For the significance of Joyce's image of the 'cracked looking glass', see Watson,
Irish Identity and the Literary Revival, Preface and Introduction.

[52] Compare e.g. 'Dresden', the opening poem in *The Irish for No,* with the
description of the reconstruction of Dresden in *The Star Factory*, 138.

ricocheting off each other in spiky trajectories. If 'eglantine' divides rapidly into a Belfast pub and Keats's pastoral sweetbriar, this is only the beginning of its experiences. The *OED* offers a further meaning of the word, citing as its authority the Anglo-Irish writer Oliver Goldsmith who uses the term in his *History of Earth and Animated Nature* to refer to 'a stone of the hardness and grain of marble'.[53] At once Carson's 'eglantine' acquires another life, independent of both the Irish pub and Keats's Ode, and, in the process, leaps to meet the porticoes of Mourne granite on the façade of the Ulster Bank. Nor is this the end, for consultation with an Irish dictionary reveals that the word 'eglantine' translates into Irish as 'fordhris', a word remarkably similar to 'for-dhorus', the Irish for a porch, porticus, or vestibule. The question of whether or not 'eglantine is alien to Ireland' thus becomes more and more complicated, as it is linked surprisingly to the granite columns which in turn represent a curious fusion of the native and the neoclassical. At this point, meanings are once again multiplying, as the origin of the granite—in the Mountains of Mourne—may also trigger thoughts of mourning, especially since the Bank's great black windows carry a reflection of the funeral parlour opposite. There may even be a suggestion, similar to that pondered over in *The Star Factory*, that 'mirrors are portals to the underworld', since the Bank's Delphic black seems to reflect signs of the deaths to come.[54] The route from 'eglantine' to the underworld may seem a bit contorted, but it offers a strange sense of half-caught significance to the 'bruised pansies', which in turn recall the unseen 'flowers at my feet'.[55]

Rather than chasing the train of ideas unfolding from the image of 'Mourne granite', however, it is perhaps easier to consider the additional resonances of the 'eglantine' and especially those arising from its association with 'the Bank'. For while the original readers of Carson's poem, who met it in the pages of *The Honest Ulsterman*, may have been struck by thoughts of

---

[53] Oliver Goldsmith, *An History of the Earth and Animated Nature*, 8 vols. (London, 1774) i. 58, which draws on Buffon's account of the layers of earth uncovered at the hundred-foot-deep well at Marly.

[54] *The Star Factory*, 266.

[55] The complexities are already sufficient without pursuing the significance here of Wordsworth's 'Ode: Intimations of Immortality', with its memorable image of 'The Pansy at my feet' (54).

the local urban landscape, those approaching from the English tradition might be led more naturally to think of Keats and Shakespeare. Although the opening lines allude to the end of Keats's 'Ode to a Nightingale', the second stanza of Carson's poem is much more indebted to Keats's fifth:

> I cannot see what flowers are at my feet,
>   Nor what soft incense hangs upon the boughs,
> But, in embalmed darkness, guess each sweet
>   Wherewith the seasonable month endows
> The grass, the thicket, and the fruit-tree wild;
>   White hawthorn, and the pastoral eglantine;
>   Fast fading violets cover'd up in leaves;
>   And mid-May's eldest child,
>   The coming musk-rose, full of dewy wine,
>   The murmurous haunt of flies on summer eves.[56]

Keats's Ode provides an ironic backdrop for Carson's urban flowers, which unfold sporadically from 'Chlorine Gardens'. Beyond these lines, though, lies *A Midsummer Night's Dream*, and the well-known speech describing Titania's bower:

> I know a bank where the wild thyme blows
> Where oxlips and the nodding violet grows,
> Quite over-canopied with luscious woodbine,
> With sweet musk-roses, and with eglantine.[57]

Although the connection with Carson's poem is perhaps over-contrived, even an oblique link to Shakespeare's 'bank' with its 'eglantine' is intriguing. For in *A Midsummer Night's Dream*, the bank is the place where resistance can be overcome, where female denial is turned into enthusiastic compliance, and where 'no' effectively becomes 'yes'.

Titania's bower is in many ways wildly dissimilar to the Ulster Bank, but the faint linguistic association may be just enough to suggest that the banks of Belfast do not merely provide local scene-painting in 'The Irish for No'. Indeed, a

---

[56] 'Ode to a Nightingale', 41–50, *John Keats: The Complete Poems*, ed. Miriam Allott (London and New York, 1970).

[57] *A Midsummer Night's Dream*, ed. Harold F. Brooks (London and New York, 1979) ii. i. 249–52. Miriam Allott notes Keats's debt to this passage in her edition of the *Complete Poems*; for an interesting related discussion of Keats's reliance on 'memory, not sight' see Helen Vendler, *The Odes of John Keats* (Cambridge, Mass., and London, 1983), 84.

further link between 'eglantine' and economics is implicit in another of the literary associations that may strike the reader of the poem. For the plant appears not only in Keats's 'Ode to a Nightingale', but also in his earlier romance, 'Isabella, or the Pot of Basil'. In the tale he adapts from Boccaccio of young love destroyed by family opposition, Keats presents the eglantine on the lips of the heroine's wealthy brothers:

> Today we purpose, aye, this hour we mount,
>   To spur three leagues towards the Appenine.
> Come down, we pray thee, ere the hot sun count
>   His dewy rosary on the eglantine.[58]

This is their invitation to the hapless Lorenzo, whom they lure away and murder on account of his love for their sister Isabella. The motivation for the killing is never entirely clear, though the descriptions highlight their jealous natures and obsession with wealth ('these money-bags'). Again, it may seem fanciful to be recollecting Keats's exotic romance in an overtly modern urban setting, but as soon as 'Isabella' begins to float across 'The Irish for No', strange connections start to form in the mind of the reader. For the fate of young Lorenzo, whose last hours are spent travelling with his murderers, is not wholly unlike that of the 'victim' in Carson's poem, who was 'last seen having driven over half | Of Ulster'.

If this parallel strikes the reader, then so may the temptation to search for further connections that might somehow make sense of the perplexing fragments that form 'The Irish for No'. Is the 'corporal' in fact the unnamed Romeo in stanza one? Is his death the result of a cross-sectarian relationship? Like so many of the thoughts inspired by the poem, these are questions rather than solutions and, appropriately in the context, lead only to further questions. For once 'Isabella' has entered the scene, the thought of the wealthy brothers may point more readily to the 'Belfast business-man' or the unidentified 'they' of the last stanza, thus suggesting a connection between these mysterious events and the couple at the beginning. Whatever the explanation (if any), the memory of the murdered Lorenzo activates a story-telling impulse in the reader and hints at larger narratives behind the fleeting images in the poem. Gradually,

---

[58] 'Isabella; or, The Pot of Basil', XXIV.

the four stanzas seem connected by more than the curiously shifting voice of the speaker, even though the larger structures remain invisible.

If the reader begins to feel reassured by making out meanings from such tiny details, however, the sense of relief is kept in check by the thought that any emerging narrative may reflect nothing more than defensiveness. In the face of confusion and violent fragmentation comes a counter impulse towards clarification and restoration. Here are the strewn bits of human lives—let us try and put them back together. But the poem itself continues to resist such desires, refusing consolatory efforts by undermining the grounds on which they might be based. One word is, after all, a rather minimal foundation on which to erect a critical structure for interpreting the entire poem. As soon as this is acknowledged, then the trails of meaning issuing from the 'eglantine' disintegrate, while the fanciful structures vanish. We cannot, after all, see what flowers or other things may be hidden in the surrounding darkness.

Given Carson's outspoken criticism of *North*, the likelihood of finding in his own representation of modern Belfast anything amenable to such quasi-mythological interpretation seems slim. If Heaney had been pilloried for finding it 'necessary to explain, to justify . . . lives in terms of his myth', then it is hardly likely that Carson would adopt a similar approach to the Troubles, glossing over the differences between his society and that depicted in 'Isabella' merely, as he puts it, 'for the sake of the parallels'.[59] The very refusal to offer consoling analogies, or to use literary allusions in ways that reassure the reader, however, does not preclude from his work the possibility of other kinds of parallel worlds. The 'parallels' in Carson's own work may not be designed to help readers make sense of the unfamiliar by pointing to an earlier instance of something similar, but seem rather to take the form of parallel universes, occasionally open to the literary traveller. This is how many of the quotations and memories operate in *The Star Factory*, and what its author seems to prize most in the work of others. Carol Reed's 1947 film of *Odd Man Out*, for example, is praised for offering just this kind of multi-layered experience:

[59] 'Escaped from the Massacre?', 184.

Mason is entering a jail delirium again . . . and we are reminded again of Reed's elegant deployment of sound to hint at other, parallel dimensions. The sound-track pulses with the noise of the city, which is punctuated, at important desultory intervals, by the bass saxophone fog-note of the escape-vessel, and the aforementioned boom of the Albert Clock. Reed's ear has picked up a cue from this passage in Green's novel, and has amplified it, so that it becomes an aural map:

> The others were silent. They were listening to the passage of police cars in the neighbouring streets. The sounds were lifted by the rising wind and carried over the whole district. Occasionally a shriek ascended like the thin tip of a flame twisting and detaching itself to float away and expire or become obliterated by the noisy passing of a private car or lorry on the main road. From somewhere far distant, the sound of a tramcar speeding along a straight road was audible like the noise of life itself in all its indifference to the personal tragedy. A train's whistle blew for several seconds, and this was followed by the clang of shunting-wagons in the marshalling-yard. And from the docks came the slow majestic note of a ship's siren.[60]

The 'parallel dimensions' signalled here by the various distinctive sounds are the other stories that are unfolding contemporaneously in the larger 'fractious epic' of Belfast. But the phrase also refers to the earlier novel by F. L. Green from which Reed's film has been created, itself an independent world but one nevertheless possessed of vital points of contiguity. Once again reading and listening become interdependent activities, in the shifts from page to screen to page, which are enabled by the key details of car engines, town clocks, and ship's sirens. These are the aural images that 'hint at other, parallel dimensions'. They thus have the power to affect not only the characters in both the novel and the film and their respective audiences, but also the readers who encounter the images through the pages of one who has seen the film and read the book. It is not a question of one familiar world and an imaginary one to which access is sometimes possible, but rather of many worlds oddly connected.

Carson's prose is patterned with glimpses of other narratives, and revels in the moments when one strand crosses with another. His poetry too is filled with words that act as portals, enabling the reader to slip momentarily from one kind of existence to another, even though the contingent world is in danger of dissolving, or of metamorphosing into something else at any moment. The connections are not, however, linear in the sense of following causal steps through time. And hence, perhaps, the reader's lack of faith in finding a satisfactory narrative explanation for the various fragments that make up 'The Irish for No'. Even if the word 'eglantine' takes us to 'Isabella' and then on to possible stories behind the different scenes, the very circuitousness of the route so far seems to check the possibility of finding a clear road ahead. Indeed, the multiplicity of associations for the 'eglantine' suggests 'parallel dimensions' far more readily than it does a single, hidden narrative. Thus the different transactions in the poem seem not so much the key moments in one story, but rather different episodes in the larger 'epic' of Belfast. It is, after all, rather difficult to determine the order of events in 'The Irish for No', since the late evening walk at the beginning flashes back to 'the long sigh of the afternoon' which is in itself a response to an earlier incident. The final stanza, too, is retrospective at first, but by the end its present tense dominates the earlier stanzas which seemed to have taken place later. Since the disturbing images may well derive from a radio or television report—perhaps heard by the poem's speaker that evening—the general sense is of parallel, rather than necessarily sequential, events.

Crucial to Carson's strategy of undermining the dominance of linear time and causal connection is his use of quotation from Keats. For the speaker of 'Ode to a Nightingale' largely addresses his subject in the present tense until the penultimate line, 'Was it a vision or a waking dream?' Closure comes as the birdsong dies away and the isolated speaker is left in the dark. Keats's question thus comes at the end of his poem, and reflects on the experience that the speaker has been articulating. Carson, however, opens 'The Irish for No' with this memorable line, and subsequently incorporates earlier moments from the 'Ode'. The temporal slippings of his own poem are thus emphasized by the reordering of Keats's lines, for now '*I cannot see what flowers are at my feet*' comes after the question of the 'vision or a waking dream?', while Carson's version of Keats's putative drinking and leaving the world unseen seems already to have taken place. If, initially, Keats's poem seems an earlier piece of work, finished and remote, it rapidly becomes apparent that in 'The Irish for No' normal temporal assumptions may be in need of radical revision. Keats's Ode was composed more than a century before Ciaran Carson was born, but if its existence within the new poem depends on the memory of the slightly inebriated speaker, then it will only appear gradually and in pieces.

For the reader, however, each broken snatch has the capacity to suggest the familiar whole, which then becomes a 'parallel dimension': a separate world continuing simultaneously, and providing an alternative set of experiences to that unfolding in 'The Irish for No'. The quotations from Keats function in ways akin to those train whistles and noisy cars in F. L. Green's novel, that provide paths into Reed's film and eventually into Carson's *Star Factory*: they hint at 'other, parallel dimensions' which are ultimately 'indifferent to the personal tragedy'. Unlike Mangan's response to Shelley, Carson is not engaged in an imaginary conversation with Keats, for the English poet himself seems indifferent and irrelevant to the situation at hand. Keats's poem, however, is half-present throughout, stimulating the reader's awareness of an alternative world. Just as the speaker in 'The Irish for No' overhears the couple at the window and opens up a glimpse of their personal drama through reported speech, so his reader catches odd lines from the 'Ode to a Nightingale' which bring to mind things quite detached from the immediate action.

If in *The Star Factory* the shifts from one narrative to another are frequent and carefully developed, however, in this poem the possibility of removal opens only to foreclose at once. Even the moment where the harbour slips away to perilous seas and 'we' seem to borrow the capacity to 'leave the world unseen' remains largely unrealized. It is not just the movement to the shocks of the next stanza, however, that checks the flight from Larne Harbour, but the very sound that seems, syntactically, to enable the movement in the first place. For the 'fog-horn' here does not signal the presence of an 'escape vessel' as in *Odd Man Out*, so much as the strange word 'forlorn' in Keats's 'Ode to a Nightingale':

> The same that oft-times hath
> Charmed magic casements, opening on the foam
> Of perilous seas in fairy lands forlorn.
>> Forlorn! The very word is like a bell
>> To toll me back from thee to my soul self!   (68–72)

The proximity of the 'perilous seas' makes it difficult to avoid the aural similarity between Keats's 'forlorn' and Carson's 'fog-horn':

> So the harbour slips away to perilous seas as things remain unsolved; we listen
> To the *ex cathedra* of the fog-horn, and *drink and leave the world unseen*—

The Ode's 'Forlorn' operates like a bell, symbolizing a return from artistic reverie to the immediate world of sickness and mortality. Its ghostly presence in 'The Irish for No' thus works against the overt desire to drink and leave the world unseen by reminding readers of the counter-movement towards closure in 'Ode to a Nightingale'. Indeed, this is perhaps the point in Carson's poem where Keats's Ode presses most closely, its pre-established pattern beginning to influence the very movements of 'The Irish for No', rather than merely existing in a parallel dimension. For, ironically, the non-quotation of 'fog-horn' serves as a more direct allusion than other complete phrases from the Ode. But it is not the imagined boom that connects Carson's image to that of the 'Nightingale'; rather the sound of the word itself prompts the recollection of Keats's 'forlorn'.

Just as the quotations from Keats help to undermine the linear logic of causality in Carson's poem, so too this sound effect upsets habitual assumptions. For the connections rely not on the reader's ability to summon up a specific sound in the mind from the image of the ship's siren, but rather on the workings of assonance and alliteration. Normal relationships between words and objects, signifiers and signified are thus disrupted, as the reader hears both the sounds of the harbour and the voice of Keats's speaker. The 'aural map' of this poem turns out to have more complicated co-ordinates than those charting the physical landscape of Northern Ireland. Interestingly, Carson's exploration of the power of sounds here gives his poem a curious affinity with one of the key critical debates of the early 1980s, in which mythologizing readings of Keats, that tended to uphold the nightingale as a transcendent symbol capable of uniting human beings across the ages, came under attack.[61] Paul de Man seized on 'the very word, forlorn' to argue that this key transition in Keats's Ode revealed its status as a form of linguistic play in which words functioned not as signs, but as sounds.

Although Carson's poem does not follow de Man down the deconstructive path, it is possible to see a related awareness of the ways in which words operate through sound in poems, and often send out multiple and even contradictory signals to the reader as a result. The word 'Chlorine', for example, means something quite different from 'Cloreen', but they are linked through their physical presence in the street plan of Belfast and through their obvious aural resemblance. Sounds have the ability to connect the otherwise detached, as 'bruised' and 'funeral' look forward to the 'afternoon', but also give a backward glance at 'you'. In the early morning balance of the last stanza, the rhyme with 'crossed' tips the probability in favour of 'frost' rather than 'dew', while the oil can 'still spills' to meet the pervasive creosote 'smell'. Rhyme, assonance, and alliteration create further connections between words already laden with different possibilities. The lines through the poem criss-cross and interweave, as the multiple meanings derived from different contexts are hooked into new patterns of sound.

Carson's awareness of the power of sound, which emerges so clearly in his comments on Reed's 'aural map' as well as in his own writings, may reflect his musical talents, but it is also worth remembering the importance of sound to Keats. In a sonnet written two or three weeks before the 'Ode to a Nightingale', for example, Keats examined the 'dull rhymes' of the English language which seemed to call for the creation of 'Sandals more

[61] See Murray Krieger, 'A Waking Dream: The Symbolic Alternative to Allegory', *Words about Words about Words: Theory, Criticism and the Literary Text* (Baltimore, 1988) and Paul de Man, "Murray Krieger: A Commentary', *Romanticism and Contemporary Criticism: The Gauss Seminar and Other Papers*, ed. E. S. Burt, Kevin Newmark, and Andrzej Warminski (Baltimore and London, 1993), 181–7; de Man comments that 'the word *forlorn* looks very much like the word *foghorn*', 186. For useful discussion of the debate between Murray Krieger and Paul de Man, see James O'Rourke, *Keats's Odes and Contemporary Criticism* (Gainesville, Fla., 1998), 25–9.

interwoven and complete | To fit the naked foot of Poesy'. It is thus possible to see the complicated stanzaic structure of his great odes as part of an attempt to work within the English literary tradition, transforming its 'chains' into an intricate aural pattern. The 'Nightingale', especially, with its careful rhyme scheme, assonance, and alliteration ('With beaded bubbles winking at the brim', 17), achieves aural effects that seem to strive after what Helen Vendler has described as 'pure sound'.[62] For although Keats's rhymes have attracted hostile criticism over the years, as in the notorious 'deceiving elf' (whose appearance struck Kingsley Amis as 'doubly unwelcome' and Robert Bridges as a 'disastrous' consequence of the choice of 'self for a rhyme-word'), the sound of the Ode is a vital dimension.[63] In a poem where 'there is no light' (38), sight becomes powerless, while all the other senses are intensified: hence the speaker's need to guess the identity of the flowers, his consciousness of aches, pains, and thirst, and above all the sound of the nightingale's song. To convey such experience to the reader, who has only the sight of the words on the page, careful strategies are required so that the sense can be stimulated virtually, through the imagination. Keats's attention to metre, rhyme, assonance, and alliteration in this poem is thus especially careful; and sensitive readers over the years have consistently responded to its 'musical' qualities. Bridges, for example, was particularly struck by Keats's ability to capture the nightingale's song with its 'pleading and tender passionate overflowing in long drawn-out notes, interspersed with plenty of playfulness and conscious exhibitions of musical skill'.[64] But the sounds cannot be separated entirely from the meaning, since associative links through the poem are forged from recurrent consonants, key words, and rhymes, as in the fourth stanza which harks back to the first:

[62] Vendler, *Odes of John Keats*, 95.

[63] Kingsley Amis, 'The Curious Elf: A Note on Rhyme in Keats', *Essays in Criticism*, 1 (1951), 191; 'A Critical Introduction to Keats', *Collected Essays, Papers, etc., of Robert Bridges*, 10 vols. (London, 1927–36), iv. 130. Bridges's interest in the aural qualities of poems can be seen in several of the essays in Vol. IX of this edition.

[64] 'A Critical Introduction to Keats', *Collected Essays*, iv. 129. See also Vendler's discussion in *Odes of John Keats*, ch. 3.

Away! Away! For I will fly to thee,
    Not charioted by Bacchus and his pards,
But on the viewless wings of Poesy,
    Though the dull brain perplexes and retards. (29–34)

The acknowledgement that the desire to fly is hindered by the 'dull brain' recalls the 'pains' of the Ode's first line, which are akin to the effects of drinking 'some dull opiate to the drains'. The recollection also links the alternative kinds of escape offered respectively by wine and poetry to the opening distinction between the 'full-throated ease' of the nightingale and the speaker's desire for 'a beaker full of the warm south, | Full of the true, the blushful Hippocrene'. The two stanzas are linked through content, as ideas from the beginning are revisited in stanza four, but the reader's capacity to connect them is stimulated by the aural reminiscences of 'dull brain' and the recurrence of 'full', which rhymes perfectly with itself and imperfectly with 'dull'.

In addition to the internal connections that bind the Ode together, however, line 33 also carries echoes of Milton's 'viewless wing' from 'The Passion' and Shakespeare's 'viewless winds' from *Measure for Measure*. Although the latter is not a perfect match, the resemblance is close enough to enable the words to serve as a portal to one of the darker moments in *Measure for Measure*, where the young Claudio contemplates his execution and a possible future 'imprison'd in the viewless winds'.[65] Keats's metaphor is thus deepened by the recognition that the 'viewless wings' are themselves drawn from the very poets who might be offering the means of escape from the present, though the associations of each resonance are different. For where Milton's poem discusses the difficulty of finding an appropriate form to address the sublime subject of Christ's Passion, and, indeed, confesses its failure through remaining unfinished, the line from *Measure for Measure* is part of Claudio's speech on the fear of death. Keats's echo thus intro-

---

[65] *Measure for Measure*, III. i. 123. Eamonn Grennan has pointed out that the subsequent 'become a sod' also echoes the fear expressed in the same speech that Claudio will 'become | A kneaded clod', 'Keats's *Contemptus Mundi*: A Shakespearean Influence on the "Ode to a Nightingale"', *Modern Language Quarterly*, 36 (1975), 272–92, 276. These echoes are also discussed by O'Rourke, who also describes 'dull brain' as a 'flash echo' from Macbeth's 'My dull brain was wrought | With things forgotten', *Macbeth*, I. iii. 151–2, *Keats's Odes*, 17.

duces ideas of poetic failure and death, even as his line appears to offer a means of escape from these very difficulties. Just as his own 'forlorn' resounds behind Carson's 'fog-horn' so Milton and Shakespeare are there in the background of his 'Ode to a Nightingale', contributing to its texture and also, at times, complicating its meaning through the subtle intrusion of their 'parallel' worlds.

If Keats's 'forlorn' and its associated context ruffles the surface of Carson's poem, so the flight of 'Poesy' in his own 'Ode' is checked by the very 'viewless wings' on which it depends. And once this kind of uncertainty is discerned within the 'Ode to a Nightingale', its position in 'The Irish for No' becomes even less secure. For instead of representing the completeness and stability of a dominant literary tradition, Keats's poem with its dense pattern of 'oblique borrowings' reveals a fragmentary and ironic quality, which impedes its own movement.[66] Indeed, its final lines,

> Was it a vision or a waking dream?
> Fled is that music—do I wake or sleep?

can be read as a statement of profound doubt about the entire poem, rather than merely as a philosophical musing over the relative 'reality' of the mundane world and that of imaginative transcendence. The poem is after all, riddled with paradox, since the lack of light means that the experience must be recollected rather than immediate, making the first-person constructions illusory. The reader too is forced into the paradoxical position of silently reading a text that asserts the absence of the visual in favour of the aural. However, the dense echoes in the 'Ode' point to the importance of reading and even seem to suggest that experience is largely constituted from books, as for example when the flowers of the fifth stanza turn out to be culled from the pages of earlier writers rather than the garden in Hampstead. Even the central image of the nightingale comes laden with literary association, from Keats's contemporaries, Wordsworth and Coleridge, their predecessors, Milton and Shakespeare, and back through the centuries to Ovid. It is this very richness of poetic usage that renders the bird 'immortal', but at the same time challenges its existence, for by the end of

[66] O'Rourke, *Keats's Odes*, 3.

the poem the reader is uncertain whether the speaker has heard a bird, or merely read about the nightingale's song in poetry. Was it a vison or a waking dream? By this stage, we do not even know what 'it' is.

Once the 'Ode' is situated in an Irish context, the complexities multiply even more startlingly. Since the nightingale does not travel as far as Northern Ireland, the difficulty of whether readers in Belfast can imagine the birdsong that Keats's speaker may or may not be hearing is intensified. The question of whether 'it' was a vision or a waking dream is thus even harder to determine. In 'The Irish for No', it rapidly becomes apparent that the recollection of Keats has not been inspired by a bird in any case, but rather by the voice of the woman at the window. Readers of Carson's poem are thus faced immediately with the question of whether the opening line carries the layers of association already accrued in Keats's Ode, or whether these have somehow been shed in the trip across two centuries and the Irish Sea. For where readers who have approached Keats's Ode from the English tradition have unpacked from his enigmatic line references to *A Midsummer Night's Dream*, *The Tempest*, Wordsworth's 'Immortality Ode', Hazlitt's *Lectures*, and Ann Radcliffe's *Romance of the Forest*, readers who encounter the words for the first time in Carson's poem may not even think immediately of Keats.[67] The line, after all, has a rhythmic quality that instantly marks it as poetry, but its situation in a colloquial monologue does not instantly emphasize the importance of its source. It is only later, as more quotations from the 'Ode' appear, that its presence as a parallel dimension becomes obvious. The response of readers who first encountered 'The Irish for No' in the pages of *The Honest Ulsterman* might well have been coloured by memories of Carson's well-publicized criticisms of *North*, and thus found in the opening line references to poems by Seamus Heaney, 'Vision' and 'A Waking Dream'.[68] Others approaching the poem from the Irish context, but less concerned with Carson's dialogue with Heaney, may read the quotation from Keats in

[67] For commentary, see Miriam Allott's edition of the *Complete Poems*; also useful are M. R. Ridley, *Keats's Craftsmanship: A Study in Poetic Development* (London, 1933), and O'Rourke, *Keats's Odes*.

[68] 'Vision', *Door into the Dark*, 33; 'A Waking Dream', *Station Island* (London, 1984), 112.

relation to the Gaelic *aisling* tradition, and thus see the response to the woman at the window in Belfast as an ironic inversion of the Irish genre.[69] As the poem unfolds, initial associations may be confirmed or modified, but the question remains as to whether these layers of possibility are part of the poem or part of the reader's mind.

Rather than approach this question in terms of a problem, however, it is perhaps more fruitful to consider it in relation to Carson's fascination with parallel dimensions, or indeed with Keats's aesthetic ideals. For despite the obvious and immediate differences between the modern, urban, colloquialism of 'The Irish for No' and the deeply literary, timeless, English pastoral, both poems are characterized by irony, indeterminacy, and intertextuality. Indeed, although Keats's line clearly does not take the form of an epigraph, it nevertheless serves ultimately as a surprisingly fitting introduction to Carson's poem. It is, after all, the line that seems to embody Keats's celebrated aesthetic ideal of 'negative capability', which he broached in a letter to his brothers: 'at once it struck me what quality went to form a Man of Achievement especially in Literature & which Shakespeare posessed so enormously—I mean *Negative Capability*, that is when a man is capable of being in uncertainties, Mysteries, doubts, without any irritable reaching after fact & reason.'[70] This was the capacity Keats so admired in Shakespeare, and which he found frustratingly absent in many other great writers: 'Coleridge, for instance, would let go by a fine isolated verisimilitude caught from the Penetralium of mystery, from being incapable of remaining content with half knowledge.' Although Keats's musings are open to a variety of interpretations, the sense that 'half-knowledge' may indeed be the optimum condition for the creation of literature sheds light on the questions that emerge from his own poetry. For where the last lines of the 'Ode to a Nightingale' might be read as a sceptical qualification of the entire poem, which has the effect of achieving closure through demolition, they may also be seen as an attempt to embody the rare qualities apparent in Shakespeare's drama.

[69] On the Irish aisling tradition, see Gerard Murphy, 'Notes on Aisling Poetry,' *Éisge*, 1 (1939–40), 40–50; Joep Leerssen, *Mere Irish and Fíor-Ghael: Studies in the Idea of Irish Nationality, its Development and Literary Expression prior to the Nineteenth Century* (Cork, 1996), 216–20.
[70] To George and Thomas Keats, 21 Dec. 1817, *Letters*, i. 193–4.

Instead of moving towards a resolution, in which the meaning of the Ode becomes clear and translatable, Keats's poem concludes with questions which leave his readers in the midst of uncertainties, mysteries, doubts. In other words, the reader of the 'Ode to a Nightingale' has something in common with the cat in 'The Irish for No' who is left 'debating whether *yes* is *no*'.

The notion that the ability to remain in the midst of doubts and uncertainties is the mark of the greatest poetry may in itself have seemed somewhat ironic in mid-1980s Belfast, but it is interesting to discover that Carson explicitly evokes the idea of 'negative capability' in the later *Star Factory*. As he muses on his own 'hook-and-eye principle' of writing, comparing it with the knitting skills of his sister and mother, he is led on to a surreal meditation on the construction of a 'Fair Isle cardigan'. The thought of the Viking settlement leads on to an Early Irish poem:

> Bitter the wind tonight,
> combing the sea's hair white:
> from the North, no need to fear
> the proud sea-coursing warrior.

I like this version by John Montague for its nice internal assonantal rhymes based around the *ee* of the sea sound, its enjambement of *fear*, giving it all a shivery impression; and I think the phrase 'negative capability' could be bandied about here, since we can see these Vikings even though they don't exist for now.[71]

Keats's well-known term thus appears at the very heart of Carson's exploration into his own writing practices, side by side with material from the Irish tradition, translated into English by another twentieth-century Irish poet. Montague's translation is admired for just the kind of aural qualities that characterize the work of Keats and Carson himself, while Keats's aesthetic ideal is evoked in praise of the kind of poetry that enables its readers to see things that do not exist. Carson's chapter closes with the passage quoted earlier in this discussion, which recalls his own bilingual upbringing, and the dreamlike state he remembers from childhood, when 'wavering between languages' he would allow his 'disembodied self to drift out of the window' to the

---

[71] *The Star Factory*, 230. The quotation is from 'The Vikings', in John Montague (ed.), *The Faber Book of Irish Verse* (London, 1974), 60.

Star Factory, 'where words were melted down and like tallow cast in new moulds'.

Rather than see the quotations from Keats in 'The Irish for No' in terms of a postcolonial rejection of a resented and now irrelevant tradition, then, it is possible to trace a more ambiguous relationship, in which two apparently dissimilar poems are linked by their very uncertainties. The uncertainties, however, are not flaws; instead they reveal the imaginative possibilities in poetry that remains content with 'half-knowledge'. Just as the title of Carson's poem becomes more and more interesting once the reader recognizes that there is no Irish for No, so too the 'Ode to a Nightingale' fascinates through its elusiveness and indeterminacy. The final irony of 'The Irish for No' may be that just as English perceptions of the Irish are based on fundamental misunderstandings, so too the commonly held Irish views of the English may be similarly askew: that, although the English attitude may be characterized as clear, unbending, and unequivocal, in fact the very poet set up as quintessentially English in his approach to the Irish is one who celebrated doubts and uncertainties. For it was Keats who most famously saw the capabilities of the negative.

7

Seamus Heaney and the Caught Line

xliv

All gone into the world of light? Perhaps
As we read the line sheer forms do crowd
The starry vestibule. Otherwise

They do not. What lucency survives
Is blanched as worms on nightlines I would lift,
Ungratified if always well prepared

For the nothing there—which was only what had been there.
Although in fact it is more like a caught line snapping,
That moment of admission of *All gone*,

When the rod butt loses touch and the tip drools
And eddies swirl a dead leaf past in silence
Swifter (it seems) than the water's passage.[1]

In 1985 the pupils of Wesley College, Dublin, were so moved by the images of famine-stricken children in Ethiopia that they decided to join in the money-raising efforts by writing to a number of well-known people and asking them to name a favourite poem. The response was rapid and rewarding, and so a series of poetry collections was put together, whose proceeds went towards famine relief in the Third World. Some years later when Penguin Books agreed to publish a selection of the poems and letters, Seamus Heaney was asked to contribute a Foreword. It was a timely request, for here was an extraordinary instance of one of his personal preoccupations—the capacity of poetry to cross into the public domain. Through the *Lifelines* anthology, various poems were fulfilling John Keats's Romantic ambition of 'doing the world some good', though not perhaps in

---

[1] From the 'Squarings' section of Seamus Heaney, *Seeing Things* (London, 1991), 104.

quite the way their authors might have anticipated.[2] Heaney's introduction nevertheless points to the situation of writers 'at the intersection of the public and the private', and although his remark relates specifically to the personal choices of those living writers who had responded to the request from Wesley College, it also reflects his profound concern with the relationship of poetry to society, of the individual to the general, of the local to the universal.[3]

As Heaney considered the poems in the volume and the 'famous people' who had selected them, he was reminded of two earlier occasions which epitomize for him the fundamental importance of poetry to the world. One is the moment recorded by the Greek writer George Seferis, when he recognized that certain poems are 'strong enough to help', the other a fictional scene in which Ford Madox Ford's character, Christopher Tietjens, counters the terrifying experience of trench warfare with thoughts of George Herbert and in the process his 'sense of value in the face of danger is both clarified and verified by the fleeting recollection of a couple of his favourite lines'.[4] These lifelines are offering help of a different kind from the practical aid that issued from sales of the anthology, but by focusing attention on these striking moments, Heaney encourages readers to see the poems in the new volume occupying a similarly vital role in the minds of those whose choices they represent. Indeed, the collection as a whole 'testifies in its own uninsistent fashion to the ways in which individuals still continue to recognize that some part of the meaning of their lives is lodged in the words and cadences of cherished passages of verse'.

This approach to poetry is reminiscent of Robert Burns's comforting suggestion to Mrs Dunlop that certain passages of

[2] Keats to Woodhouse, 27 Oct. 1818, *Letters*, i. 387.

[3] Seamus Heaney, 'Foreword' to Niall Macmonagle (ed.), *Lifelines*, p. xiv.

[4] Ibid. p. xiii. Heaney refers to a passage in Seferis's *Journals* recording his powerful encounter with the work of the Greek poet, Constantine Cavafy, but see also Walter Kaiser's remarks on Seferis's eventual painful rejection of Cavafy, who 'in time of stress is not strong enough to help', George Seferis, *A Poet's Journal: Days of 1945–1951*, trans. Athan Anagnostopoulos, ed. Walter Kaiser (Cambridge, Mass., and London, 1974), p. xii. Heaney also mentions that it was the English poet, Jon Stallworthy, who drew his attention to the passage from Ford; see The Bodley Head Ford Madox Ford, 4 vols. (London, 1963), iv: *Parade's End*, 416.

verse have an extraordinary capacity to soothe and strengthen: 'Do you know, I pick up favorite quotations, & store them in my mind as ready armour, offensive, or defensive, amid the struggle of this turbulent existence.'[5] In a rather similar way, Heaney encourages modern readers to nurture those 'cherished passages' so vital to inner well-being. A few years earlier, when interviewed about the merits of learning poetry by heart, Heaney had responded with remarks that suggest a belief even stronger than Burns's in the psychological value of favourite passages. Remembered lines for Heaney are not just a form of protective clothing, but seem to constitute a mental blood-stream: 'they are capillaries, back into the original parts of yourself and I think for the whole personality, the more linkages there are between one stage and another, the better you are psychically. The ultimate justification for memorisation is a unity in your own life.'[6] Learning poetry is a means to inner health and, interestingly, the words of others have the capacity to open 'channels back into the original parts of yourself'. This is perhaps what Heaney sees happening in *Parade's End*, when the crucial recollection of Herbert means that the soldier's self-respect is 'clarified and verified', his confidence in the future renewed.

For poets, especially, personal favourites are of fundamental importance, not only in the puzzle to recognize the 'meanings of their lives' or as 'ready armour', but also because new compositions are fed by earlier poems. Heaney regards the selection by almost every poet in the *Lifelines* anthology as being 'corroborative of some aspect of his own published work', a comment which testifies to his own faith in the benefits of reading and recollecting.[7] There is no sense of the past master representing a burden to the living, as the reader-writer is seen as being both strengthened and confirmed in his own endeavour. Favourite lines have the power to 'corroborate', 'clarify', and 'verify': verbs which seem to present poetry as the revelation and embodiment of truth. Once absorbed, particular passages maintain a self-authenticating and life-affirming presence in the mind, unfailingly ready at moments of crisis.

---

[5] Burns to Mrs Dunlop, 6 Dec. 1792, *Letters*, ii. 165. See Ch. 1, above.

[6] McSweeney, 'The Poet's Picture of Education', 139.

[7] 'Foreword' to *Lifelines*, p. xiv.

The significance of the new anthology thus lies not merely in its incidental capacity to generate financial aid, but also in its massing together of poems that are manifestly 'strong enough to help' their individual readers.

These bold claims for poetry are closely related to the more extensive discussion which formed the inaugural lecture delivered by Seamus Heaney as Professor of Poetry at the University of Oxford in 1989. Here Heaney confronted specifically the perennial question of how 'poetry's existence as a form of art relates to our existence as citizens of society', and attempted to elucidate his own views on the 'redress' of poetry. Here too George Seferis was invoked, but this time the help offered by strong poetry was considered in a larger exploration of the exhilarating experience of reading. At its best, poetry offers

the undisappointed joy of finding that everything holds up and answers the desire that it awakens. At such moments, the delight of having all one's faculties simultaneously provoked and gratified is like gaining an upper hand over all that is contingent and (as Borges says) 'inconsequential'. There is a sensation both of arrival and of prospect, so that one does indeed seem to 'recover a past' and 'prefigure a future', and thereby to complete the circle of one's being. When this happens, we have a distinct sensation that (to borrow a phrase from George Seferis's notebooks) poetry is 'strong enough to help'.[8]

The redress of poetry can be felt in such revelatory moments of reading, when the awakened reader is suddenly satisfied and gratified and vitally 'complete'. The experience is thus akin to remembering favourite lines, and the sense of inner unity that comes as the mental capillaries open and the blood flows freely. For although Heaney's emphasis on key 'moments' may suggest a rather fleeting kind of assistance, the pleasure of reading brings with it an uplifting sensation 'both of arrival and prospect'. It is as if the energy generated in reading poetry is at once reactivating stored resources and laying down supplies for the future.

Heaney's title is in itself reminiscent of Shelley's great *Defence of Poetry*, but his focus on the idea of 'redress' suggests an even more dynamic force.[9] For where Shelley felt the need to

---

[8] Seamus Heaney, *The Redress of Poetry: Oxford Lectures* (London, 1995), 9.
[9] Bernard O'Donoghue has pointed to a Shelleyan influence on Heaney's earlier

leap to the aid of poetry and fend off all comers, Heaney's notion of 'redress' demonstrates a belief in the self-sustaining power of poetry and its ability to offer help to the reader. So while some of Heaney's celebratory observations are reminiscent of Shelley's stirring essay, much of his lecture is devoted to a quieter discussion of the 'undisappointing' poetry of George Herbert.

Heaney's defence of poetry relies partly on his ability to convey to his audience the deep and almost physical pleasure to be gained from reading Herbert's lyrics. The words of the seventeenth-century poet, so salutary to Ford's struggling protagonist, also have the power to affect new readers, eliciting 'the catch in the breath' or sending 'the reader's mind sweeping and veering away in delighted reflex'.[10] The perfectly controlled lyric verse strikes Heaney as perhaps the best 'example of that fully realized poetry . . . a poetry where the co-ordinates of the imagined thing correspond to and allow us to contemplate the complex burden of our own experience'.[11] Herbert's is thus a profoundly personal poetry, which demands participation from the reader in order to work properly. Nor is this merely a question of a sympathetic response to the rhythms and imagery, or to the religious outlook embodied in the finely crafted lines. Active participation often requires an alertness to the linguistic possibilities of the simplest words, as demonstrated by Heaney's comments on the two meanings of 'rest' that operate in 'The Pulley'. While part of the poem's power is invested in the reader's ability to understand the wordplay, the clarity of the pun ensures that every reader will respond appropriately and thus share the impetus towards the beautifully balanced conclusion. 'The Pulley' is uncluttered but not remotely simplistic: 'in its unforced way', Heaney comments, 'it does contain within itself the co-ordinates and contradictions of experience, and would be as comprehensible within the cosmology of Yin and Yang as it is amenable to the dialectic of thesis, antithesis, and synthesis'.[12] Herbert's poetry, in other words, is prized not

lecture series, *The Government of the Tongue* (London, 1988), with its preoccupation with 'poetry's power to legislate', *Seamus Heaney and the Language of Poetry*, 136.

[10] Heaney, *The Redress of Poetry*, 12, 16.
[11] Ibid. 10.
[12] Ibid. 12–13.

merely as a repository of embodied emotion, but also for its strong, internal logic: the self-bracing quality of a poetry strong enough to brace the reader.[13]

As a defence of poetry's importance to society, Heaney's emphasis on the private experience of reading may initially seem a little contradictory. The inner life of contemplation has often been placed in opposition to the active life, an antithesis that may present a hard moral dilemma to poets caught in periods of national crisis. Coleridge, for example, acutely conscious of the war with France, felt duty call him from 'delicious solitude' to 'go, and join, heart, and hand, | Active and firm, to fight the bloodless fight | Of Science, Freedom, and the Truth in Christ'.[14] Something of this obligation also haunts Heaney, emerging painfully in *Station Island* when the ghost of his second cousin, Colum McCartney, recalls the day he was killed by Loyalist gunmen:

> You were there with poets when you got the word
> and stayed there with them, while your own flesh and blood
> was carted to Bellaghy from the Fews.[15]

Through the words of the accusing ghost, who charges his famous relation with drawing 'the lovely blinds of the *Purgatorio*', Heaney countenances the possibility that poetry can be an excuse for evasion.

The passage alludes to Heaney's earlier elegy for his murdered cousin, 'The Strand at Lough Beg', which had taken three lines from Dante as its epigraph and echoed them at its close.[16] In *Station Island*, he is revisiting his own poem to

---

[13] It is worth comparing Heaney's memories of how he and schoolfriends 'braced themselves linguistically' for *The Ambleside Book of Verse* ('Burns's Art Speech', 218) with his comments on the 'upright, resistant, and self-bracing entity' of poetry in *The Redress of Poetry*, 14.

[14] 'Reflections on having left a Place of Retirement', 58–63. When the poem first appeared in the *Monthly Magazine*, II (Oct. 1796), 712, the title was 'Reflections on entering into Active Life'. Coleridge subsequently embarked on a series of public lectures on the contemporary political situation. His earlier career in the dragoons, when he adopted the name of Silas Tomkyn Comberbache, had been neither long nor distinguished.

[15] Heaney, *Station Island*, 82.

[16] 'The Strand at Lough Beg' appeared in *Field Work* (London, 1979), 17–18. For discussion see O'Donoghue, *Seamus Heaney and the Language of Poetry*, 85–6; Corcoran, *The Poetry of Seamus Heaney*, 94–5; Michael Parker, *Seamus Heaney: The Making of the Poet* (London, 1993), 159–61.

question whether its reliance on quotation had somehow been an avoidance measure and a betrayal of truth: 'You saw that, and you wrote that—not the fact', as the dead man points out. The speaker, who has spent so much of his life reading and thinking, thus finds himself in the dock with the gunmen:

> You confused evasion and artistic tact.
> The Protestant who shot me through the head
> I accuse directly, but indirectly, you
> who now atone perhaps upon this bed
> for the way you whitewashed ugliness and drew
> the lovely blinds of the *Purgatorio*
> and saccharined my death with morning dew.

The strong admonishment meted out to the penitent speaker reveals not only a profound uncertainty about the value of intellectual and aesthetic pursuits, but also an awareness of the far less comfortable workings of the memory. As recollections of earlier poetry mix guiltily with thoughts of violent death and family grief, the speaker is racked with self-doubt. The old charges against Heaney's tendency to mythologize the Troubles and place brutality at one remove are once again being levelled, but this time in an internalized debate with his 'own flesh and blood'.[17]

The question of how 'poetry's existence as a form of art relates to our existence as citizens of society' is a major part of the probing meditation of *Station Island*, and is posed long before the appearance of Colum McCartney. Early in the volume, the half-ironic, half-guilty 'Away from it All' places the reader 'in full view of the strand' to witness the cooking of lobster and to catch the late evening debate after the meal.[18] Once again, the recourse to other writing seems doubtful and evasive:

> and quotations start to rise
>
> like rehearsed alibis:
> *I was stretched between contemplation*
> *of a motionless point*
> *and the command to participate*
> *actively in history.*
>
> 'Actively? What do you mean?'

---

[17] See Ch. 6, above for Carson's attack on *North*.
[18] *Station Island*, 16–17.

The italicized lines are taken from a passage by the Polish poet Czeslaw Milosz, which deals explicitly with the guilty feelings that often afflict those of a contemplative nature, prone to self-accusations about 'political passivity'.[19] Milosz describes the anguish he felt after a hostile review of his poetry by a critic who accused him of wanting to 'keep his hands clean'. The pain derived not from a sense of injustice or malice, but because the attack had penetrated his own 'inner discord'. It is clear from Milosz's account that the life of contemplation leads not unproblematically to inner peace because of the guilt it simultaneously fosters, especially in situations where others are on trial for their beliefs. The fascination with the transcendent may, in certain circumstances, seem little more than an excuse for being mealy-mouthed or silent. Hence Milosz's memorable comment: 'I was stretched, therefore, between two poles: the contemplation of a motionless point and the command to participate actively in history; in other words, between transcendence and becoming. I did not manage to bring these extremes into a unity, but I did not want to give either of them up.'[20]

Although Milosz's words possess a disarming honesty in their original context, the way in which they intrude into Heaney's poem, introduced by the jingling rhyme and uneasy image of 'rehearsed alibis', suggests profound doubt about their legitimacy. It is as if they have been called up to win an argument, to justify a position which even the pleader finds unconvincing. Quotation here seems almost a parodic prefiguring of the affirmative corroboration celebrated in *The Redress of Poetry*, offering the speaker not a lifeline but a cover. Since the borrowed sentence is poised on the predicament of the instinctively private poet faced with the demands of history, there is an implicit association between contemplation, passivity, and self-deception—'*Actively*? What do you mean?'

If the contemplative life has been set up as an alternative to the active life, then perhaps it is another name for passivity, which for the creative writer might mean mere imitation, or

[19] Czeslaw Milosz, *Native Realm: A Search for Self-Definition*, translated from the Polish by Catherine S. Leach (London and Manchester, 1981), 125.

[20] Ibid. It is also worth noting Heaney's acknowledged sympathy with the Polish writer: 'Milosz I just find enormously close', from a conversation with Neil Corcoran, quoted in Corcoran, *The Poetry of Seamus Heaney*, 260.

borrowing from earlier literature. The dilemma faced in *Station Island* is not only a question of a withdrawal from or entrance into public events, then, but also of artistic integrity. For the life of the mind, nourished by reading and encouraged by Catholic tradition, may lead to a reverential attitude to authority and a kind of self-abasement not altogether conducive to creative writing. The pilgrim of *Station Island* has also to grapple with the possible contradictions of learning from past examples and becoming an independent voice.

These difficulties are acknowledged directly, but the journey is never without hope. Even the lobster in 'Away from it All', lifted out of his element and about to be 'plunged and reddened', is 'fortified' as well as 'bewildered'. And Colum McCartney is not the only shade to appear; for the sequence ends with the ghost of James Joyce, dismissing the 'peasant pilgrimage' and urging self-confidence and renewed creativity:

> You lose more of yourself than you redeem
> doing the decent thing. Keep at a tangent.
> When they make the circle wide, it's time to swim
>
> out on your own and fill the element
> with signatures on your own frequency,
> echo soundings, searches, probes, allurements,
>
> elver-gleams in the dark of the whole sea.[21]

In a passage that reconciles respect for earlier figures with the natural desire for independence and originality, the long poem concludes, while the next section of the volume begins 'Take hold of the shaft of the pen'.[22] Guilt about opting for the life of the mind is finally assuaged through mental effort, while, paradoxically, the way to independence is revealed through the words of another writer.

The soul-searching of *Station Island* may seem far removed from the light and life-embracing lectures delivered by Heaney in the years after its publication. It is perhaps the very capacity for this kind of dark misgiving, however, that gives the later lecture on 'The Redress of Poetry' its full force. For Heaney's celebration of the private experience of reading lies at the heart of the larger question concerning poetry's role in society, while

---

[21] *Station Island*, 93–4.
[22] Ibid. 97, 'The First Gloss', which is the first poem in Part Three, 'Sweeney Redivivus'.

his account of its 'redress' is prefaced by careful remarks about the dangers of pressing poetry into public debate. While he remains fully alert to the primary meaning of poetry's redress 'as an agent for proclaiming and correcting injustices' and the particular demands this has placed on twentieth-century Irish poets, he is at pains to point out, nevertheless, that in pursuing such an aim, 'poets are in danger of slighting another imperative, namely, to redress poetry *as* poetry, to set it up as its own category, an eminence established and a pressure exercised by distinctly linguistic means'.[23] Poetry's power does not lie in its ability to enter into political debate, but rather in its role as poetry.

Such a view marks a clear development from the slightly more defensive position outlined in an interview with Seamus Deane some years earlier, when the English ideal of the 'well-made poem' had seemed distinctly suspect. Despite his clear acknowledgement of the contemporary confrontation between Britain and Ireland, however, he was resistant even at that point to the possibility of poetry becoming propaganda. In response to questioning about the political obligations of Northern Irish poets, Heaney had replied that

the poet's force now, and hopefully in the future, is to maintain the efficacy of his own 'mythos', his own cultural and political colourings, rather than to serve any particular momentary strategy that his political leaders, his paramilitary organization or his own liberal self might want him to serve. I think that poetry and politics are, in different ways, an articulation, an ordering, a giving of form to inchoate pieties, prejudices, world-views or whatever. And I think that my own poetry is a kind of slow, obstinate, papish burn, emanating from the ground I was brought up on.[24]

The Redress of Poetry is similarly attuned to the importance of the poet maintaining 'his own cultural and political colourings', but the emphasis is rather more inclusive. For although he recognizes that certain writers, whether from Ireland, the West Indies, or Newcastle, might find that 'their education in Shakespeare or Keats was little more than an exercise in alienating them from their authentic experience', he is now

[23] *The Redress of Poetry*, 5–6.
[24] 'Unhappy and at Home: Interview with Seamus Heaney', Seamus Deane, *The Crane Bag* 1/1 (1977), 61–7, 62.

warning that 'that argument should not obliterate other truths'.[25] Hence the justification for someone whose passport is green, still finding deep pleasure in traditional English lyrics.

It is through Heaney's personal understanding of the feelings of a colonized people that he is able to argue his case so persuasively, for he is not denying that poetry such as George Herbert's, 'so domiciled within a native culture and voice, so conscripted as a manifestation of the desirable English temperament', was regarded by many as an incarnation of 'the civilities and beliefs which England, through the operations of its colonial power, sought to impose upon other peoples'. Such a view, eloquently expressed in polemical essays such as Sean Golden's 'Post-Traditional English Literature', is not dismissed so much as balanced against another kind of argument based on the inherent truth of certain poetry. 'My point has to be this,' Heaney observes, 'even the most imposed-upon colonial will discern in the clear element of Herbert's poetry a true paradigm of the shape of things.'[26] Admiration for Herbert among readers whose own 'cultural and political colourings' may be very different does not then constitute a betrayal but rather an honest response to genuine complexity. Indeed, the denial of aesthetic influences and attractions for political reasons can be as damaging as the unthinking imitation of an imposed culture, since it is a form of deception. The greatness of Joyce, who appears in *Station Island* as the voice of independence, is now shown to derive partly from his capacity to allow English literature its riches, even as he challenged its authority.

The real heroes of this lecture, however, are figures such as Czeslaw Milosz and Osip Mandelstam, both writers who suffered under Communism but, as Heaney has observed elsewhere, nevertheless retained an 'inner freedom' nourished by and blossoming into poetry.[27] Indeed, it is the idea of hope, as defined by the Czech liberation leader and poet Vaclav Havel, that corroborates Heaney's own view of poetry's redemptive powers:

[25] *The Redress of Poetry*, 7.
[26] Ibid. 9–10.
[27] Ibid, 4. Seamus Heaney, 'Osip and Nadzhda Mandelstam', *The Government of the Tongue*, 71–88, 72; see also in the same volume, 'The Impact of Translation', 36–44. Corcoran suggests that Heaney 'finds in the Eastern bloc poets an analogous case for the Irish writer', *The Poetry of Seamus Heaney*, 147.

it is a dimension of the soul, and it's not essentially dependent on some particular observation of the world or estimate of the situation . . . It is an orientation of the spirit, an orientation of the heart; it transcends the world that is immediately experienced, and is anchored somewhere beyond its horizon. I don't think you can explain it as a mere derivative of something here, of some movement, or of some favourable signs in the world. I feel that its deepest roots are in the transcendental, just as the roots of human responsibility are . . . It is not the conviction that something will turn out well, but the certainty that something makes sense, regardless of how it turns out.[28]

Again and again, Heaney turns to other poets for corroboration of his own deeply felt beliefs, drawing on their words to clarify and verify his thoughts. But his faith in the importance of poetry is founded on a recognition that not everyone in the world feels, thinks, or behaves alike. It is, indeed, from the bewildering awareness of contrary influences that poetry emerges, to make sense.[29]

The celebration of poetry that allows for the 'complex burden of experience' continues in the first volume of poetry to be published by Heaney after his stirring lecture on 'The Redress of Poetry'—*Seeing Things*. Early in the collection, a poem for Ted Hughes entitled 'Casting and Gathering' describes the contrasting sounds made by fishermen on either side of a river:

> One sound is saying, 'You are not worth tuppence,
> But neither is anybody. Watch it! Be severe.'
> The other says, 'Go with it! Give and swerve.
> You are everything you feel beside the river.'[30]

The two actions seem to be set up as opposing symbols of creative release and sceptical restraint, one perhaps associated with the Irish tradition ('On the left bank, a green silk tapered cast | Went whispering through the air, saying *hush* | And *lush*, entirely free'), the other with English control ('A sharp ratcheting went on and on | Cutting across the stillness'). And yet this separation, which recalls both 'The Ministry of Fear' in *North*

---

[28] *The Redress of Poetry*, 4–5, quoting from Vaclav Havel, *Disturbing the Peace* (London, 1990), 181.

[29] In his critical study of Heaney and contraries, Henry Hart suggests that 'At the root of his work is a multifaceted argument with himself', *Seamus Heaney: Poet of Contrary Progressions* (New York, 1992), 2.

[30] *Seeing Things*, 13.

and several of the essays in *Preoccupations*, is soon shown to be based on a false perception.[31] The speaker comments, 'I have grown older and can see them both', suggesting the balanced detachment of one who prefers not to take sides, since both are necessary. By the end, the two actions are presented as part of one larger pursuit:

> I love hushed air, I trust contrariness.
> Years and years go past and I do not move
> For I see that when one man casts, the other gathers
> And then *vice versa*, without changing sides.

To 'trust contrariness' suggests an attitude similar to that expressed in *The Redress of Poetry*, with its praise of Joyce for his capacity to challenge and admire the English tradition, and of Herbert for compositions that contain 'the co-ordinates and contradictions of experience'. The physical actions in 'Casting and Gathering' which serve as a metaphor for creative writing are also related to the later meanings of 'redress' that bring the lecture to its conclusion. The final association of this rich word that Heaney singles out as an aspect of poetry is taken from hunting: 'To bring back (the hounds or deer) to the proper course'. This is the meaning which has least bearing on politics, society, or ethical obligations, but it is the one that Heaney finally emphasizes and even re-creates as he turns suddenly to the crucial element of poetry's capacity to 'surprise'. As once used by huntsmen, the verb 'to redress' was, according to Heaney, 'a matter of finding a course where something un-hindered, yet directed, can sweep ahead into its full potential'.[32] In just this way, the action of casting can represent the powerful release of energy at once free, and yet under control—like the lines of the most accomplished lyric verse.

Seeing Things reveals this fascination with sudden revelations of innate capacity; the volume is propelled by 'shadow-boosts' and 'hums with transparency'.[33] But still the more sceptical

---

[31] See Ch. 6, above for the earlier awkwardness about the South Derry 'hush' in 'The Ministry of Fear'. English and Irish influences are seen as 'masculine' and 'feminine' in Heaney's essay 'Belfast', but see also 'The Makings of a Music' where it is Yeats as opposed to Wordsworth who is deemed 'masculine', *Preoccupations: Selected Prose 1968–1978* (London, 1980), 33–7, 61–78.

[32] *The Redress of Poetry*, 15.

[33] 'A Basket of Chestnuts', 'Wheels within Wheels', *Seeing Things*, 24, 46.

voice remains, while the 'heaviness of being' explored in 'Foster-
ling' seems hard to shed especially since many of the poems
were written after the death of Heaney's father.[34] In 'Casting
and Gathering', contrariness seems perfectly under control, as
two sides of one fully realized activity. At other moments, the
poetry has a more equivocal tone and almost seems to be
questioning its own capacities. Once the celebration of surprise
becomes a recurrent motif, however, the reader is perhaps even
more startled by its absence.

One of the most interesting poems in *Seeing Things*, certainly
for the purposes of this study, is '*All gone into the world of
light?*', the untitled forty-fourth poem in the 'Squarings'
sequence ('Squarings?—In the game of marbles, squarings |
were all those anglings, aimings, feints and squints | You were
allowed before you'd shoot'[35]). At first it seems to embody
exactly the kind of balance so admired in *The Redress of Poetry*,
as the apparent gloom of the mundane words 'All gone' is
instantly lifted and poised against the mysterious 'world of
light'. Response to the opening words is complicated, however,
by the recognition that they represent a quotation from the
seventeenth-century poet Henry Vaughan, whose well-known
elegy begins:

> They are all gone into the world of light!
>   And I alone sit ling'ring here:
> Their very memory is fair and bright,
>   And my sad thoughts doth clear.[36]

The poem explores the mourner's sense of being left in lonely
misery, while those who have departed are 'walking in an air of
glory'. Despite the speaker's frustration and unhappiness, how-
ever, Vaughan's poem concludes with a prayer for ultimate
union with God:

> O Father of eternal life, and all
>   Created glories under thee!
> Resume thy spirit from this world of thrall
>   Into true liberty.

---

[34] 'Fosterling', *Seeing Things*, 50.
[35] 'iii', *Seeing Things*, 57.
[36] 'They are all gone into the world of light', Henry Vaughan, *The Complete
Poems*, ed. Alan Rudrum (Harmondsworth, 1976), 246.

> Either disperse these mists, which blot and fill
>   My perspective (still) as they pass,
> Or else remove me hence unto that hill,
>   Where I shall need no glass.

Since *Seeing Things* is largely concerned with the desire for perfect vision, with glimpses of the transcendent and with various kinds of communion with the dead, Vaughan's poem does not seem out of place. It also begins with explicit reference to the power of memory to 'clear' sad thoughts, and may thus be fulfilling a role similar to that offered by Herbert to Ford Madox Ford's troubled character, clarifying and verifying the speaker of the new poem in a moment of need. Indeed, it might well be just the kind of strongly constructed poem that would have the capacity to encourage constructive meditation, in the same way that Heaney sees favourite poems as being 'corroborative' of new work by those in whose minds they lodge so securely.

Although Heaney's poem begins with a direct reference to Vaughan, however, the tone of his poem is different altogether. For where Vaughan's opening line seems emphatic and unequivocal, Heaney's is doubtful and tentative. The removal of the subject, 'They' immediately places the emphasis on the fact of absence rather than the distinct memory of those who have disappeared, while the insertion of a query and 'Perhaps' prepares the reader for a more sceptical and regretful approach. Rather than being welcomed as a poem that might illuminate the new speaker's experience, Vaughan's appears to be dismissed as ultimately unconvincing:

> *All gone into the world of light?* Perhaps
> As we read the line sheer forms do crowd
> The starry vestibule. Otherwise
> They do not.

For those unfamiliar with Vaughan's poem, the lines work as a gloss, indicating that the opening words are part of an existing poem. The emphasis on reading, however, immediately distances the opening image, which is transformed from the confident apostrophe of the seventeenth-century original to a strangely archaic idea of 'sheer forms' in a 'starry vestibule'. Vaughan's clear vision is dismissed as nothing more than an image, which may work for some readers, but not for others, including, it seems, the speaker who has conjured it up.

The failure seems all the more disappointing, because of the desire to enter into Vaughan's vision sympathetically, to reach out for the lifeline he might be offering. Instead of being strong enough to .help, the earlier poem seems to have vanished with those it lamented, leaving the modern speaker conscious of a deeper absence—the 'moment of admission of *All gone*', the 'nothing there'. Contrariness here seems to consist of nothing more than a rejection of one strongly held view: this may represent an honest response to something perceived as false, but it does not seem to offer any consolation to the speaker. Rather than having his faculties 'simultaneously provoked and gratified', the reader in the poem is immune to the memory of Vaughan's words, remaining emptily 'Ungratified if always well prepared'. Nor is it immediately obvious why this should be so, for why begin with a poem that apparently does not meet those standards of 'total adequacy' sought by every reader? Why evoke a poem so clearly, only to dismiss it as inadequate? The shift from the imagery of reading to night-fishing in this poem suggests isolation rather than good-humoured debate, and so it seems that the help of poetry has been looked for and found wanting.

At first it might seem that Heaney is adopting a strategy similar to Ciaran Carson's, as he picked out a line from Keats to submerge in the modern city of Belfast. Carson's engagement with the English ode, however, turns out to be more complicated and rather less dismissive than it initially seems. In the case of Heaney, too, whose remarks on the attitude of the colonial writer in *The Redress of Poetry* are so careful, unequivocal resistance to a poem on the grounds of its Englishness seems unlikely. Given Heaney's overt admiration for English lyric poetry, the perceived inadequacies of Vaughan's line can hardly represent the response of the 'imposed-upon colonial' glaring back at a dominant and irrelevant culture. Perhaps, then, the distance felt in his poem is not a question of geography or nationality, but rather of history or religion. Perhaps '*All gone into the world of light?*' is acknowledging that the vision of the seventeenth-century mystic is not fully accessible to the modern reader whose sense of God is so much less certain?

If Vaughan's lyric is being rejected for these reasons, then Heaney's response might be placed in the company of a poem such as Philip Larkin's 'Aubade', which dismisses religion as a 'vast moth-eaten musical brocade | Created to pretend we never die'.[37] Heaney's 'starry vestibule' has a touch of this attitude to beliefs now deemed archaic, while his transformation of Vaughan's 'faint beams in which this hill is dressed, | After the sun's remove' to the 'lucency' of blanched worms suggests a similarly bleak emphasis on physical decay rather than heavenly bliss. When Heaney lectured on Larkin's 'Aubade' the year before *Seeing Things* was published, however, he drew the audience's attention to Milosz's indignant response to the poem, and the Polish writer's criticism of Larkin for betraying poetry which 'has always been on the side of life'.[38] Although Heaney is alert to the technical quality of Larkin's poem, which goes some way to counter Milosz's charge, he still goes on to uphold the value of more affirmative kinds of poetry in the face of 'Larkin's attractively defeatist proposition'.[39] It would perhaps be surprising then to find Heaney writing a poem of his own at the same time, which seems to take as its premiss the failure of the life-affirmative and visionary in the face of the doubtful and material.

Since the tone of the poem is intensely private, it is perhaps more likely that the disappointment expressed is that of the mourner denied the consolation he had sought. Of all crises, bereavement is perhaps the most testing of poetry's capacity to provide redress.[40] Heaney's equation of poetry with hope and fortification is so very forward-looking, while grief is inevitably preoccupied with the past. Corroboration and verification, too, may not be quite what is wanted when the fact of something that has happened is still too painful to accept. Mourning, moreover, is so focused on the sense of a unique individual, that

[37] 'Aubade' was published in the *Times Literary Supplement*, 23 Dec. 1977; the text quoted here is from Philip Larkin, *Collected Poems*, ed. Anthony Thwaite (London, 1988), 208–9.

[38] 'Joy or Night: Last Things in the Poetry of W. B. Yeats and Philip Larkin', *The Redress of Poetry*, 146–163, 158. Milosz's remarks appeared in 'The Real and the Paradigms', *Poetry Australia*, 72 (October 1979), 18–24.

[39] *The Redress of Poetry*, 163.

[40] On the consolation of poetry after bereavement, see Stephen Gill's account of Leslie Stephen turning to Wordsworth as 'the only consoler' after the death of his wife, *Wordsworth and the Victorians* (Oxford, 1998), 215.

an existing elegy is unlikely to be entirely adequate to the
personal calamity. If Heaney's speaker has been reminded of
Vaughan at a time of personal bereavement, it seems that the
seventeenth-century elegist is not strong enough to help.

To read the poem as an expression of grief may seem a little
fanciful when it is taken out of the volume in which it originally
appeared. When approaching it in the context of *Seeing Things*,
however, the reader of '*All gone into the world of light?*' is
already open to the numerous ideas that have been flowing
through the earlier poems, marked by recurrent phrases,
images, and forms. The failure of vision recorded here, as the
speaker remains

> Ungratified if always well prepared
> For the nothing there—

is all the more moving once recognized as an echo of an earlier
moment of personal illumination. For in the last part of the title-
poem, 'Seeing Things', Heaney had described the day in which
his father had almost drowned in the local river, but then
emerged, shaken and alive:

> That afternoon,
> I saw him face to face, he came to me
> With his damp footprints out of the river,
> And there was nothing between us there
> That might not still be happily ever after.[41]

The isolation of the later poem is intensified by the memory of
this transfiguring encounter when father and son were 'face to
face' on the banks of the river, with 'nothing between us there'.
The 'nothing' of '*All gone into the world of light?*' encompasses
both the loss of personal vision and the now permanent loss of
Heaney's father. And once the personal dimension of the
recourse to Vaughan's elegy becomes apparent, its failure to
console is all the more painful.

But if '*All gone into the world of light?*' seems to suggest the
inadequacies of poetry, its very allusiveness is countering the
sense of disappointment. Although the recollection of the
moment in 'Seeing Things' where Heaney's father had emerged
dripping from the driving accident serves to make the 'nothing'

---

[41] 'Seeing Things', *Seeing Things*, 18.

of the later poem even emptier, it is also sending the reader back through the earlier pieces in an active quest for meaning. Nor is the pursuit complete when the reader arrives at the title-poem, for the passage in 'Seeing Things' that lies behind poem 'xliv' is itself freighted with allusive possibility. The recollection of the 'face to face' encounter by the river sends the reader further back to the very opening pages of the volume, where the translation from Virgil reveals the figure of Aeneas praying to the Sibyl of Cumae for 'one look, one face-to-face meeting with my dear father'.[42]

The longing for reunion with the lost father thus acquires a heroic dimension and, crucially, a sense of purpose: for the grieving Aeneas is set a task in order to achieve his desire. If he can pluck the golden bough, he will be able to descend to the underworld, but, as the Sibyl warns, 'to retrace your steps and get back to upper air, | This is the real task and the real undertaking'. To revisit the dead is one thing, but to retrace these steps and return to life and 'upper air' is even harder. In *Seeing Things*, Heaney is visiting the dead through his translations and allusions to earlier texts, and in doing so perhaps struggling with more immediate, personal losses. He is also, however, freeing his own distinctive voice, which cannot survive if it remains submerged in the Underworld with Dante and Virgil. The volume accordingly celebrates a re-emergence into the light— the 'Time to be dazzled and the heart to lighten'[43]—but it nevertheless makes clear from the start that such 'lightening' is part of an arduous and often uncertain process.

If many of the poems celebrate the sudden liberation of energy from constraint, others move more cautiously, acknowledging the possibility of vacancy and of vision withdrawn. The reader shares in both the remembered moments and the reflection of recurring ideas and images, progressing with care or occasional recklessness when a surprising connection strikes. The exhilaration of sudden seeing, however, has as its corollary the sense of longing that precedes and follows the moment when truth became visible. Aeneas's desire for a 'face-to-face meeting' wells up from his deep consciousness of loss and continuing absence, while the last poem in the 'Squarings' sequence concludes with

---

[42] 'The Golden Bough' (*Aeneid*, VI. 98–148), *Seeing Things*, 1–3.
[43] 'Fosterling', ibid. 50.

'what escaped'.[44] This is also what makes the encounter on the riverbank so powerful, as the reader shares the sense of marvel at this rare moment when desire is fully gratified.

The memory of fulfilled desire haunts the rest of the volume, increasing the frustration in '*All gone into the world of light?*', when the speaker remains 'Ungratified'. And yet the allusiveness that transforms the reader's disappointment into active participation also works to reduce the very sense of distance apparently created by Vaughan's poem. For if the phrase 'face to face' links Heaney to Aeneas, it also evokes the very different tradition of the Bible. The speaker who saw his father 'face to face' recalls St Paul's longing for unclouded communion with God, 'For now we see through a glass, darkly; but then face to face.'[45] This is of course the very text alluded to by Vaughan as he imagines finally being swept up to 'that hill, | Where I shall need no glass', and so the recollection of 'Seeing Things' that is prompted by '*All gone into the world of light?*' has the curious effect of bringing the latter poem closer to the source it appears to reject as inadequate. Through the play of allusion, Heaney's reader moves back and forth through the volume and its guiding texts to find startling reunions where they are least expected. When read out of context, '*All gone into the world of light?*' seems to cast Vaughan's line as a powerful statement of unproblematic belief, but the circuitous return to its closing stanza, through internal and external allusions, reminds the reader that the earlier poem and, indeed, St Paul's epistle both express a similar longing for light and union. For behind St Paul's memorable summary of the human condition lies the Old Testament certainty of Jacob, who could say, after his struggle, 'I have seen God face to face.'[46] If St Paul's reference to seeing God directly stemmed from a recognition that the normal human condition was one of obscured vision, then the speaker of '*All gone into the world of light?*' may perhaps take some comfort from Vaughan. A longing for communication with the divine is not, after all, an exclusively modern phenomenon.[47]

[44] 'xlviii', ibid. 108.
[45] 1 Cor. 13: 12.
[46] Gen. 32: 30.
[47] St Paul's own experience of heavenly light is described in Acts 9: 3–8. It was nevertheless regarded as miraculous and extremely rare even by medieval

As the speaker in Vaughan's lyric begins to seem less remote, so the distance between the two poems shrinks. Rather than being 'All gone', Vaughan's poem reappears, not in the shape of an alien consciousness informed by strange inaccessible notions, but more as the voice of a suffering human being, acutely aware of his incompleteness and longing to be made whole. In apparently rejecting Vaughan's words, Heaney's poem has in fact encouraged his reader to look at them again and, perhaps, on closer inspection to see the poem more clearly. The inadequacy was perhaps within the reader rather than the poem, just as Coleridge had suggested in 'Dejection' when the inefficacy of 'outward forms' is seen as a consequence of inner failing. Where Coleridge had articulated a profound creative inertia through the idea of seeing without feeling, however, Heaney emphasizes the importance of sight.

One of the poems placed near the beginning of *Seeing Things* is 'Field of Vision', which describes a woman 'who sat for years | In a wheelchair, looking straight ahead | Out of the window'.[48] As it unfolds, we learn that she is 'steadfast as the big window itself' and thus the reader is invited to look not at her, but into her:

> Face to face with her was an education
> Of the sort you got across a well-braced gate—
> One of those lean, clean, iron, roadside ones
> Between two whitewashed pillars, where you could see
>
> Deeper into the country than you expected
> And discovered that the field behind the hedge
> Grew more distinctly strange as you kept standing
> Focused and drawn in by what barred the way.

What appears to be inaccessible is suddenly offering glimpses of a hitherto unimagined world, the very barrier to communication being the enabling talisman. This is another transfiguring, face-to-face moment, but not one that comes through accident or after a hard journey. The poem records rather the slowly dawning revelation that rewards contemplation and that more careful, active looking into the apparently mundane.

theologians. For St Thomas Aquinas's view of the '*raptus*' and '*visio dei*', see Robert Leet Patterson, *The Conception of God in the Philosophy of Aquinas* (London, 1933), 483–91.

[48] 'Field of Vision', *Seeing Things*, 22.

The need to look and look again is impressed on the reader from the opening pages of the volume where the Sibyl urges Aeneas to 'look up and search deep', to the later 'Squarings' where the very emptiness of the prospect compels the eye ('But once you turned your back on it, your back | Was suddenly all eyes like Argus's. | Then when you'd look again, the offing felt | Untrespassed still, and yet somehow vacated').[49] In the title-poem, 'Seeing Things', the central section, which forms the prelude to the 'face-to-face' meeting with Heaney's 'undrowned father', reveals both the necessity and reward of intelligent looking:

> *Claritas*. The dry-eyed Latin word
> Is perfect for the carved stone of the water
> Where Jesus stands up to his unwet knees
> And John the Baptist pours out more water
> Over his head: all this in bright sunlight
> On the façade of a cathedral. Lines
> Hard and thin and sinuous represent
> The flowing river. Down between the lines
> Little antic fish are all go. Nothing else.
> And yet in that utter visibility
> The stone's alive with what's invisible:
> Waterweed, stirred sand-grains hurrying off,
> The shadowy, unshadowed stream itself.
> All afternoon, heat wavered on the steps
> And the air we stood up to our eyes in wavered
> Like the zig-zag hieroglyph for life itself.[50]

The startling visual clarity of the stone carving in the sunlight is matched by the language; but although the lines are 'Hard and thin and sinuous', they are also brimming with life. It is the 'utter visibility' that makes the stone 'alive with what's invisible', and which enables the observers to participate momentarily in the divine. In this key passage, the visual is vitally important, not merely in aesthetic terms, but as a means of discovering the spiritual in the physical. In a remarkable moment that seems to invert the petrifying powers of the Medusa, stone comes to life, as the hard, dry, bright surface turns to shadowy water, rippling with activity. If the reader is initially arrested by the dazzling physical façade, deeper mean-

---

[49] 'xlvii', ibid. 107.   [50] 'Seeing Things', ibid. 17.

ings become visible as soon as he is able to look 'down between the lines'.

For the very first word, '*claritas*', carries physical and spiritual, religious and literary associations. Heaney's readers are likely to be reminded immediately of Joyce's Stephen Dedalus grappling with the philosophy of Thomas Aquinas, as part of his Catholic education. Dedalus concludes that the deepest aesthetic pleasure comes from the experience of '*claritas*', a spiritual state which he describes as the 'instant wherein that supreme quality of beauty, the clear radiance of the esthetic image, is apprehended luminously by the mind which has been arrested by its wholeness and fascinated by its harmony'.[51] Joyce's character interprets this aspect of beauty, whose importance for Aquinas was entirely theological, in aesthetic and intuitive terms, explaining the 'scholastic *quidditas*, the *whatness* of a thing' through reference to Shelley's account of the mind in creation as a fading coal. In his *Defence of Poetry*, Shelley had distinguished poetry from reasoning on the grounds that it could not operate according to the will:

A man cannot say 'I will compose poetry'. The greatest poet even cannot say it: for the mind in creation is as a fading coal which some invisible influence, like an inconstant wind, awakens to transitory brightness: this power arises from within, like the colour of a flower which fades and changes as it is developed, and the conscious portions of our natures are unprophetic either of its approach or its departure.[52]

Although the 'fading coal' image suggests the operation of an external power—something akin to the Wordsworthian 'sweet breath of Heaven' with its powerful anterior tradition of divine inspiration—Shelley makes plain that the power 'arises from within'.[53] Despite the unconscious workings of the creative

[51] James Joyce, *A Portrait of the Artist as a Young Man*, ed. Seamus Deane (Harmondsworth, 1992), 217. Wimsatt commented that Joyce 'in that freely romantic rendering of Thomist aesthetic . . . has misapplied the Thomist specific *quidditas*, but that while doing this he has placed the correct accent on radiance or *claritas*—the radiant epiphany of the whole and structurally intelligible *individual* thing', *The Verbal Icon*, 270–1. For helpful discussion of Joyce's interpretation, see W. T. Noon, *Joyce and Aquinas* (New Haven and London, 1957).

[52] Shelley, *A Defence of Poetry*, 503–4. For the idea of 'whatness' in Aquinas's thought, see 'De Ente et Essentia', trans. by Timothy McDermott, *Thomas Aquinas: Selected Philosophical Writings* (Oxford and New York, 1993), 92–3.

[53] Wordsworth, *The Prelude* (1805), 41. See also Abrams, *The Correspondent Breeze*.

mind, Shelley's account attempts to illuminate an internal, human phenomenon, though one which is also represented as 'divine'. There is no mention in his *Defence* of the idea of 'claritas', but his eloquent thoughts on poetry, 'the interpenetration of a diviner nature through our own', reveal striking similarities to those of Joyce's young artist. The idea emerging from *A Portrait* is thus of an experience of startling radiance, as the very essence of an object is revealed, and can be felt by the artist when the 'image is first conceived in his imagination'.[54]

Since, for Heaney, '*claritas*' is the word inspired by the sight of a bright cathedral and the clear figure of Jesus being baptized, it also seems to encompass more than a purely aesthetic radiance. The glory of this great sculpted church lies not merely in the physical delight of bright sunlight, nor in the contemplation of the form, though both of these are crucial elements of the startling moment re-created in the poem. Those who are seeing within the poem seem somehow to mirror the very image of baptism:

> And the air we stood up to our eyes in wavered
> Like the zig-zag hieroglyph for life itself.

The lines reflect the carved figure of Jesus, who 'stands up to his unwet knees', momentarily uniting the seer and the seen. Here, stone turns into waves, while heat and air 'waver': the four elements instantaneously balanced and harmonious, and symbolic of life and creation.

Often the revelation of what is going on 'between the lines' is prompted by a fleeting recollection, through a key word such as '*claritas*', or a biblical reference, as here, to the baptism of Jesus. Whether the reader is prompted to memories of Joyce and through him to Shelley, or whether he is struck more readily by the thought of Christ infused by the Holy Spirit, the physical description of the church is suddenly flooded with light and meaning. The very means to such experiences, however, also constitute a possible obstacle, because always the reader is attended by doubt. Are the allusions an integral part of the poem, or are they merely arbitrary connections existing only in the mind of the reader? Is Heaney's father really haunting '*All gone into the world of light?*' and does he bring with him

[54] Joyce, *A Portrait of the Artist*, 231.

Aeneas and St Paul? In other words, is the reader apprehending what is there, or merely seeing things? For the sceptical colloquialism is embodied in Heaney's title just as firmly as the more visionary association, thus unsettling the reader and his perception of the volume. It is thus hard to determine whether Heaney is presenting himself in visionary company, or whether he is adopting the voice of twentieth-century irony, questioning the illusions of the past.

Since the volume begins with Virgil and ends with Dante, it might be safe to assume that what comes between will be aiming high. However, the very decision to begin with a translation has a certain ambiguity. While it might suggest an invocation of the epic voice, it could equally well be seen as a form of disguise— an assumption of someone else's clothes, to hide a lack of substance. The discovery that the first original poem in the volume depicts the shade of Philip Larkin—'A nine-to-five man who had seen poetry'—is hardly guaranteed to sustain the heroic atmosphere of Aeneas's descent into the Underworld. If anything, the appearance of Larkin seems to ironize the entire enterprise, especially when he begins to quote Dante:

> I alone was girding myself to face
> The ordeal of my journey and my duty
> And not a thing had changed, as rush-hour buses
> Bore the drained and laden through the city.[55]

The creation of Larkin returning from the dead with Dante as his guide only to be faced with rush-hour traffic and tired commuters could be seen as an ironic English rebuke to Heaney's swishing Virgilian opening—the severe reeling in that is needed after casting a line. However, the image of Larkin on his 'Journey Back' recalls another of Heaney's lectures, in which he had imagined the English poet composing a version of the *Divine Comedy*, beginning 'not in a dark wood, but a railway tunnel half-way on a journey down England'.[56] In this lecture, although Heaney casts Larkin's 'Aubade' as an 'inferno proper', he refuses to accept it as the end of the line. Instead he argues that Larkin 'also had it in him to write his own version of the

---

[55] 'The Journey Back', *Seeing Things*, 7. Larkin's shade quotes from Dante's *Inferno*, II. 3–5.
[56] 'The Main of Light', *The Government of the Tongue*, 15–22, 22.

Paradiso', and devotes much of the lecture to those passages where light and life predominate. Larkin's shade in *Seeing Things* may be sceptical, but it is not therefore destructive to the visionary. Indeed, his surprising presence seems almost a condition of true vision, since he represents for Heaney that 'unfoolable mind' whose rare moments of hope are made all the more powerful by the surrounding gloom.

In 'The Main of Light', Heaney praises Larkin for the way 'he sifts the conditions of contemporary life, refuses alibis and pushes consciousness towards an exposed condition', while still retaining 'a repining for a more crystalline reality'.[57] The account resonates with the terms of Heaney's own poetry, revealing a deep admiration for the hard truth and 'unconsoled clarity' of Larkin's work, despite the uncongenial character of some of his views. Among the poems singled out for its inclusion of a Joycean epiphany is 'Here', which Heaney quotes as follows:

> Here silence stands
> Like heat. Here leaves unnoticed thicken,
> Hidden weeds flower, neglected waters quicken,
> Luminously-peopled air ascends;
> And past the poppies bluish neutral distance
> Ends the land suddenly beyond a beach
> Of shapes and shingle. Here is unfenced existence:
> Facing the sun, untalkative, out of reach.[58]

Interestingly, Heaney omits the two words that begin this final verse, presumably because they represent the end of a stanza-straddling sentence. Once restored, however, the stanza begins 'Loneliness clarifies', thus making Larkin's epiphany seem as consequent on clarification as Heaney's later apprehension of 'what's invisible'. Rather than proving a malign or mocking presence in *Seeing Things*, then, Larkin perhaps has the capacity to clarify and verify Heaney's poetry, corroborating the new work and being acknowledged as a vital, if unexpected, influence. The surprise of Larkin is oddly consistent with the re-perception of the woman in 'Field of Vision', whose revelation is all the more satisfying for being unobvious.

[57] 'The Main of Light', *The Government of the Tongue*, 16.
[58] Ibid. 19. 'Here' was the first poem in Philip Larkin's *The Whitsun Weddings* (London, 1964).

Heaney's desire to find glimpses of the *Paradiso* in the work of Larkin should encourage his readers to trust the possibilities they find emerging in his poetry. For although 'seeing things' may suggest that there is really nothing to be seen, the prevailing sense of the volume is that the marvellous is always there and ready to be revealed in the mundane, if only one were looking. Unlike 'Aubade', in which death inhabits 'the edge of vision | A small unfocused blur', Heaney's vacancies are explicitly *vacated*: 'As if a lambent troop that exercised | On the borders of your vision had withdrawn | Behind the skyline to manoeuvre and regroup.'[59] There is rarely a sense that emptiness has never been filled, that absence does not imply earlier or future presence. The image of the angler

> Ungratified if always well prepared
> For the nothing there—which was only what had been there

is thus all the more surprising—and hence the reader's impulse to pursue the echo in 'nothing there', and to find what has surely disappeared.

Even without the memory of 'nothing between us there', the shift from Vaughan's poem to the imagery of fishing which occurs with the blanched 'worms' brings a host of earlier associations. Although the poem seems to develop the image of an angler failing to catch anything, the metaphor charges the empty surface with meaning through raising thoughts of what has gone before. Indeed, in the passage beginning '*Claritas*', what happens 'down between the lines' is imaged by 'little antic fish'. Fish are, of course, a traditional symbol of Christ, while in Irish mythology it is Finn Mac Cumhail's success in catching the salmon of knowledge that endows him with divine wisdom.[60] Whether or not the reader is aware of such associations, however, it is evident from 'Seeing Things' that the antic fish are symbols of life not always visible, whose sudden revelation is akin to religious experience. These ideas hardly lessen the sense

---

[59] 'xlvii', *Seeing Things*, 107.

[60] On fish as a symbol of divine life in Christian and Eastern cultures, see Jessie Weston, *From Ritual to Romance* (Cambridge, 1920), ch. 9. The story of Finn and the salmon has been retold many times: see e.g. T. F. O'Rahilly, *Early Irish History and Mythology* (Dublin, 1946), 318–40; Charles Squire, *Mythology of the British Isles* (London, 1905), 210–11.

of despair when the angler finds the fish 'all gone' rather than 'all go', but they nevertheless deepen the significance of his attempt, transforming the act of fishing into an act of faith.

The little antic fish are particularly visible in the title-poem because it appears after four other poems in which fishing provides the dominant metaphor. 'The Pulse', for example, celebrates 'the effortlessness of a spinning reel', and the sheer exhilaration of casting a line, which is reiterated in 'Casting and Gathering'.[61] In 'A Haul', on the other hand, it is the Norse god Thor's failure to hold on to the great world serpent that creates 'A Milky Way in the Water' and an extraordinary sensation of freedom for the fisherman.[62] In each poem, fishing seems a means to the marvellous, but the power of the experience has nothing to do with *catching* fish.

Rather more sombre associations emerge in 'Man and Boy', where childhood memories of fishing lessons rapidly move to a contemplation of Heaney's father as a boy, on the day that *his* father died:

> My father is a barefoot boy with news,
> Running at eye-level with weeds and stooks
> On the afternoon of his own father's death.
>
> The open, black half of the half-door waits.
> I feel much heat and hurry in the air.
> I feel his legs and quick heels far away
>
> And strange as my own—when he will piggyback me
> At a great height, light-headed and thin-boned,
> Like a witless elder rescued from the fire.[63]

From the down-to-earth memory of salmon-fishing, the poem has moved to thoughts of Aeneas rescuing Anchises from the burning Troy. For a moment, child and grandfather become one, in their shared dependence on the linking father, whose very dominance is made all the more poignant by the knowledge that two of the generations are already gone, and that neither father nor grandfather can now be saved physically.

The task of writing has been represented so memorably in Heaney's work as a successor to agricultural labour, however,

---

[61] 'The Pulse', 'Casting and Gathering', *Seeing Things*, 11, 13.
[62] 'A Haul', ibid, 12.
[63] 'Man and Boy', ibid, 15–16.

that this poem, too, can be seen as an act of rescue and memorial. In 'Digging', the physical strength and skill of father and grandfather was celebrated by their heir, who had 'no spade to follow men like them', and therefore digs with his pen.[64] In the later volume, *Seeing Things*, the preoccupation with light and water perhaps makes the spade less useful, and so his father's skill in fishing is a more appropriate metaphor for the writing son. Nor would Heaney be the first to draw an analogy between writing poetry and fishing, as is clear in the following passage from what is undoubtedly the most famous literary account of fishing, Izaak Walton's *The Compleat Angler*:

Angling is somewhat like *Poetry*, men are to be born so: I mean with inclinations to it, though both may be heightened by discourse and practice, but he that hopes to be a good *Angler* must not only bring an inquiring, searching, observing wit; but he must bring a large measure of hope and patience, and a love and propensity to the Art it self; but having once got and practis'd it, then doubt not but *Angling* will prove to be so pleasant, that it will prove to be like Vertue, *a reward to it self.*[65]

Walton's analogy is strikingly apposite, with its emphasis on the qualities of hope and patience, characteristic of both angler and poet, and the celebration of the self-rewarding nature of their art. The emphasis on poetry as an art, too, provides an important corrective to the heady Shelleyan metaphors of invisible influences, since Walton draws attention to the need for 'practice'. Men may be born with an inclination to this pursuit, but their natural abilities still need to be 'heightened by discourse and practice', an attitude in keeping with the subtitle of Walton's famous book: '*the Contemplative Man's Recreation*'.

The idea of poetry as an activity which, like angling, requires constant practice in order to provide fulfilment had already been introduced by Heaney in one of the poems published in *The Haw Lantern*. 'The Daylight Art' takes the story recounted by Plato in the *Phaedo*, of Socrates spending his last days putting into verse any of Aesop's *Fables* that came to mind. The

---

[64] 'Digging', *Death of a Naturalist* (London, 1966), 1–2. This is the poem chosen by Heaney to stand at the beginning of each selected edition.

[65] Izaak Walton and Charles Cotton, *The Compleat Angler, Or the Contemplative Man's Recreation*, ed. John Buxton (Oxford, 1982), 37–8. Heaney's familiarity with Walton can be seen in 'The Salmon Fisher to the Salmon', *Door into the Dark*, 6.

reason given by Plato for this surprising eleventh-hour interest is in turn put into verse by Heaney:

> And this was not because Socrates loved wisdom
> and advocated the examined life.
> The reason was that he had had a dream.[66]

All his life, Socrates had been misinterpreting the recurrent dream, which had been telling him 'Practise the art, which art until that moment I he always took to mean philosophy'. With the approach of death, however, Socrates turned at last to poetry and, too late to master the art, spent his last working hours versifying Aesop. In the closing stanzas of his own short poem, Heaney wittily adopts the classical 'beatus ille' to observe:

> Happy the man, therefore, with a natural gift
>
> For practising the right one from the start—
> poetry, say, or fishing; whose nights are dreamless;
> whose deep-sunk panoramas rise and pass
>
> like daylight through the rod's eye or the nib's eye.

The Horatian ideal of the 'happy man', as manifest in Heaney's poem, is thus remarkably close to Izaak Walton's notion of the man born with a natural inclination towards and possessed of the character to perfect his chosen art, be it fishing or poetry.

With the parallel between poetry and angling in mind, tightened as it is by remarks in *The Redress of Poetry* and the frequent references in *Seeing Things*, the meaning of the short poem '*All gone into the world of light?*' begins to amplify. In particular, the word 'line', carefully occurring three times in the poem, takes on far more significance when seen as a reference to both poetry and fishing. It is not so much what is happening 'between the lines', but rather within them. For the two meanings of 'line' operate a little like the pun on 'rest' which Heaney had so admired in Herbert's 'The Pulley', both working in a dynamic equilibrium.

---

[66] 'A Daylight Art', *The Haw Lantern* (London, 1987), 9. Cf. Plato, *Phaedo*, 60–1, trans. David Gallop (Oxford, 1975), 4–5. Neil Corcoran points out that Heaney's lecture, 'Atlas of Civilisation', *The Government of the Tongue*, 54–70, begins with the same classical anecdote, *The Poetry of Seamus Heaney*, 138.

As soon as the fishing imagery is seen primarily in relation to poetry rather than religious belief, the meaning of the poem alters dramatically. Instead of maintaining the sense of spiritual vacancy, the 'nightlines I would lift' begin to suggest literary borrowing and thus disappointment of a rather different kind. The rejection of the opening image now takes on a new complexion, as a 'lifted line' which offers no gratification because it belongs to another poem—not because that poem is a failure. It is rather like the 'rehearsed alibis' in 'Away from it All', which stand out guiltily amid the scenes of cooking and killing. Vaughan's line is a 'caught line', which snaps because it is out of place and unworkable in the new poem.

Again, Walton's *The Compleat Angler* offers an interesting insight as it describes a fishing lesson in which the experienced *piscator* lends his own tackle to a novice. The apprentice is almost successful, but the fish gets away, snapping the line. The episode leads the *piscator* to draw a parallel with the preacher who lent his curate one of his favourite sermons, only to find that the congregation dislike it thoroughly:

> *though the borrower of it preach'd it word for word, as it was at first, yet it was utterly disliked as it was preached by the second to his Congregation: which the sermon-borrower complained of to the lender of it, and was thus answered; I lent you indeed my* Fiddle, *but not my* Fiddlestick; *for you are to know, that every one cannot make musick with my words, which are fitted for my own mouth. And so, my Scholar, you are to know, that as the ill pronunciation or ill accenting of words in a Sermon spoils it, so the ill carriage of your line, or not fishing even to a foot in a right place, makes you lose your labour.*[67]

Walton's point is that although words (or fishing tackle) can be borrowed, ability and skill cannot; so each may learn from a master, but must still develop his powers independently. Wholesale borrowing inevitably results in artistic failure and can gratify neither the speaker nor his audience. It is no good stealing something in order to compensate for a personal sense of deprivation—and thus the line snaps.

The *piscator*'s advice to the novice is curiously reminiscent of the shade of James Joyce, who rebukes and inspires the pilgrim-poet of *Station Island*:

---

[67] *The Compleat Angler*, 102.

What you must do must be done on your own
so get back into harness. The main thing is to write
for the joy of it.[68]

The passage, already discussed above, is of great relevance to
Seeing Things as a whole, and in particular to '*All gone into the
world of light?*', since Joyce's voice is 'eddying with the vowels
of all rivers'—an image that contributes positively to the other-
wise potentially dark 'eddies' of the later poem. The shade of
Joyce is also represented leaning on an ash plant, which not
only recalls his own creation, Stephen Dedalus, but also takes
the reader of *Seeing Things* to one of the many poems in the
later collection inspired by Heaney's father. 'The Ash Plant' in
Seeing Things is inspired by Patrick Heaney's stick; but grafted
on to the family possession is the image of Stephen Dedalus,
whose development into an artist occurs in a series of personal
illuminations, or moments of '*claritas*'.

The father figure who haunts *Seeing Things* is not only a
blood relation, for when the shade of Joyce appeared in *Station
Island*, the speaker greeted him 'Old father'.[69] Aeneas's prayer
for a face-to-face meeting with his father may reflect a personal
longing on the part of the translator, but recollection of
Heaney's earlier creation of shades suggests that more compli-
cated allegiances are also being confronted. It is, indeed, signifi-
cant that the ash plant in *Seeing Things* should be described as a
'silver bough', since in Celtic mythology this is the passport to
the Tir-nan-Og, the Otherworld normally inaccessible to
mortals.[70] The image also recalls Aeneas's search for the golden
bough, which fulfilled the same function in classical mythology,
transporting the living to the realms of the dead and facilitating
the crossing from the everyday world into the unknown.
Significantly, the golden bough is a 'special gift' desired rather
than feared by the hero, whose own capacities will be magnified
through its possession.[71] Both Joyce and Patrick Heaney are
represented as possessors of walking sticks, but far from
suggesting weakness the 'silver bough' emerges from the web of

---

[68] *Station Island*, 92–3.
[69] Ibid. 93; cf. Joyce, *A Portrait of the Artist*, 276.
[70] 'The Ash Plant', *Seeing Things*, 19. See also F. Marian McNeill, *The Silver Bough*, Vol. I (Edinburgh, 1989), 105–6.
[71] 'The Golden Bough', *Seeing Things*, 3.

allusions as a symbol of strength that can be passed on to the next generation.

Although in *Station Island*, the figure of Joyce might have represented the overwhelming burden of past genius ('his voice eddying with the vowels of all rivers'), the words he utters suggest an impulse towards a new originality. Stephen Dedalus had drawn on the teachings of the philosophers and theologians for his 'own use and guidance' in preparation for doing 'something' for himself 'by their light', and so now Heaney makes Joyce's advice curiously self-occluding, since the voice of the shade urges the later poet to swim free of the past.[72] The encouragement to be independent, however, means that, in place of an Oedipal struggle, the younger poet is invited to learn from the wisdom of his elders, in order to find his own voice.

Rather than conveying a sense of helplessness in the face of time and death, then, it is also possible that the concluding lines of '*All gone into the world of light?*' represent a sudden sweep of power:

> And eddies swirl a dead leaf past in silence
> Swifter (it seems) than the water's passage.

Since so many of the poems in *Seeing Things* develop images of 'giddy strange assistance' it is not strange to find something similar occurring here, though the paradox, as in all the other instances, is that the assistance is self-generated. For the very representation of uncertainty and loss in the poem is countered by the extraordinary control of its form and the internal balance of the lyric. This is the work of a highly accomplished poet, who has learned his art through years of practice and through the study of earlier masters. In evoking the shade of Joyce in '*All gone into the world of light?*', Heaney is really recalling his own image of Joyce and the words he had placed in the mouth of the 'Old Father'. As he observes in the last poem of the 'Squarings' sequence,

> what's come upon is manifest
> Only in the light of what has been gone through.[73]

---

[72] See Noon, *Joyce and Aquinas*, 19–21 for discussion of Dedalus's approach to early authority.

[73] 'xlviii', *Seeing Things*, 108.

Just as Aeneas had to visit the shades of the dead before return-ing to 'upper air' and the great task ahead, so Heaney seems to suggest that discovery is at least partly the result of accumulated knowledge and experience.

Even the 'dead leaf' in the closing lines may be a positive image when seen in the light of 'what has been gone through'; for while a literal reading may suggest death and hopelessness, a more literary interpretation is likely to charge the image with life and possibility. For Shelley had transformed the 'dead leaf' in his 'Ode to the West Wind', from an image of despair to one of tumultuous creativity, making the last section of the poem (which, like Heaney's, draws on the Dantean terza rima) a climactic prophecy of new life:

> Drive my dead thoughts over the universe
> Like withered leaves to quicken a new birth!
> And by the incantation of this verse,
>
> Scatter, as from an unextinguished hearth
> Ashes and sparks, my words among mankind!
> Be through my lips to unawakened Earth
>
> The trumpet of a prophecy! O Wind,
> If Winter comes, can Spring be far behind?[74]

If Heaney's 'dead leaf' is really Shelley's, then his image, too, may suggest the quickening of a new birth. Indeed, the leaf might symbolize any earlier poem—Vaughan's, Virgil's, Dante's, Larkin's—swirling in the voice of the reader-writer.

Rather than representing the failure of a poem based on borrowed tackle, then, the snapping of the 'caught line' in '*All gone into the world of light?*' may after all be supremely posi-tive. Perhaps it represents the moment of breaking free from other men's words or, indeed, of following Joyce's advice to 'Let go, let fly, forget. | You've listened long enough. Now strike your note'.[75] In 'A Haul', it is after all the moment when the line snaps that creates an image very similar to the 'elver-gleams in the dark of the whole sea' at the conclusion of Joyce's speech:

> But the big haul came to an end
> when Thor's foot went through the boards

---

[74] Shelley, 'Ode to the West Wind', 63–70.   [75] *Station Island*, 93.

> and Hymer panicked and cut
> the line with a bait-knife. Then
> roll-over, turmoil, whiplash!
> A Milky Way in the water.[76]

'That moment of admission of *All gone*' may be a similar moment of unexpected opportunity, when unsuccessful angling gives way to a rush of mysterious movement. For the effect of the line snapping in 'A Haul' is mind-opening and intensely enlightening:

> The hole he smashed in the boat
> opened, the way Thor's head
> opened out there on the sea.
> He felt at one with space,
>
> unroofed and obvious—
> surprised in his empty arms
> like some fabulous high-catcher
> coming down without the ball.

Thor's experience anticipates that depicted in 'The Skylight', when a similar cutting through of something solid and familiar results in a miraculous enablement, as 'extravagant | Sky entered and held surprise wide open'.[77] Paradoxically, Thor's failure to hold on to what he has caught transforms him into 'some fabulous high-catcher', and so perhaps the ungratified speaker of '*All gone into the world of light?*' is similarly translated once his line snaps.

The lifeline offered by earlier verse is not, after all, something to hang on to in preference to independent exploration, but rather a guide whose memory enables new motion. Thor's startling sense of elevation results from letting go, but the force of his new experience comes from the weight of his quarry. The contrary impulses in 'The Haul', like those in '*All gone into the world of light?*', epitomize the internal dynamism of the entire volume, which in turn corresponds to the aesthetic ideals of *The Redress of Poetry*. The sense of poetry as an art, somewhat like fishing, also emphasizes the vital recreational element, which balances the seriousness of the other associations of 'redress'.

---

[76] 'A Haul', *Seeing Things*, 12.

[77] 'The Skylight', *Seeing Things*, 37. The sonnet is part of the 'Glanmore Revisited' section, which alludes to the 'Glanmore Sonnets' published in *Field Work*, 33–43.

The repeated play on 'lines' turns reading into another kind of game, and offers the exhilaration of high-catching through the unexpected recognition of a pun or an allusion. The contemplative pursuit of reading poetry thus becomes an active mental exercise, and one which becomes more and more fulfilling with practice. Poems that emphasize reading by beginning with an obvious reference to another poem are invitations to imaginative participation, since they present such a flattering parallel to their own readers. If a writer such as Heaney is propelled so demonstrably into creative action by reading, then the imagination of every reader must surely be stirred in some way? Very few will produce new poems of such quality, but the rewards of an active, creative response to the text are, in themselves, supremely gratifying.

Epilogue

George Mackay Brown

All Souls

'There are more Hamnavoe
    folk in the kirkyard
Than there are walking the
    Hamnavoe street'—
My father used to say that,
    and I a child.

Death was a door
    that never had opened,
I had no dread of the skull
    beyond
Nor of ghosts that troubled
    some of the living.

Today a throng of good
    ghosts visit me,
Coming at the bellstroke of
    the prayer *de mortuis*
A host so numerous I
    can't name them all.
Name seven, as the
    second sun of November
    comes cold in at the
    window
And a November cloud
Rattles first hailstones on
    bereft gardens.
Name Peter Esson, tailor,
    presiding from his bench
Over sailors' nightly anthologies,
    stories
Rooted in Shanghai,
    Rio, all ports between,

And Peter stitching a
    Sabbath suit for some
    farmer.
Name Attie Campbell, whose
    every utterance
Brimmed the ears of beermen
    with joy
As his mug brimmed with
    tawny Barleycorn fleeces.
Bring Edwin Muir:
    he in age with the chalice of childlight still.
Bring John Folster, fisherman
    who gathered haddocks
    and lobsters
From the thunder-bruised
    Atlantic
Into his frail boat, then
    read his books by
    lamplight,
A lonely gentle pier-dweller.
Summon John Shearer, teacher,
    kinder to his stumbling
    pupils
Than to those who moved
    dextrously
Through the labyrinth of his
    little lab.
Come Peter Leith, farmer,
    turning the leaves of
    books
As familiarly as furrows
In a farm, generations-old, above a loch.
Sing an unknown brother,
    whose bead of light went out
Before the first star.

How many crowd today
    at the kirkyard gate!
Such fragrances filled Hamnavoe's
    closes and piers!
Seventy-year-old tongue
    of dust
Say a blessing now, once more
    in early November.

Mary Jane Mackay, died 3
November 1967.
At her name's telling,
  a light breaks
  still
On older Hamnavoe
  faces.
In this year's flower-time
She'd have garnered
  a hundred summers.

2 November 1991

Bibliography

ABRAMS, M. H., *The Mirror and the Lamp: Romantic Theory and the Critical Tradition* (New York, 1953).
——*The Correspondent Breeze: Essays on English Romanticism* (New York, 1984).
ADDISON, JOSEPH, *The Spectator*, ed. Donald F. Bond, 5 vols. (Oxford, 1965).
ALEXANDER, J. H., *Two Studies in Romantic Reviewing: Edinburgh Reviewers and the English Tradition: The Reviewing of Walter Scott's Poetry 1805–1817*, Salzburg Studies in English Literature: Romantic Reassessment, 49, 2 vols. (Salzburg, 1975).
——*Marmion: Studies in Interpretation and Composition*, Salzburg Studies in English Literature: Romantic Reassessment, 30 (Salzburg, 1981).
ALLINGHAM, HELEN, and DICK, STEWART, *The Cottage Homes of England* (London, 1909).
AMIS, KINGSLEY, 'The Curious Elf: A Note on Rhyme in Keats', *Essays in Criticism*, 1 (1951), 191.
ANDERSON, BENEDICT, *Imagined Communities: Reflections on the Origin and Spread of Nationalism*, rev. edn. (London, 1991).
ANDERSON, JAMES, 'Poems chiefly in the Scottish Dialect. By Robert Burns', *Monthly Review*, 75 (1786), 442.
APPLEYARD, J. A., *Coleridge's Philosophy of Literature* (Cambridge, Mass., 1965).
AQUINAS, THOMAS, *Selected Philosophical Writings*, trans. by Timothy McDermott (Oxford, 1993).
ASHTON, ROSEMARY, *The Life of Samuel Taylor Coleridge* (Oxford and Cambridge, Mass., 1996).
ATTRIDGE, DEREK, *The Rhythms of English Poetry* (London, 1982).
AUSTEN, JANE, *Jane Austen's Letters*, ed. Deirdre Le Faye, 3rd edn. (Oxford, 1995).
BAILLIE, JOANNA, *The Dramatic and Poetical Works of Joanna Baillie* (London, 1851).
BAKHTIN, M. M., *The Dialogic Imagination*, ed. Michael Holquist, trans. Caryl Emerson and Michael Holquist (Austin, Tex., 1981).
BARMAN, CHRISTIAN, *Architecture* (London, 1928).
BARTH, J. ROBERT, 'Theological Implications of Coleridge's Theory of Imagination', in Christine Gallant (ed.), *Coleridge's Theory of Imagination Today*, 3–13.

BARTH, J. ROBERT, *Coleridge and Christian Doctrine* (Cambridge, Mass., 1969).

BARTON, BERNARD, *Household Verses* (London, 1845).

BASKER, JAMES G., 'Scotticisms and the Problem of Cultural Identity in Eighteenth-Century Britain', in John Dwyer and Richard B. Sher (eds.), *Sociability and Society in Eighteenth-Century Scotland* (Edinburgh, 1993).

BATE, JONATHAN, *Shakespeare and the English Romantic Imagination* (Oxford, 1986).

—— and JACKSON, R., *Shakespeare: An Illustrated Stage History* (London, 1989).

BATE, W. J., *From Classic to Romantic* (Cambridge, Mass., 1946).

—— *John Keats* (Cambridge, Mass., 1963).

—— *The Burden of the Past and the English Poet* (London, 1971).

BEARD, MADELEINE, *English Landed Society in the Twentieth Century* (London, 1989).

BEATTIE, JAMES, *The Minstrel; or, The Progress of Genius. A Poem* (London, 1771).

Belfast Streetfinder (London, 1999).

BHABHA, HOMI, *The Location of Culture* (London, 1994).

BLAIR, HUGH, 'A Critical Dissertation on the Poems of Ossian' (1763), in James Macpherson, *The Poems of Ossian*, ed. Howard Gaskill (Edinburgh, 1996), 343–99.

—— *Lectures on Rhetoric and Belles Lettres*, 2 vols. (London and Edinburgh, 1783).

—— *Sermons*, 5 vols. (Edinburgh and London, 1777–1801).

BLOOM, HAROLD, *The Anxiety of Influence: A Theory of Poetry* (New York, 1973).

—— *A Map of Misreading* (Oxford and New York, 1975).

—— (ed.), *Seamus Heaney* (New Haven and New York, 1986).

—— (ed.), *Blaise Pascal* (New York and Philadelphia, 1989).

BOGDANOR, VERNON, *Devolution in the United Kingdom* (Oxford, 1999).

BOSWELL, JAMES, *The Life of Samuel Johnson* (1791), ed. G. B. Hill, rev. L. F. Powell, 6 vols. (Oxford, 1934–50).

BRENNER, R., and BRENNER, G., *Gambling and Speculation: A Theory, A History, and a Future of Some Human Decisions* (Cambridge, 1990).

BRIDGES, ROBERT, *Collected Essays, Papers, etc. of Robert Bridges*, 10 vols. (London, 1927–36).

BRINKLEY, ROBERT, and HANLEY, KEITH (eds.), *Romantic Revisions* (Cambridge, 1992).

BROWN, GEORGE MACKAY, *An Orkney Tapestry* (London, 1969).

——— *Following A Lark* (London, 1996).

——— *For the Islands I Sing: An Autobiography* (London, 1997).

——— *Northern Lights: A Poet's Sources* (London, 1999).

BROWN, MARY ELLEN, *Burns and Tradition* (London, 1984).

BROWN, TERENCE (ed.), *Celticism* (Amsterdam and Atlanta, Ga., 1996).

BUCHAN, DAVID, *A Scottish Ballad Book* (London, 1972).

——— *The Ballad and the Folk* (London, 1972).

BURNS, ROBERT, *Poems Chiefly in the Scottish Dialect* (Kilmarnock, 1786).

——— *Poems Chiefly in the Scottish Dialect*, enlarged edn. (Edinburgh, 1787).

——— 'Humanity: An Ode', *Gentleman's Magazine*, lxiv/2 (1794), 748–9.

——— *The Poems and Songs of Robert Burns*, ed. James Kinsley, 3 vols. (Oxford, 1968).

——— *First Commonplace Book*, ed. Raymond Lamont Brown (Wakefield, 1969).

——— *The Letters of Robert Burns*, ed. J. De Lancey Ferguson, rev. 2nd edn., ed. G. Ross Roy, 2 vols. (Oxford, 1985).

——— *The Songs of Robert Burns*, ed. Donald A. Low (London, 1993).

BUTLER, MARILYN, *Romantics, Rebels, and Reactionaries: English Literature and its Background 1760–1830* (Oxford, 1981).

——— (ed.), *Burke, Paine, Godwin, and the Revolution Controversy* (Cambridge, 1984).

BUTT, JOHN, 'The Revival of Scottish Vernacular Poetry in the Eighteenth Century', in F. W. Hilles and Harold Bloom (eds.), *From Sensibility to Romanticism: Essays presented to Frederick A. Pottle*, (New York, 1965).

BYRON, LORD, *The Complete Poetical Works of Lord Byron*, ed. Jerome J. McGann, 7 vols. (Oxford, 1980–1993).

CARLSON, JULIE A., *In the Theatre of Romanticism: Coleridge, Nationalism, Women* (Cambridge, 1994).

CARLYLE, THOMAS, 'The Life of Burns. By J. G. Lockhart', *Edinburgh Review*, 48 (1828), 267–312.

——— *On Heroes, Hero-Worship and the Heroic in History* (London, 1841).

CARPENTER, HUMPHREY, *W. H. Auden: A Biography*, rev. edn. (London, 1983).

CARROLL, LEWIS (Charles Lutwidge Dodgson), *Alice's Adventures in Wonderland* (1865), *The Annotated Alice*, ed. Martin Gardner, rev. edn. (Harmondsworth, 1970).

CARSON, CIARAN, 'Escaped from the Massacre? *North* by Seamus Heaney', *The Honest Ulsterman*, 50 (1975), 183–6.

—— *The New Estate* (Belfast, 1976).

—— 'The Irish for No', *The Honest Ulsterman*, 82 (1986), 3–4.

—— 'Third Degree for Mr Reid. *Katerina Brac*', *The Honest Ulsterman*, 82 (1986), 86–7.

—— *The Irish for No* (Dublin, 1987).

—— *Belfast Confetti* (Dublin, 1989).

—— *First Language* (Dublin, 1993).

—— *Last Night's Fun: A Book About Irish Traditional Music* (London, 1996).

—— *The Star Factory* (London, 1997)

CHILD, F. J. (ed.), *The English and Scottish Popular Ballads* (1882), facsimile edn., 5 vols. (New York, 1956).

CHORLEY, HENRY, *Memorials of Mrs Hemans*, 2 vols. (London, 1836).

CHRISTIANSEN, J., *Coleridge's Blessed Machine of Language* (Ithaca and London, 1981).

CHUTO, JACQUES, *James Clarence Mangan: A Bibliography of his Works* (Blackrock, 1999).

COLERIDGE, SAMUEL TAYLOR, *Poems on Various Subjects* (Bristol, 1796).

—— *Fears in Solitude* (London, 1798).

—— *Sibylline Leaves: A Collection of Poems* (London, 1817).

—— *The Poetical Works of Samuel Taylor Coleridge*, ed. E. H. Coleridge, 2 vols. (Oxford, 1912).

—— *The Collected Letters of Samuel Taylor Coleridge*, ed. E. L. Griggs, 6 vols. (Oxford, 1956–71).

—— *The Notebooks of Samuel Taylor Coleridge*, ed. Kathleen Coburn, 6 vols. (Princeton and London, 1957–).

—— *The Collected Works of Samuel Taylor Coleridge*, gen. editor Kathleen Coburn. Volumes consulted:

—— *The Friend*, ed. Barbara E. Rooke, 2 vols. (Princeton and London, 1969).

—— *The Watchman*, ed. Lewis Patton (Princeton and London, 1970).

—— *Lectures 1795 on Politics and Religion*, ed. Lewis Patton and Peter Mann (Princeton and London, 1971).

—— *Lay Sermons*, ed. R. J. White (Princeton and London, 1972).

—— *On the Constitution of the Church and State*, ed. John Colmer (Princeton and London, 1976).

—— *Biographia. Literaria*, ed. James Engell and W. J. Bate, 2 vols. (Princeton and London, 1983).

—— *Lectures 1808–1819 On Literature*, ed. R. A. Foakes, 2 vols. (Princeton and London, 1987).

—— *Shorter Works and Fragments*, ed. H. J. Jackson and J. de R. Jackson (Princeton and London, 1995).

—— *Coleridge's Dejection: The Earliest Manuscripts and the Earliest Printings*, ed. Stephen M. Parrish (Ithaca, 1988).

COLLEY, LINDA, *Britons: Forging the Nation 1707–1837* (London, 1992).

The Comet (1831–2).

CONNOLLY, S. J. (ed.), *Kingdoms United? Great Britain and Ireland since 1500: Integration and Diversity* (Dublin and Portland, Oreg., 1999).

COPLEY, STEPHEN, and WHALE, JOHN (eds.), *Beyond Romanticism: New Approaches to Texts and Contexts 1780–1832* (London, 1992).

CORCORAN, NEIL, 'One Step Forward, Two Steps Back: Ciaran Carson's *The Irish for No*', in Neil Corcoran (ed.), *The Chosen Ground: Essays on the Contemporary Poetry of Northern Ireland* (Chester Springs and Bridgend, 1992), 213–33.

—— *The Poetry of Seamus Heaney*, rev. edn. (London, 1998).

COWARD, NOEL, *Middle East Diary* (London and Toronto, 1944).

—— *Operette* (London, 1938).

—— *The Noel Coward Song Book* (London, 1953).

COWPER, WILLIAM, *The Letters and Prose Writings of William Cowper*, ed. J. King and C. Ryskamp, 5 vols. (Oxford, 1979–86).

CRAIG, DAVID, *Scottish Literature and the Scottish People 1680–1830* (London, 1961).

CRAWFORD, ROBERT, *Devolving English Literature* (Oxford, 1992).

—— (ed.), *Robert Burns and Cultural Authority* (Edinburgh, 1997).

—— (ed.), *The Scottish Invention of English Literature* (Cambridge, 1998).

CRAWFORD, THOMAS, *Burns: A Study of the Poems and Songs* (Edinburgh and London, 1960)

—— David Hewitt and Alexander Law (eds.), *Longer Scottish Poems*, Volume II: *1650–1830* (Edinburgh, 1987).

CRONIN, MICHAEL, *Translating Ireland: Translation, Languages, Cultures* (Cork, 1996).

CUMBERLAND, RICHARD, *Memoirs* (London, 1806).

CURRAN, STUART, *Poetic Form and British Romanticism* (Oxford, 1986).

DAICHES, DAVID, *The Paradox of Scottish Culture* (London, 1964).

DANTE, *The Divine Comedy of Dante Alighieri*, trans. by John D. Sinclair, 3 vols. (London, 1939).

DARLEY, GILLIAN, *Octavia Hill: A Life* (London, 1990).

DARWIN, BERNARD, 'Introduction', *The Oxford Dictionary of Quotations* (Oxford, 1941).

DAVIS, LEITH, *Acts of Union: Scotland and the Literary Negotiation of the British Nation 1707–1830* (Stanford, 1999).

DAWSON, P. M. S., *The Unacknowledged Legislator: Shelley and Politics* (Oxford, 1980).

DEANE, SEAMUS, 'Unhappy and at Home: Interview with Seamus Heaney', *The Crane Bag*, 1/1 (1977), 61–7.

—— (ed.), *The Field Day Anthology of Irish Writing*, 3 vols. (Derry, 1991).

—— *Strange Country: Modernity and Nationhood in Irish Writing since 1790* (Oxford, 1997).

DEKKER, GEORGE, *Coleridge and the Literature of Sensibility* (London, 1978).

DE MAN, PAUL, *The Rhetoric of Romanticism* (New York, 1984).

—— *Romanticism and Contemporary Criticism: The Gauss Seminar and Other Papers*, ed. E. S. Burt, Kevin Newmark, and Andrzej Warminski (Baltimore and London, 1993).

DIGBY, KENELME, *Two Treatises: In the one of which the Nature of Bodies; In the other, the Nature of Man's Soule, is looked into: in way of discovery of the Immortality of Reasonable Soules* (London, 1645).

DOBSON, MICHAEL, *The Making of the National Poet: Shakespeare, Adaptation and Authority 1600–1769* (Oxford, 1992).

DONNE, JOHN, *The Complete English Poems*, ed. A. J. Smith, corrected edn. (Harmondsworth, 1973).

DORSON, RICHARD M., *The British Folklorists: A History* (Chicago and London, 1968).

DOUGLAS, GAVIN, *Translation of Virgil's Aeneid*, ed. David Coldwell, 4 vols. (Edinburgh and London, 1957–64).

DOWDEN, EDWARD, *The Life of Percy Bysshe Shelley*, new edn. (London, 1896).

DRYDEN, JOHN, *The Oxford Authors: John Dryden*, ed. Keith Walker (Oxford and New York, 1987).

The Dublin Penny Journal, 1832–3.

Dublin University Magazine, 1834–49.

DUFF, WILLIAM, *An Essay on Original Genius* (London, 1967).

DUFFY, CHARLES GAVAN (ed.), *The Ballad Poetry of Ireland* (Dublin, 1845).

—— (ed.), *The Spirit of the Nation* (Dublin, 1845), facsimile edn. with introduction by John Kelly (Poole and Washington, DC, 1998).

—— *Four Years of Irish History, 1845–1849* (London, 1880).

—— *Young Ireland: A Fragment of Irish History, 1840–1850* (London, 1880).

DUNBAR, WILLIAM, *The Poems of William Dunbar*, ed. John Small,

2 vols. (Edinburgh and London, 1893).

DUNN, DAVID, ' "A Very Scottish Kind of Dash": Burns's Native Metric', in Robert Crawford (ed.), *Robert Burns and Cultural Authority*, 58–85.

EAGLETON, TERRY, *Heathcliff and the Great Hunger* (London and New York, 1995).

—— *Crazy John and the Bishop and Other Essays on Irish Culture* (Cork, 1998).

Edinburgh Review, I (1755).

ELIOT, T. S., *The Complete Poems and Plays of T. S. Eliot* (London, 1969).

ENGELBERG, KARSTEN KLEJS, *The Making of the Shelley Myth: An Annotated Bibliography of Criticism of Percy Bysshe Shelley, 1822–1860* (London, 1988).

FANON, FRANTZ, *Black Skin, White Masks* (London, 1991).

FARMER, RICHARD, *An Essay on the Learning of Shakespeare: Addressed to Joseph Cradock, Esq.*, 2nd edn. (1767), in D. Nichol Smith (ed.), *Eighteenth Century Essays on Shakespeare* (Glasgow, 1903), 162–215.

FAVRET, M., and WATSON, N., *At the Limits of Romanticism: Essays in Cultural, Feminist and Materialist Criticism* (Bloomington, Ind., 1994).

FERGUSON, SAMUEL, 'Hardiman's Irish Minstrelsy', *Dublin University Magazine*, III (1834), 465–78; IV (1834), 152–67, 447–67, 514–30.

FERRY, ANNE, *The Title to the Poem* (Stanford, 1996).

FIELDING, PENNY, *Writing and Orality: Nationality, Culture, and Nineteenth-Century Scottish Writing* (Oxford, 1996).

FISHER, CLIVE, *Noel Coward* (London, 1992).

FOERSTER, D. M., *Homer in English Criticism: The Historical Approach in the Eighteenth Century* (New Haven, 1947).

FORBES, WILLIAM, *An Account of the Life and Writings of James Beattie*, 2. vols. (Edinburgh, 1806).

FORD, FORD MADOX, *Parade's End, The Bodley Head Ford Madox Ford*, 4 vols. (London, 1963).

FOSTER, ROY, *Modern Ireland 1600–1972* (Harmondsworth, 1988).

FOWLER, DAVID C., *A Literary History of the Popular Ballad* (Durham, NC, 1968).

FRUMAN, NORMAN, *Coleridge: The Damaged Archangel* (New York, 1971).

FURNISS, AVERIL SANDERSON, *The Homes of the People* (Oxford, 1925).

GALLANT, CHRISTINE (ed.), *Coleridge's Theory of Imagination Today* (New York, 1989).

GERARD, ALEXANDER, *An Essay on Genius* (London, 1774).

GIBBONS, LUKE, 'The Sympathetic Bond: Ossian, Celticism and Colonialism', in Terence Brown (ed.), *Celticism*, 273–91.

—— *Transformations in Irish Culture* (Cork, 1996).

GILL, STEPHEN, *William Wordsworth: A Life* (Oxford, 1989).

—— 'Wordsworth's Poems: The Question of Text', in Robert Brinkley and Keith Hanley (eds.), *Romantic Revisions*, 43–63.

—— *Wordsworth and the Victorians* (Oxford, 1998).

GIROUARD, MARK, *Life in the English Country House: A Social and Architectural History* (New Haven and London, 1978).

—— *The Return to Camelot: Chivalry and the English Gentleman* (New Haven and London, 1981).

GOLDEN, SEAN, 'Post-Traditional English Literature: A Polemic', *The Crane Bag*, 3/2 (1979), 7–18.

GOLDMANN, LUCIEN, 'The Wager: The Christian Religion', in Harold Bloom (ed.), *Blaise Pascal*, 53–80.

GOLDSMITH, OLIVER, *An History of the Earth and Animated Nature*, 8 vols. (London, 1774).

—— *The Collected Works of Oliver Goldsmith*, ed. A. Friedman, 5 vols. (Oxford, 1966).

GOLLANCZ, VICTOR (ed.), *A Year of Grace* (London, 1950).

—— *From Darkness to Light: A Confession of Faith in the Form of an Anthology* (London, 1956).

GRAVIL, R., NEWLYN, L., and ROE, N. (eds.), *Coleridge's Imagination: Essays in Memory of Pete Laver* (Cambridge, 1985).

GREEN, ROGER LANCELYN, *Andrew Lang: A Critical Biography* (Leicester, 1946).

GRENNAN, EAMONN, 'Keats's Contemptus Mundi: A Shakespearean Influence on the "Ode to a Nightingale"', *Modern Language Quarterly*, 36 (1975), 272–92.

GROOM, NICK, *The Making of Percy's Reliques* (Oxford, 1999).

HAGER, ALAN (ed.), *Understanding Romeo and Juliet* (London, 1999).

HART, HENRY, *Seamus Heaney: Poet of Contrary Progressions* (New York, 1991).

HASLETT, MOYRA, *Byron's Don Juan and the Don Juan Legend* (Oxford, 1997).

HAY, IAN, 'The Lighter Side of Life: VII. The Father of the Man', *Blackwood's Magazine*, cxcvi (Oct. 1914), 458–66.

HAYLEY, BARBARA, 'Irish Periodicals from the Union to the Nation', Anglo-Irish Studies, II (1976), 83–103.

HAZLITT, WILLIAM, *The Complete Works of William Hazlitt*, ed. P. P. Howe, 21 vols. (London, 1930–4).

HEANEY, SEAMUS, *Death of a Naturalist* (London, 1966).
—— *Door into the Dark* (London, 1969).
—— *Wintering Out* (London, 1972).
—— *North* (London, 1975).
—— *Field Work* (London, 1979).
—— *Preoccupations: Selected Prose 1968–1978* (London, 1980).
—— 'An Open Letter' (1983), *Ireland's Field Day* (London, 1985), 23–32.
—— *Station Island* (London, 1984).
—— *The Haw Lantern* (London, 1987).
—— *The Government of the Tongue: The 1986 T. S. Eliot Memorial Lectures and Other Critical Writings* (London, 1988).
—— *The Redress of Poetry* (Oxford, 1990).
—— *Seeing Things* (London, 1991).
—— 'Foreword', Niall Macmonagle (ed.), *Lifelines: An Anthology of Poems Chosen by Famous People* (Harmondsworth, 1993).
—— *The Redress of Poetry: Oxford Lectures* (London, 1995).
—— 'Burns's Art Speech', in Robert Crawford (ed.), *Burns and Cultural Authority*, 216–33.
—— *Opened Ground: Poems 1966–1996* (London, 1998).
HEATH, WILLIAM, *Wordsworth and Coleridge: A Study of their Literary Relations in 1801–1802* (Oxford, 1970).
HEMANS, FELICIA, *Records of Woman, with Other Poems*, 2nd edn. (Edinburgh, 1828).
—— *The Works of Mrs Hemans, with a Memoir by her Sister*, 7 vols. (Edinburgh, 1839).
HENLEY, W. E., *The Works of W. E. Henley*, 7 vols. (London, 1908).
HENNESSY, THOMAS, *A History of Northern Ireland 1920–1996* (London, 1997).
HENRYSON, ROBERT, *Poems*, ed. Charles Elliott (Oxford, 1963).
HERBERT, GEORGE, *The English Poems of George Herbert*, ed. C. A. Patrides (London, 1974).
HERON, ROBERT, 'Memoirs of the Life of the Late Robert Burns', *Monthly Magazine*, 3 (1797), 213–16, 552–62.
HIBBERD, JOHN, *Salomon Gessner: His Creative Achievement and Influence* (Cambridge, 1976).
HILL, OCTAVIA, *Homes of the London Poor (1875) and The Bitter Cry of Outcast London: An Inquiry into the Condition of the Abject Poor* (1883), facsimile edn., ed. A. Mearns (London, 1970).
HOGG, THOMAS JEFFERSON, *The Life of Percy Bysshe Shelley* (London, 1858).
HOLLANDER, JOHN, *The Figure of Echo* (London, 1981).
—— (ed.), *Poetics of Influence* (New Haven, 1988).

HOLMES, RICHARD, *Shelley: The Pursuit* (London, 1974).
—— *Coleridge: Early Visions* (London, 1989).
HOPKINS, GERARD MANLEY, *The Poetical Works of Gerard Manley Hopkins*, ed. Norman H. Mackenzie (Oxford, 1990).
HUME, DAVID, *The Letters of David Hume*, ed. J. Y. T. Grieg, 2 vols. (Oxford, 1932).
HUNT, LEIGH, *Lord Byron and Some of his Contemporaries* (London, 1828).
HUTCHEON, LINDA, *A Theory of Parody: The Teachings of Twentieth-Century Art Forms* (New York and London, 1985).
HUTCHINSON, SARA, *The Letters of Sara Hutchinson*, ed. Kathleen Coburn (London, 1954).
HYDE, DOUGLAS, 'The Necessity for De-Anglicising Ireland', *The Revival of Irish Literature: Addresses by Sir Charles Gavan. Duffy, KCMG, Dr George Sigerson, and Dr Douglas Hyde* (London, 1894), 117–61.
Ireland's Field Day (London, 1985).
JACK, R. D. S., 'Burns as Sassenach Poet', in Kenneth Simpson (ed.), *Burns Now*, 150–66.
JAFFÉ, HANS L. C., *Picasso* (New York, n.d. [1973?]).
JEFFREY, FRANCIS, 'Records of Woman, with Other Poems by Felicia Hemans; The Forest Sanctuary, with other Poems by Felicia Hemans', *Edinburgh Review*, 50 (1829), 32–47.
JEWITT, L. and HALL, S. C., *The Stately Homes of England* (London, 1874).
JOHNSON, SAMUEL, *The Oxford Authors: Samuel Johnson*, ed. Donald Greene (Oxford, 1984).
JONES, R. F., *Ancients and Moderns: A Study of the Rise of the Scientific Movement in Seventeenth-Century England* (St Louis, 1936).
JOYCE, JAMES, *A Portrait of the Artist as a Young Man*, ed. Seamus Deane (Harmondsworth, 1992).
JOYCE, P. W., *English as we Speak it in Ireland*. 2nd edn. (London and Dublin, 1910).
KEARNEY, RICHARD, 'Between Politics and Literature: The Irish Cultural Journal', *The Crane Bag*, 7/2 (1983), 160–71.
—— *Myth and Motherland* (1984), in *Ireland's Field Day*, 61–82.
—— 'Between Conflict and Consensus', *The Crane Bag*, 9/1 (1985), 87–9.
KEATS, JOHN, *The Letters of John Keats 1814–1821*, ed. Hyder E. Rollins, 2 vols. (Cambridge, Mass., 1958).
—— *John Keats: The Complete Poems*, ed. Miriam Allott (London, 1970).

KERRIGAN, JOHN, 'Hand and Foot', *London Review of Books* (27 May 1999), 20–3.

KIBERD, DECLAN, *Anglo-Irish Attitudes* (1984), in *Ireland's Field Day*, 83–105.

—— *Inventing Ireland: The Literature of the Modern Nation* (London, 1995).

KIDD, COLIN, *Subverting Scotland's Past: Scottish Whig Historians and the Creation of an Anglo-British Identity, 1689–c.1830* (Cambridge, 1993).

KINGHORN, A. M., 'The Literary and Historical Origins of the Burns Myth', *Dalhousie Review*, xxxix (1959), 76–85.

KIRKLAND, RICHARD, *Literature and Culture in Northern Ireland since 1965: Moments of Danger* (London, 1996).

KLANCHER, JON, *The Making of English Reading Audiences, 1790–1832* (Madison, Wis., 1987).

KNOX, W. J., *Decades of the Ulster Bank* (Belfast, 1965).

LANDOR, W. S., *The Poetical Works of Walter Savage Landor*, ed. Stephen Wheeler, 3 vols. (Oxford, 1937).

LANG, ANDREW, *The Poetical Works of Andrew Lang*, ed. Mrs Lang, 4 vols. (London, 1923).

LARKIN, PHILIP, *Collected Poems*, ed. Anthony Thwaite (London, 1988).

LEADER, ZACHARY, *Revision and Romantic Authorship* (Oxford, 1996).

LEERSSEN, JOEP, *Mere Irish and Fíor Ghael: Studies in the Idea of Irish Nationality, its Development and Literary Expression prior to the Nineteenth Century* (Cork, 1996).

—— *Remembrance and Imagination: Patterns in the Historical and Literary Representation of Ireland in the Nineteenth Century* (Cork, 1996).

LEVINE, J., *The Battle of the Books: History and Literature in the Augustan Age* (London, 1991).

LEVINSON, M., *The Romantic Fragment Poem: A Critique of a Form* (Chapel Hill, NC, 1986).

LLOYD, DAVID, *Nationalism and Minor Literature: James Clarence Mangan. and the Emergence of Irish Cultural Nationalism* (Berkeley and Los Angeles, 1987).

LOCKE, JOHN, *An Essay Concerning Human Understanding* (1690), ed. P. H. Nidditch (Oxford, 1975).

LOOTENS, TRICIA, 'Hemans and Home: Victorianism, Feminine "Internal Enemies", and the Domestication of National Identity', *PMLA*, 109 (1994), 234–53.

LOW, DONALD A. (ed.), *Robert Burns: The Critical Heritage* (London and Boston, 1974).

LOW, DONALD A. (ed.), *Critical Essays on Robert Burns* (London, 1975).

MCCALL, JOHN, *The Life of James Clarence Mangan*, ed. Thomas Wall, facsimile edn. (Blackrock, 1975).

MACCARTHY, DENIS FLORENCE, 'Recent English Poets: John Keats', *The Nation*, III/157 (11 Oct. 1845), 858–9; IV/159 (25 Oct. 1845), 27.

—— 'Recent English Poets: Percy Bysshe Shelley', *The Nation*, IV/167 (20 Dec. 1845), 154; IV/168 (27 Dec. 1845), 171–2.

—— *A Book of Irish Ballads* (Dublin, 1846).

—— *Shelley's Early Life from Original Sources* (London, 1872).

MACCORMACK, W. J., *Ascendancy and Tradition in Anglo-Irish Literary History from 1789 to 1939* (Oxford, 1985).

MACCUE, KIRSTEEN, 'Burns, Women and Song', in Robert Crawford (ed.), *Robert Burns and Cultural Authority*, 40–57.

MACDONAGH, OLIVER, *States of Mind: A Study of the Anglo-Irish Conflict 1780–1980* (London, 1983).

MACDONALD, DWIGHT (ed.), *Parodies: An Anthology from Chaucer to Beerbohm and After* (London, 1961).

MCFARLAND, THOMAS, *Romanticism and the Forms of Ruin: Wordsworth, Coleridge, and the Modalities of Fragmentation* (Princeton, 1981).

MCGANN, JEROME J., *The Romantic Ideology: A Critical Investigation* (Chicago, 1983).

—— Literary History, Romanticism, and Felicia Hemans', *Modern Language Quarterly*, 54/2 (1993), 215–35.

MCGRATH, NIALL, 'Ciaran Carson: Interview with Niall McGrath', *Edinburgh Review*, 93 (Spring 1995), 61–6.

MCGUIRK, CAROL, *Robert Burns and the Sentimental Era* (Athens, Ga., 1985).

MCINTYRE, IAN, *Dirt and Deity: A Life of Robert Burns* (London, 1995).

MACKAY, CHARLES, *Voices from the Crowd*, 3rd edn. (London, 1846).

MACKENZIE, HENRY, Untitled review of Robert Burns's *Poems Chiefly in the Scottish Dialect*, *The Lounger*, 97 (9 Dec. 1786), 385–8.

MACMANUS, M. J., *First Editions of Thomas Moore* (Dublin, 1934).

MACMONAGLE, NIALL (ed.), *Lifelines: An Anthology of Poems Chosen by Famous People* (Harmondsworth, 1993).

MCNEILL, F. MARIAN, *The Silver Bough*, vol. i (Edinburgh, 1989).

MACPHERSON, JAMES, *The Poems of Ossian*, ed. Howard Gaskill (Edinburgh, 1996).

MCSWEENEY, SIOBHAN, 'The Poet's Picture of Education', *The Crane Bag*, 7/2 (1983), 134–42.

MAGNUSON, PAUL, *Coleridge and Wordsworth: A Lyrical Dialogue* (Princeton, 1988).

MANDLER, PETER, *The Fall and Rise of the Stately Home* (New Haven and London, 1997).

MANGAN, JAMES CLARENCE, 'The Dying Enthusiast to his Friend', *The Comet* (5 Aug. 1832).

—— 'The Dying Enthusiast to his Friend', *Dublin Penny Journal*, I (5 Jan. 1833), 244.

—— 'Faust and Other Minor Poems of Goethe', *Dublin University Magazine*, VII (1836), 278–302.

—— 'Literae Orientales', *Dublin University Magazine*, X (1837), 274–92; XI (1838), 291–312; XII (1838), 328–46; XV (1840), 377–94; XXIII (1844), 535–50; XXVII (1846), 43–57.

—— 'The Autobiography of James Clarence Mangan', Royal Irish Academy Library, MS 12/P/18.

—— *The Prose Writings of James Clarence Mangan*, ed. D. J. Donoghue (Dublin, 1904).

—— *The Collected Works of James Clarence Mangan: Poems 1818–1837*, ed. Jacques Chuto, Rudolf Patrick Holzapfel, Peter Mac Mahon, Pádraic Ó Snodaigh, Ellen Shannon-Mangan, Peter Van de Kamp (Blackrock and Portland, Oreg., 1996).

MANNING, SUSAN, 'Burns and God', in Robert Crawford (ed.), *Robert Burns and Cultural Authority*, 113–135.

MASEFIELD, JOHN, *Poems* (London and Toronto, 1946).

MEDWIN, THOMAS, 'Memoir of Shelley', *Athenaeum*, 247 (21 July 1832), 472–4; 248 (28 July 1832), 488–9; 249 (4 Aug. 1832), 502–4; 250 (11 Aug. 1832), 522–4; 251 (18 Aug. 1832), 535–7; 252 (25 Aug. 1832), 554–5.

MEE, JON, 'Anxieties of Enthusiasm: Coleridge, Prophecy, and Popular Politics in the 1790s', *Huntington Library Quarterly*, 60/1, 2 (1998), 179–203.

MELLOR, ANNE K., *Romanticism and Gender* (New York and London, 1993).

MERCIER, VIVIEN, *Modern Irish Literature: Sources and Founders*, ed. Eílis Dillon (Oxford, 1994).

MILOSZ, CZESLAW, *Native Realm: A Search for Self-Definition*, trans. Catherine S. Leach (London and Manchester, 1981).

MILTON, JOHN, *The Complete Shorter Poems*, ed. John Carey (London, 1968).

MODIANO, RAIMONDA, 'Coleridge and Wordsworth: The Ethics of Gift Exchange and Literary Ownership', in Christine Gallant (ed.), *Coleridge's Theory of Imagination Today*, 243–56.

MONTAGUE, JOHN (ed.), *The Faber Book of Irish Verse* (London, 1974).

MOONIE, MARTIN, 'William Greenfield: Gender and the Transmission of Literary Culture', in Robert Crawford (ed.), *The Scottish Invention of English Lierature*, 103–115.

MOORE, THOMAS, *Irish Melodies, and a Melalogue upon National Music* (Dublin, 1820).

—— *The Life and Death of Lord Edward Fitzgerald*, 2 vols. (London, 1831).

MORRISON, BLAKE, *Seamus Heaney* (London, 1982).

MULDOON, PAUL, *Meeting the British* (London, 1987).

—— *Madoc* (London, 1990).

MURISON, DAVID, 'The Language of Burns', in Donald A. Low (ed.), *Critical Essays on Robert Burns*, 54–69.

MYERS, F. W. H., *Human Personality and its Survival of Bodily Death* (London, 1903).

NEWLYN, LUCY, *Coleridge, Wordsworth, and the Language of Allusion* (Oxford, 1986).

—— *Paradise Lost and the Romantic Reader* (Oxford, 1993).

—— 'Coleridge and the Anxiety of Reception', *Romanticism*, 1/2 (1995), 206–38.

NOON, W. T., *Joyce and Aquinas* (New Haven and London, 1957).

NORTON, CAROLINE, *A Voice from the Factories* (London, 1836).

NUTTALL, A. D., *Openings: Narrative Beginnings from the Epic to the Novel* (Oxford, 1992).

O'DONOGHUE, BERNARD, *Seamus Heaney and the Language of Poetry* (Hemel Hempstead, 1994).

O'DONOGHUE, D. J., *The Life and Writings of James Clarence Mangan* (Dublin, 1897).

O'FARRELL, PATRICK, *Ireland's English Question: Anglo-Irish Relations 1534–1970* (London, 1971).

O'FERRALL, FERGUS, *Catholic Emancipation: Daniel O'Connell and the Birth of Irish Democracy* (Dublin, 1985).

O'GLAISNE, RISTEÁRD, 'Irish and the Protestant Tradition', *The Crane Bag* 5/2 (1981), 33–44.

O'NEILL, MICHAEL (ed.), *Shelley* (London, 1993).

—— *Romanticism and the Self-Conscious Poem* (Oxford, 1997).

—— (ed.), *Literature of the Romantic Period: A Bibliographical Guide* (Oxford, 1998).

O'RAHILLY, T. F., *Early Irish History and Mythology* (Dublin, 1946).

O'ROURKE, James, *Keats's Odes and Contemporary Criticism* (Gainesville, Fla., 1998).

ORSINI, G. N. G., *Coleridge and German Idealism* (Carbondale, Ill., 1969).

OWENSON, SYDNEY, LADY MORGAN, *The Lay of an Irish Harp* (London, 1807).

PARKER, E. W. (ed.), *The Ambleside Book of Verse* (London, 1949).

PARKER, MICHAEL, *Seamus Heaney: The Making of a Poet* (London, 1993).

PARKER, REEVE, *Coleridge's Meditative Art* (Ithaca, 1975).

PASCAL, BLAISE, *Pensées*, trans. by A. J. Krailsheimer, rev. edn. (Harmondsworth, 1995).

PATTERSON, ROBERT LEET, *The Conception of God in the Philosophy of Aquinas* (London, 1933).

PAULIN, TOM, *A New Look at the Language Question* (1983), in *Ireland's Field Day*, 3–22.

—— *Ireland and the English Crisis* (Newcastle upon Tyne, 1984).

—— *The Day Star of Liberty: William Hazlitt's Radical Style* (London, 1998).

PEACOCK, THOMAS LOVE, *The Halliford Edition of the Works of Thomas Love Peacock*, ed. H. F. Brett-Smith and C. E. Jones, 10 vols. (London, 1924–34).

PERCY, THOMAS, *Reliques. of Ancient English Poetry*, 3 vols. (London, 1765).

—— *The Percy Letters: The Correspondence of Thomas Percy and David Dalrymple, Lord Hailes*, ed. A. F. Falconer (Baton Rouge, 1954).

—— *The Percy Letters: The Correspondence of Thomas Percy and William Shenstone*, ed. Cleanth Brooks (New Haven and London, 1977).

PERRY, SEAMUS, *Coleridge and the Uses of Division* (Oxford, 1999).

PINKERTON, JOHN, *Scottish Poems*, 3 vols. (Edinburgh, 1792).

PIRIE, DAVID, 'A Letter to [Asra]', in Jonathan Wordsworth and Beth Darlington (eds.), *Bicentenary Wordsworth Studies in Memory of John Alban Finch* (Ithaca, 1970), 294–339.

PITTOCK, MURRAY, *Poetry and Jacobite Politics in Eighteenth-Century Britain and Ireland* (Cambridge, 1994).

PLATO, *Phaedo*, trans. David Gallop (Oxford, 1975).

PODMORE, FRANK, *Apparitions and Thought Transference* (London, 1894).

POPE, ALEXANDER, *The Twickenham Edition of the Works of Alexander Pope*, general editor John Butt, 11 vols. (London, 1938–68).

PRATT, LYNDA, 'A Coleridge Borrowing from Southey', *Notes and Queries*, NS 42 (1994), 336–8.

RAMSAY, ALLAN, *The Ever-Green*, 2 vols. (Edinburgh, 1724).

—— *The Tea-Table Miscellany*, 4 vols. (Edinburgh, 1723–37).

RAMSAY, ALLAN, *Poems by Allan Ramsay and Robert Fergusson*, ed. A. M. Kinghorn and A. Law (Edinburgh and London, 1974).

REED, BERTHA, *The Influence of Solomon Gessner upon English Literature* (Philadelphia, 1905).

RICHTARIK, MARILYNN, *Acting Between the Lines: The Field Day Theatre Company and Irish Cultural Politics 1980–1984* (Oxford, 1994).

RICKS, CHRISTOPHER, *The Force of Poetry* (London, 1984).

—— *T. S. Eliot and Prejudice* (London, 1988).

ROLLINS, HYDER, E. (ed.), *The Keats Circle: Letters and Papers, 1816–1878*, 2 vols. (Cambridge, Mass., 1948).

ROSE, MARGARET, *Parody: Ancient, Modern, and Post-Modern* (Cambridge, 1993).

ROSE, MARK, *Authors and Owners: The Invention of Copyright* (Cambridge, Mass., 1993).

ROSS, MARLON, *The Contours of Masculine Desire: Romanticism and the Rise of Women's Poetry* (New York and London, 1989).

RUOFF, GENE, *Wordsworth and Coleridge: The Making of the Major Lyrics 1802–1804* (London, 1989).

SACKS, PETER, 'Last Clouds: A Reading of "Adonais"' *Studies in Romanticism*, 23 (1984), 380–400.

—— *The English Elegy: Studies in the Genre from Spenser to Yeats* (Baltimore, 1985).

SAID, EDWARD, *Beginnings, Intention and Method* (New York, 1975).

—— *Culture and Imperialism* (London, 1993).

SAMBROOK, JAMES, *James Thomson 1700–1748: A Life* (Oxford, 1991).

SCHOENBAUM, S., *Shakespeare's Lives* (Oxford, 1970).

SCOTT, A. F., *The Poet's Craft* (Cambridge, 1957).

SCOTT, WALTER, *Minstrelsy of the Scottish Border*, 2 vols. (Kelso, 1802).

—— *Minstrelsy of the Scottish Border*, 2nd edn., 3 vols (Edinburgh and London, 1803).

—— (ed.) *Minstrelsy of the Scottish Border*, ed. T. F. Henderson, 4 vols. (Edinburgh, 1902).

—— *Marmion* (Edinburgh and London, 1808).

—— *Poetical Works*, ed. J. Logie Robertson (Oxford, 1904).

SEFERIS, G., *A Poet's Journal: Days of 1945–1951*, trans. Athan Anagnostopolous, ed. Walter Kaiser (Cambridge, Mass., and London, 1974).

SHAKESPEARE, WILLIAM, *The Arden Shakespeare*, general editor Richard Proudfoot. Volumes consulted:

—— *Othello*, ed. M. R. Ridley (London and New York, 1958).

—— *Measure for Measure*, ed. J. W. Lever (London and New York, 1965).

—— *As You Like It*, ed. Agnes Latham (London and New York, 1975).

—— *A Midsummer Night's Dream*, ed. Harold F. Brooks (London and New York, 1979).

—— *King Lear*, ed. R. A. Foakes. (London, 1997).

SHANNON-MANGAN, ELLEN, *James Clarence Mangan: A Biography* (Blackrock and Portland, Oreg., 1996).

SHELLEY, PERCY BYSSHE, *Posthumous Poems*, ed. Mary Shelley (London, 1824).

—— 'Adonais. An Elegy on the Death of John Keats, Author of "Endymion", "Hyperion", etc.' *Athenaeum*, 97 (1829), 544–5.

—— *The Beauties of Percy Bysshe Shelley, Consisting of Miscellaneous Selections from his Poetical Works: The Entire Poems of Adonais and Alastor, and a revised edition of Queen Mab, Free from all Objectionable Passages* (London, 1830).

—— *The Masque of Anarchy*, ed. Leigh Hunt (London, 1832).

—— *The Poetical Works of Percy Bysshe Shelley*, ed. Mary Shelley, 4 vols. (London, 1839).

—— *The Letters of Percy Bysshe Shelley*, ed. Frederick L. Jones, 2 vols. (Oxford, 1964).

—— *The Poetical Works*, ed. Thomas Hutchinson, rev. edn. G. M. Matthews (Oxford, 1970).

—— *Shelley's Poetry and Prose*, ed. Donald Reiman and Sharon B. Powers (New York and London, 1977).

—— *Shelley's Adonais: A Critical Edition*, ed. A. D. Knerr (New York, 1984).

—— *The Poems of Shelley*, Vol. I: *1804–1817*, ed. G. M. Matthews and Kelvin Everest (London, 1989).

—— *The Prose Works of Percy Bysshe Shelley*, Vol. I, ed. E. B. Murray (Oxford, 1993).

SHERIDAN, THOMAS, *A Course of Lectures on Elocution* (London, 1762).

SIMONSUURI, K., *Homer's Original Genius: Eighteenth-Century Notions of the Early Greek Epic 1688–1798* (Cambridge, 1979).

SIMPSON, KENNETH, *The Protean Scot: The Crisis of Identity in Eighteenth-Century Scottish Literature* (Aberdeen, 1988).

—— (ed.), *Burns Now* (Edinburgh, 1994).

SOUTHEY, ROBERT, *Poems of Robert Southey*, ed. Maurice Fitzgerald (London and New York, 1909).

The Spectator, see Addison, Joseph.

SPERRY, STUART, *Keats the Poet* (Princeton, 1973).

STILLINGER, J., 'Keats's Extempore Effusions and the Question of Intentionality', in Robert Brinkley and Keith Hanley (eds.), *Romantic Revisions*, 307–20.

—— *Coleridge and Textual Instability: The Multiple Versions of the Major Poems* (New York and Oxford, 1994).

STONES, G., and STRACHAN, J. (eds.), *Parodies of the Romantic Age*, 5 vols. (London, 1998).

STRONG, ROY, BINNEY, MARCUS, and HARRIS, JOHN, *The Destruction of the Country House 1875–1975* (London, 1974).

SUTHERLAND, KATHRYN, 'The Native Poet: The Influence of Percy's Minstrel from Beattie to Wordsworth', *Review of English Studies*, NS 33 (Nov. 1982), 414–33.

SWIFT, JONATHAN, *The Poems of Jonathan Swift*, ed. Harold Williams, 3 vols. (Oxford, 1937).

THOMAS, DYLAN, *Poet in the Making: The Notebooks of Dylan Thomas*, ed. Ralph Maud (London, 1965).

THOMSON, DERICK S., *An Introduction to Gaelic Poetry* (London, 1977).

THOMSON, JAMES, *The Seasons*, ed. James Sambrook (Oxford, 1981).

THUENTE, MARY, *The Harp Re-strung: The United Irishmen and the Rise of Irish Literary Nationalism* (Syracuse, 1994).

TRUMPENER, KATIE, *Bardic Nationalism: The Romantic Novel and the British Empire* (Princeton, 1997).

TUCKER, S., *Enthusiasm: A Study in Semantic Change* (Cambridge, 1972).

TYLER, LUTHER, 'Losing A Letter: The Contexts of Coleridge's "Dejection: An Ode"', *English Literary History*, 52/2 (1985), 419–45.

VANCE, NORMAN, 'Text and Tradition: Robert Emmet's Speech from the Dock', *Studies*, lxxi (Summer 1982), 185–91.

VAUGHAN, HENRY, *The Complete Poems*, ed. Alan Rudrum. (Harmondsworth, 1976).

VENDLER, HELEN, *The Odes of John Keats* (Cambridge, Mass., and London, 1983).

—— *The Music of What Happens: Poems, Poets, Critics* (Cambridge, Mass., 1988).

WALTON, IZAAK, and COTTON, CHARLES, *The Compleat Angler, Or the Contemplative Man's Recreation*, ed. John Buxton (Oxford, 1982).

WATERSON, MERLIN (ed.), *The Country House Remembered* (London, Melbourne, and Henley, 1985).

WATSON, GEORGE, J. B., *Irish Identity and the Literary Revival: Synge, Yeats, Joyce and O'Casey*, 2nd edn. (Washington, DC, 1994).

—— 'Celticism and the Annulment of History', in Terence Brown (ed.), *Celticism*, 207–20.

WATSON, JAMES, *Watson's Choice Collection of Comic and Serious Scots Poems*, ed. Harriet Harvey Wood, 2 vols. (Edinburgh and Aberdeen, 1977, 1991).

WATSON, WILLIAM J. (ed.), *Bardachd Ghaidhlig: Gaelic Poetry 1550–1900*, 3rd edn. (repr. Inverness, 1976).

WAUGH, EVELYN, *Brideshead Revisited* (London, 1945).

WEBB, T., 'Religion of the Heart: Leigh Hunt's Unpublished Tribute to Shelley', *Keats–Shelley Review*, 7 (1992), 1–61.

—— ' "A Noble Field": Shelley's Irish Expedition and the Lessons of the French Revolution', in Nadia Minerva (ed.), *Robespierre and Co.*, 3 vols. (Bologna, 1990), 553–76.

WEINBROT, HOWARD, *Britannia's Issue: The Rise of British Literature from Dryden to Ossian* (Cambridge, 1995).

WENDLING, RONALD C., *Coleridge's Progress to Christianity: Experience and Authority in Religious Faith* (Lewisburg, Pa., and London, 1995).

WHALLEY, GEORGE, *Coleridge and Sara Hutchinson and the Asra Poems* (London, 1955).

WHEELER, KATHLEEN, *The Creative Mind in Coleridge's Poetry* (London, 1981).

WHITE, NEWMAN IVEY, *Shelley*, 2 vols. (New York, 1940).

WIMSATT, W. K., *The Verbal Icon: Studies in the Meaning of Poetry* (Lexington, Ky., 1954).

WITHERS, CHARLES, *Gaelic in Scotland, 1698–1981* (Edinburgh, 1984).

WITTIG, KURT, *The Scottish Tradition in English Literature* (Edinburgh and London, 1958).

WOLFSON, SUSAN, *Formal Charges: The Shaping of Poetry in British Romanticism* (Stanford, 1997).

WORDSWORTH, DOROTHY, *The Grasmere Journals*, ed. Pamela Woof (Oxford, 1991).

WORDSWORTH, JONATHAN, 'The Infinite I AM: Coleridge and the Ascent of Being', in R. Gravil, L. Newlyn, and N. Roe (eds.), *Coleridge's Imagination*, 22–52.

—— *The Bright Work Grows: Women Writers of the Romantic Age* (Poole and Washington, DC, 1997).

WORDSWORTH, WILLIAM, *The Cornell Wordsworth*, general editor Stephen Parrish. Volumes consulted:

—— *The Salisbury Plain Poems*, ed. Stephen Gill (Ithaca, 1975).

—— *Home at Grasmere*, ed. Beth Darlington (Ithaca, 1977).

—— *Poems, in Two Volumes and Other Poems, 1800–1807*, ed. Jared R. Curtis (Ithaca, 1983).

WORDSWORTH, WILLIAM, *Peter Bell*, ed. John E. Jordan (Ithaca, 1985).

—— *Lyrical Ballads* (1798), ed. James Butler and Karen Green (Ithaca, 1992).

—— *The Prelude 1799, 1805, 1850*, ed. M. H. Abrams, Jonathan Wordsworth, and Stephen Gill (New York, 1979).

—— *The Oxford Authors: William Wordsworth*, ed. Stephen Gill (Oxford, 1984).

—— *Lyrical Ballads*, ed. Michael Mason (London, 1992).

WU, DUNCAN, *Wordsworth's Reading, 1770–1799* (Cambridge, 1993).

YEATS, W. B., *The Poems*, ed. Daniel Albright (London, 1990).

—— *Yeats on Yeats: The Last Introductions and the 'Dublin' Edition*, ed. Edward Callan (Mountrath, 1981).

YOUNG, EDWARD, *Conjectures on Original Composition* (1759), ed. Edith Morley (Manchester, 1918).

YU-LAN, FUNG, *A Short History of Chinese Philosophy*, ed. Derk Bodde (New York and London, 1948).

Index